MW00345807

Winged Sabres

Winged Sabres

One of the RFC's Most Decorated Squadrons

Robert A Sellwood

Pen & Sword
AVIATION
AN IMPRINT OF PEN & SWORD BOOKS LTD.
YORKSHIRE – PHILADELPHIA

First published in Great Britain in 2018 by
Pen & Sword Aviation
An imprint of Pen & Sword Books Ltd
Yorkshire - Philadelphia

The National Archives is the official archives and publisher for the UK Government,
and for England and Wales. We work to bring together and secure the future of the public record,
both digital and physical, for future generations.
The National Archives is open to all, offering a range of activities and spaces to enjoy, as well as our
reading rooms for research. Many of our most popular records are also available online.

ISBN: 9781526729576

A CIP catalogue record for this book is available from the British Library.

Typeset in INDIA By Geniies IT & Services Private Limited
Printed and bound in the UK by TJ International

Pen & Sword Books Ltd incorporates the Imprints of Pen & Sword Books Archaeology, Atlas,
Aviation, Battleground, Discovery, Family History, History, Maritime, Military, Naval, Politics,
Railways, Select, Transport, True Crime, Fiction, Frontline Books, Leo Cooper, Praetorian Press,
Seaforth Publishing, Wharncliffe and White Owl.

For a complete list of Pen & Sword titles please contact

PEN & SWORD BOOKS LIMITED
47 Church Street, Barnsley, South Yorkshire, S70 2AS, England
E-mail: enquiries@pen-and-sword.co.uk
Website: www.pen-and-sword.co.uk

or

PEN AND SWORD BOOKS
1950 Lawrence Rd, Havertown, PA 19083, USA
E-mail: Uspen-and-sword@casematepublishers.com
Website: www.penandswordbooks.com

This book was written for my mother
in proud memory of the father
she never knew.

Driver T2/10816 George Tester, ASC attached 20 Squadron RFC
Probationary Aerial Gunner

and his pilot, Captain John Santiago Campbell, Argyll & Sutherland
Highlanders and RFC

who were together killed in action on 28 September 1917.

'We Will Remember Them'

Contents

Introduction and Acknowledgements

The catalyst for this book was my own family history and how the events of more than a century ago played a pivotal part in it. My Scots-born grandfather George Tester was killed in action while flying as an air gunner in the First World War. He left a wife Isabella and daughter, Mary, who was barely two. Three years later, his widow died of tuberculosis and my five-year-old Mum was adopted by her late father's sister, Aunt Helen, and her husband, Gilbert Thorns, who lived near London. They passed on his medals to her when she was old enough to appreciate them but all she then knew was that he had been killed in action on 28 September 1917 while serving with the Royal Flying Corps.

In 1996, nine years after my own father's death, Mum remarked that I was lucky to be able to visit my Dad's grave from time to time as she did not know where her own father lay – or even if he had a proper grave. Touched by her remark, my sister Rosemary and I began a hunt that culminated in the three of us standing at the side of his war grave at the Pont du Hem Military Cemetery in northern France, where he lies beside his pilot and fellow Scot, Captain John Santiago Campbell. This profoundly moving experience was rendered even more poignant as we listened to the nightly sounding of the Last Post at the Menin Gate in Ypres a few hours later. We knew from his war grave details that George was serving with 20 Squadron RFC when he was killed and, once back in England, I found I could not let the matter rest. I wanted to know more about my grandfather and the squadron he flew and died for. So began a family history quest that soon developed into a much larger project.

Following some helpful advice from much published aviation historian Norman Franks, I visited the National Archives at Kew and studied the 20 Squadron Record Books for 1917, a war diary by any other name, and soon realised that 20 Squadron had been far above average in its achievements. Given the almost daily air battles against great odds, the grim toll of casualties and the stunning victory totals, I realised that 20 Squadron was clearly an elite unit. But when I searched for 20 Squadron's Record Books for 1916 and 1918, I found that, apart from a few pages, they had been forever lost when the squadron transferred to India in 1919. In their absence, I began to look further afield.

I tracked down a copy of N.J. Roberson's *The History of No 20 Squadron RFC and RAF*, a limited-edition book published in 1987 mainly for serving and ex-members. It told 20 Squadron's story from the unit's formation in 1915 through to the mid-1980s but only the first 25 pages related to the First World War. I then studied Norman Franks' 1970s articles about 20 Squadron published in the First World War Aviation Historical Society quarterly magazine, *Cross & Cockade International*, and found that, while his articles provided much fuller information about 20 Squadron's lengthy victory and casualty lists, it was still not enough. Although I now knew a lot more about the squadron's exploits than when I had started, I still knew very little about the men who carried them out and almost nothing about the hopefully sound military reasons that lay behind their missions. I decided that the full story of one of the most decorated and successful of all the two-seater fighter squadrons on the Western Front deserved to be told. With that in mind, I began to research the higher-echelon records and casualty reports at Kew that were likely to relate to 20 Squadron. There were many. In addition, I received much help from the Imperial War Museum, the RAF Museum at Hendon and the Commonwealth War Graves Commission. My grateful thanks are due to all these institutions and their very helpful staffs.

I have also been exceptionally lucky in receiving the help I have from the descendants of some of 20 Squadron's men and many others who have helped out of interest. These include Jamie Tyrell, from Belfast, regarding his grandfather's service and Lorraine Colvill-Jones, in Argentina, who recently published a book about her great-uncle, Tommy Colvill-Jones, titled *Your Ever Loving Son*. Mrs Hope Iaccaci (now Hope Thayer) was equally generous in providing help with my research on her father, the American 20 Squadron ace Paul Iaccaci and his brother August. So too, my gratitude to Chris Boucher, John Colbert, Michael Scott and Simon Burbidge with regard to their own ancestors. Also deserving my warmest thanks are Mark McCall, his sister Dee Arkell and their cousin Tom McCall for their unstinting research and help regarding Malcolm McCall and Clement Boothroyd, and Major Les Donnithorne for his help with Randolph White's story. Similarly, I would like to thank Nick Forder and Tony Grange-Bennett, both long-standing members of *Cross & Cockade International*, for their help and interest. I also gratefully acknowledge the help of the many members of The Great War Forum at *http://1914-1918. invisionzone.com/forums* and *theaerodrome.com*. Of several who helped me on these forums, I would particularly like to thank Frank Olnyk for helping me to access German War Diaries held in the US National Archives. Likewise, my gratitude to Russ Gannon for his willing and expert help in tying in some of 20 Squadron's victory claims with lesser known German losses, and Alex Revell for his help with James McCudden's logbook.

I also obtained four published works, now out of print, by ex-20 Squadron members. These are *Flying Fury* by James T. McCudden, *Wings Over France* by Harold Hartney, *With a Bristol Fighter Squadron* by Walter Noble and *Flying an Ugly Duckling* by Michael Cambray. To help fill the remaining gaps I have happily been able to turn to a fine collection of more recently published works by Grub Street and other publishers. In order to better understand 20 Squadron's activities in terms of the ground war, I have learned from many informative documents at the National Archives as well a number of published works, although to mention them all here would take more space than is available. I have tried to annotate the narrative whenever I have used official documents, the help of the squadron members' descendants or any of the foregoing published works and a more complete listing can be found in the bibliography. I sincerely hope I will be forgiven if I have unintentionally missed any notations and acknowledgements I should have made. It was not deliberate.

Finally, my sincere thanks are due to my long-suffering sisters Rosemary and Marian for their encouragement and proof-reading and my niece Lisa and her husband Des for driving me around the battlegrounds and war cemeteries of northern France. I would also like to thank my equally long-suffering friends Alex Hall and Felice Wechsler and Mike and Pat Gwynne-Smyth for their continual help and encouragement.

The British System for Confirming
Aerial Combat Victory Claims

The British policy of the continual air offensive during the First World War meant that most operations were conducted over enemy territory, while the German fliers were fewer in number and adopted a more defensive stance to try to prevent these incursions. This meant that most (some estimates say over 80 per cent) of aerial combats took place over enemy territory and therefore most of the downed aircraft fell there too. This made it almost impossible for the RFC and later RAF commanders to firmly establish whether an enemy aircraft had been destroyed or not. That being so, they were forced to adopt a less exacting attitude to British pilots' victory claims than that of the Germans, who could easily count the wrecked British aircraft lying on their territory. Provided there were witnesses such as other nearby pilots or soldiers watching from the ground, a claim was usually 'confirmed' and awarded to the pilot by higher authority when it included any of the following descriptions of the enemy aircraft at the end of a particular fight. These included an enemy aircraft *driven down* so that it was no longer a threat, *forced to land* so it could not complete its mission, shot down looking like it was *out of control*, shot down *in flames*, shot down and *broke up in the air* or, lastly, shot down and *was seen to crash*. The *driven down* and *forced to land* categories had fallen out of use by 1916, while *out of control* claims were often still being accepted as decisive through to the end of the war. This policy was probably intended to encourage pilots undertaking highly dangerous missions over enemy territory and was perhaps a hangover from the days when the fact of an enemy running away was considered a victory. So pilots were awarded a 'victory' rather than a 'kill': a term that did not really become popular until the Second World War and required the confirmed destruction of an enemy aircraft. Such a system could not be used to accurately measure the number of enemy aircraft actually destroyed in air combat, but it was the only system we had.

A century later it may be thought that we can easily clarify things by checking the British records (which are still largely intact and can be examined by anyone visiting the National Archives at Kew) against the German records of a similar type. But that is not really true as, apart from the German records of those who died (which often do not even include the cause of death, location or unit number) very few German air service records, unit war diaries or any similarly relevant records can now be found. Almost all were probably destroyed by allied bombing during the Second World War.

Of the 628 or more combat victory claims submitted by 20 Squadron's pilots, observers and aerial gunners, more than 460 were accepted as confirmed at a senior level and included in the RFC and RAF communiqués for the relevant dates. In so doing, the communiqués make a strong case for 20 Squadron having been the highest-scoring British squadron in the Great War. However, there are other contenders for the title and, with the fog of war made murkier by the mists of time, we will probably never know much more about the exact totals and who shot down who than we know right now.

Chapter 1

Beginnings – January 1916

When 20 Squadron was first formed in September 1915 at Netheravon, on Salisbury Plain, Wiltshire, it was in order to counter an alarming new threat in the air that nobody could have foreseen. The first year of war had seen the Royal Flying Corps aviators convince all but the most obdurate of the British and French generals of the value of aerial reconnaissance as a means of seeing what the German armies were doing. Firstly, they had spotted and reported the whereabouts of the German armies and allowed the British Expeditionary Force to prepare for the Battle of Mons in late August 1914. Then a couple of weeks later they had spotted the German First Army's eastwards turn north of Paris that led to the invader being stopped at the Battle of the Marne. The British and French generals quickly came to rely on these early aeronauts for up-to-the-minute intelligence of the enemy's movements. In 1915 the BEF's commander, General (later Field Marshal) Sir Douglas Haig, commented that the RFC's photographic work just before the Battle of Neuve Chapelle had given him a far greater knowledge of the enemy's defence lines and dispositions than any general had ever known before.

Weather permitting, the RFC had maintained and gradually improved on its reconnaissance abilities throughout the fateful first few months of war but in summer 1915 its work had been rudely interrupted by a new German super-weapon: the single-seat Fokker E-I Eindecker monoplane scout. This was the first aeroplane of any nationality to be fitted with a machine-gun synchronised to fire between the whirling blades of its propeller. Until then, most airmen flying even the latest aeroplanes had been armed only with pistols or rifles. Although a few had experimented with poorly mounted machine-guns with a very limited field of fire, their practical usefulness was almost totally negated by the guns' extra weight, which seriously impaired those early flying machines' performance. As a result, meetings with enemy aeroplanes had usually resulted in an exchange of friendly waves rather than bullets and there had been few casualties. With this new German development, the aeroplane itself became a weapon and all the pilot had to do was point its nose at the target. Now adventurous young German flyers such as Oswald Boelke and Max Immelman were busily making themselves famous by shooting down as many British and French aeroplanes as they could find. The British press called it the 'Fokker Scourge' and many RFC crews dubbed themselves 'Fokker Fodder' as the German pilots took the British and French air strategy by the throat and slowly began to squeeze the life out of it – and of many of its finest men.

The best aeroplane the British could put up against the Fokkers at this time was the two-seat Vickers FB 5, or 'Gun-bus', which was already in service. This was a 'pusher' type aircraft, the engine and propeller being behind the crew, in which the observer, armed with a drum-fed Lewis gun, sat in the front of the nacelle so that he could fire forwards or sideways. The Gun-bus was slower and less manoeuvrable than the Fokkers, though, and although some of its crews achieved success with the type, it was not good enough to face the up-rated Fokker E-II and E-III variants that soon appeared and quickly began to push the Gun-buses into the ground. Something better was required and, in the absence of a British synchronising gear, the RFC experimented with two more 'pusher' types, while the French tried the more conventional tractor-engine layout. One such British 'pusher' was the single-seat De Havilland DH2 with a Lewis-gun fixed in front of the pilot to fire straight ahead; while a small French designed single-seat tractor-biplane, the Nieuport 11 'Bebe', carried a Lewis gun on the top wing firing above the propeller-arc. Both proved quite successful against the Fokkers but, being single-seaters, they were not much use for reconnaissance work, which required an observer to take notes and use a camera. For that job, the Royal Aircraft Factory substantially modified the Farman Experimental No.2 (FE2) two-seat 'pusher' aircraft and later re-designated it as the 'Fighting Experimental No.2'. Although superficially similar in appearance to the earlier Gun-bus, the FE2B that went into production was larger, faster, stronger and more manoeuvrable. Armament consisted of a single Lewis gun that the observer could move around his cockpit to any one of six different mountings and the FE2B quickly proved itself against the Fokkers, matching them in speed and having better manoeuvrability. The FE2B was also much stronger and could absorb more damage than the Eindecker. The FE2B began its operational life attached to various squadrons in ones and twos. Then, when its effectiveness became apparent, it was decided to form a new squadron equipped only with FE2Bs to take the fight to the Germans, clear them from its sector of the sky and then carry out its primary role of reconnaissance as the airborne eyes of the BEF.

So 20 Squadron came into being out of grim necessity. The unit was formed on 1 September 1915 from the enlargement of 7 Reserve Aeroplane Squadron at Netheravon under the command of Captain C.W. Wilson MC, whose job was to bring the new squadron up to fighting strength and ability before taking it to France. Captain Wilson had joined the fledgling RFC before the war and, despite receiving a fractured jaw and other minor head injuries in an aeroplane crash in May 1914, he recovered enough to be able to return to duty with 5 Squadron six weeks later. After being appointed a flight commander in September 1914, he was mentioned in despatches by Field Marshal Sir John French in the *London Gazette* of 9 October that year for his work over France at the start of the German onslaught. Now he faced the even more daunting responsibilities of forming his own fighting squadron, assisted by a small group of officers helped by the skilled tradesmen of the other ranks, led by Acting Warrant Officer (Technical) Bertie Billing. A former turner from Sudbury, Suffolk, Billing had enlisted in the regular army in June 1908, aged nineteen. After transferring to the RFC as an Air Mechanic Second Class in July 1912, he rapidly rose through the ranks, making Corporal in July 1914 and Sergeant just three months later, immediately before being sent to France. A year later, he was posted to 20 Squadron at Netheravon, where his experience, efforts and expertise would come to be recognised by all who served with the squadron. His posting was fortuitous for him on a more personal level too, as it allowed him to marry his sweetheart, Hilda Mary, on 4 November 1915.

The Squadron began to receive the first of its FE2Bs shortly before Christmas 1915 and flying training on them began immediately. Newly promoted Major Wilson busied himself not only with ensuring that his pilots became proficient on the FE2B before they went to France but also with a thousand other matters that had to be dealt with. Stores and supplies had to be requisitioned and sorted for road transport and shipping, including three spare 160 hp Beardmore engines, fifteen Lewis guns and several Sterling Wireless sets in addition to tents, bedding, medical supplies, tools for the mechanics, initial food rations, cooking equipment, other weapons and ammunition. The pilots were to fly out to France in the squadron's collection of eight FE2Bs and four BE2Cs, while the other officers and men and all the supplies were to travel by road, by ferry and then by road again. Once in France the four BE2Cs were to be exchanged for FE2Bs currently held on the strength of other squadrons. It required considerable feats of organisation but Major Wilson had arranged things so that the road transport would leave more than a day before the aeroplanes were flown out in order to ensure that the mechanics and all their supplies would be ready and waiting at Clairmarais aerodrome, near St. Omer, Pas de Calais.

Things did not turn out quite as planned, however, and when on 24 January 1916 the aeroplanes touched down at Clairmarais as per instructions, the pilots found that the road transport column was still at Rouen. Blocked roads, fuel shortages and all the other confusions of war organisation meant that the main body of personnel did not arrive at Clairmarais until the 26 January and the supplies the following day. Even so, by that date all the aircraft, most of the supplies and 99 NCOs and other ranks were in place – although Warrant Officer Billing was not. He had arrived in France on 26 January as ordered but a sharp-eyed RFC staff officer had recognised him and, realising the need for a man of his talents at the Aircraft Depot at St. Omer, had promptly issued fresh orders. Bertie Billing was transferred to the Aircraft Depot and, despite Major Wilson's protests, would remain there until August 1917. Two more pilots arrived on January 29, at which time the nominal roll consisted of the following officers:

Pilots	Observers
Capt. J.R. Howett RFC (SR)	Capt. E.W. Forbes (Warwick Reg't)
Capt. E.P. Graves (Royal Field Artillery)	Capt. A.I.F. Duff (Dorset Reg't)
Lt. C.W.E. Cole-Hamilton (2nd Royal Scots)	Lt. F. Billinge (Manchester Reg't)
Lt. R.H. Anderson (12th Rifle Brigade)	2/Lt. H.F. Champion (Rifle Brigade)
2/Lt. I.R. Heywood (Royal Engineers)	2/Lt. C.J. Pile (Royal Field Artillery)
2/Lt. L.A. Newbold (Essex Reg't)	2/Lt. G.E. Chancellor (W. Surreys)
2/Lt. N.G. McNaughton RFC (SR)	2/Lt. A.H. Dickinson (N. Cyclist Bn)
2/Lt. P.G. Scott (Gloucester Reg't)	2/Lt. D.B. Gayford (W. Surreys)
2/Lt. J.R. Kirton (KOSB)	2/Lt. G. Exley (Yorkshire Light Inf.)
2/Lt. R.F.S. Morton RFC (SR)	2/Lt. S. Maller (Royal Dublin Fus.)
2/Lt. C.E.H. James (Welsh Reg't)	2/Lt. G.P.S. Reid (Seaforths)

Also now at Clairmarais was 2/Lt. E. W. Wright, Equipment Officer.

One thing that did go to plan was the exchange of the squadron's four BE2Cs for FE2Bs, so that the squadron now had twelve FE2Bs and a prototype single-seat Martinsyde Scout, Serial No 4735, for evaluation. The FE2Bs on strength included the following serial numbers: A5202, A5204, A5643, A6328, A6329, A6331, A6332, A6333, A6336 and A6338. Clairmarais aerodrome was situated at the edge of the forest after which it was named, about twenty-six miles from the front lines of the Ypres Salient and was close to the Aircraft Depot at St. Omer and the important rail junction at Hazebrouk. The supplies and the ground crews were all in place, the flyers and flying machines all set to go. The enemy was just over the horizon. And 20 Squadron, attached to 2nd Wing RFC, was ready for war.

******

Chapter 2

Learning to Fight – February 1916

On 3 February 1916, the honour of being the first of 20 Squadron's flyers to cross the lines on a real mission fell to Lieutenant Robert Hutchison Anderson and Second Lieutenant Chancellor in FE2B A6328, along with Second Lieutenants Newbold and Gayford in A5202 and Second Lieutenants Scott and Exley in A6331. The six men had flown up to 15 Squadron's base at Droglandt, about ten miles to the northeast, the previous evening, so as to be ready to provide an escort for that unit's early reconnaissance.

The hard-hit 15 Squadron was equipped with BE2Cs and it was these already obsolete machines that had borne the brunt of the Fokker scourge so far. It might well be said that their crews had been flying something akin to suicide missions because, with a maximum speed of only 72 mph, the BEs could not run away from the Fokkers – and once caught they tended to stay that way. Defensive armament was a single Lewis gun handled by the observer. But as he was seated in front of the pilot and surrounded above and to either side by wings and struts, with the propeller in front of him and the pilot directly behind, his field of fire was extremely limited. However, even that was not the sum of the BE's liabilities as a fighting machine. It had been designed to be inherently stable, which was ideal for note-taking and photography in a reconnaissance machine that would not meet any opposition but was disastrous in an aeroplane that would have to fight its way to and from the target area. 'Inherently stable' is the precise opposite of 'highly manoeuvrable' and it was the latter quality that all war pilots were rapidly learning was vital in an aeroplane required to fight its way out of tight corners.

The sight of the three sturdy FE2Bs escorting them must have been somewhat reassuring to the BE2 crews as they worked their way across their lines. The reconnaissance set off at 08.15, and the six young men who sat in their FE2Bs high over the German side of the lines were the first of the many that would fly 20 Squadron's faithful 'Fees', as the FE2Bs were affectionately dubbed, into battle and right now they must have had mixed feelings on their very first foray against the enemy. It can also be supposed that Major Wilson had mixed feelings as he anxiously awaited their safe return. He need not have worried though, for at 10.30 the three FE2Bs hove into sight over Clairmarais and came in to land. They had not met the enemy in the air but they had accomplished their mission.

Half an hour later, three more FEs rose into the sky and headed out towards the lines. Led by Captains Graves and Forbes in A6333, the machines were eastward bound on an offensive patrol (termed an 'OP'): in other words, looking for trouble. They all returned at 13.20 without having found any, although this might have come as something of a relief to all six men, the remaining four being Second Lieutenant McNaughton and Air Mechanic Second Class Kinder in A6332 and Lieutenant Cole-Hamilton and Captain Duff in A5643. Apart from some more local flying that included new pilot arrival Lieutenant Renton with Corporal May as his observer/aerial gunner, that was the extent of 20 Squadron's first day of operations. If any of those involved felt a sense of anti-climax at the day's end they would not have to wait long for it to be dispelled. First contact with the enemy came just two days later.

The German two-seater LVG reconnaissance aircraft had already taken a look at the RFC's aircraft depot at St. Omer and its pilot now headed north before turning towards the little town of Cassel situated at the top of one of two conical hills that jutted upwards from the otherwise flat and featureless Flanders plains. The town made an excellent landmark for aviators, from which it was easy to locate the rail yards at Hazebrouk after which, his mission completed, the German pilot would then be able to make a straight run for the safety of his own side of the lines. But other eyes were also searching towards Cassel from among the drifting broken clouds, and they belonged to Captain Howett of the RFC.

James Howett was flying the Martinsyde aircraft 20 Squadron was evaluating and, as it had a better speed and rate of climb than the FE2B, he had taken it up as soon as HQ had telephoned to warn the squadron of the German intruder. Now he was relishing his position. Rapidly overhauling the LVG and opening the throttle wider, he gently pulled the control column back a little so as to climb a bit higher than his quarry before beginning his attack at 9,500ft over Cassel with a height advantage of some 2,000ft. Stick forward a bit, throttle wide open, and the Martinsyde began its accelerating rush of pursuit, with Howett opening fire when he got to about 200 yards range. The LVG dived immediately, accelerating to about 100mph, while its observer fired off a succession of machine-gun bursts at the British Scout. British anti-aircraft batteries below now joined the assault, their white bursts of smoke punctuating the sky around the German intruder and Howett was confident he could catch the LVG and finish the job – but just at the crucial moment he ran out of ammunition.

The Martinsyde was armed with a single Lewis machine-gun fitted to the aircraft's top wing. The gun was reliable enough if properly maintained but had the disadvantage of carrying its ammunition – just 47 rounds at that time – in a drum-shaped cylinder that had to be replaced whenever it was necessary to reload. Aircraft gun-mountings were very primitive at this time and replacing the drum meant that the pilot had to stand up in the cockpit and reach forwards and upwards so as to remove the used drum with one hand while replacing it with a new one held in his other hand. In the meantime, the only control he had over his aeroplane came from gripping the control column between his knees. This was an extremely dangerous and difficult drill to perform and Captain Howett found it quite impossible. Bitterly disappointed, he sank back into his seat and turned for home[1]

The Squadron would have to wait a little longer for its first combat victory and, when it came, it would fall to a FE2B. As for the Martinsyde, that would soon be returned to the depot and, although it was apparently not much use for aerial combat, the type would later find more favour as a light bomber. Captain Howett's encounter over Cassel had been just one more minor incident among many along the Ypres front. If it was notable in any way, it was only by the facts that it involved his squadron's first air combat and that nobody got hurt. Things would not stay that way for long.

On 7 February, shortly before 09.00, two of 20 Squadron's FE2Bs were escorting a BE2C reconnaissance machine well behind the German lines over Roulers, ten miles northeast of Ypres. The town straddled vital road and rail junctions in continuous use by the Germans for the supply and reinforcement of their armies, so day-to-day information on what was happening there was crucial to the British commanders in making their own dispositions. The Germans could be expected to do everything in their power to prevent the reconnaissance being successful and, this being so, the British flyers were particularly on the alert for enemy machines as they circled over the town. It fell to Lieutenant Frank Billinge, Second Lieutenant Reid's observer in FE2B A6331, to be the first to spot the approaching danger. Two Fokker monoplanes and four unidentified biplanes were closing rapidly. One of the monoplanes swept in to attack the BE2C on Billinge's left, making a steep spiral around it and passing about 300 feet below and in front of his machine. Billinge opened fire as it did so and saw it suddenly sideslip and fall away behind the British formation, trailing smoke from its engine. A second German Fokker opened fire on Billinge's FE2B but its shots went wide. Then the Germans broke off their attack, leaving the British formation to finish its reconnaissance. The Squadron's first fight with the fearsome Fokkers was over. Although the Fokker that had gone down smoking had not been seen to crash, it seemed certain that it had been damaged and put to flight and, for that reason, it was officially recorded as an 'out of control' victory for Reid and Billinge[1].

The following week passed without any decisive combats, but there was a change in the command structure when the RFC reorganised itself into brigades, with each one attached to a particular army. Thus 1 Brigade was attached to the British First Army, 2 Brigade was attached to the British Second Army and so on. Each brigade consisted of two 'wings' with different responsibilities and each wing of several squadrons. A brigade's 'corps wing' was responsible for local tactical reconnaissance, close co-operation with the local troops on the ground and artillery observation, while its 'army' wing was responsible for longer-range strategic reconnaissance, aerial combat and bombing of enemy ground targets. The current reorganisation meant that 20 Squadron was now attached to 11 (Army) Wing, 2 Brigade RFC and, being a fighter-reconnaissance unit, could look forward to carrying out all of the army wing's roles at different times – and all at once on some occasions!

******

It may be useful at this point to acquaint the reader with a general overview of what strategic reconnaissance involved in those early days. What exactly were the observers looking for as their pilots flew them over enemy lines and what skills were involved? Basically, they were looking for any changes in the enemy's positions that might pose a direct or indirect threat. These included increases in road and rail movements, new trenches, artillery positions or machine-gun nests and any obvious reinforcement or withdrawal of large numbers of troops. It was crucial that the airmen knew what to look for and accurately recorded all that they saw. The men who carried out this duty had to be fit enough to remain vigilant while flying in an open cockpit in often freezing conditions. They needed good eyesight and the ability to concentrate on their tasks even when enemy bullets and anti-aircraft shells were ripping holes in the fabric of their aeroplanes. If they were afraid, they had to put that to the back of their minds while they scrutinised the ground below, made meticulous notes on whatever they saw and simultaneously scanned the sky for enemy aircraft.

The pilots too had to be equally calm and collected. They had to keep the aircraft flying as straight and level as possible over the target area regardless of enemy anti-aircraft fire, taking care to avoid violent evasive manoeuvres that might cause their observers to miss something important or the photographs to be blurred. Like their observers, they too had to look out for enemy aircraft and be ready to fight or flee as the situation demanded. Above all, the two airmen had to understand and have confidence in each other. Because the noise of the engine made normal conversation impossible, they had to develop a system of sign language that was instantly understandable, both in the relative calm of note-taking and photography and in the heat of battle. Teamwork was the essence of a good reconnaissance, and calm nerves and a quick mind were essential tools for survival.

The squadron's primary role was strategic reconnaissance deep behind the enemy lines and often enduring anti-aircraft fire over enemy territory for two or three hours at a time. Their problems did not simply end when they turned for home, for the return trip usually meant flying into the prevailing westerly wind that had the effect of considerably slowing down those early aeroplanes. It made the trip from base to the target area a short one, while the return trip was long. They were still being fired at from the ground and the danger of a sudden attack by enemy aircraft was ever present. If they were shot down and somehow survived the resultant crash or forced landing, the best they could hope for would be to spend the rest of the war in a prison camp. That was the nature of the job. As for the people who did the job, although all of 20 Squadron's pilots and qualified observers in those early days were commissioned officers, it would be wrong to assume that they all came from similar backgrounds.

Flight-Commander Captain Evelyn Paget Graves, single and aged 25, was born in India in 1890, the son of the Honourable A.E.P. Graves. Educated at Lancing College in Sussex, he was originally commissioned into the Royal Field Artillery and graduated at the Central Flying School in October 1914. On the other hand, Captain E. Webster Forbes had been the manager at a Walsall leather-works before the war, was married and came to the RFC via the Royal Warwickshire Regiment, Territorial Army. Another married officer was 30-year-old Captain Ian Archibald James Duff from Inverness. Originally commissioned into the Dorsets, he had qualified as an observer just two weeks before the squadron flew to France. Although born in London, FE2B pilot Norman George McNaughton had been a rancher in the Argentine before the war. Lieutenant Frank Billinge, an observer, was the son of Manchester grocers William and Amy Billinge, and gave his occupation as that of a 'clerk in Holy Orders' at St. Mary's Rectory in Manchester when enlisting just after the outbreak of war. Commissioned into the 3 Manchester Regiment, he transferred to the RFC in September 1915. Ralph Imray Kirton was the son of Dr Charles and Mrs Lillian Kirton, of Honor Oak, London, and was educated at the King's School, Canterbury from May 1911 to July 1914. He originally enlisted in 1914 in the 10 (Service) Battalion Royal Fusiliers before being commissioned into the King's Own Scottish Borderers. In September 1915 he transferred to Royal Flying Corps. Hilary Francis Champion had journeyed from South Africa to serve the mother country, while Observer John Cyril Pile represented the titled aristocracy, being the 18-year-old son of Sir John Devereux Pile. Another of the squadron's 'founder members' to have returned to England from abroad following the outbreak of war was R.H. Anderson. Married with two children, his family staying in Edinburgh, Anderson was an inventive mining engineer who had gained his qualifications in such diverse establishments as Michigan College of Mining and Leeds and Edinburgh universities. While Geoffrey Chancellor, Frank Maller and Douglas Gayford had been drilling with the Inns of Court OTC before the war, the much-travelled Anderson had been working as a sampler and surveyor in mines as far apart as Peru and the Transvaal. At 33, he was the oldest of the pilots and observers, very inventive and nearly twice Gayford's age, the latter being only 17 when he flew to France.

When in England, Lieutenant Anderson had been struck by the clumsy inefficiency of the early gun mountings on the FE2Bs and set about improving them. The result was that the squadron flew out to France with some of their machines fitted with new gun mountings that would give them a much better chance against the Fokkers. The modified FE2Bs were fitted with five 'Anderson mountings' in the observer's cockpit, so that the Lewis gun could be moved from one to the other as required in order to meet attacks from any direction except behind. The 'Anderson arch' checked that threat. This was an arch-shaped brace secured to the floor of the nacelle between the observer and pilot, to which was attached a telescopic pillar gun-mounting that allowed the observer to fire a second Lewis gun backwards over the top wing. The pillar also incorporated a release catch within the pilot's reach, so that he too could use the gun if the observer was killed or wounded.

Such were the varying types who made up the squadron's roster of pilots and observers. But such differences did not stop them from working together. For example, when the squadron flew a reconnaissance escort over Courtrai on 13 February 1916, the miner/inventor Lieutenant Anderson carried 18-year-old Etonian Second Lieutenant Geoffrey Ellis Chancellor as his observer. By 15.30 the formation had crossed the lines south of Ypres and had reached an altitude of 9,000ft when Chancellor noticed a dark coloured biplane with distinct black crosses approaching from slightly above and to the left of him and opened fire as the enemy machine closed. The German then swung around behind the FE and Chancellor hurriedly switched the Lewis gun to the rear mounting and fired another burst. However, the range being about 300 yards, his fire had no apparent effect and the German flew off unharmed[1]. Ten minutes later, a cream coloured German two-seater attacked the formation from behind. Second Lieutenants P.G. Scott and F.S. Maller in A6331 turned their FE around to assist the one behind them and Maller emptied a whole drum of 47 bullets into the attacker's fuselage that caused it to break off its attack before plunging earthwards in a vertical nose-dive, the British crew losing sight of it as it fell[1].

More attacks came between Menin and Halluin when an Albatros two-seater came in on the left of A6336, crewed by Second Lieutenant Kirton and Lieutenant Billinge. The Albatros opened fire from about 350 yards but as Billinge fired his reply, the German pilot evidently decided that discretion was the better part of valour and turned away northwards. A few minutes later a German Rumpler two-seater dived in close behind A6336, firing all the time, and Kirton banked the FE over in two tight circles before the two machines flew nose to nose with Billinge firing off one-and-a-half drums in quick bursts that forced this German also to make off.

The next attack came around 16.30, when a new enemy approached. According to combat reports submitted both by Billinge and the crew of the 15 Squadron BE2C, Lieutenant Adams and Corporal Edwards, and RFC Communiqué No 30, the German machine was a twin-engine two-seater pusher-type. Once again, the German attacked the formation from the rear and, after firing a red flare to warn the other machines, Kirton quickly turned his FE to meet the enemy. The fight came to close quarters and Billinge fired his last burst at only 30 yards range. The German machine at once turned away and dived and, according to one of the FE crews who had turned to help on seeing Billinge's flare, it fell to the ground just west of Mouscron for 20 Squadron's second combat victory.

Appalling weather meant that the Brigade was unable to undertake any serious flying over the next two days and, early in the morning of 15 February, a gale blew down all 20 Squadron's iron hangars, wrecking three FE2Bs, damaging five lorries and seriously injuring one of the mechanics. The winds moderated in the afternoon, however, and some patrols and tactical reconnaissances were able to fly before it closed in again the following day. However, 20 February brought more success. Second Lieutenants L. Heywood and H. Champion were flying A6338 at around 10,000ft over Neuve Eglise when they spotted and dived on a German LVG reconnaissance aircraft. Champion opened fire at a range of about 300 feet and hit the German machine's engine, causing its propeller to stop. The LVG then went down in a steep glide towards Deulemont and, when they saw their stricken foe preparing to land about eight miles north of Lille, they broke off the chase and turned for home. Allowing their enemy to escape with their lives was an act of chivalry quite in keeping with the standards of the day but, as the war continued and the body count rose, such notions became more and more out-dated. The FE2's return trip was uneventful until Heywood and Champion reached Bailleul and found it being bombed by three more German machines. They were unable to get in close enough for decisive combat, though, and the bombers made off towards their own territory without loss[1].

******

On 21 February 1916 the Germans launched a major attack against the French in the south and the mass slaughter of Verdun began. In northern Flanders, the war continued much as it had done over the previous months and the only thing that day brought to 20 Squadron was another inconclusive brush with the enemy when McNaughton and Chancellor exchanged fire with a Fokker monoplane over Roubaix at around 08.25[1]. Apart from that, the squadron was kept on its toes over the next few days by repeated dawn stand-bys in readiness for an imminent air offensive planned by brigade HQ. Snow sweeping in from the north prevented any but the most foolhardy from getting airborne, however, and it was not until the end of the month that the weather moderated enough to allow a resumption of flying – on a day that brought the squadron's first losses.

At 07.00 on 29 February 1916, four FE2Bs set out for a reconnaissance over the enemy aerodromes at Gheluwe, Halluin and Moorseele. Second Lieutenants Newbold and Champion were flying together in the reconnaissance machine A6338, escorted by the other FEs, and things first started to go wrong when two of the escorts were forced to drop out with engine trouble, leaving only the FE flown by Lieutenant Cole-Hamilton to protect A6338. It was raining when they crossed the lines at 6,000ft over Ypres and, after passing over the first two German aerodromes, they were approaching Moorseele when a lone Fokker attacked them. Cole-Hamilton soon drove it off but not before it had hit and damaged Newbold and Champion's FE in the cylinder water jacket. As A6338 began to lose height, it was attacked by another Fokker and an Aviatik – and was rendered completely defenceless when Champion's gun froze up as the rain on it turned to ice. Their engine gave up when they were at 4,000ft east of Menin and a company of German infantry opened fire as the FE descended. Champion quickly destroyed his notes and maps before dismantling the gun and scattering its parts over the countryside just before they landed in a field right next to the German infantry, where both men were immediately captured and taken to German XIII Army HQ at Wevelghem,. The German victory was credited to a 'Vfw Wass' (VizeFeldwebel being the equivalent of sergeant).

It was on that sombre note that 20 Squadron completed its first full month at the front. It had been a good start: four combat victories against one loss was a reasonable balance by any standard and, with the likely exception of Newbold and Champion, Major Wilson and his men must have felt considerable satisfaction with what they had achieved. They had met the Fokkers and found them to be not quite as fearsome as they might have expected. They had faced the enemy's bullets and returned their fire with deadly effect. They had every reason to feel confident about the future.

******

Note

1.   Combat Report.

Chapter 3

Holding the Line – March/April 1916

In the first week of March, 20 Squadron fought off a number of attacks while carrying out its bread-and-butter reconnaissance work and in the second week it was noticed that the Fokkers were starting to attack in groups with their leaders' aeroplanes carrying identification streamers. A late-morning reconnaissance escort on 9 March saw five FE2Bs come under repeated attack. The first attack was by four Rumpler two-seaters that approached the formation on its outward flight just west of Tournai. One of them got on the tail of A6358, flown by Cole-Hamilton and Nicholls, but was forced to break off when Cole-Hamilton sharply turned his machine around to allow Nicholls to fire off one-and-a-half Lewis drums at the enemy before making off and rejoining his colleagues near Lille to await a more propitious moment[1]. Scott and Exley, flying A6340, were having difficulty keeping up with the others as the patrol turned over Tournai. The four Rumplers seized the chance for a second attack, with one of them diving at the FE from its left rear and zooming scarcely thirty feet over their heads. The other FE crews quickly turned to help Scott and Exley as Captain Howett and Sergeant May in A6339 engaged one of the Germans head-on. As the two machines rushed towards each other, Sergeant May emptied a drum towards the Rumpler. Captain Howett saw the tracers hitting the enemy aeroplane as the German also opened fire. As Sergeant May continued firing, after replacing the empty ammunition drum, he was hit in the leg by one of the German bullets and collapsed in the nacelle[1]. Howett hurriedly broke away and turned for home, while Cole-Hamilton and Nicholls – who had just shot up a Rumpler at close range and sent it plunging earthwards in an out of control vertical nose-dive – drove off a Fokker monoplane that was shooting-up Heywood and Gayford's FE A6356. They were just too late, however, and could only watch helplessly as Heywood and Gayford went down to a crash landing near La Bassee, a few miles south of Lille[1].

According to Douglas Gayford's post-war report on the circumstances of his capture, they had just brought down a LVG when the Fokker attacked them wounding Heywood in the foot and Gayford in his back, both arms and right leg. Both their guns had jammed and, following the inevitable forced landing, they were immediately taken prisoner and packed off to hospital at Seclin. Gayford's wounds proved too serious for the Seclin hospital and, from there, he was moved first to Douai before further treatment at Aachen allowed him to be transferred to a Prisoner of War camp at Gutersloh and eventually Crefeld. He spent much of his captivity in hospital and underwent six operations, one of them without anaesthetics, before being repatriated on 8 December 1918. First commissioned into the Royal West Surrey Regiment in July 1915 at the tender age of 16 years and three months, he was six weeks short of his eighteenth birthday when he was captured. Semi-crippled, his body still riddled with splinters the German doctors had been unable to remove, he appealed for help from the Air Ministry. But the Ministry refused him flying pay arrears as he was not a qualified observer when he was shot down. Instead he was given a wound gratuity of just £35 per annum valid only until March 1920 because the military doctors had written up his wounds as being 'serious and permanent' rather than 'very serious and permanent'[2]. Leo Heywood, a 24-year-old from Bromley, Kent, had transferred into the RFC from the Royal Engineers and had been with 20 Squadron since its formation at Netheravon in 1915. After the war, he too was required to complete a report on the circumstances of their capture in which he supported Gayford's claim for the LVG shot down immediately before they were themselves brought down.

As the remaining British machines began the return trip, one of the Rumplers made a final attack on Scott and Exley's machine over Blandain but Exley hit it with a full drum of bullets at only 10 yards range. Heavy smoke suddenly poured from the German's engine and the Rumpler dropped away in a spinning nosedive before crashing in a field[1]. Although only four of the original five FEs made it home and Sergeant May had been wounded, the squadron had, if Heywood's and Gayford's claim is correct, shot down two of the enemy. One confirmed German loss that day was that of two-seater crew Lieutenant Erwin Friedel and Gerhardt Freiherr von Gayl from Flieger-Abteilung 18 who were killed near Lille[3]. In addition, with Cole-Hamilton and Nicholls claiming an 'out of control' victory, 20 Squadron's hardest fight so far could probably be fairly described as having ended in a draw.

On 14 March a whirling dogfight brought the squadron another casualty. Captain Howett was leading the reconnaissance escort in A6339 when at 08.00, flying at 8,000ft between Thourout and Roulers, he noticed a Fokker monoplane taking off from the nearby aerodrome at Gits. As he watched it, an anti-aircraft shell exploded close to the FE2, knocking Frank Billinge to one side with blood streaming from shrapnel in his right eye. Howett could do nothing to help him except keep a wary eye on the now climbing Fokker. It was as well that he did so, for as soon as the German monoplane reached their height it attacked. Howett now fired off a red flare to warn the rest of the patrol and turned towards the German with the other FEs following. His combat report mentions how Billinge continued to make 'excellent shooting' from a range of about 500ft despite only being able to see out of his left eye. The Fokker pilot seems to have been deterred by this aggressive display and dived away. A few minutes later, two more Fokkers came up to start another scrap. Once again the FEs turned to meet the enemy, who responded in the same way as before by diving away. The British pilots dived down in pursuit but after dropping about 1,000ft the Fokkers soared up again and returned to the attack. Howett's machine seemed to be their primary target – perhaps having been identified as the patrol leader because of the streamers his aircraft bore – and the attack came in from behind. At least eight bullets hit the FE before Howett could bring it around to face the attack as the Fokker shot over the top of them. Another attack came in from the front and, as Billinge opened fire, the two machines rushed towards each other nose to nose, passing with no more than ten feet to spare. Then it was over.

One of the Fokkers had sported black and white streamers and, according to McNaughton and Chancellor, it had dived vertically for at least 2,000ft after being fired on by Second Lieutenant Morton and Corporal May in A6459[(1)*]. Streamers identifying the leader's aeroplane were now in use by both sides, but the use of flares seems to have been limited to the British side. If the flight leader fired a red flare, it signalled that he was about to attack the enemy or that he wanted to rally his formation after it had become broken up, while a red flare fired by anyone else signalled an enemy attack. A white flare from the leader's machine was the 'washout' signal, indicating that the patrol should return home, while a green flare signalled that the pilot who had fired it was returning to base due to shortage of petrol, engine trouble or battle damage.

Such methods were again put to the test during the late morning of 18 March when a formation of five FEs carried out a reconnaissance over Tourcoing. Six Fokker monoplanes and four two-seaters took up station above and behind the 'Fees' but held off from attacking immediately, while for their part, the British formation also 'kept their powder dry', since their primary mission was a successful reconnaissance and any unnecessary air fighting might jeopardise its success. The Germans, however, were merely awaiting their chance and it came as the British crews concentrated on a formation turn over Courtrai. Two Fokkers swept down on McNaughton's machine, A6332. The British pilot immediately fired off a red flare and turned his machine to fly straight at the nearest enemy while his gunner, Air Mechanic Second Class Talbot, opened fire and forced it to swerve away. Having seen the flare, the other 'Fees' also turned to the attack. The Germans now backed off until the formation was over Menin before attacking again. Captain James and his Mancunian gunner Corporal James Stringer, flying A5206, had just sent one Fokker down with smoke streaming from its engine when they noticed A6328 very low down gliding towards the lines, closely pursued by a Fokker. They and another FE immediately dived to the rescue and after driving the German away climbed back up to rejoin the formation. There was nothing more they could do for Anderson and Forbes in the evidently stricken A6328 except to circle around in the hope that their colleagues might somehow join up with them again. Anderson's machine did not come back up, though, and eventually the leader fired a white flare to signal the others to follow him home[1]. By the time they had all landed safely at Clairmarais they had no doubt given up Anderson and Forbes for lost – but such thoughts were premature. For Anderson somehow coaxed his damaged aeroplane back across the lines and came down in fields south of Ypres, missing two trees by a hairsbreadth as he landed. Second Lieutenant Kirton was repatriated to England after being wounded in the arm and leg and after a Medical Board review he was classified as permanently unfit for flying except below 5,000ft. In early 1917 he became a test pilot at the Vickers factory, flying more than seventy types of aircraft until he was killed in a Sopwith Dolphin accident on 22 November 1918. In January 1919 he was awarded the Air Force Cross[3].

******

As if the problems created by the enemy, the weather, and the general unreliability of early aero-engines were not enough, RFC squadrons all along the front had recently found themselves contending with a new danger: friendly fire, although the phrase had yet to become well known. Aeroplanes were such a recent phenomenon that very few people, soldiers and civilians alike, could recognise one type from another. Many ground troops had suffered being on the receiving end of accurate artillery fire directed onto their position by a German aeroplane circling overhead, so it was hardly surprising that with most of the British machines spending much of their time out of sight deep behind enemy lines the soldiery began to regard all aeroplanes as hostile and fired at them on sight. The number of such incidents had now reached dangerous proportions and an order went out for each squadron to supply a quota of officers to visit the trenches on a regular basis to teach the ground troops the rudiments of aircraft recognition and to liase with their fellow officers in the infantry and artillery as to what they needed from the RFC. A number of 20 Squadron's officers were temporarily released from flying duties for a few days at a time in this regard.

Bad weather prevented operations between 22 and 27 March, while on 31 March the FE2 crew of 20 Squadron must have been bitterly disappointed to have successfully carried out their photographic mission only to have the camera destroyed by enemy anti-aircraft fire while they were on their way home. Such incidents usually meant that the mission would have to be repeated, perhaps immediately after landing and refuelling.

One other significant event for the squadron during March was Major Wilson being posted home. His replacement was Major G. J. Malcolm, formerly of the Royal Field Artillery, who came to 20 Squadron with considerable military and flying experience. Having first been commissioned in the Royal Field Artillery in August 1911, the Manitoba-born University of London graduate's interest in aviation led to him gaining his Royal Aero Club pilot's certificate at Brooklands on 5 November 1913. After transferring to the Royal Flying Corps early the following year, he saw action over Belgium and France in the earliest months of the war for which, again like his predecessor, he was mentioned in despatches. Another experience he shared with Major Wilson was that of crashing, with his flying career coming close to a premature end on 20 March 1915 when his engine failed just 150 feet over the aerodrome at Bailleul in France. With no height to regain control, he plunged headlong into the ground, fracturing his ribs, his jaw and the base of his skull. He only regained consciousness four days later at 7 Stationary Hospital, Boulogne. Following convalescence in England, he was promoted to captain and posted to flying instructor duties with 9 Squadron at Dover and in November 1915 he moved to Hounslow to take temporary command of the newly formed 27 Squadron. From there he was ordered to France to take over 20 Squadron[5].

Also reporting to 20 Squadron at about this time was Major Malcolm's fellow Canadian: 32-year-old former mechanical engineer Lieutenant Trafford Jones, a 1906 University of Toronto graduate in applied science. The married younger son of the late George A. Jones, he originally enlisted in the Canadian Army Service Corps and was first stationed at the Second Divisional Ammunition sub-park in May 1915 before being sent to England where he transferred to the Royal Flying Corps. His older brother Henry, a Boer War veteran whose wife and children were living in California, was serving as a driver with 6 Brigade, Canadian Field Artillery[6]. Trafford Jones would probably have got on well with Robert Anderson as the two shared a mutual interest in all things mechanical. But where Anderson designed gun-mountings, Trafford Jones turned his mind to the unwieldy tricycle undercarriage of the FE2B and invented a new set-up that substantially strengthened the main undercarriage legs and replaced the front wheel with a tail wheel.

Major Malcolm and Trafford Jones had arrived at 20 Squadron at a time when the RFC was starting to recover from its struggle during the Fokker scourge and the spring of 1916 saw the formation of more DH2 and FE2 squadrons and two months later the introduction of two new aeroplanes. One was the British Sopwith One and a Half Strutter, a tractor engine two-seater that came with the distinction of being the first British aircraft type to be fitted with a synchronised Vickers machine-gun firing through the propeller, as well as a Lewis gun in the observer's rear cockpit. The other was the agile French-designed Nieuport 17, a successor to the Nieuport 11-16 series, carrying a forward-firing Lewis gun on the top wing. These developments soon led to the Germans finding their airspace invaded by ever-increasing numbers of British and French fighting scouts, most of them superior to the Fokkers. The advantage gained by these new aircraft and squadrons was far from total, however, and would prove only a temporary one for the allies before German aircraft development and tactical changes started to reverse the trend in late summer.

April 1 brought a skirmish over the Salient for Captain Graves and Second Lieutenant Aked in A5202. The 20-year-old Henry Leslie Coutley Aked, from Harrogate, was a former student at Magdalene College and had served as a platoon sergeant with Radley College OTC until December 1914 before he was commissioned into 8 Battalion West Yorkshire Regiment on 7 January 1915 from which he later transferred to the RFC. At about 10.45 they were keeping a watchful eye on two German biplanes approaching a British reconnaissance machine over Polygon Wood and, their attention thus distracted, were suddenly surprised by the chatter of a machine-gun as an Aviatik two-seater swooped in close, its observer aiming his gun forward between the Aviatik's wings as it approached. Fortunately though, this was not an easy shot and the bullets went wide of the FE, allowing Graves to quickly turn towards his attacker and drive him off eastwards. Fifteen minutes later this was followed by another attack when a Fokker swept down on them from above and behind before passing over their heads under a hail of machine-gun bullets from Aked's Lewis gun. Both machines now turned to rush at each other and, although the German evidently had spirit, making two or three attacks in all, Graves recorded in his combat report afterwards that his opponent seemed to be something of a novice in that he did not appear to handle his machine quickly enough or to be much good with his gun. This may have been a trifle unfair, as it appears neither Graves nor Aked could keep their own guns on the German. The combat eventually ended without result and both machines went their separate ways[1].

There was another brush with the enemy the following day when Robert Anderson and recently arrived observer Lieutenant Herbert James Hamilton met a German machine over Ypres. The 21-year-old observer from Stroud Green, London, had worked in the silk trade before the war before enlisting in the Artists Rifles in 1913 and had seen action in Flanders from October 1914. Later commissioned in 1 Battalion the Duke of Cornwall's Light Infantry in August 1915, he transferred to the RFC in February 1916. Now he was in his first serious air fight, throughout which his efforts were frustrated by gun jams. The fight ended inconclusively and a disgusted Hamilton bemoaned the fact that his aircraft was not fitted with the Anderson mounting, which would have made clearing the gun jams and dealing with the enemy much easier[1]. In fact, eighty Anderson mountings had been ordered for the RFC by April 1916 but due to production difficulties in England, very few had actually arrived. So most of 20 Squadron's FE 's were still equipped with earlier designs[7]. The lack of a quick release mechanism when firing from the high rear pillar made changing the drums and clearing jams very difficult.

The first twenty days of April brought little but a series of inconclusive skirmishes for the squadron that at least gave the flyers more valuable experience. This casualty free co-existence had to end sometime, though, and on 21 April two FE2Bs on a reconnaissance escort got the worst of a fight over Zonnebeke, just to the south of where the famous Tyne Cot Memorial now stands. His pilot having been wounded, it fell to Air Mechanic First Class Samuel Catton, Norman McNaughton's gunner in A6332, to write the combat report afterwards and describe how they were attacked by a large biplane that opened fire at the somewhat optimistic range of 400 yards. Just as McNaughton began to turn towards their attacker, he was hit in the leg and stomach yet still managed to turn for home and reach the safety of the British lines before making a hurried landing, in which Catton was slightly injured and McNaughton was packed off to hospital. Fortunately, his stomach wound was not as serious as it might have been. Captain James and Second Lieutenant Exley were also lucky to avoid serious injury when they were forced to land near Ypres after being shot up by two Fokkers.

Such fighting as there was on 23 April brought only more frustration, when two of the Squadron's FEs were unable to catch two Rumplers carrying out a reconnaissance over Armentieres. The following day ended differently. Five FEs set out for the morning reconnaissance and after climbing to 9,500ft the 'X-shaped' formation flew northeastwards out over Poelcappelle. Morton and Billinge had been entrusted with carrying out the photography in A6339 and thus flew in the centre of the 'X'— a well-practised formation for 20 Squadron in which all the other machines took station in relation to the one with the camera. The patrol leaders, Graves and Chancellor, were flying 50 to 100 feet higher than A6339 and positioned themselves slightly ahead and to the right of Morton and Billinge, while Second Lieutenant Scott and Corporal Gawthrop in A6340 took up a similar position on the left. Meanwhile, the rear points of the 'X' were covered by Captain James and Second Lieutenant Exley in A5206 on the right and Second Lieutenant Dabbs and Corporal Ward in A6373 on the left, both machines flying approximately 500 feet higher than their leaders.

This type of formation, apparently a 20 Squadron invention, had a number of advantages. The first was that the pilot of the reconnaissance machine had all-round protection where he could see the observers of the machines ahead of him and any signals they made, as well as watching for signals from his own observer who had a clear view downwards. The second advantage was that, being higher, the pilots of the rear-most machines could easily keep a careful eye on all three machines in front of them. For their part, the observers of all the FEs except the reconnaissance machine – who would be taking the photographs – faced backwards to watch out for an attack from behind. Hand signals were used between the pilot and his observer: a clenched fist indicating enemy aircraft, while a thumbs-up indicated friendly machines. Other well-rehearsed signals between the two could be used to indicate anything from gun jams to engine problems.

Thus were the five FEs spaced out as they passed over Poelcappelle, then Staden where they turned roughly southeast towards Roulers, several miles behind the German lines. The trouble began as they approached the town. A German two-seater, thought to be a Rumpler, attacked Scott and Gawthrop's machine on the front left but broke off its attack in the face of Gawthrop's return fire. The whole formation then began a right turn over Roulers, but Scott and Gawthrop's machine lagged back, perhaps anticipating another attack by the Rumpler, and the formation was loosened a little. Just as the turn was finished, a Fokker came diving down on Captain James's machine at the right rear of the 'X' and broke off from its attack after a brief exchange of fire. Frank Billinge was now busily taking photographs of Roulers Station and while he did so another German machine, an unidentified biplane, attacked Captain James from behind. As his pilot swung the FE around, Exley sent a stream of tracers into their attacker so that smoke immediately poured out from the biplane's engine and it fell away in a vertical spin, its speed increasing steadily and the fabric tearing back from its wings seconds before it smashed into the ground[1]. But the fight was not over. Two more small fixed-engine biplanes that Second Lieutenant Dabbs described as being very much faster than the FEs swept down from the left front. They failed to hit any of the FEs as they dived through the hail of British fire and one that went down apparently out of control was confirmed by the watching Guard's Division as having fallen near Passchendaele[1]. Despite continuous attacks from all directions, the British flyers held their formation and saw off all comers. Then, having finished their work over Roulers, they turned for home taking the same route as before and making several formation turns over Staden to enable Billinge to take photographs of that area. As they did so, two more biplanes dived in to attack Scott and Gawthrop again and by the time they crossed the lines they had lost 3,000ft in the fighting and their machine had been badly shot about.

Major Malcolm prepared a Resume of Combat Reports for HQ 11 Wing afterwards and noted that flares had played their part once again. Scott's signal over Staden had alerted the whole escort to his danger and caused them to turn together straight at the two German scouts and drive them off. In drawing conclusions from the fight, Major Malcolm was of the firm opinion that the Germans' inability to penetrate the FEs tightly kept formation enabled Lieutenant Billinge to concentrate on the photography, which was carried out successfully while the gunners on the aircraft around him kept the enemy at bay[8]. Frank Billinge's combat report mentioned that the German anti-aircraft stopped just before the German aeroplanes launched their attack. This became a recurrent feature of the war in the air and pilots quickly learned that whenever so-called 'Archie' stopped, danger was imminent. He also reported that he did not at first notice the German aeroplanes, as he was too busy taking pictures.

So the fight ended with two more victories to the Squadron's tally. The two-seater shot down by James and Exley may well have been that of Offizierstellvertreter (warrant officer) Karl Ritter and Oberleutnant (first lieutenant) Dietrich Freiherr von Kanne of Flieger Abteilung (reconnaissance squadron) 41, who were both listed as killed in action over Roulers that day[4]. Then there was the biplane scout sent down out of control by Graves and Chancellor. But what were the 'small fixed engine biplanes' that they had seen? They were new to 20 Squadron's experience and were probably Halberstadt single-seat scouts. These had made their first appearance over the front in February 1916 and were now being encountered in increasing numbers. Although they were not much faster than the FE in level flight, their main advantage lay in their great strength and diving ability. Nonetheless, they were not overwhelmingly popular with their pilots and their heyday quickly passed when the first Albatros single-seaters began to appear later in the year.

April 24 also brought good news of an unexpected kind when RFC Communiqué No 34 announced that Hilary Champion, who had been posted missing on 29 February, had reported to RFC Headquarters on 23 April after escaping from Germany with another officer, Lieutenant H. S. Ward of 16

Squadron. The prisoners bribed one or more Germans into supplying them with civilian clothing and seized the chance to escape when the train taking them to the PoW camp at Heidleburg stopped at Villingen. As their guards stood around chatting on the platform, the two men jumped down from the other side of the train and disappeared. After arriving at the Swiss frontier the following morning, they were repatriated to England. Hilary Champion did not return to 20 Squadron, though. After being mentioned in despatches for his exploits, he went on to become a pilot and flight commander with 9 Reserve Squadron, finishing the war with the rank of temporary major. His pilot on 29 February, Lieutenant Newbold, also survived the war and in 1919 was mentioned in a report for valuable services in captivity.

The good news of Champion's escape was balanced five days later by the squadron's first combat fatality. On 29 April, a 20 Squadron reconnaissance formation was over Quesnoy when a Fokker attacked A6332 from the left. At this crucial moment, the FE's engine started to splutter and as Second Lieutenant Sampson hurriedly switched fuel tanks his aerial gunner Samuel Catton fired a red flare to alert the formation and then a quick burst of half a drum aimed at the German. The Fokker swung around onto their tail, firing hard and as Catton clambered up and returned fire from the back mounting, the FE's engine cut out completely. Sampson fired a green flare and turned for the lines and, as he did so, Catton fell back into his cockpit hit by bullets in the back and leg. Sampson managed to glide the stricken FE back over the lines and survived the resultant crash-landing in a ploughed field one-and-a-half miles southwest of Poperinghe but 19-year-old Samuel Catton, from Cheshire, was already dead. In a cruel twist of fate, the young aerial gunner was killed on the very day that the official notification of his qualification as an observer was published[9]. It was unusual for a mere air mechanic to receive this qualification and there is little doubt that he would have soon been promoted had he survived.

It was a sobering moment for everyone in the squadron. So far, all their losses – just four men, in fact – had been posted missing and were actually safe as prisoners of war. Samuel Catton was the first to die and is buried at Lijssenthoek Military Cemetery, not far from Poperinghe. Even when dead, authority still had one more trick to play on him in the shape of a simple clerical error. Many of the reports of the time were hand-written in pencil and this can always lead to misreading later. In Catton's case, the mistake was over his name, with the unfortunate result that, when the then Imperial War Graves Commission placed the standard headstone on his grave at Lijssenthoek cemetery during the 1920s, the stone was inscribed with the name Cotton instead of Catton and was also written that way in their records. So it remained for the next ninety years until the author spotted the mistake in 2006. The CWGC acted promptly on being presented with the evidence and Catton's gravestone and the commision website now bear his correct name. All the same, one cannot help but wonder how the mistake affected his mother and other family members over the years – and fear how many of those years were spent searching for a grave that bore the wrong name.

******

The Squadron had acquitted itself well during April but the month did not end without acrimony. Regular officers like Major Malcolm were not used to having their wishes questioned, least of all by temporary 'war only' subordinates. Equally, it must have been difficult for talented and enthusiastic civilians with no previous military experience to adapt to the curious ways and customs of the army. Major Malcolm had evidently recognised Robert Anderson's unique technical abilities and had offered to second him to the role of 'Officer in Charge of Experimental Work' at the squadron. Having made the offer with good intentions, he was probably taken aback by Anderson's rejection of it on the grounds that even if any of his ideas were taken up, he would not be consulted as to any modifications or alleged improvements to his inventions! Major Malcolm was even less pleased when Anderson put his complaints about the system in writing and asked that he should forward the letter to Major General Hugh Trenchard, General Officer Commanding the RFC on the Western Front, which Malcolm refused to do. So Anderson sent the letter direct to General Trenchard without other authority. The result was a summons to Brigade Headquarters and a personal dressing-down from Brigade Commander Brigadier-General Webb-Bowan.

Shortly after this, Anderson was given leave in England, following which he was appointed as the first flying officer to be attached to the new RFC Experimental Station at Orford, Suffolk. While there, he found his earlier complaints borne out by the discovery that his gun-mounting designs had been altered by the manufacturers for easier production and the changes had made the mountings less efficient. The lack of consultation annoyed him intensely, especially in view of the fact that the factory changes put lives at risk. He was not the kind of man to treat such foolery lightly and his uninvited personal appearances at various generals' offices to argue his case quickly turned the remainder of his career into a testimony to his own determination to get things put right, regardless of who he upset. However, he was setting himself against an officialdom that, regardless of the issues involved, had no patience with anyone who dared to question higher authority. The net result was that despite his clear dedication and technical brilliance, Anderson was in February 1917 required to resign his commission on the grounds of ill health – the unusual diagnosis being 'mental irritability'. It would seem that the army had taken offence and wanted rid of him but could find no grounds for disciplinary action. In succumbing to pressure from above, the medical officer who examined Anderson wrote of him:

> He suffers from too brilliant an intellect to be a successful military officer. He is a genius and like many of his class cannot possibly understand why he is not allowed to use his brains…were I asked my opinion of this case I should strongly urge him being sent back to civilian life where his extraordinary gifts would render him extremely useful to the country.

Robert Anderson then retired from the service, but was permitted to retain the rank of honorary Lieutenant[10]. Another officer to leave the squadron in April was Second Lieutenant Frank Maller. A 'founder member' observer, his logbook shows that up to and including 10 April he had carried out 21 operational flights including offensive patrols, reconnaissance and photography missions and bomber escort duties. He had also assisted in sending down a Rumpler out of control in the fight of 13 February. Originally commissioned into the Royal Dublin Fusiliers, he was now returning to his former unit.

******

Notes

1. Combat report.
2. WO 339/38332 & AIR 76 Officer's Service Record for Douglas Gayford.
3. Kirton: from King's School, Canterbury Roll of Honour.
4. *Casualties of the German Air Service* by Norman Franks, Frank Bailey and Rick Duiven (Grub Street Press).
5. WO 339/8138 – Major Malcolm's Officers Service Record.
6. Trafford Jones Attestation Papers and other information courtesy of Veterans Affairs Canada http://www.veterans.gc.ca.
7. AIR 1/1085/204/5/1727 – Gun Mountings.
8. AIR 1/1827/204/202/15 – Resume of Combat Reports 29/4/1916.
9. Auth. B.213 29.04.1916 – AIR 79, Samuel Catton's Service Record.
10. WO 339/31428 – Robert Anderson's Officers Service Record.

******

Chapter 4

Chivalrous Combats – May/June 1916

Adverse weather limited flying during the first half of May but on 16 May 1916 Second Lieutenant Trafford Jones was shot and killed and his observer Captain Forbes was hit in his lung and shoulder when A6359 was badly shot up in a fight over Ypres. That should have been the end of it except that, despite his wounds, Captain Forbes somehow managed to climb over the high cockpit structure behind him and reach into the pilot's cockpit. Taking over the controls, he then brought A6359 down to a safe landing on the British side of the lines in an exploit for which he was awarded the squadron's first decoration, the Military Cross. But this was little compensation for the loss of a man like Trafford Jones. The FE2B, A6359, was fitted with his new undercarriage and the fact that this made landings easier had no doubt contributed to his observer's survival. Perhaps the best memorial to the Canadian pilot was the RFC order of 15 October 1916 which instructed that his undercarriage should henceforth be fitted to all FE2Ds[2]. Trafford Jones was 20 Squadron's first pilot fatality and the first of many Canadians who would fly and later die with the squadron as the war continued. He left behind his wife, Madeline, and is buried at Reninghelst New Military Cemetery at Poperinghe. His loss would not be the only one to grieve his family, for on 21 October that year they would also lose his older brother Henry, killed in action serving with the Canadian Artillery near Vimy Ridge.

On 19 May, a 20 Squadron offensive patrol (OP) had reached 10,500ft over Passchendaele when Lieutenant Maxwell and Air Mechanic First Class D.A. Stewart in A5247 closed with a German two-seater, believed to be an Aviatik, some 200 feet above them and they fired up at it as it passed over their heads. The German machine suddenly lost height and, as Maxwell turned the FE back for a second attack, he came alongside the enemy so that Stewart was able to fire another three drums into it. Stewart had to change his ammunition drums by hand, of course, and at this altitude his fingers were so nearly frozen that he fumbled the next change and the empty ammunition drum flew back over his head and smashed the FEs propeller, effectively leaving them without an engine. Maxwell had no choice but to break off the action and glide back over the British side of the lines to a forced landing. Their last view of their adversary was as it dived away at increasing speed, its fate unknown[1].

The remaining FEs continued with the patrol and twenty minutes later were over Poelcappelle when Lieutenant A. D. Pearse and Air Mechanic First Class Hodder in A5248 spotted a German machine, its type not being recorded, edging towards them. As it grew closer the FE on their right suddenly turned in pursuit and, as Pearse did likewise, two more German machines appeared. One stayed out of range while the second closed in on the other FE, which suddenly started to go down towards the lines, evidently damaged. The first German they had sighted now came around to finish him off but Pearse immediately dived at it and the German swung around to attack them nose to nose. Being slightly higher than the German, it was perhaps a little easier for the British crew to aim their guns as the two machines closed, for after they opened fire the German side-slipped violently and went into a nose dive. The other two Germans now kept their distance and Pearse turned for the lines to guard his stricken comrade's tail until they were safely across. Men of the British 14 Corps had also been watching the fight from the ground and confirmed seeing the German aircraft fall on the German side of the lines[3].

Two days later the pilot of A6340, Second Lieutenant J.N. Francis, was wounded and had to break off from a fight between Boisinghe and Messines and make a forced landing near Poperinghe[1]. Then an afternoon patrol on the same day brought more bad luck when three FE2Bs and the two BE2Cs they were escorting on a photo reconnaissance of the Lille defences were turning for home over Menin. Flight Commander Captain C.E.H. James was flying his FE2B on the right of the 'X' shape formation in A5206 when a Fokker attacked the BE2C behind him. James immediately fired a red flare and turned to its assistance but quickly found himself under attack from both sides by two more Fokkers. Unfortunately, through concentrating on the turn manoeuvre, no one else saw Captain James's signal flare and it was only by chance that Lieutenant Cole-Hamilton suddenly realised that his machine was no longer present. Hurriedly turning back again, he saw his leader's FE going down fast, apparently in pursuit of a Fokker. But as the escort's first duty was to their vulnerable charges and there were several other Fokkers in the immediate vicinity, they could not go down to assist him. Meantime, Captain James's machine was hit in the crankcase and petrol tank, the magneto wires were shot through and the engine had stopped. Still a long way from the trenches he could only go down and, during the descent, his FE was hit yet again: this time by artillery or anti-aircraft fire that badly damaged its tail. Despite that, he managed to bring the FE down under control in a field near Zandwoorde but, as it was filled with

German infantry, there was no time for the 21-year-old ex-Border Regiment pilot or his observer, Lieutenant Aked, to set fire to their aircraft before they were taken prisoner and the FE was captured.

Cole-Hamilton and Billinge ended their combat report by noting that the missing FE climbed badly and was always lower than the other FE2Bs. However, watching anxiously from above as Captain James's FE landed, they could have been forgiven a wry smile when they then saw the German victor's machine glide in to land alongside the FE. For Fokker pilot Leutnant Wilhelm Frankl of FA 40 must have misjudged the wind or the terrain and his moment of triumph was somewhat soured as he clipped the ground with his propeller and overturned his aeroplane. As the British flyers turned for home, they would have been comforted by the thought that Captain James had made an apparently safe landing and this was confirmed a couple of weeks later when a German aeroplane dropped an undated message over the British lines that read:

> To the Royal Flying Corps, Bailleul,
>   Captain Hilton James and Lieutenant Aked were defeated in an aerial fight on the 21st and are in honourable captivity. They are completely unwounded.[4]

It was a brave attempt to keep a sense of chivalry in the increasingly bitter conflict –and provides an interesting contrast with the Second World War where it concerns the identity of the victorious German flyer. For 22- year-old Wilhelm Frankl was Jewish and, in being so, was unique in the history of the Imperial German Air Service. Having been at the front since May 1915, he was starting to make a name for himself and by the time he was killed in action in April 1917 he had collected a total of twenty combat victories and became the only German Jew ever to be awarded the *Pour le Merite*, or 'Blue Max' as it was commonly known.

For 20 Squadron, the first few months at the front had proved very successful and Major Malcolm's high regard for his squadron was reflected in his letters home. While modestly writing that his only role was to answer the telephone and issue orders to older and better fellows to go and do jobs he claimed he dared not do himself, he added that he was proud to command what he believed to be the best squadron in the corps and that this was due entirely to his officers and men. Although they had suffered casualties, he felt they had made the Germans pay dearly for them. When they were not flying or working on the ground, the officers and men could enjoy musical recreation – with, he claimed, the photographic section possessing the loudest gramophone in the corps – while the squadron Pierrot troupe that the sergeant major had organised provided further entertainment.

Continuing, he wrote that next to its skills in air fighting his squadron took greatest pride in the quality of its aerial photography over every town one cared to imagine up to twenty miles behind the German lines from Lille to the sea. He also wrote how he was looking forward to the unit receiving the new and more powerful FE2D aircraft with its 250HP Rolls Royce engine. Once they arrived, he wrote, 'life in the German Flying Corps round here will be even less worth living than it is at present'.[5]

******

The soon to arrive FE2D referred to by Major Malcolm was only marginally faster than the FE2B it would replace, as the increase in horsepower was somewhat offset by its increased weight of 3,470lb against the FE2B's 3,037lb. Even so, the extra power did allow it to carry heavier loads including three Lewis guns in place of the original one or two, plus more bombs and cameras. Annoyingly though, its arrival in France was marred by an upset that infuriated many on the British side when it was captured intact by the Germans after its pilot, Lieutenant S.C.T. Littlewood, inadvertently landed at the German airfield of Haubourdin in very poor weather. Despite the setback, more FE2Ds were delivered over the coming weeks. The first arrived the following day and, by the end of June, 20 Squadron had thirteen on charge. In the meantime, the closest fight of this period came on 8 June.

Two FEs were patrolling at 10,000ft over Boisinghe when they noticed two German biplanes approaching the lines from the southeast. The enemy machines sheared off on spotting the FEs and flew north of them crossing the lines over the floods just north of Boisinghe. Lieutenants Scott and White in FE2B A6340 caught up with them just after they crossed the lines and fired a red flare to attract the attention of the other 'Fee' A6364, whose crew, Second Lieutenants J.B. Blackwood and Norman Caton, seemed unaware of the developing situation. Then came a nasty shock for Scott and White, for no sooner had they fired their flare than the two German machines, which were about 1,000ft higher than the FE, dived straight towards them firing through their propellers. The German fire was accurate, completely riddling A6340, before they managed to get it back over the lines to a very heavy landing at Clairmarais, in which it was further damaged as the under-carriage collapsed. The German machines were described as being of unknown type but, once again, were probably Halberstadt scouts[1].

Part of the RFC's response to the appearance of the fast new German scouts was to increase the strength of its frontline squadrons from twelve to eighteen aircraft, with pilot strength rising to twenty with an accompanying ground-crew increase of three more corporals, six fitters and six riggers. In 20 Squadron's case, the increase was not completed until late July[6]. There were also some personnel changes. Norman Caton returned to the Royal Field Artillery on 12 June 1916 and the next notable date in the squadron's affairs came on 16 June 1916 with the arrival of two replacement pilots from across the Atlantic.

Lieutenant Harold E. Hartney was a Toronto barrister who had initially served with the Saskatoon 105 Fusiliers in 28 Battalion Canadian Expeditionary Force. He had married his bride, Irene, in Canada on 11 November 1914 and had volunteered for the RFC while his unit was undergoing infantry training in England the following year. Irene joined him in England during July when they spent what free time he had in a rented cottage overlooking Hythe, Kent. It was while stationed near there that Hartney got his first real experience of war during a Zeppelin raid that left eighteen of his battalion dead and reinforced his desire to become a flyer. Accepted on his second application, Hartney joined the RFC on 21 October 1915 and soon qualified as a pilot. However, his departure to France was delayed by a severe bout of rheumatic fever involving hospitalisation and a lengthy convalescence, so it was not until June 1916 that he finally received his embarkation orders.

Hartney's arrival at the Squadron was eventful. According to his published memoir *Wings Over France*, his companion was an American flyer who, during the train journey across France, had expressed grave misgivings about the safety of the heavy 'Fees' they were destined to fly. After rashly repeating his complaints to their new CO, Major Malcolm swiftly ordered him to return from whence he came. He did not want him in his squadron.

Hartney then presented himself in a more acceptable fashion, and the CO's anger immediately subsided. Major Malcolm welcomed him to the squadron and told him that he would be assigned to A Flight, adding for good measure that he should get in as much flying as he could before he went into action. In the event, that turned out to be just two flights before he was sent out on his 'Cook's Tour' of the Front on 21 June. Flying with Lieutenant Dewar as his gunner and with another 'Fee' as escort, he was shown the lines from the North Sea to a point somewhere south of Clairmarais during which he experienced his first taste of 'Archie', as anti-aircraft fire had been popularly dubbed. Thereafter he would be a fully participating member of the squadron in all respects[7]. As for his observer: 23-year-old Alexander Dewar had also crossed the Atlantic to help the motherland, for, although born in Edinburgh, he had emigrated to Canada before the war and had seen volunteer service in the 19 Alberta Dragoons while working as a cattle rancher. He was posted as an observer on probation on 1 April 1916 and to 20 Squadron on the 17 April.

Squadron commanders were not meant to cross the lines or take any other unnecessary risks as it was felt that their experience was of more importance to the RFC than individual heroics. However, Major Malcolm was not the type to order his men to take risks that he was not prepared to share. Thus, having availed himself of some excuse, he and his observer Second Lieutenant G. E. Chancellor were airborne close to the lines near Ypres at about 11.45 on 22 June. On seeing two German LVG reconnaissance machines over our side of the lines, Major Malcolm immediately went in to the attack, quickly firing off two drums at one of the LVGs, which replied in kind, courtesy of its own observer in the rear cockpit. At this point, a FE8, a small British single-seat 'pusher' fighter similar to the DH2, came up and joined in the attack, only to quickly break off and plunge earthwards out of control. Major Malcolm continued the fight and, after about five drums had been fired, the LVG went down very quickly towards its own lines as if he had been hit[1]. As to the FE8, Major Malcolm's description of its fall had, unfortunately, been entirely accurate. It belonged to 29 Squadron, another of 2 Brigade's units and was being flown by Captain L.H. Sweet when it was hit by some of the German observer's bullets. It fell all the way to the ground and Captain Sweet was killed.

******

Although the River Somme was well to the south of 20 Squadron's area of operations, there was still room for them to play a secondary role in the coming battle that would be fought there. Air activities around Ypres might have useful effects by drawing German attention away from the steady movement of British reinforcements to the Somme. By attacking the northern balloon line and preventing German reconnaissance aircraft from spying over the area, the resultant weakening of British defences there might go unnoticed. In the last week of June 1916, 2 Brigade's squadrons were assigned the job of destroying all the German observation balloons on their section of the front. This was no small task but, if successful, they would have poked out one of the German army's eyes.

Attacking observation balloons was not easy. They were usually heavily defended by anti-aircraft positions and could frequently be punctured by hundreds of bullets without any apparent effect. The raids would therefore involve both machine-gun attacks with incendiary bullets and dropping phosphorous bombs as the main weapons. According to Harold Hartney, the attack went ahead on 30 June and 20 Squadron was assigned to escort the BE bombers in the assault. Lieutenant Hartney, recording his memories of his first operational mission, describes how the attack was not without its tragic-comic side, with the phosphorous bombs on the first two BEs exploding during take-off and destroying five machines and two hangars. His own FE2D, was unscathed, however, and the raid went ahead regardless.

Once across the lines, Hartney watched the bombs rain down on the German positions – without any hitting their target, it has to be said – when out of the clouds came another biplane bearing two black crosses on its wings diving for the safety of German territory. It was a Rumpler two-seater, to which Hartney gave chase. However, when his gunner, Air Mechanic First Class Hodder, signalled that his guns had jammed, he was forced to break off the attack as the German gunner was now spraying them with machine-gun fire. Hartney's FE was the only one of the Squadron to meet the enemy in the air that day and, although he was praised in the mess afterwards, his own view was that the whole thing had been a complete flop. This view was underlined by the fact that not a single enemy balloon had been destroyed anywhere along the front throughout the whole day. Such a result was extremely disappointing for all concerned but, given the facts that an accurate bomb-sight had still to be invented and that attacking such heavily defended targets was in any case so extremely hazardous, it should not, perhaps, have come as a complete surprise[7].

When evening fell, Hartney and the other officers were called to a special briefing at which they were told what their duties would be the following morning. It would be the morning of 1 July 1916, the first day of the Battle of the Somme. By mounting continuous patrols between Armentieres on the British side of the lines and Lille well inside the German lines, it was hoped the RFC on the Ypres front would succeed in keeping the German units based there so busy that they would not be able to help their beleaguered forces further south. As Major Malcolm put it to his men: 'We must knock the Germans out of the air.'[7] They would take him at his word.

******

Notes

1.   Combat Report.
2.   *Windsock International:* Vol.10/6, Dec 1994.
3.   AIR 1/1579/204/81/2 – 2nd Brig. War Diary, RFC Communiqués and C/R.

4. AIR 1/435/15/273/11 – Fate of Missing Airmen, Messages dropped by Germans.
5. Major Malcolm's Letters, by kind permission of Nick Boles.
6. AIR 1/1001/204/15/1258-60 – Policy and Organisation August 1915 to March 1917.
7. *Wings over France* by Harold E. Hartney.

Chapter 5

Triumphs and Tragedies – July 1916

At 04.15 on Saturday 1 July, the five FE2s detailed to escort a bombing raid from Bailleul trundled slowly across the grass at Clairmarais and into the air. When they had gained some height they formed up in 20 Squadron's distinctive 'X' formation with the flight leader's FE, containing Lieutenant Spratt and Corporal Stringer, in the centre of the 'X'. The FE2Ds flown by Lieutenants Birch and Lascelles and Lieutenants Blackwood and White took up station just ahead to the right and left of the flight leader, while Harold Hartney and Air Mechanic Second Class 6717 A.O. Stanley in FE2D A3 took up position behind and to the left with Lieutenant Tyrell and Air Mechanic First Class Hodder on the right. The formation then made its way to Bailleul for the agreed rendezvous but, after circling around for 25 minutes without seeing any of the bombing machines, they left for the lines without them, crossing over just south of Armentieres.

The German reaction was immediate. First one Fokker came up to harry them and, no sooner had they driven it off, another came up from Lille. This one dived right through the centre of the formation, firing at the leader, then straight into a hail of fire from Corporal Stringer that caused it to suddenly loop and spin down out of control. The FEs then turned northeast and, after driving off two more Fokkers between Menin and Courtrai, came under attack from two more that swooped down on Tyrell's machine on the right rear of the 'X' and forced him out of the formation. Hartney immediately fired a red flare to attract the others and swung his own FE around to help Tyrell. But the result was to split the 'X-formation' in two, with Hartney's and Tyrell's machines forced into an eastward running fight, while the main formation continued northeast but was also under attack. Lieutenant Birch managed to bring down a Fokker that crashed to the ground near Mouveux and, while doing this, was also able to keep sight of Hartney's and Tyrell's machines in the distance. Still the attacks came in on Lieutenant Spratt and the two FEs remaining with him, while Hartney's and Tyrell's machines grew ever more distant, fighting hard all the way.

According to Hartney's combat report, his separation from the main formation led him into nine successive combats. The first of these was when he turned to assist Tyrell, getting behind one of the Fokkers with Stanley firing short bursts until it suddenly dived away with heavy smoke pouring from its engine. Hartney now tried to turn to rejoin the patrol over Tourcoing but was prevented from doing so as another Fokker dived on his tail. Some hurried side-slipping and a left turn brought the Fokker into close range, and Hartney followed it down with Stanley firing hard until it fell away apparently out of control. Another attack prevented them from seeing its fate but was driven off after some adept diving, sideslipping and a complete right-hand circle brought the Fokker within range. In the brief respite that followed, Hartney again turned to try to rejoin the formation, which was in his own words 'scattered high and southwards', but again came under attack from the rear. Another full circle brought this machine into their sights and a burst of fire sent it too diving away. A further attack ended in a similar way as Hartney tried to regain some of the height he had lost. The Germans appeared to be learning fast from their lack of success and, at exactly the moment Stanley signalled yet another attack from behind, Hartney spotted a second Fokker diving in to attack them from the front. A long-range burst of fire from the FE forced it to swerve away but, even as it did so, a stream of bullets from the Fokker behind hit the FE's engine, which at once began to lose power. Despite that, Hartney managed to turn on the enemy once again and a withering burst from Stanley seemed to hit the pilot, who lurched up in his seat and collapsed, and the Fokker spun away earthwards.

The Germans were still not giving up though. Two more now came in to attack A3 from either side and, while Stanley tried to keep them at bay with his one remaining Lewis gun, the other having jammed, Hartney tried to nurse the stricken FE towards the lines, its engine steadily losing power all the way. It was a long time since he had seen Tyrell's machine and his relief must have been indescribable when another of the patrol's FEs finally came up alongside to help drive off the Fokkers. All Hartney wanted now was to get home in one piece and, after signalling the other FE of his intentions, he continued towards the trench-lines. Both of Stanley's guns had now jammed and, with the engine almost dead, the only thing Hartney could do was to glide westwards as level as possible, his machine now only having 6,000ft altitude and still being well east of the lines. Now came the last attack, again from behind and, at Stanley's signal, Hartney swung the battered FE around one last time. 'Fee' and Fokker now raced at each other nose-to-nose but, with a collision imminent, Stanley swung his jammed Lewis gun around as if to open fire on the Fokker, which immediately swerved away and dived off towards Lille.

All they had to do now was to get back over the lines but, with the battle-scarred machine barely responding to the controls, they must have both endured many heart-stopping moments as German anti-aircraft guns now joined in the assault. They finally crossed the lines with black clouds of German 'Archie' bursts mushrooming all around them and, with their engine having seized due to the oil and water systems being hit, they came down to an unexpectedly successful landing on the main road between Armentieres and Bailleul. There, according to Hartney's own account in *Wings over France*, the two flyers, officer and non-com, hugged each other wildly in exultation and relief. It had been a desperately near run thing[1, 2].

But what of the others? They had also been heavily engaged, and one of the retreating Fokkers had strayed towards the lines where it was spotted by Guy Reid and Captain Dixon-Spain in FE2D, serial number A11, who had watched the fighting from a distance while carrying out a line patrol. They now attacked the lone Fokker and sent it crashing to earth just north of Comines, at trench map reference 28.P.28[1]. A married man from Hythe, in Kent, 27-year-old former lecturer and draughtsman Captain Gerald Dixon-Spain had been with 20 Squadron since March. First commissioned in the 23 Royal Fusiliers he had served as a Battalion Musketry Officer with the Hampshire Regiment in 1915 and attended the Senior Officers Course at Staff College. Following that, he commanded an infantry company in France before transferring to the RFC. Lieutenant Scott and Second Lieutenant Exley also met the enemy that morning while patrolling over Ypres. First they attacked two enemy two-seaters above the German trenches at St. Eloi and forced one to land, then fought another two a little later. But this second fight proved less decisive as, according to their combat report, the enemy seemed disinclined to fight[1].

Once everyone had found their way back to Clairmarais and their reports had been analysed, Lieutenants Birch and Lascelles were credited with the Fokker they shot down and saw crash near Mouveux in the early stages. Another 'destroyed' claim was granted to Guy Reid and Captain Dixon-Spain, and two 'out of control' victories were officially credited to Harold Hartney and Air Mechanic Stanley for their efforts, with one more being awarded to Lieutenant Spratt and Corporal Stringer. It had been a good day for 20 Squadron. Its airmen had been credited with shooting down five Fokkers and forcing a two-seater to land, without loss. Apart from Tyrell being wounded, it was exactly what Major Malcolm had ordered!

******

On 4 and 5 July 1916, the squadron saw the arrival of two replacement pilots. They were 18-year-old Second Lieutenant E.D. Spicer, from Parkstone, Dorset, and Second Lieutenant Brian Laidley Dowling, a former engineer from Sydney, Australia, who had surrendered his captaincy in the Australian Army Service Corps on transferring to the RFC. Two events were recorded on Saturday 8 July: one of less importance than the other and both being overshadowed by unrelated events on the following day. In the first of Saturday's events, Second Lieutenant Birch took off across wind in FE2D A10 for a practice photography flight but hit some standing corn and was injured as the machine overturned[3], while the second event revolved around a new Sergeant Pilot reporting to Major Malcolm. Unremarkable though the young sergeant may have looked, his future would turn out to be most significant. For this young man was none other than Sergeant James T. McCudden who, having started his RFC service as a lowly Air Mechanic, had proved his worth as an observer before being rewarded with pilot training. Nobody would have guessed that this quiet and serious young NCO would go on to become one of the RFC's most celebrated aces. McCudden achieved more than fifty combat victories on DH2s and SE5s, the rank of major and a VC before his untimely death in a flying accident in 1918. For now, he would have to be content with a month flying FE2s at 20 Squadron that would, in comparison to his future as a scout pilot, pass quite peacefully. But Major Malcolm and Sergeant McCudden's acquaintance would be unexpectedly cut short.

The following morning, Sunday 9 July, McCudden made his first practise flight on a FE2D while others flew a patrol during which Lieutenant Chancellor experienced a show of flying fellowship between enemies after he tried to engage a Fokker monoplane. His pilot having out-manoeuvred the German and got the 'Fee' into a good firing position Chancellor was mortified to find that both his guns had jammed and, as his aircraft rapidly overtook and passed the Fokker, he gave the German a wave instead of a burst of gunfire. Whether the German was in an identical predicament is not known but he responded by waving back and flying away. The fact that the German had not immediately returned to the attack probably saved Chancellor's and his pilot's lives but it was only a temporary reprieve for the young observer. Later on in the day, Major Malcolm decided to bring over A20, one of the new FE2Ds that had just been delivered to the aircraft depot, and took Chancellor along with him. They took off northeastwards over the wood by the aerodrome and were scarcely fifty feet up when the engine failed and the aircraft plunged down into the trees and burst into flames, killing both men.

It was a devastating blow for the squadron. The loss of the popular CO was bad and Geoffrey Chancellor would also be sorely missed. Having been one of the squadron's founder members when it arrived in France at the end of January 1916, the Eton educated ex-OTC sergeant was just eighteen when he died. The war could not be stopped in sympathy, of course, and operational flying continued as usual even as Major Malcolm's replacement was on his way. In addition to night bombing raids against enemy supply dumps, railways, bridges and billets, some valuable night reconnaissances were carried out on 9 and 10 July that kept track of German troop and rail movements from the northwest. These were later shown to be part of a German army division's move to the Cambrai/Marcoing area in the south[4].

The new CO of 20 Squadron arrived on the 10 July. Major William Mansfield was the 30-year-old son of Lieutenant Colonel the Honourable H.W. Mansfield, from Old Catton, Norwich, and had originally been commissioned in the Shropshire Light infantry in 1909. He had attended the Central Flying School in January 1914, and, along with a number of other early RFC pilots, he had been mentioned in despatches for his service in the very early days of the war. By December 1914, he had been gazetted as a temporary captain and flight commander and in February 1915 he was awarded the DSO. This was followed on 27 March 1916 by the *London Gazette* announcing his appointment as Temporary Major and Commanding Officer of No.39 Squadron in England. Now he was in France again and one of his first duties was to supervise the funeral arrangements for Major Malcolm and Lieutenant Chancellor. Major Mansfield paraded the entire squadron for the following day's service at the French Souvenir Cemetery at St. Omer, also attended by a brigadier and five other staff officers.

******

Sergeant McCudden and Major Mansfield were not the only new arrivals at 20 Squadron as three new flight commanders had also been posted in. Two of them had transferred from 25 Squadron, which also flew FE2Bs. The first to arrive, back in May, was Captain Reginald Stuart Maxwell, or 'George' as he preferred to be called. He was credited with having forced down an Aviatik two-seater while with 25 Squadron and would prove just as combative with his new unit. Shortly afterwards he was joined by fellow ex-25 Squadron pilot Captain George Ranald Mcfarlane Reid. Reid had been commissioned into the 4 Battalion (Special Reserve) Argyll and Sutherland Highlanders in August 1914 and had been sent to France with the 2 Battalion Royal Highlanders (The Black Watch) in January 1915. He fought at Neuve Chapelle where his batman was killed by a sniper and on 9 May of that year he was himself wounded in the head by a sniper at the battle of Festubert. Sent home to recuperate, he subsequently transferred to the RFC. He returned to France in February 1916 on being posted to 25 Squadron, in which he scored three combat victories. He later wrote that he liked the FE2Bs very much, although he found them 'a little slow'. His new squadron with the slightly faster FE2Ds with their more powerful engines 'did similar work to 25 but went further afield on their better aeroplanes'.[5].

So 20 Squadron now had two pilots named Reid on the roster, the other one being squadron founder member Guy Patrick Spence Reid who, with Frank Billinge as his observer, had distinguished himself by claiming 20 Squadron's first combat victory on 7 February 1916. The third new flight commander was 19-year-old Captain Guy Teale. The son of Herbert Greenwood and Virginia Mary Teale, of De Vere Gardens, Kensington, London, he had previously served with the Buffs and as an instructor at the Central Flying School. In November 1915 he had gone to France with 18 Squadron, which then flew the Vickers FB5 'gun-bus' but had recently converted to the FE2B. The fact that a mere 19-year-old could have done so much and risen to captain so quickly says much for his qualities – but also the casualty rates being suffered at this time. Another new arrival around this time was 23-year-old former mining engineer Lieutenant J.K. Stead from Everdon, Redcar, Yorkshire, who had seen previous service as a subaltern with 4 Yorkshire Regiment before transferring to the RFC and qualifying as a pilot.

The funerals behind them, 20 Squadron's men began to settle back into the familiar routine of patrols, with McCudden flying five patrols with Lieutenant Lascelles, Lieutenant Statt and Corporal Stringer as his observers by 19 July. On the following day – just as it seemed everything was getting back to normal – tragedy struck again. Five FEs took off at 05.30 on an OP led by Captain Maxwell but within a few minutes a thick ground mist rolled in from the northwest and covered the land from horizon to horizon. The FEs flew this way and that and became separated in their efforts to get their bearings, eventually landing wherever they could. Captain Maxwell and Sergeant McCudden managed to get their machines down safely, the latter in a field near St. Pol, but Captain Teale and Corporal Stringer were both killed trying to land A18 in the mist at Roellecourt, while the other two FEs also crashed causing serious injuries to all concerned. Captain Blatherwick and Air Mechanic Stanley (A16) and Lieutenant D.S. Davies eventually recovered but Davies's gunner, Corporal 3836 William Moore did not. After being repatriated to England with serious spinal injuries, he died on 1 September 1916 and, as far as is known, is the squadron's only member killed on active service to have been buried in his hometown: at All Saints Cemetery at Fleet, Hampshire. The two other fatalities, James Stringer and Guy Teale, were buried at St. Pol. Corporal 10068 Stringer came from Moston, Manchester, and after ten years service had been invalided out of the Royal Navy before enlisting in the RFC in October 1915. He left a wife, Ada, and their one child, Frances.

The following day brought James McCudden his very first experience of aerial fighting as a pilot. At 09.00 that morning he and Lieutenant C.C. Statt were patrolling over Bethune in FE2D A6 at 11,000ft when he noticed a Rumpler being shelled by British anti-aircraft fire. With an early show of the aggressive spirit for which he would later become famous, McCudden turned to attack the German intruder and opened fire at a range of about 250 yards. The German was having none of it and immediately turned eastwards for the safety of his own lines. McCudden followed hopefully but it was a lost cause. As his combat report concluded: 'A6 being a slow machine was left behind.'[1]

After another week of fairly uneventful patrols and reconnaissances, 20 Squadron's last conclusive fight that month came on 29 July when Captain G.R.M. Reid and Lieutenant L.H. Scott were patrolling in FE2D A22 at 8,000ft over Zandwoorde. There they closed to within 20 yards of two Rumplers and opened fire on one of them but Reid took little pleasure in the clear-cut victory that resulted. He later wrote:

I dived on a German biplane and opened fire: either we hit him and removed his wings or he was startled into the fatal dive, which tore them off. As I watched the poor young chaps hurtling to their deaths I had all sorts of emotions, with pity overshadowing the triumph.'[1, 5]

The German's death-dive was witnessed by the crew of another FE accompanying them, and two German flyers who died that day over Zandwoorde were Leutnant D. R. Rudolf Kisker, a 27-year old pilot with FA.3, and his observer, Oberleutnant Eberhard Freiherr Von Holtz[6]. In the absence of any other claims, it would seem that the two sets of records probably match.

******

Notes

1. Combat Report.
2. *Wings over France* by Harold E. Hartney.

3. AIR 1/967/204/5/1097: Pilot and Observer Casualties.
4. AIR 1/689/21/20/20: 20 Squadron History.
5. Memoir of Air Vice Marshal Ranald McFarlane Reid: Documents Archive of the I.W.M. Reproduced by kind permission.
6. *Casualties of the German Air Service* by Franks, Bailey & Duiven.

Chapter 6

First Aces – August/September 1916

O ne of the highest accolades that a pilot of the First World War could receive was to become known as an 'ace': a pilot who had shot down five or more enemy aircraft. In France and Germany, the pilot who achieved this status could expect the highest gallantry awards with his name and photograph in all the major newspapers and, in short, something akin to the cult personality celebrity status of the present day. The more reserved British authorities seemed, for a while at least, to resist using the term and discouraged the lionisation of particularly successful individuals above the many who also served and often died with far less fanfare. Gallantry medals would be awarded and reported in the traditional manner when appropriate but, other than in the most exceptional circumstances, the names of the highest scoring British and Empire aces would not become well known until much later in the war.

By the end of July 1916, a number of British, French and German pilots had achieved five or more victories, almost all of them flying single-seat scout aeroplanes. Max Immelman and Oswald Boelke were household names in Germany while Charles Nungesser enjoyed similar fame in France. The British, had their names been publicised as widely, could include Lanoe Hawker and Albert Ball in the list, to which would soon be added some of 20 Squadron's pilots. Captain G.R.M. Reid had already scored three victories with 25 Squadron and, since his transfer, had added two more on 29 and 31 July, bringing him up to the magic number five. He had thus become an ace, although in terms of scores achieved only within 20 Squadron, his two victories put him on an equal footing with four others: the captain's namesake Second Lieutenant G.P.S. Reid, along with Second Lieutenant P.G. Scott, Lieutenant Harold Hartney and observer Second Lieutenant G.A. Exley. As yet, nobody had achieved 'ace' status for victories scored only within 20 Squadron but, this would not remain the case for much longer. In fact, as the fighting on the Somme rumbled on in the south, the beginning of August 1916 brought 20 Squadron three victories in three days. On Tuesday 1 August Second Lieutenant D. H. Dabbs and Air Mechanic Stewart engaged a lone Fokker over Moorslede at around four in the afternoon. Dabbs opened fire at about 150yds and saw his tracers pour into the enemy machine between the engine and pilot. The Fokker went into a dive and, seeing no other enemy machines in the vicinity, Dabbs dived after it with Stewart firing continuously. The Fokker did not level out and crashed into a field just south of Poelcappelle. DH2 pilot, Second Lieutenant Brearly of 29 Squadron and another FE that had been racing to help in the fight confirmed its fall[1].

Observer Lieutenant E. H. Lascelles was wounded by anti-aircraft fire on 2 August but this was followed by two more victories for the squadron the next day. In the first of these, Second Lieutenant Guy Reid and Captain Dixon-Spain, noticed an Aviatik two-seater approaching the lines from Ledeghem and a Fokker coming up from Menin. Both places were roughly southeast of the FE and Reid attacked the Fokker head-on. Guy Reid fired off two-and-a-half drums from his fixed gun as the two machines rushed towards each other at a combined speed of about 180mph. Just as a collision seemed inevitable the German dived away and passed under the FE's wheels with only a few feet to spare. Reid now swung the FE around to take on the Aviatik and, after forcing it to flee back towards Roulers, he again dived on the Fokker, which had flattened out some 2,000ft below, sending it down further in a spinning nose-dive until they lost sight of it against the background land colours. Moments later, the German anti-aircraft gunners opened up on them in a furious bombardment and, since the German 'Archie' seldom fired at British machines when their own aircraft were in the immediate vicinity, it might be assumed that the Fokker had either crashed or landed. Whatever the case, they were awarded an 'out of control' victory, making Reid's third and Dixon-Spain's second[1]. The 'fixed gun' used by Reid was a recent addition to the FE2D's arsenal designed by Captain Dixon-Spain. In brief, a pillar gun mounting had been fitted inside the right-hand wall of the pilot's cockpit carrying a Lewis gun fixed to aim straight ahead that was fired by means of a Bowden cable. It would be officially accepted and named as the 'Dixon-Spain Gun Mounting' and would be recommended to all FE2D squadrons[4].

Forty minutes later, Captain Maxwell and Air Mechanic Stewart were carrying out an altitude test at 10,000ft above the lines near Ypres when they spotted an approaching German two-seater. Maxwell did not recognise the type and described it as a biplane that was rather fatter than a Rumpler with a stationary engine and the observer seated behind the pilot, which may well have described a Roland CII. The enemy observer opened fire as they approached and, as the FE began to return fire, the German pilot turned back in a zigzag dive with the FE in hot pursuit. This was a bad mistake as it allowed Maxwell to close the gap. The pursuit now turned south with both machines firing at each other almost continuously and, after about ten minutes, they had come down to 5,000ft with the enemy clearly in difficulties. The German pilot then seemed to lose control and his aircraft went into a steepening dive before crashing into the ground close to some trees on the edge of a field just north of Gheluvelt. It had taken Maxwell and Stewart twelve-and-a-half drums of ammunition to win the victory and although, as in so many cases, there is no firm evidence as to the identity of the downed German crew, they were credited with a hostile machine destroyed. However, their satisfaction at the result was probably slightly dented when Maxwell's combat report was returned with a curt, unsigned note pencilled-in at the bottom, presumably from a brass-hat at Wing or Brigade HQ, which read: 'Inform Maxwell that tests should not be carried out over the trench line.' Taking a possibly faulty machine into an area swarming with Germans was probably not the wisest move, although one has to admire the spirit[1].

On 7 August James McCudden flew his last two FE2D flights, carrying ground crew NCOs, Corporal Farmer and Corporal Hughes, on separate test flights of A6 following an overhaul. A few hours later, he was practising over Abeele in a DH2 single-seat scout after his transfer to 29 Squadron. He had flown a total of fifteen hours on FE2Ds with 20 Squadron but, as shown in his logbook,[2] he had by this time completed a total of 150 hours 30 minutes flying time as a pilot. Thus the future ace would start his career at 29 Squadron with a great deal more flying time behind him than most new scout pilots – and it would stand him in good stead.

It was around this time that Major Mansfield received a request from Headquarters for a report on the fighting techniques used in 20 Squadron. His reply of 13 August[3] makes some interesting points. In answering the first question regarding enemy formations, he wrote that the enemy seldom used any formation but that the leader carried streamers for quick identification in a dogfight. He was able to say much more concerning 20 Squadron's methods, clearly explaining all the advantages of the 'X-shape' formation in which each pilot and observer watched every other machine and the leaders were thus able to set the speed of the formation to that of the slowest. Not only that but the pilot of the camera carrying aeroplane in the middle of the 'X' could watch the two escorts ahead without having to look around, which was good as he also had to keep an eye open for any signals from his own observer.

Adjusting the speed of the formation to the slowest was essential in ensuring that no one became isolated and thus an easy target. It was also the policy adopted by the Admiralty in the case of shipping convoys. As to the 'X' formation itself: Major Mansfield's lucid explanation of its benefits provides a good clue as to why the Germans found it so difficult to deal with the FEs. With regard to German and British methods of attack, Major Mansfield noted that the Germans usually attacked in a dive from the rear and, perhaps reflecting the problems the Fokker pilots were finding in fighting the FEs, he added that recently the attacks on his aircraft had been very half-hearted and easily thwarted. In turning to the British method of attack, Major Mansfield echoed the great German Ace Oswald Boelke and his famous dicta: The general principles, he wrote, were to attack a forward firing aircraft from above and behind, whereas a rearward firing aircraft should be attacked from above and in front so the enemy observer could not easily bring his gun to bear, adding that the usual enemy tactic on being attacked was to dive for safety.

Despite the last comments, it would be very wrong to draw the conclusion that the German pilots lacked courage. Diving away was not just an escape mechanism. It was also an invitation to rash or inexperienced pilots to leave the FE formation and dive down low in pursuit, where they would then become isolated and a much easier target for the Germans. Diving away might also be common sense. The Fokkers were simply not a match for the FE2D and even the Halberstadt biplanes, despite their strength and manoeuvrability, were not invincible. However, if a Halberstadt pilot could lure a FE2 into diving after it, he might then be able to use his dive energy to suddenly zoom up and make a second attack on the British plane.

The next question was perhaps framed in order to help the senior officers improve pilot training. Here Major Mansfield pointed out that the main problems in formation flying arose because there were so many things for a new pilot to think about. He had to keep control of his machine, maintain his formation, watch for enemy aircraft, note his route by reference to landmarks and watch his observer for any signals. All these things had to be done continually and simultaneously and, with experience, the ability to do so instinctively would come in time for every pilot. At least Major Mansfield's men had a good chance of living long enough to gain that experience, for the 'X' formation used by his squadron seems to have been designed with that very thing in mind. As to the new pilot in combat, the Major felt that the newcomer's main difficulty lay with aircraft recognition where they needed to be quicker in recognising the type of enemy aircraft and thus from which angle to attack. It is to be hoped that due note was taken of his views and that training was adapted to include greater emphasis on formation flying and aircraft recognition, particularly of enemy aircraft.

Second Lieutenant Dewar marked a day of achievement on 15 August when, with his probation ended, he was officially allowed to 'put up his wing' after becoming a fully-fledged observer. The next day, Major Mansfield was again putting pen to paper: this time in answer to HQ's concerns over gun jams, (or jambs as they then called them) having left Lieutenants Pearce and Findlay temporarily defenceless in A7995 during a fight with two Fokkers over Fortuin the previous day. The first jam, the Major wrote, was caused by a defective cartridge case, causing the extractors to break off at the rim and stop the bolt action from functioning. The second one was due to the cartridge dropping down into the bolt instead of being ejected properly, although Findlay was able to clear this one. Faulty ammunition was often the result of poor quality-control systems at the factories, sometimes resulting from cost-cutting greed on the part of the manufacturer but, often as not, from ignorance of the standards required. In an effort to avoid such problems in the air, many pilots and observers insisted on loading their guns themselves before a patrol and became quite meticulous in checking every bullet and the free working of the guns. It was time consuming but it was time well spent. Temperature extremes were another common cause of jams, when unsatisfactory lubricants would thicken or freeze at great altitudes and the moving parts of the gun would quickly overheat and seize up when it was fired. These problems were not the only ones and more would come to light as the war dragged on.

Despite the promising start to the month, bad weather severely curtailed operations throughout the rest of the month and it was not until the 31 August that 20 Squadron was able to add to its victory tally. At around 09.10 two FEs – A19 flown by Captain George Reid and Second Lieutenant L.H. Scott and A14 flown by Second Lieutenant Guy Reid and Captain Dixon-Spain – spotted a Rumpler two-seater north of Ypres. No sooner had they driven it off eastwards than they saw another two approaching and attacked one each. These were also driven off, closely followed by two more over the Langemark area. Shortly afterwards they came up against a new type: a lone rotary powered two-seater biplane they thought to be of Fokker design. The crew of this aeroplane made four determined attacks, with both crew members firing from front and rear, before Second Lieutenant Scott was able to get in a burst of fire that caused clouds of black smoke to pour from their engine. The German dived away steeply and was not seen to flatten out despite several apparent attempts to do so, but neither was he actually seen to crash. Even so, the smoke and lack of control were good enough for Brigade HQ and they awarded an out of control victory to the British crew[1]. The actual identity of the enemy aircraft type remains a mystery, however, as Fokker built very few two-seat aircraft in the Great War and those they did deliver, such as the C.1 and B.1 types, were mainly sent to the Austrians or used for training.

So August drew to an end with observers Frank Billinge, George Exley and Herbert Hamilton transferring out of the squadron to train as pilots but with only one of them surviving the war. Frank Billinge went on to fly DH2 scouts in France with 32 Squadron before finishing the war as a captain in 56 Squadron and George Exley, a former member of the Pharmaceutical Society, was killed in action with 29 Squadron on 14 January 1917. Meanwhile, Herbert Hamilton, who had originally been commissioned in the Duke of Cornwall's Light Infantry in August 1915, went on to reach the rank of captain and flight commander in France before he was killed in an air accident in England on 13 June 1918. In early September, Lieutenant P.G. Scott returned to England to become a test pilot at the Royal Aircraft Factory at Farnborough and was followed out of the squadron on 8 September by Alexander Dewar. After returning to England for a well-earned week's leave in London, Dewar was admitted to hospital with an infection that persisted on and off for the next few months, following which he transferred out of the RFC and returned to the Royal Field Artillery. Harold Hartney also embarked for leave in England on 8 September, although his pleasure at being re-united with Irene and their baby daughter was to prove short-lived when, having been home for just three hours, he received a telegram recalling him to the front.[5] .

******

Quietly successful reconnaissances on the first two days of September presented a false picture of the month ahead, which saw the pace quicken as the German Air Service responded to the RFC's increasing violations of its airspace. The first fight came at 13.30 on September 3 when Second Lieutenants Dabbs and Dewar were attacked by a Fokker monoplane at 9,000ft over Rumbeke. The Fokker dived on them from an advantage of about 1,500ft but as soon as the FE turned and opened fire, the Fokker swerved aside and dived away steeply. The dive turned into a spin and the Fokker crashed into the north bank of the Roulers-Issegham canal, one-and-a-half miles east of Roulers[1]. Another victory came at 12.45 two days later when Guy Reid and H.M. Golding, flying A19, ran into two Fokker biplanes escorting a two-seater over Passchendaele. The Germans came down on them in an attack from behind but Reid's manoeuvrings prevented it from getting into a decent firing position, while Golding was able to let fly with an accurate half-drum burst over the top wing that quickly sent it diving away, belching smoke from its engine. While Reid turned his attention to the escorting Fokkers, a second FE2D, A4 flown by Second Lieutenant C.

Gordon Davis and Corporal S. Birch, followed the two-seater down to 4,000ft, hitting the observer and forcing the pilot to make a hurried landing in the countryside near Passchendaele[1]. Curiously, Reid and Golding's combat report is dated 5 September, while that of Gordon Davis and Corporal Birch is dated the following day, although both reports stipulate the same time and place and identical descriptions of the fight. As a result, RFC communiqués announced two separate victories, one to each crew, for what was clearly only one enemy aircraft forced to land.

The award of a victory to Second Lieutenant Guy Reid put his score at five claimed within 20 Squadron, thus making him the first true 20 Squadron 'ace'. But such loose interpretations of combat reports and victory claims at HQs would become a recurrent feature in RFC and later RAF communiqués throughout the war and created the impression that far more enemy aircraft were actually destroyed than was really the case. The unforeseen consequence of this was the bitter post-war controversy among air historians of all the belligerent countries that continues to this day. But as this narrative unfolds, the reader will see that both sides were guilty of over-claiming. The fog of war crept everywhere and deliberate dishonesty had very little to do with it.

On 8 September there were two more skirmishes, including a casualty. Air Mechanic Stanley had returned to the squadron after recovering from the injuries he received on 20 July and was flying with Captain Maxwell in A29, when they turned back a LVG south of Lille[1]. The casualty came immediately after a later engagement. Second Lieutenant Dabbs and Air Mechanic Dearing had just sent an Aviatik two-seater side-slipping into the clouds apparently out of control when their FE was hit by ground fire that sent shrapnel ripping through Dabbs's arm and the FE's petrol piping and radiator. The FE rapidly began to lose height but, while Dearing strafed the German trenches 700ft below them, Dabbs was able to glide it back across the lines to a safe forced landing in a field near Fleurbaix. However, this was in full view of a German artillery emplacement whose gunners quickly laid down a barrage of shells all around the grounded machine and Dabbs was hit in the leg by shrapnel as Dearing helped him from the cockpit. The grounded FE was left untouched by the enemy artillery fire, however, and was eventually brought back to the aerodrome by road after being recovered under fire in the early evening by Captain Maxwell and a party of five mechanics.

Despite the best efforts of Second Lieutenants Guy Reid and H.M. Golding in picking no less than four separate but indecisive fights with enemy machines in the course of one patrol on 9 September, 20 Squadron's next decisive victory did not come until 10.45 on the 17 September. Captain Maxwell and Air Mechanic Stanley were patrolling at 13,000ft over Passchendaele in A29 when they sighted an enemy two-seater heading towards the British lines about 4,000ft below them. Maxwell craftily continued his steady southward course for a while so as to fool the German into thinking they had not seen him and could then position himself to attack from out of the sun. Having gained this advantage, he then dived down on the enemy machine and opened fire at a range of about 100yds. The two-seater dived away to the southeast with the FE following close behind and, after receiving about five drums of bullets from its pursuer, spun into the clouds above a small wood south of Bousbecque. Maxwell and Stanley did not follow it right down but circled slowly above, peering down intently until a gap in the clouds revealed the German machine smashed to pieces close by the southeast corner of the wood[1].

With 19 September came personnel movements rather than fighting. Captain Deuchar escaped with a sprained back and a slight knee injury after a forced landing. Brian Dowling returned to England for Home Establishment duties as an instructor, while the 21-year-old Canadian, Lieutenant R.W. White, was embarking for France from England as an observer replacement. Former Ontario law student Randolph Wilbur White had first arrived in France as a Second Lieutenant with the 21 Battalion CEF in September 1915 and had soon after been transferred to the 4 Brigade Machine-gun Company, where he reputedly stripped a Colt machine-gun in nine seconds flat. He continued to serve with that unit until June 1916 when he returned to England to train as an observer in the RFC. He would see action with 20 Squadron within days of his arrival.

The last ten days of September brought several more fights, with 2 Brigade's squadrons flying continuous missions behind enemy lines. A detailed reconnaissance carried out by 20 Squadron on 23 September over Haubourdin, Ronchin, Tournai, Mouscron, Menin, Courtrai, Inglemunster and Roulers brought intelligence of increased German road transport. It also brought another combat victory when at 17.25 Lieutenant Sydney Alder and Air Mechanic Alexander in A24 were dived on from behind by a Fokker that then swept on down in front and below them. Alder immediately dived in pursuit, firing until the hostile aeroplane went into a vertical dive and crashed into the ground southeast of Roulers between Ouchene and Rumbeke[1].

In the first engagement on Sunday 24 September, an unidentified two-seater was driven back over the German side of the lines but escaped in a long fast dive which left the FEs far behind. Then one hour later at 11.45, a Fokker biplane dived on Captain G.R.M. Reid's machine, A39, at 14,000ft northwest of Menin but was driven down streaming black smoke by a combination of Scott's return fire and a fusillade from Lieutenant Alder and his observer Randolph White in A24. They watched it go down but eventually saw it flatten out near the ground and make off under control. Five minutes later, Alder and White attacked a Rumpler that was seen to go into a steep dive, turn over in the air and crash two miles southwest of Courtrai[1]. The FEs continued their patrol and were at 13,500ft over Roulers when a Fokker dived on Reid and Scott, its opening fire hitting the FE in several places. While Scott replied in kind, Reid pulled up the nose of the FE into a stall and fired a drum of ammunition from his own fixed gun at 30 yards range as the Fokker passed over them. The tracers seemed to pour into the Fokker just in front of the pilot, which went into a steep dive with Reid following closely. Alder and White in A24 and Pearce and Findlay in A19 were also firing as it went down and it was finally seen by all three FE crews to crash into a ploughed field one-and-a-half miles south of the German aerodrome at Rumbeke[1]. This must have seemed an exciting start to life as a 20 Squadron observer for Randolph White. He had been with the squadron less than a week and already he had played a part in two combat victories.

But 26 September brought a loss. At 07.30 that morning, Second Lieutenant Livingstone and Air Mechanic Dearing were patrolling at 12,000ft near Ypres in A8 when Livingstone dived on a lone German machine 2,000ft below them but, as he frankly recorded in his combat report, he dived too far and found it necessary to go alongside the hostile aeroplane in order to regain height. Both machines were firing at each other at this point and, as the FE climbed above the German machine at close range, the enemy observer's answering fire hit both the British flyers, wounding Livingstone in his ankle and Dearing in the neck and head. Livingstone brought the machine down to a successful forced landing just south of Vlamertinghe but it was too late for Dearing, a single man from Shoreham, Sussex, who died shortly afterwards and is buried at Lijssenthoek Military Cemetery, Poperinghe[1]. If it was any consolation to his pilot, it seems the German machine had also been badly shot-up, for as the RFC communiqué for that day reported: 'Information has been received that an Albatros fell near where Lieutenant Livingstone's combat took place.'

Worsening weather over the last few days of September brought just two more inconclusive combats, and the month was brought to a very satisfactory conclusion when it was announced that Captain G.R.M. Reid and Captain Dixon-Spain were each to receive the Military Cross.

******

Notes

1. Combat Report.
2. James T. McCudden's Logbook: my thanks to Alex Revell.
3. AIR 1/1827/204/202/13: report by Major Malcolm.
4. AIR 1/1085: Gun Mountings.
5. *Wings Over France* by Harold Hartney.

Chapter 7

Eclipse of the EindeCkers – October/December 1916

Albert Stanley was posted back to England for pilot training on 10 October and poor weather meant that the first success of the month did not come until 16 October. The guns of Captain G.R.M. Reid and Second Lieutenant L.H. Scott diving A39 onto an LVG sent it spinning out of control until they lost sight of it. Two pilots of 29 Squadron confirmed this and it was recorded as an 'out of control' victory for Captain Reid.

There was no fighting during the next few days of patrols and reconnaissances and, even though 20 October brought several fights, they were inconclusive. If any conclusions could be drawn from them they would have centred on the ever-increasing numbers of German scouts they were facing. The Fokker Eindeckers were still around but they were now gradually being replaced by faster and better designed biplane scouts, such as the Halberstadt and Fokker D series scouts that were being met in increasing numbers. These later types were not to be scorned at but, they too would soon be replaced by an even deadlier scout: the Albatros DI.

There were not only more German scouts in the sky but they were also better organised. For while the Fokker monoplanes had originally been attached to reconnaissance units in ones and twos, they and the newer types were now being reorganised into fighter squadrons, just like the RFC. The first of these German fighter squadrons – the Jagstaffeln, or Jastas as they became known – had been formed in the Somme area during August but on 12 September another new unit, Jasta 8, was formed at Rumbeke near Roulers. In 1917 it would rank along with Jasta 18 as one of 20 Squadron's most relentless enemies. Jasta 8 was equipped mainly with Halberstadt scouts at this time, while the slightly later formed Jasta 18 would get Albatros scouts from the start.

On 21 October Second Lieutenants G.G. Callander and H. Soulby made a forced landing on the British side of the lines after Callander was wounded in the face and arm during separate fights with a Fokker scout and a LVG two-seater. It was not a total defeat though, as the officer commanding 25 Field Battery RA reported having seen the LVG go down apparently out of control after the fight[1]. The only New Zealander known to have served with 20 Squadron up to this time, 18-year-old Geoffrey Callander, was subsequently hospitalised. He returned to England for convalescence from where he was posted to other units on other fronts, during which time he was awarded the Italian Silver Star and in June 1919 the Air Force Cross.

Fighting around midday resulted in two more victories when Captain G.R.M. Reid and Second Lieutenant Scott were patrolling over Comines in A39 with Second Lieutenant E.D. Spicer and Sergeant S. Birch in A8. After attacking one of two LVG's and sending it down out of control Captain Reid turned his attentions to the second one. While he was watching the second machine and his observer watched the first one fall and crash, another Fokker dived on them from the front and shot up their engine and rudder controls. Reid managed to turn the FE away by using the ailerons and the Fokker sheared off as Spicer's FE came diving down, firing on him. The Fokker dived away streaming smoke and flattened out near Becelaere but Spicer thought the smoke came from the German's exhaust pipe so did not claim a victory. Reid and Scott then struggled back across the lines in their damaged FE and, as they crossed the trenches, the epicyclic gear and propeller both broke off and fell away and they force-landed[1]. Lieutenant Scott was left at the scene in charge of a recovery party, and an officer of the Manchester Regiment recovered the FEs epicyclic gear. He told Scott that he had watched the fight from the ground and could confirm their victory over the LVG they had attacked. He then added that he had also watched Spicer's attack on the Fokker immediately afterwards and saw it fall in flames. Lieutenant Scott subsequently reported this to Major Mansfield who, after interviewing Spicer, sent off an additional report to Brigade HQ that resulted in Spicer being credited with the 'flamer'.

Although pilots and observers would fly with whoever they were told to fly with, it was clear that some of them had their preferences, hence the frequent partnerships of Reid and Scott and Alder and White. Another such rapidly developing partnership was that of Harold Hartney and Wilfrid Jourdan, their bond no doubt cemented by mutual interests. Although he had been born in the Channel Islands, Jourdan had emigrated to Canada and was studying law in Vancouver when war broke out. After first serving with the 89 Canadian Infantry Battalion and then as a Sapper with 2 Tunnelling Company of the CEF, he was commissioned into the RFC and appointed as a probationary observer with 20 Squadron from 28 September. His and Hartney's mutual interests in Canada and the law made them natural comrades and they were up together again at 08.15 on 22 October when they intercepted a Rumpler flying at 12,000ft near Messines that escaped by diving away safely to the east. Another inconclusive scrap on the

29 October brought the month's fighting to an end as the weather closed in yet again. This allowed November 1916 to begin with an all-too-short lull, although the squadron continued its reconnaissance patrols whenever the weather allowed.

******

Considering the lack of training that observers and aerial gunners had received in the course of the war so far, it is perhaps something of a wonder that 20 Squadron and other similar units had been able to achieve the results they had. Some senior officers including Field Marshal Sir John French and Field Marshal Sir Douglas Haig, who had replaced him as Commander in Chief on the Western Front, had at least recognised the potential of aerial reconnaissance after taking part in peacetime army manoeuvres. Both men realised that pilots had to be taught to fly but, being unfamiliar with the skills involved, they left the matter to other pilots. Even then, among most of the pilots, it was thought that observer training was something that could be done 'on the job' with a squadron, as if it was simply a question of a man with reasonable eyesight looking down and making notes of what he saw. In addition, given the flimsy construction and limited capabilities of aeroplanes in August 1914, most pilots and senior officers that year thought the idea of aerial combats involving several aeroplanes armed with machine-guns as beyond belief. So at the start of the war the employment and training of non-commissioned ranks as aerial gunners had not even been suggested. No one foresaw how quickly aviation would develop in the pressure cooker of war. Observers had to recognise fortifications and barbed wire entanglements from high above and learn how shadows could either reveal or conceal what the enemy was doing, depending on the time of day and the angle from which one looked at it. They learned how to take accurate photographs of the ground from a height of several thousand feet and change the awkward camera plates with frozen fingers while the aeroplane rocked and rose and fell with every nearby anti-aircraft explosion – and still keep an eye on every quarter of the sky for the sight of an approaching enemy. It was very different to old style cavalry reconnaissance and it took a while for their experiences to be evaluated by their commanders and translated into a sensible training scheme.

Most observers were either posted to squadrons direct from their battalions or were posted to squadrons in England just before they were sent to for France, where they learnt whatever they could in the limited time available. It was only in the autumn of 1916 that an observer section was formed at the wireless school at Brooklands with an output of about twenty observers per month. The training dealt mainly with wireless, artillery and machine-gun work[2], and the system was gradually improved throughout the remainder of the war. At about the same time, the question of gunnery training began to be taken seriously. It was now obvious that sitting in a gun emplacement on the ground firing a machine-gun at closely packed waves of advancing infantry was an entirely different matter to trying to hit a small fast-moving, twisting, turning target in the sky while your own emplacement – your aeroplane – was also twisting and turning to avoid the enemy's bullets.

It had long been a well established principle in hunting and war that one had to fire ahead of moving targets such as grouse, rabbits or galloping cavalrymen lest your bullets pass behind them. But exactly how far ahead should you aim when trying to hit a distant aeroplane flying at around 100 miles-an-hour? And how far down would gravity cause your bullets to fall before they reached the target? Aerial gunnery was now starting to be recognised as an essential skill for pilots and observers alike and both needed to know how to aim, fire and if necessary maintain their guns in the air. A conference of squadron commanders in England in November 1916 suggested that there should be a distinction between qualified observers (who achieved their qualification largely by a mixture of training and experience at the Front), and 'gunner-observers' whose main role was gunnery. It had already been decided that two-seater squadrons should each have an extra establishment of six rank and file gunner-observers and the conference recommended that this should be recognised as a senior trade deserving the rank of corporal or sergeant. It was also suggested that gunner-observers should have a distinctive badge in the same way as pilots and qualified observers. While higher authority immediately rejected the idea of an air gunner's badge, most of the other recommendations were accepted. In addition to firing practice on the ground and in the air, the training of gunner-observers should include the mechanism, stripping, care and cleaning of the Lewis gun, as well as map reading, reconnaissance duties, artillery observation and registration, air tactics and use of the 'ring sight'. At the end of their training, pupils had to carry out two cross-country flights of between twenty and forty miles each, for which they were given a small map to mark up any road transport or trains and other points of interest. They were then rigorously tested about the features on the ground they had flown over[3]. On 22 December the first batch of ten trained gunner-observers passed-out from the gunnery school at Hythe. In the meantime, aerial gunners drawn from the ranks were already playing a full part in 20 Squadron's activities. The role of the observers, who were at that time nearly all officers, is perfectly illustrated in the detail of the following typical reconnaissance report filed by Hartney and Golding on 9 November 1916.

Time	PLACE	OBSERVATION
5.35am	Crossed Lines	
5.40am	MENIN	One train going to TOURCOING
5.41am	MENIN	One train approaching from North
5.42am	COURTRAI	One train entering from NE, one train going to SE
5.53am	COURTRAI	One train approaching from SE
5.58am	ROUBAIX	One train going East seen from HELCHIN
6.07am	MENIN	One train going to COURTRAI.
6.07am	COURTRAI	One train going to MENIN
6.10am	TOURCOING	One train going to HALLUIN
6.12am	HALLUIN	One train leaving for S.
6.14am	RECKEM	There appeared a large oblong set of lights which flashed on several times, as if signalling to show position. This was apparently a set of lights right round the aerodrome.
6.15am	TOURCOING	Two trains with steam up.
6.18am	ROUBAIX	One train approaching from S. One leaving for S.
6.20am	LILLE	One train leaving for North.
6.22am	LILLE	Two trains with steam up, in ST. SAVEUR Station.
6.23am	LILLE	One train going SE, from HELLEMMES
6.24am	LILLE	One train leaving HELEMMES for SE
6.25am	HAUBOURDIN	One train going to LILLE
6.27am	MADELAINE	One train leaving for West.
6.28am	HELLEMMES	One train leaving for East. One approaching from East.
6.29am	LILLE	One train approaching St. SAVEUR from North and one from South and one train leaving for North.
6.31am	ROUBAIX	One train going to LILLE
6.34am	MENIN	One train entering from North. One train leaving for East.
6.35am	WERVICQ	One train going to COMINES.
6.37am	HALLUIN	One train going to South.
6.38am	COURTRAI	One train approaching MENIN.
6.41am	BECELAERE	One train with two engines approaching from East.
6.42am	HOUTHEM	One train going Northwest.

BOUSBECQUE: There is a bridge or pontoon across the river here. It has no road leading away either side, nor were any tracks observed. The river here has not flooded surrounding fields, as along most of the way. The position of the bridge is Sheet 28.Q.34.b.7.4. Good visibility. No H.A. encountered. The FE was shelled with Tracer A.A. shells over Lille. These appeared to come from about Sheet 36.K.33.b. White and yellow tinsel was first fired and when we gave no response shelling commenced.

Hartney and Golding had spent sixty-seven minutes making their meticulous notes, under fire for most of the time, while flying slowly around an area the enemy considered of primary importance and had probably been lucky in not meeting any hostile aircraft. The next day's morning reconnaissance would be slightly less fortunate.

At 09.40 on Friday 10 November, Second Lieutenant R.W. Reid was patrolling over Menin at 14,000ft in A32 when he spotted a Halberstadt scout diving at him from the right front. At the same time his gunner, Air Mechanic First Class H. Alexander, saw another diving from the left front. Reid immediately turned slightly right and pulled the FE's nose upwards to allow his gunner to fire at the first Halberstad but Alexander was already aiming at the one to the left. As it was, the first one misjudged his dive and passed harmlessly overhead while the second made good shooting, hitting Alexander in his right arm on its first pass. Despite this, Alexander managed to get to the back mounting and aim the gun with his left hand as the Halberstadt swung around behind them. But the German was quicker and his bullets shot the Lewis gun out of Alexander's hand and wounded him in his side. The Halberstadt then swerved away and made off, its comrade having already disappeared, and Reid was able to bring his stricken observer home[1].

Given the shorter days and wintry weather, there was little in the way of serious fighting for the remainder of the month, although there were several skirmishes. One of these was on 15 November when Sergeant Birch was hit in the arm by a German bullet while his pilot, Second Lieutenant R.B. Wainwright, took on a Halberstadt two-seater approaching Ypres. The Halberstadt went down in a vertical nose-dive with its propeller stopped and its engine smoking and, although Wainwright and Birch were unable to watch it all the way down to the ground owing to thick mist, they were at least credited with an 'out of control' victory[1].

Second Lieutenant J.N. Francis and Lieutenant F.R.C. Cobbold had a lucky escape on 16 November when they were attacked over the northern sector by three enemy scouts from above and behind. Cobbold and the leading German opened fire at about the same time and, although the German machine broke off as if hit and dived away to safety, the other two kept up the attack from either side of the FE's tail. Part of the FE's propeller and controls were soon shot away and, with the engine vibrating dangerously and the machine close to becoming uncontrollable, Francis turned towards Poperinghe, sideslipping to avoid the fire of the still pursuing Germans before eventually coming down in a crash-landing on the British side of the lines about four miles east of Abeele. Both men walked away uninjured, while the victory over them was awarded to Unteroffizier (equivalent to corporal) W. Seitz of Jasta 8, marking Jasta 8's first definite encounter with 20 Squadron[1, 4]. The 22-year-old Felix Rudolph Chevalier Cobbold was a recent arrival at the squadron but was accustomed to enemy fire. A Kent man, he had served in the junior division of the Westminster OTC before being commissioned into the Suffolk Regiment in September 1914 but was wounded at the Battle of Loos on 26 September 1915. He transferred to the RFC in August 1916 following his recovery.

Another new pilot recently arrived at 20 Squadron was Sergeant Tom Mottershead, DCM who had transferred over from 25 Squadron in which he had flown the older FE2B. He had first distinguished himself with that squadron by being credited with a combat victory over a Fokker Eindecker above the Somme battlefields, for which he was awarded the Distinguished Conduct Medal. Later he made a daring attack on an enemy aerodrome in which he and fellow Sergeant-Pilot Sydney Attwater (soon to follow him to 20 Squadron) had landed on the German airfield and taxied across it while their observers machine-gunned the sheds. At 08.30 on 17 November he was patrolling at 12,000ft near Armentieres in A30 when he saw a LVG cross the lines about 3,000ft below him. He and his observer, Second Lieutenant G.N. Dennis, dived on the German and opened fire but the LVG promptly retreated east again, its observer keeping up a rapid fire[1].

Heavy fog appeared on the night of 5-6 December and persisted throughout the week and into the next, except for a few hours on 11 December when 20 Squadron were able to pinpoint the location of a German heavy artillery piece on the eastern edge of Houthulst Forest. It had been pounding British ground positions for several days and, now that it been located, the British artillery could reply in kind.

Fog closed in again soon afterwards and lasted until the skies finally cleared on 16 December. Although there were two fights that day, they ended inconclusively but were notable for including two more new observers on the squadron roster: Captain R.M. Knowles, who had previously served with 3 Battalion Norfolk Regiment, and Lieutenant D.B. Woolley, who came from Sussex. The weather now became so consistently poor that very little flying was possible all along the Western Front except on the odd day here and there until

26 December, Boxing Day, when several reconnaissances were flown. The most serious incident came on 27 December when two squadron newcomers, Second Lieutenant D.C. Cunnell and Captain C.M. Carbert, were hit by anti-aircraft fire which set their FE2D A36 alight. Fortunately they were already down to 1,000ft over the British side of the lines and were able to make a speedy forced-landing at Berthen. This team again illustrated the diversity of the crews flying with the RFC. Neither was a regular officer. Donald Cunnell had been born into a Norfolk farming family and served in the OTC before being commissioned into 20 Battalion Royal Fusiliers, while Canadian Charles Carbert was the son of an Ontario doctor and gave his own occupation as that of 'clerk'.

Later on in the day, Second Lieutenants R.B. Wainwright and H.R. Wilkinson were attacked by two Halberstadt scouts while carrying out an OP over Poelcappelle but managed to send both down apparently out of control. Captain Blackwood had been promoted to Flight Commander on 12 December and he and his observer, Second Lieutenant Bronskill, were attacked by two more Halberstadts over Zonnebeke. One of them dived on the FE's tail and scored several hits but Bronskill's return fire from the back mounting sent the Halberstadt falling away to crash south of Zonnebeke while its companion broke off the action and escaped[1] Canadian Frank Bronskill, aged 26, was a former bank clerk from Ontario, who had served in a local militia regiment before the war.

******

Earlier in December Harold Hartney, by now an experienced veteran of six months war flying, was offered the choice of accepting a lengthy tour of duty in England or taking ten days leave before returning to the squadron as a captain and flight commander. Taking the latter choice, he set off for his leave on 10 December and returned on Christmas Day. Captain Maxwell was another to be granted leave in December but he did not return to the squadron. His promotion to major brought him the command of 18 Squadron and he would soon learn that he had also been awarded the MC for his previous work. Two more permanent departures in December were Captain G.R.M. Reid and Lieutenant L.H. Scott, both men being decorated and posted back to Home Establishment, with Reid receiving a bar to the MC he had been awarded in June and Scott getting his own MC. Sergeant Mottershead was also given leave and returned early in the New Year[5].

So 1916 drew to a close. It had been an eventful year. In addition to some of the squadron's airmen having established themselves as 'aces' and with the training changes already mentioned, the RFC's experiences with the much faster

Halberstadt and Albatros scouts from September onwards had set alarm bells ringing at Headquarters. So severe had been the losses over the Somme and so gloomy did the future look that on 29 September 1916 Major General Trenchard had written to the War Office complaining about the poor quality of the current British aeroplanes generally and forecasting a very bloody time in the spring of 1917 if something was not done urgently. In mentioning the offensive policy he rightly saw as the only way of maintaining predominance in the air and the fact that our own machines were outclassed in speed and maximum height, he went on to itemise various specific measures he regarded as crucial. These included engine upgrades for all DH2, FE 8 and Sopwith aeroplanes, the provision of five FE2D squadrons with the 250hp Rolls Royce engines and five squadrons of the French-designed SPAD single-seaters with Hispano Suiza engines. He ended the letter with the words: 'Unless every effort is made to overcome this difficulty, we shall be unable to maintain next spring our ascendancy in the air, the moral effect of which on the rest of the army is of such vital importance'[6]. Trenchard's forebodings were well founded, anticipating the looming tragedies of 'Bloody April, 1917' with quietly under-stated accuracy. The alarm bells were certainly ringing and he could only hope that others back in England could also hear them.

The FE2's obsolescence was beginning to tell and, as if that was not enough, some of 20 Squadron's more proficient flyers had recently been transferred to other units and had been replaced by others who were generally less experienced, many of them fresh from training. Given the superiority of the new German scouts they would be facing, it was inevitable that they would find the going hard. Of the new pilots, Captain G.J. Mahony-Jones had served with 11 Lancashire Fusiliers before transferring to the RFC in early 1916 and, by 1 September, had risen to the rank of temporary captain and flight commander with 59 Squadron, then in England. He had a fair amount of flying under his belt but this would be his first taste of aerial combat. Another newcomer, 22-year-old Second Lieutenant Michael Woods, was a former marine engineer from Belfast who, after enlisting with the 29 London Regiment in mid-September 1914, was commissioned in August 1916. He then transferred to the RFC, qualifying as a pilot on 23 November 1916 just a month before he arrived at 20 Squadron. Also fresh from training was 25-year-old Second Lieutenant William Wright Sawden, a former clerk from Cottingham, Yorkshire, who had risen to sergeant during his five years with the TA's 5 Battalion East Yorkshire (Cyclists) Regiment. When war broke out he had enlisted with the 23 Royal Fusiliers, 1 Sportsman's Battalion and from there had found his way into the RFC.

A 'colonial' among the new observers to arrive at the squadron around this time was 21-year-old Francis Michael Myers from Johannesburg, South Africa.

An agricultural student in civilian life, he had served as a 'dresser' in the South African Veterinary Corps during the German South West Africa Campaign. He received glowing references from his commanding officer Captain Quinlan, who was himself, a lecturer in veterinary science at the school of agriculture and experimental farming at Potchefstroom. Myers made his own way to England but upon arrival was unable to get a commission in the British Veterinary Corps because he had not yet qualified as a member of the Royal College of Veterinary Surgeons. He applied for the cavalry but the machinations of the army recruiters being what they were (and maybe still are!) he was actually commissioned into the Suffolk Regiment in February 1916. This not apparently being to his liking, he transferred to the RFC. The other two new observers came from England and were Second Lieutenant Charles Frederick Drabble, a 19-year-old from Sheffield who had first been commissioned in the Durham Light Infantry, and Lieutenant Edward Barry Maule, the son of J. Percy Maule, clerk of the peace and clerk of the county council for Huntingdon. Maule had been educated at Eastbourne, Sussex, and at Uppingham School, near Leicester, and his application for a commission was recommended by no lesser personages than the Earl of Sandwich and the Mayor of Huntingdon, as well as his school housemaster. Commissioned into the Highland Light Infantry, he had been wounded in action at Neuve Chapelle on 1 March 1915. After convalescing from shell-shock and injuries to his head and spine, he transferred to the RFC.

Such were the backgrounds of the more recent arrivals at 20 Squadron. They were all new to war flying and would soon go on to face challenges and tests of courage and fortitude that are almost beyond understanding in the present age. Perhaps most astounding of all was the fact that not one of them would be found wanting in these virtues.

******

Notes

1. Combat Report.
2. AIR 1/161/15/123/15 Memorandum on the training of observers from 1915 to 1918.
3. AIR 1/129/15/40/191 Formation flying and fighting in the air – notes on.
4. *The Jasta War Chronology* by N. Franks, G. Bailey & R. Duiven: Grub Street Publishing.
5. AIR 1/1579/204/81/2, 2nd Brigade War Diaries.
6. AIR 1/1001/204/5/1260 Policy and Organisation of RFC in France.

Chapter 8

The Way to Glory – January 1917

Major Mansfield had no doubt been kept informed of the dangers posed by the new German Albatros scouts, so when high winds and low clouds prevented almost all offensive air operations on the first day of 1917, he sent up most of his pilots and observers, especially the new intakes, for aircraft tests and a mixture of formation and reconnaissance training, gunnery practice and mock combats in preparation. The next day dawned clear and cold at Clairmarais and operations could not be avoided. But the patrols were largely uneventful and the weather closed in again the following day.

Thursday 4 January was also uneventful apart from Harold Hartney going up in A38 to test a new wireless receiving set issued to 20 Squadron as part of ongoing field trials. The practise of pilots and observers using airborne wireless transmitters and Morse code to communicate with the ground forces, particularly for artillery observation, was well established. But so far it had been limited to one-way signals from aircraft to ground, with no facility for the aircraft to receive return messages. By the winter of 1916/17, experiments were afoot to see if such wireless telegraphy, or W/T as it became known, was a practical proposition – which also raised the question of whether it could also eventually be used between aircraft. The Mk II transmitter designed by Captain Prince of the Royal Engineers was joined with a receiver designed by Mr. Matthieu of the Signals Experimental Establishment and both were put into production[2], with some sets being issued to squadrons for field tests. In tests that lasted over ninety minutes, he reported that the clear ground signals he received over Cassel, which was near to the local Wireless Compass Station, could still be heard several miles away at 11,000ft over Bailleul. Hartney described the work in his book *Wings over France*, his descriptions highlighting the primitive nature of the wireless sets they were testing, with a long antenna hanging behind the aircraft, and also the reflection of some signals back to the aircraft from hills and other high land features. This was possibly the first time this had been recorded, and eventually led to the much later radar and direction finding equipment that featured in the Battle of Britain and the bomber offensives during the Second World War[3].

Captain Hartney and Lieutenant Gower led up a five-strong photo-reconnaissance patrol on Friday 5 January, during which Stead and Jefferson carried the heavy wireless apparatus in A31 and found the 120ft aerial line they had to hang behind the aircraft wrapped itself around the undercarriage soon after take-off. Forced to land again to untangle it, they were probably relieved that it had not fouled the flying control surfaces or threatened other aircraft. They took off again after five minutes and soon caught up with the others. Five enemy machines were seen variously over Armentieres, Bailleul, and Chestre but the most alarming moment came when friendly anti-aircraft batteries suddenly fired on the FEs. Evidently aircraft recognition among the ground troops had not improved in the months since some of the pilots had visited the trenches in a liaison role.

Bad weather stepped in again to give the flyers a day off on 6 January but cleared the following morning; and Sergeant Tom Mottershead and Lieutenant Gower set off on an OP at 11.16 in A39, along with Second Lieutenant Marsh and Air Mechanic Lee flying A1935. As the two FE2Ds patrolled over Ploegsteert Wood, they were attacked by several of the new Albatros scouts and Mottershead's machine was hit and set alight by VizeFeldwebel (Sergeant) Walter Gottsch of Jasta 8[(4)]. As Gottsch broke away from the doomed FE, the two Britons' best hope of survival was to land and abandon the burning FE as quickly as possible wherever that happened to be – which was east of the lines. But Mottershead was not the kind of man to surrender himself, his observer or his machine to the Germans if he could possibly avoid it. Despite his own clothes now being on fire and more flames enveloping the engine and structures all around him, Mottershead kept the FE2D under control and crossed the trenches. Gower, who had been wounded in his eye, did what he could to help by playing the primitive water fire extinguisher over Mottershead. But there was little else he could do and, once the extinguisher was empty, he could only watch helplessly as his pilot struggled to keep control despite the flames.

Mottershead could have crash-landed in the trenches once over the British side but, mindful of his observer's safety, he flew on until he found a likely landing spot and circled carefully around it to make sure it was safe before bringing his machine down to what was almost a perfect landing. But the badly burned under-carriage collapsed as they touched down and the FE overturned, throwing Gower clear while trapping Mottershead under the blazing wreckage until Gower and some nearby Tommies managed to drag him out and rush him off to the nearest Casualty Clearing Station. Transferred to a field hospital, he lingered on in agony until the 11 January, when he received a visit from his old friend Sydney Attwater. Many years later, Attwater left a description of his visit in a memoir he deposited with the Imperial War Museum[5]. Mottershead tried to be cheerful despite the pain, and when Attwater drew his attention to a burning kite balloon he could see from the window, he struggled over to the window to watch it falling. It was his last sight of the war, and he died the following morning. In an unusual display of respect for a NCO, Major Mansfield paraded the whole squadron for his burial with full military honours at Bailleul.

Less than a month later, on 9 February 1917, the *London Gazette* announced the posthumous award of the Victoria Cross to the hero – the only non-commissioned member of the RFC, RNAS or RAF to receive the VC in the entire war. Thomas left behind his parents Thomas and Lucy, nine brothers and sisters, his wife Lillian and baby son Sidney Thomas. He would also be remembered in the years that followed by a Mottershead Scholarship at Halton College of Further Education in Widnes, Cheshire, and a Mottershead Road in the same town. On 2 June 1917 the King presented the Victoria Cross to the widowed Lillian and the Military Cross to Lieutenant Gower for his attempts at rescuing Mottershead from the blazing wreckage. As Mottershead's war grave headstone at Bailleul records: 'Not Once or Twice in our Rough Island Story was the Path of Duty the Way to Glory.'

Lieutenant Gower survived the war but was mentally scarred by the event for many years. After being hospitalised shortly afterwards, he was struck off the squadron's strength on 26 March 1917. There then followed several periods of ill health before he went on to become a photography equipment officer with the RAF in the Middle East, for which service he was mentioned in despatches on 5 May 1919 before being demobilised later that year.

Sydney Attwater had been 17 when war broke out but was already a skilled toolmaker and motor engineer who had just been accepted for employment by the A.V. Roe Aeroplane Manufacturing Company. Spurning the opportunities his new job offered, he immediately volunteered for the RFC and was settling in at Farnborough the following day. His evident keenness notwithstanding, the transition from civilian to soldier is never completely smooth, and the very next day he was in the glass-house for having failed to notice his name on a list of men down for duty in the breakfast kitchen – despite being unaware that such 'Orders Lists' existed, nor where to look for them. Then came two weeks of drill and basic training followed by two weeks in the workshops working on 70hp Renault aero-engines, after which he was promoted from air mechanic second class to first class. By November that year, he was with 8 Squadron in France where, despite his flight sergeant's disinterest, he succeeded in persuading his fellow mechanics to help him design and build an engine test-bed for which he was praised by his CO. This and his work on bomb racks and release devices soon led to him being promoted to corporal.

But Attwater really wanted to fly. He had already tried out the controls several times after persuading various officers to take him up with them; and when the call came for volunteers to fly as gunner–observers, he jumped at the chance, even though this would be in the obsolete BE2Cs his squadron used. His field of fire being so limited as previously described, Attwater persuaded the fitters to cut away a piece of the centre-section of the top wing and fit a gun mounting there that he could reach by standing up in his cockpit. It was not long before he was awarded the Military Medal after shooting down two German aircraft in this way, only to be wounded in the knee and sent back to England a little later. Having earlier begged his CO to put his name forward for pilot training, his desire was fulfilled when he was posted to Reading University and then to Brooklands for basic flying training. This was followed by higher instruction at Hounslow on FE2Bs before he was posted to 25 Squadron in February 1916. Twelve months later, he was with 20 Squadron and had lost his closest friend. He was carrying the torch now, but not for long[5].

More bad weather prevented any serious operations over the next few days following Mottershead's heroic sacrifice, and the squadron was restricted to test and training flights until 19 January when it moved to Boisdinghem, about 10 miles to the west of Clairmarais. The move was necessitated by the fact that, despite a new drainage system, Clairmarais had become almost impossible for flying due to frequent flooding. The new aerodrome was far from ideal, though. Although its location on the hills behind St. Omer meant it was not subject to flooding, it had such an inadequate water supply that additional supplies had to be brought up by tender every day. It was also too far behind the lines, and this led to a further move in April. For the time being, though, all the officers and men could do was make do and mend. The move was completed on Sunday 21 January and, after confining themselves to test flights on the Monday, the squadron's members were back over enemy lines by the Tuesday. Numerous patrols were flown on that and the following day, enabling the observers to report on the co-ordinates of gun flashes in the northern sector that provided our own artillery with an idea of where the enemy's artillery was positioned. They also located a new light railway behind the German lines south of Hollebeke and enemy rail and road movements. They were only once harassed by enemy scouts and there were no losses on either side.

Four more patrols were flown on the Thursday but only the last of these brought a fight when at 15.10 the five-strong formation was attacked by five Halberstadt scouts over Menin. Three of the Germans attacked Lucas and

Gilson in A32, who sent one down out of control,[1] while Wainwright and Gibbon engaged two more in A28, forcing one of them to make a controlled forced landing at Neuville, northeast of Tourcoing[1]. When the FEs reformed and turned for home, however, they realised one was missing. Sydney Alder and Randolph White had both been wounded and came down near Bousbecque, where German soldiers took them prisoner after finding the unconscious observer lying under the wrecked A34's left wing. Randolph White had been hit by bullets in his mouth and shoulder and, by coincidence, was taken prisoner on the same day he was promoted to temporary captain in the Canadian Machine-gun Corps, attached to the RFC. After spending the rest of the war in captivity, he was one of the earliest repatriations from Germany and relinquished his commission in the RAF just a week later on 4 December 1918. Two days after that, he married Marguerite Eames and returned to Canada, where he died in 1928. The Canadian military authorities attributed his early death to his war service and granted both his mother and his widow the customary 'Mothers Cross'[6]. Jasta 18's Oberleutnant Karl von Grieffenhagen claimed the victory[4].

There was more action the following day, Friday 26 January, when Captain Mahony-Jones and Lieutenant Moyes flew A1962 at the head of a six-strong patrol that was quickly reduced to four when two of the FEs had to drop out with engine trouble. Then at 15.50, shortly after crossing the lines the patrol was attacked over Westroosebeke by what they described as five Roland single-seat scouts, another new type recently introduced by the Germans. One of them dived on Stead and Gilson in A31 from behind, but they got on its tail as it swept past and emptied a whole drum into it, after which it seemed to go down out of control before turning upside down very near the ground. According to the 20 Squadron Record Book, Wainwright and Golding shot down another out of control, after which the Germans broke off the fight and got away. There were no losses as such, but Flight-Sergeant Cox was badly injured making a forced landing near to St. Marie Cappel in A35, while his observer, Second Lieutenant S.G. Fauvel, got away with a sprained ankle.

The last five days of January brought very little in the way of fighting, although Lieutenant Golding was hit in the arm after A28 was attacked from behind during a reconnaissance. The wound did not stop him shooting back and driving off his attacker, after which he calmly wrote out his report and dropped it safely over Brigade HQ. The only other noteworthy event came on 31 January when, 20 Squadron having been loaned a new RE7 reconnaissance machine (No. 2299) for trials, Second Lieutenant H.G. White and Lieutenant A.G. Stewart were detailed to return it to No.1 Aircraft Depot. They had scarcely taken off when the water pipe burst and White was forced to attempt the best landing he could, even though he could not see the ground for steam and smoke. Needless to say, it was not the best landing he ever made but at least he and his observer walked away relatively unscathed. The RE7, however, was reported as being rather 'crumpled up'.

Notes

1. Combat Report.
2. AIR/1/733/183/1 – History of RFC Wireless by Majors Orme & Prince.
3. *Wings over France* by Harold Hartney.
4. *The Jasta War Chronology* by N. Franks et al.
5. Personal Memoir of Sydney Attwater, Documents Archive, Imperial War Museum; in respect of Mottershead also see *The Air VCs* by Peter G. Cooksley.
6. R.W. White, C.E.F. service record courtesy of Les Donnithorne.

Chapter 9

Advantage 'Albatrii' – February/March 1917

On 1 February, HQ asked 20 Squadron to photograph the results of another squadron's bombing raid against the rail yards at Courtrai, roughly ten miles behind the lines. The idea was to ascertain the effects of the raid before the Germans had time to carry out repairs and was timed so that the FEs would arrive over the target just half-an-hour after the bombers had left. However, it did not seem to have occurred to HQ that the Jastas would now be alert and airborne, ready to fight off any second wave that might appear. As a result, the six-strong force led by Harold Hartney, found itself shadowed by enemy scouts all the way from Lille to Courtrai. Their numbers gradually increased as the FE formation carried out its photography and attacked as the British turned for home.

When the attack came in, Hartney managed to spin down under control and make it home with the vital photographs. In the meantime, Wilfrid Jourdan was trying to fend off two Halberstadts attacking from behind when, from the front, a third came down on his FE A31. Its first burst of fire hit John Stead in the thigh and severed an artery as Second Lieutenant Spicer, flying A28, was shot through the head and killed. The two aircraft fell from the fight closely followed by A1951, which was not only on fire but had also had its engine and controls shot through. Stead's and Spicer's uninjured observers made desperate efforts to take control of their falling machines, with Captain Carbert climbing out onto the wing to reach into his dead pilot's cockpit and bring the FE down to what should have been a safe landing. But the wheels hit a bump on the frozen ground and he was thrown off the wing and broke his neck. Meantime, Wilfrid Jourdan emulated Carbert's efforts by clambering out onto the wing so that he could reach into his pilot's cockpit and apply a makeshift tourniquet to staunch the flow of blood. Gradually the lines drew nearer, with Stead just managing to keep control of the aircraft and bring it down safely at Bailleul[1]. From there he was taken to the nearby Canadian hospital where, although the hospital padre donated his own blood in an effort to save him, gangrene set in and 24-year-old John Stead died on 4 February. Despite the flames, the engine and control problems and being wounded in his leg, Walter Reeves managed to bring A1951 down to a safe crash landing north of Lille where he and his Canadian Observer, Frank Bronskill, were promptly taken prisoner.

Although born during a family visit to Victoria, British Columbia, on 23 February 1898, Edmund Daniel Spicer was the son of Newton and Emma Spicer from Little Denstone, Parkstone, Dorset. Educated at St. Aubyn's School in Rottingdean, Sussex, and later at Marlborough College and Seafield Park Engineering College, he gained his Pilot's Certificate at Hendon in August 1915 and had been at the Front since July 1916. Charles Molyneux Carbert was the 22-year-old son of Dr G.B. Carbert of Halton County, Ontario. A close friend of Harold Hartney, he had served for two years in the 20 Halton Rifles before the war. The Germans laid the two young flyers to rest in the northwest corner of Moorseele Churchyard, from where after the war they were subsequently removed to their final resting-place at the military cemetery behind the Convent of the Holy Family. A former mining engineer from Redcar in Yorkshire, 24-year-old John Stead, who had seen previous service with 4 Battalion of the Yorkshire Regiment, was buried at Bailleul. There his comrades initially marked his grave with a cross made from the damaged walnut propeller of his aircraft, inscribed with the words 'Ad Astra'. As to Reeves and Bronskill, they were taken to Douai after capture, where Reeves's privately purchased flying kit was promptly 'confiscated' and never seen again. They then discovered that their cell had been secretly bugged with German listening devices, which they promptly destroyed, and shortly afterwards were transferred to prison camps where they survived the war. The credit for the two FEs that fell on the German side of the lines went to Jasta 8's Walter Gottsch, who had been the victor in Mottershead's famous last fight less than a month before. Three men killed and two more taken prisoner made this 20 Squadron's grimmest day of the war so far, with the possible exception of the flying accidents of 20 July 1916 – and was just a foretaste of what was yet to come.

The British armies in the south had not been idle since the end of the Somme offensive, but had embarked on a series of deliberately limited advances that had begun to pinch the Germans out of the salient into which the Somme advance had forced them. The Germans, recognising the difficulties of defending the salient, had also begun to construct a new and better defence line up to the thirty miles behind their existing lines, to which they planned to make a series of well-planned withdrawals. Other plans were also afoot, with the French now commanded by General Nivelle, organising a great offensive that he claimed would break the German lines and end the war. It was supported by a British offensive at Arras intended to draw German forces away from the French sector. Both sides' reconnaissance aircraft were actively engaged in trying to see what the other side were up to all along the front from north to south, and it fell to the fighting scouts to try to stop them. The new aircraft types the Germans had introduced were tilting the odds decidedly in their favour when it came to air fighting and 20 Squadron would suffer as a consequence.

Even so, 2 February brought some kind of revenge for the losses suffered the previous day, when Hartney and Wilkinson brought down one of three Halberstadt scouts during a fight over Lille. From another FE, Second Lieutenant Gordon Davis confirmed its crash at trench-map reference Sheet 36.J.26, on or very near the northwest outskirts of the city.[1]. The early-morning patrol of two aircraft on Saturday, 3 February was uneventful but that was not the case for the second patrol, which set off at 10.00 with Second Lieutenant Gordon Davis and Captain Knowles in A1960 and Second Lieutenants Walter and Moyes in A4. Firstly, engine trouble forced Walter and Moyes to land almost immediately, although they quickly set off again after apparently rectifying the problem. However, they then suffered a total engine failure that resulted in a forced landing near the aerodrome in which both men were uninjured but the machine badly damaged. Meantime, Gordon Davis and Captain Knowles pushed on alone, recording their deeds in the combat report they submitted afterwards. This tells of how, on reaching the lines south of Ypres at 10.45, they chased and damaged a Halberstadt that was being fired on by British anti-aircraft, watching it go spinning down towards Wervicq with its broken propeller stopped. They then chased after two unidentified enemy scouts east of Ploegsteert, promptly being attacked by another four. Gordon Davis and Knowles turned into the approaching Germans and split up their formation before isolating one and sending it down trailing smoke in a vertical dive over Wervicq. Shortly after this, they saw an enemy two-seater with a red fuselage heading towards Bailleul and eventually managed to drive it back over the lines, even though one of their guns had jammed and the other had frozen. Although they did not know it at the time, one of the two scouts they had sent down out of control was none other than 20 Squadron's now regular adversary, Walter Gottsch. He had been seriously wounded and would not trouble 20 Squadron again for several weeks, by which time Gordon Davis would have been awarded the Military Cross for his actions in the fight[1]. The remainder of the day passed uneventfully enough with thick mists on 4 February making useful patrols and observations impossible. Normal service was restored on Monday, 5 February and allowed more successful reconnaissance. Many useful observations were recorded: the new 'E-454' camera employed on one of the missions was judged to be a great success. There were no fights, however, and the day ended on a sad note as Lieutenant Lucas brought A31, Lieutenant Stead's FE2D back to Boisdinghem from Bailleul after repairs.

The increased efforts of the Germans to prevent British reconnaissance aircraft operating anywhere over their territory brought 20 Squadron yet more losses on Tuesday, 6 February. A patrol of four FEs led by Lieutenants Lucas and Gibbon in A31 had just exposed sixteen plates over the Roulers-Courtrai area when they were attacked by six enemy scout aircraft. Outclassed and outnumbered as they were, the FEs fought doggedly. Sadly, their machine and that of Woods and Maule were last seen very low over Moorslede, both harried by enemy scouts and with one of them trailing smoke. Gordon Davis's and Jefferson's efforts to help were hampered by damage to A5147: the compensating wire, main bracing wire and the main strut of the centre-section having been shot through so that they were unable go down towards them in anything steeper than a slow and careful spiral nose-dive. Second Lieutenants Pattinson and Myers in A29 could not help either, as they too were under direct attack. So only two of the four FE2Ds got home and news of the missing men came the following day, when a German aircraft dropped a message over the trenches from Jasta 8's Leutnant Traeger who, together with Rudolf von Esebeck, had been credited with shooting down the two FEs. It read:

> We inform you …that on 6 February out of a squadron of three 'Vickers DD' (250 Rolls Royce) 2 machines were shot down. In one of them, 'A31', Lt.s Gibbon and Lucas dead. In the other 'A38' Lieutenant M.E. Woods unwounded, in captivity. Lieutenant E. B. Maule is dead. Be good enough to forward enclosed letter from Lieutenant Woods.
>   We express our sympathy.
>   Lieutenant C. Traeger.'[2]

Thomas Charles Lucas was the son of Charles and Annie Lucas, of Burwell, Cambridgeshire. He had formerly served as a lieutenant with the Suffolk Regiment, transferring to the RFC in April 1916. He had been with 20 Squadron since early August 1916 and was just 19 when he was killed. John Taylor Gibbon, from Market Lavington, Wiltshire, had transferred into the RFC from the Army Service Corps. He was 29 and left a widow, Grace. Although Lieutenant Woods's letter cannot be found now, a subsequent letter to the RFC from the International Red Cross in Frankfurt mentions that he recorded that Maule had been shot through the head and stomach and died immediately after landing. A photograph enclosed with the letter shows where the Germans buried him close to where he fell, with plants set beneath the ornately inscribed wooden cross erected over his grave. This little piece of German chivalry allowed the three graves to survive the continuous heavy fighting and shelling that the area saw right up until the Armistice. As a result, the Imperial War Graves Commission was able to find and eventually relocate the three men's remains, so that Maule now rests in Hooge Crater Cemetery, while Lucas and Gibbon lie side by side in the Perth (China Wall) Cemetery at Zillebeke. The squadron had not had to wait long to learn the fates of their comrades and, although the chivalrous German message might have brought a sober kind of satisfaction to them, it would have also served to underline the fact that the Grim Reaper was ever-present.

It was now clear that even patrols of four or five FEs were going to suffer at the hands of the German squadrons equipped with the new Albatros – or 'Albatrii' as RFC pilots, many of whom had learned Latin at their public or grammar schools, had dubbed the plural of this threatening aeroplane. Knowing how heavily the odds were stacked against them, the long, lone patrols that 20 Squadron was ordered to carry out the following day must have seemed particularly daunting. Three such patrols were carried out that morning, taking the flyers far to the north of Ypres and deep over enemy territory. The gods were smiling on the squadron, though, as none of the FEs was attacked and the reconnaissances brought back a wealth of useful information about German rail movements as well as locating two German landing grounds. Two further patrols were flown in the afternoon but, apart from their observations, the only other noteworthy feature was Lieutenant Sawden's forlorn chase of an enemy machine flying high between Bailleul and Hazebrouk. Unusually, the German continued flying west, vainly pursued by the slow FE, until it crossed the coast towards England at an estimated height of 20,000ft, which was way beyond the FE's reach.

Poor visibility and gusting easterly winds hampered observations the following day, while a fight on 9 February brought 20 Squadron two more victories as a consolation for its recent losses. Five FEs set out in mid-afternoon for a photographic reconnaissance north of Ypres but were attacked by an equal force of German scouts over Houthulst Forest before they could take any photographs. Captain Blackwood and Lieutenant Soulby got a long burst into one German aeroplane, which was seen to go down by all the patrol. Just after that, another one was seen going down after a burst from both the front guns of A27 flown by Captain Hartney and Second Lieutenant Wilkinson[1]. This seemed to be enough for the Germans, who promptly broke off their attack as the FEs returned to their own side of the lines. The reconnaissance had thus been thwarted and, although 20 Squadron recorded two victories, German records do not reveal any casualties that would match the combat. That being so, one can probably assume that the pilots of the two German machines seen going down were either feigning or made successful forced landings, although, it should be emphasised that the absence of surviving German records for aircraft damaged or written-off as a result of enemy action does not make the matching of British claims and German losses any easier. Regardless of that, the photo-reconnaissance had not been successful and, to make matters worse, the next morning's photo-reconnaissance was also unsuccessful. Three of the six FEs sent up for the patrol had to return early with engine trouble and, with the patrol's strength cut by half, the mission was sensibly abandoned. A second attempt in the afternoon was slightly more successful as only two of the machines had to turn back.

The next three days of patrols were hampered by bad weather, while the morning patrol on Wednesday, 14 February went well enough, with two German scouts being driven off and a German gun battery being pinpointed to within a few yards inside a small wood northeast of the village of Draaibank. The Germans had given away their location with their gun flashes, so their position no doubt became a favoured target for their counterparts on the British side over the next few days. The afternoon patrol was not so trouble free. Harold Hartney and Wilfrid Jourdan, accompanied by Lieutenant Taylor and Second Lieutenant Myers in A15, set off at 14.00 to photograph the forest areas around Passchendaele and there met six of Jasta 18's Albatros scouts. Heavily outnumbered and badly shot up, they managed to get back over the lines, where both aircraft crashed a considerable distance apart. Hartney, Jourdan and Taylor were all seriously injured and were struck off the squadron's strength. Myers, the South African former agricultural student was killed when he and Taylor crash-landed; he is buried at Ferme-Olivier Military Cemetery near Ypres. Harold Hartney and Wilfrid Jourdan were sent back to England to convalesce, after which Hartney was unexpectedly instructed to report back to Canada and take command of the newly forming 27 American Aero Squadron. He was simultaneously transferred to the US Air Service with the rank of major and granted American citizenship, finishing the war as a colonel in command of the American 1 Pursuit Group. As for Wilfrid Jourdan, his injuries were compounded by appendicitis in May 1917, following which he continued to suffer the effects of his crash, rendering him unfit for general service for at least a year after the Armistice. Credit for downing the two FE2Ds was awarded to Leutnant Paul Strahle and Unteroffizier (corporal) Flemming as the first victories for each of these Jasta 18 men, which they reported as occurring at 17.00 German Time[3].

The following day brought 20 Squadron's final casualty of the month when Lieutenant Wainwright, piloting A5143 with Second Lieutenant Wilkinson as his observer, was wounded in the head by anti-aircraft fire but managed to get down safely at Abeele.

The first two weeks of February had not gone well; but the weather saved the squadron from even worse, when it provided the weary flyers with a well-earned rest from late afternoon on 16 February right through to Saturday, 24 February. Even then, that day was taken up entirely with new pilot instruction, gunnery practice and test flights, followed the next day by yet more bad weather that lasted to the end of the month and well into March. Among the new observers honing their skills on that Saturday was Lieutenant Gordon Dennis, who had worked as an articled pupil surveyor with the Borough Engineers Department in West Hartlepool, before transferring to the RFC from the East Yorkshire Regiment. Other newcomers were Londoner Sub-Lieutenant William Gilson RNVR and ex-Lancashire Territorial Second Lieutenant H.N. Hampson, from the Leeds suburb of Headingly. New air gunners included Sergeant Smith, Sergeant Boyd, Corporal Riach, Private Salmons and Air Mechanics Sayers and Cahill. A gunnery session was followed by a practice reconnaissance flight of seven machines and pilot instruction for recent arrivals Second Lieutenant Perry and Second Lieutenant Bacon. Offsetting the new arrivals was the departure of the very experienced Captain G.R.M. Reid, MC and Bar, who was posted back to England to take command of the training school at Norwich. He would later return to France to command 18 Squadron, which also flew FE2Ds but which were now, as he noted, 'very passé indeed, and being massacred'. Passé or not, 20 Squadron would have to put up with them until late summer and would not do so badly, all things considered[4].

******

The poor weather inherited from February meant that the first half of March passed without fights or losses, with most patrols being flown in conditions that hampered the German flyers just as much as the British. Only one uneventful patrol was possible on Thursday, 1 March and the next was not flown until the Sunday three days later. Nonetheless, a patrol of five FEs led by Captain Mahony-Jones and Captain Knowles obtained very good reconnaissance results. Despite poor visibility, they recorded enemy rail and canal movements, completing the patrol with the bombing of German positions near Château le Sars. One more patrol was flown on 6 March before the weather clamped down completely again until Saturday, 17 March. Meantime, the Germans had begun their pre-planned series of phased withdrawals to the new Hindenburg Line, retreating up to thirty miles in places and considerably shortening their defensive lines. This allowed them to concentrate their troops more effectively and, coincidentally, countered most of General Nivelle's plans – though he refused to admit it and insisted that his grand offensive should go ahead virtually unaltered.

If being a war flyer in those days of wood, wires and doped fabric could ever be regarded as normal, the weather finally allowed things to get back to normal on 17 March but, even then, only limited operations were possible. A five-strong patrol that set off on reconnaissance at 08.50 with an escort flight of 1 Squadron's Nieuport 17's saw plenty of action. Their route took them over Lille, Roubaix, Courtrai and Menin to photograph train movements before they bombed the German aerodrome at Coucou. Shortly afterwards they were attacked by five enemy scouts over Wervicq. As the Nieuports attempted to drive them off, the FE crews saw one of the enemy go down out of control, followed with the same fate by one of the Nieuports, A6617 flown by Second Lieutenant A.J. Gilson, who had been shot through the head and killed by Jasta 18's Leutnant Paul Strahle. According to Strahle's personal diary,[5] the Nieuport hit the ground with such force that its engine had to be dug out of the ground. At about the same time, Lieutenants W. Anderson and D.C. Woolley became separated from the rest of the flight and were last seen heading west between Lille and Messines. They did not return and it was not until the end of May that the squadron learned from HQ RFC – who had received the information from a repatriated Frenchman from German occupied Tourcoing – that they had been taken prisoner after being forced to land near Lambersart. Since Woolley's post-Armistice report on the circumstances of their capture makes it clear, that their aircraft was forced to land as a result of engine failure rather than enemy action[6], it is interesting that some German reports claimed that A27 was shot down by anti-aircraft fire, while a combat victory at the appropriate time and place was also submitted by Unteroffizier W. Hippert of FA (A) 227. Given that Woolley's report is perfectly clear on the subject, it might be suspected that the Germans concerned were trying it on to win some glory. Whatever was actually the case, A27 was not in one piece when it was captured. The Frenchman reported that Anderson and Woolley destroyed the machine and all its equipment before they were taken prisoner, and that the bombing raid on Coucou had destroyed four German aeroplanes on the ground and inflicted around twenty German casualties. William Anderson had been with the squadron since early February, having previously served with the 7 Cameron Highlanders, while his observer Duncan Boyd Woolley, from Sussex, had entered the RFC direct.

Another fight came in the early afternoon when three FEs led by Captain Blackwood and Sergeant Smith in A1935 saw three BE2Cs being attacked by enemy scouts over Polygon Wood. The FEs flew to their assistance but were not in time to prevent one of them going down in flames, which was probably number 6241 flown by Second Lieutenant A. Appleton and Corporal A. Cooper of 6 Squadron, who were both killed. Blackwood and Smith then dived to the rescue of another BE2C seen fleeing west with a German on its tail and chased the enemy down to 1,500ft over Becelaere, where it was last seen spinning earthwards before they lost sight of it below the FE's wing[1]. Captain Blackwood identified the German aircraft as Roland scouts in his combat report but they were most likely Albatros DIIIs, because the victory over the BE crew was awarded to Oberleutnant Grieffenhagen of Jasta 18 which appears not have had any Rolands on its strength. Jasta 18 recorded no casualties that day, although Greg van Weingarten's book *Jasta 18 – The Red Noses* notes that Leutenant Flink of that unit survived after being shot down and crashing near Reckem.

******

The RFC preparations for the coming offensive had now matured into preliminary air operations aimed at gathering information and disrupting and dislocating the enemy's lines of communication. Just to the southwest of Lille lay the important railway junction and goods yards at Sainghin and, although Sunday, 18 March brought worsening visibility, it did not deter 20 Squadron from sending out a patrol of six FEs to successfully bomb the railway before returning safely to Boisdinghem. They might well have done a great deal more had the weather not clamped down again until 22 March when the one patrol that was able to fly was forced to return after an hour. The reconnaissance was successfully repeated the following morning but brought another casualty. Former chartered accountant Herbert Fordred was wounded by ground fire and, after hospital and convalescence, survived the war as armaments officer with 27 Squadron. This reconnaissance was followed by a ten-strong bombing raid against Courtrai goods station, escorted by five of 1 Squadron's Nieuports; the FEs carrying out an OP along the valley of the River Lys after dropping their bombs. The only casualty came when Air Mechanic Second Class Riach was wounded in the hand by a piece of anti-aircraft shrapnel. After that, there was little else to report for the rest of the month, due to bad weather again preventing almost all flying. Although many of the more experienced (and tired) pilots and observers might have welcomed this, it did not come without a fee. At the end of March an order from GHQ brought word of increased responsibilities that would come into effect as soon as the weather allowed, in which the reconnaissance area of Second Army was to be enlarged to include Dixmunde, Beerst, Thourout, Thielt, Tournai, Seclin and Aubers[7].

This meant that April would see 20 Squadron extend its operations both north and south, bringing yet more fighting. As it was, the squadron had recorded eleven victories in the last three months at a cost of eight dead, seven captured and eleven wounded or injured. At first glance, a total of 26 casualties of all kinds, involving perhaps 13 aircraft, might not seem an unreasonable score when set against the eleven victories that were claimed – but the truth was less palatable. In only four of these victories was it claimed that an enemy aircraft was destroyed or crashed and, unknown to the British, in nearly every case the German pilots involved had survived uninjured and would soon be back in the air. The way to glory seemed to be a bloody one.

******

Notes

1. Combat Report.
2. AIR 1/435/15/273/11 – Messages Dropped by German Aircraft.
3. *The Jasta War Chronology* by N. Franks et al.
4. Personal Memoir of Air vice Marshal Sir Ranald Mcfarlane Reid, KCB: Documents Archive, Imperial War Museum.
5. Diary of Paul Strahle: *Cross & Cockade* Volume 11 No. 4.
6. WO 339/109852 – Officer's Service Record.
7. AIR 1/1001/204/5/1258 – Reports and instructions on aerial reconnaissance in France.

Chapter 10

'Bloody April' 1917

By now, 20 Squadron was not alone in having suffered at the hands of the new Albatros scouts. Mounting British air losses were starting to affect morale throughout the Royal Flying Corps and, all along the front, pilots and observers alike complained bitterly about the inferiority of their machines compared to the enemy's. The problem was exacerbated by the fact that most new pilots arriving at their squadrons had barely been given time to learn how to fly. To expect them to fight in out-dated aeroplanes without any real combat training was, in the opinion of many experienced flyers, simply asking too much. In addition, the need to protect the fledglings, while at the same time trying to carry out successful missions and return alive themselves, put added and sometimes almost intolerable pressure on the veterans.

On the ground, the British Army was gearing up for its planned assault on Vimy Ridge scheduled for 9 April. Local air supremacy was essential regardless of cost, and up-to-date photographs were desperately needed of the German positions at Arras and of everything else north and south that could have a bearing on the coming battle. As a result, a full-scale air offensive was planned for 1 April with the intention of clearing the skies of German aeroplanes so as to allow the British bombers and 'art-obs' (as artillery observations were generally termed) machines to carry out their work unhindered. In the event, except for a few limited operations, the seemingly permanent bad weather meant that no real operational flying was possible that day, although it cleared just enough the next day for four FEs from 20 Squadron to start out at 07.45 on a south offensive patrol (termed an 'SOP'). They soon had to return, however, as southwesterly wind gusts of 40 to 50 miles an hour and thick clouds at 6,000ft prevented any worthwhile observations. The strong winds continued over the next two days and it was not until 5 April that the air offensive got properly off the ground, with 20 Squadron playing a memorable role.

While the squadron's early patrol saw little enemy activity in the air or on the ground, a second OP that set off at 09.52 led by Captain Mahony-Jones and Captain Knowles in A1961 was more eventful. Having chased a lone German machine down to 700ft over Courtrai, they found themselves under attack by nine more. In a running fight, the patrol leaders brought down two Halberstadt scouts out of control without loss: the first over Courtrai and the second over Houthulst[1, 3, 7]. Meantime, a south OP that took off at 10.15 fought two Albatros scouts at 10,000ft over St. Eloi. Second Lieutenant Bacon's and Lieutenant Soulby's A1943 was immediately hit in the radiator causing them to descend to a successful forced landing at Abeele. Second Lieutenant Lawson's and Sergeant Clayton's A1942 was also badly shot about and they too followed Bacon's machine down to a forced landing in the nearby countryside. Second Lieutenant White and Private Allum, flying A6385, had a different experience though.

In his combat report, White described how he throttled back and lifted the nose of his machine so that it stalled as one of the 'Albatrii' dived on him, allowing Allum to fire about two-thirds of a drum into it as it swept overhead. The Albatros went into a steep dive with fuel vapour streaming behind it and, with the FE in hot pursuit, it flattened out and glided down to a forced landing in a ploughed field on the British side of the lines near Neuve Eglise, about three miles east of St. Eloi. Because most fighting took place over the enemy lines, it was a rare achievement to bring down an enemy aircraft on the British side and was a certain cause for celebration. After landing back at Boisdinghem, White and Allum learned that their opponent, Leutnant Josef Flink of Jasta 18, had only sustained a hand wound. His machine, Albatros DIII No. 1942/16, had been captured more-or-less intact and given the British captured aircraft designation number G/20. This was Flink's second and last experience of being shot down. Had he not been put out of the war by White and Allum, he might well have gone on to become a high-scorer for the Germans, having already been credited with two confirmed victories since first joining his unit in February 1917[1, 3, 4, 7].

Private Allum was involved in even heavier fighting the following day when nine FEs were detailed to bomb the German ammunition and supply dump at Ledeghem, near Moorseele. This time, he was flying with Second Lieutenant Perry in A6370, and they were just getting into line for the bomb-run when a Halberstadt scout suddenly appeared above and in front of them. The FE crew opened fire as the Halberstadt dived across their left front and tried to get round onto their tail. But Perry's flying skills were up to the challenge and the German pilot suddenly found the FE on *his* tail. Perry kept close behind the Halberstadt, still firing as it tried to dive away until it 'went straight down to the ground and struck it still diving' just south of Ledeghem dump at map reference 28.L.8.c[1]. In the meantime, Smart and Hampson had got lost in the thick clouds and sleet and, after about ten minutes searching for the others, they attacked three

Halberstadt scouts they had spotted over to their left. Two of these immediately turned right and made their way around to attack the FE from behind, while the third Halberstadt came straight at them. Hampson opened fire as it did so and saw the German pilot duck down in his cockpit as if he had been hit, following which the Halberstadt dropped away emitting clouds of smoke and steam. Hampson then turned on the other two Halberstadts and fired half a drum into the left-hand machine, which 'dropped into a spinning nose-dive and disappeared into a cloud', while the third one escaped in a spiral dive[1].

Elsewhere, in what now became a running fight with around half a dozen German scouts, things did not go so well and A6358 was seen going down partly on fire. The FE seemed to flatten out but Smith and Hume were both killed when it crashed near Bellewarde, the German victor once again being Walter Gottsch of Jasta 8 – back from hospital and out for blood[4, 5]. The only other casualty was Air Mechanic Second Class Sayers who received a slight head wound from anti-aircraft fragments. Second Lieutenant Roland Smith, 19-year-old son of Alderman J Smith, JP, from Lancaster, had originally been commissioned into 3 Battalion King's Own Yorkshire Light Infantry and had only been with the squadron since 24 March following his graduation as a pilot in mid-January. His observer, former Royal Navy officer Ronald Hume, son of Henry S. Hume from London, had also been with 20 Squadron less than three weeks when he was killed. Neither of their bodies was recovered, and both are remembered at the Arras Flying Services Memorial.

The morning of 7 April brought another fight and even worse casualties. Two bombing raids were launched against Mouveux aerodrome, the initial raid being carried out with little opposition while the afternoon raid was not so fortunate. Having left two of the hangars at Moveux in flames, the formation was re-crossing the lines when it was attacked by the Albatros scouts of Jastas 18 and 28. Lieutenant Lawson's FE2D A6400 was assailed on all sides by nine enemy scouts and would have certainly been lost had not Captain Mahony-Jones turned to his rescue. By this time, A6400 had been badly hit and Mahony-Jones's intervention gave Lawson the chance to make a forced landing on the British side, a German victory being claimed by Leutnant Walter von Bulow of Jasta 18[5]. That left the FE of Mahoney-Jones and Captain Moyes to take on the Albatrosses alone. Hemmed in on all sides, the FE single-handedly scattered the enemy machines several times with aggressive rushes before eventually falling in flames. Its heroic struggle against impossible odds was closely watched from the ground by the men of 34 Battalion, Australian Infantry – who so admired the crew's bravery that their adjutant was moved to write to RFC HQ to put their heroism on record:

The Commanding Officer 34th Battalion AIF has asked me to express a deep sense of admiration which was inspired by the gallant flying of an airman, apparently belonging to a squadron under your command. About 6pm on the evening of 7th instant two of our planes were engaged with nine of the enemy. One plane was damaged, and the other, although retreat looked possible, turned and fought. Several of the enemy planes scattered. Our plane was hit and immediately burst into flames. The scene was witnessed by the men of this Battalion from the trenches, and the conspicuous bravery was much spoken of by them, and is sure to foster a spirit of emulation for our men to strive hard, in their parts, to act in the same heroic and self-sacrificing manner as this gallant airman. The true bravery of your fine Corps was thus strikingly brought home to our men.[3]

Mahony-Jones and Moyes were not the only casualties, for although Lieutenant Lawson had got his FE safely down in friendly territory his observer, Lieutenant H.N. Hampson had been mortally wounded and died soon afterwards. He was buried at Bailleul, and after the war the remains of Mahony-Jones and Moyes were also transferred there from the German cemetery where they were originally laid to rest. Mahony-Jones had served with 11 Lancashire Fusiliers before joining the RFC, while Moyes, a former construction engineer from Edinburgh, had served in the ranks of 9 and 6 Battalions the Royal Scots before gaining his commission. The German victory over them was credited to Jasta 28's Offizierstellvertreter (equivalent to warrant officer) M. Muller. The first week of 'Bloody April' 1917 had been a hard one and, although the following two weeks would not be quite as trying, the month would not end without further casualties.

Sunday 8 April was cloudy but fine and 20 Squadron was tasked with an attack on Reckem aerodrome. This was carried out without major mishaps, while in another foray Robertson and Fauvel claimed an Albatros scout shot down out of control[3]. The following day was less eventful as most of the squadrons were grounded by snow, mists and freezing rain that swept the battlefields even as the infantry went 'over the top' to start the Battle of Arras.

******

The primitive facilities at Boisdinghem had long been a source of complaint, and on 15 April the squadron abandoned the place and moved to St. Marie Cappel, about one mile southeast of Mont Cassel. The new aerodrome was situated on farmland directly south of the village of St. Marie Cappel and ran approximately north to south, bordered by the road to Cassel on its west perimeter and a lane leading to nearby St. Sylvestre Cappelle on the east. Apart from enjoying better water supplies and other facilities, the new aerodrome was also closer to the front, and easier to find because of the nearby prominent landmarks of Mont Cassel and Mont Des Cats. It was a popular move for the men of 20 Squadron but the same could not be said for those already in residence. The existing incumbent, 45 Squadron, was junior to 20 Squadron so was forced to make way for their seniors, abandoning their wooden huts and metal hangars for tents and canvas Bessoneau hangars in the middle of a very cold spring. Captain Norman Macmillan MC remarked on this in his book *Into the Blue* and told how they later forgave the newcomers when they realised what a fine squadron they made.

The move was completed with all speed but, in the event, the haste was unnecessary as continuing bad weather delayed the second phase of the Battle of Arras by two days, until Monday, 23 April. Only one flight each day was possible on the Friday and Saturday but the Sunday brought an increase in activity with the squadron successfully completing three reconnaissance missions. The last one was an OP of ten FEs sent out over Lille, during which twenty-one plates were exposed through gaps in the clouds over the city's important railway stations and junctions. The patrol was mainly noteworthy for including several new arrivals at the squadron and was made up as follows:

> Sergeant Attwater & Second Lieutenant Davies in A19
> Second Lieutenant Dalziel & Air Mechanic Second Class Sayers in A6392
> Second Lieutenants Bacon & Lewis in A23
> Lieutenants Hay & Nicholson in A5143
> Lieutenant Satchell & Second Lieutenant Tod in A5149
> Captains Thayre & Cubbon in A6390
> Captain White & Second Lieutenant Fauvel in A6391
> Lieutenant Stevens & Lieutenant Gilson in A6393
> Lieutenant Cunnell & Second Lieutenant Wilkinson in A1965
> Second Lieutenants Heseltine & Houghton in A6403

Captain Frederick J.H. Thayre, a 23-year-old married man, from Littlehampton, Sussex, had served with the Honourable Artillery Company before transferring to the RFC in July 1915. He was then sent to France and, having claimed his first and so far only victory on 18 March 1916 with 16 Squadron, was mentioned in despatches in the *London Gazette* before being promoted to captain and flight commander a month later. Sandhurst trained Indian Army officer Captain Francis Richard Cubbon, aged 25, would soon become his regular observer; he had previously served with the 72 Punjabis, the Yorks & Lancs Regiment and the Royal Warwickshire Regiment. The recently promoted Captain Hugh Granville White was, of course, the same person who with Private Allum had wounded and captured Leutnant Flink of Jasta 18 on April 5. Canadian observer Lieutenant Harry Reid Nicholson, aged 21, was the son of William and Mary Elizabeth (nee Billington) Nicholson from Hamilton, Ontario, and had studied engineering at the University of Toronto. After serving four months with 13 Regiment of Militia he joined 1 Canadian Pioneer Battalion and was attached to the RFC as an observer on probation on 8 February 1917. Five days later he embarked for England for a one-month observer's course after which he was sent to France.

******

The postponed offensive was finally launched at 04.45 on Monday, 23 April 1917. Third Army was ordered to advance north and south of the Scarpe while the Canadian Corps of First Army was to take the line from Gavrelle to Acheville[6]. For their part, 20 Squadron carried out a number of unopposed reconnaissance flights during the day – but it was only the lull before the storm, for the following day brought a savage fight.

At 06.14 that morning, seven FEs set out to escort seven of 45 Squadron's Sopwith Strutters on a photo-reconnaissance mission north of Ypres. The reconnaissance itself was completed without incident but at 07.55 on the return leg the two formations were intercepted by a large number of Albatros scouts. As the Sopwiths continued across the lines with their vital photographs the FEs turned to hold off the Germans, four of which attacked A6385 flown by Captain Johnston and Lieutenant Nicholson. Perry and Sayers immediately turned to their rescue, driving off two of the attackers and sending a third down apparently out of control. But the fourth Albatros managed to get on their tail and shoot up their engine before Sayers could get up on the locker and drive it away with a few rounds over the top wing. Perry then turned A6403 towards the lines again and made a successful forced landing on the British side near Ypres. Later, he and Sayers learned that the men of No. D276 Battery, Royal Field Artillery had seen their Albatros catch fire as it went down out of control[1].

Meanwhile, the original attackers from Jastas 8 and 18 were now joined by three more led by Vizeflugmeister (equivalent to Aviation Chief Petty Officer) Wirtz of Marine-Feldjagdstaffel No.1 (MFJ-1). In the course of the confused melee that followed, Lieutenant Robertson and Captain Knowles had the extremely unpleasant experience of being badly shot-up and their machine A5144 set alight while still at a great height. But in a heroic endeavour that almost mirrored Tom Mottershead's feats back in January, Robertson, despite being wounded in two places, managed to keep control of his FE2 down to a height of about 200 feet. Knowles jumped clear just before it crashed, and then rushed over in time to pull Robertson out alive from under the burning wreckage. Lieutenant R.E. Johnson and Captain Cubbon were also in the thick of things in A6392 and after their safe return put in claims for two more enemy machines destroyed and out of control[7].

But A6385 did not return. Although a German message dropped over the lines later confirmed the deaths of 21-year-old Captain Alfred Johnston, from Bedford, and ex-Canadian Pioneer officer Lieutenant Harry Nicholson, the details of their passing remained unknown for many years until it was recently possible to study MFJ-1's captured War Diary[8]. This revealed that it was Wirtz who had shot up and set alight Robertson's and Knowles's machine, and that almost immediately afterwards he had collided head-on with A6385, the two machines plunging headlong to the ground close to Becelaere, killing all three airmen. It is likely that the Germans buried Johnston and Nicholson close to where they fell but the area was shelled and fought over repeatedly throughout the war and their graves were destroyed. Both are remembered at the Arras Flying Memorial.

Despite their casualties, 20 Squadron had done their job well. All of 45 Squadron's Sopwiths, with whose safety 20 Squadron had been charged, returned safely with their photographs – any one of which might have subsequently saved many British lives on the ground. Additionally, one Albatros had been destroyed in flames while another two had been claimed as shot down. Robertson's and Knowles's escape from death had, of course, been close to miraculous and provided yet another illustration of the admiration the RFC elicited from the ground troops, as shown in a letter received by 20 Squadron from the Commanding Officer of D/103 Battery, RFA:[9]

I beg to report that an aeroplane, No.5144, belonging to your squadron landed in flames on my battery position about 8am this morning and was totally destroyed. The machine burst into flames at a great height and was landed safely within our lines owing to the gallant conduct and great presence of mind of the two occupants, the pilot Lieutenant Robertson RFC, and observer Captain Knowles RFC. Though both these officers were wounded, the pilot rather seriously in two places, and both were burned slightly, they managed to keep the flames under control until within 200 feet of the ground. Knowles then jumped clear just before the machine turned over, and pulled Robertson from under the burning wreckage. Captain Knowles was full of praise at the manner in which Lieutenant Robertson piloted him safely to ground.

Dated 24/4/1917;

(Signed) James Abbey; Major, RFA: OC D/103 RFA

As to the Germans: in addition to MFJ-1's loss of Vizefeldwebl Wirtz, Jasta 18's Leutnant Fritz Kleindienst was shot down in flames and killed at Korentje, about seven or eight kilometres south of Becelaere, which ties in with Perry's claim and its confirmation by the Royal Artillery. A second Jasta 18 casualty was its CO, Rittmeister Karl von Grieffenhagen, who is listed as having been severely injured in a forced landing after combat[5]. This probably matches one of the two victories credited to Lieutenant Johnson and Captain Cubbon, while their second claim could refer to a German who feigned damage or injury to escape their fire. The total of three British victory claims was therefore a fair reflection of the actual German losses. The same cannot be said of the German victory claims, where it seems that the authorities were perhaps a little over-zealous in their attempts to balance the books after losing two dead and another severely injured. In fact, the German Army and Marine commanders awarded their pilots a total of five victories in a fight that had actually seen the British lose just two aircraft destroyed and a third damaged. Jasta 8's Offizierstellvertreter Walter Gottsch and Leutnant W. Junck were both awarded victories for having shot down FE2s over Ypres and east of Ypres respectively at 09.10 German time. Jasta 18's Leutnant Walter von Bulow was awarded another for a FE2D shot down over Ypres at 09.40 German time[5]. In addition, the German Naval authorities posthumously credited Wirtz with having shot down Robertson and Knowles in flames, and with another combat victory resulting from his collision with Johnston and Nicholson moments later. In the light of this, it seems fair to credit Johnston and Nicholson with a victory for their collision with Wirtz, since it will never be known for sure whether the collision was accidental or the result of a deliberate ramming. It may well be that the Germans granted these victory awards in good faith. The British had long experienced the difficulties involved in confirming victory claims made by their pilots for fights taking place over enemy territory or close to the front lines, so it is very likely that the Germans experienced similar problems in which the proverbial fog of war forever clouded the facts. Whatever the truth of it, the 'official' scoreboard has provided posterity (and those who defend the then British system of awarding combat victories) with an interesting riposte to those who still allege that the British victory lists were deliberate lies created for propaganda purposes.

******

More bad weather brought a brief respite to 20 Squadron by preventing any flying on April 25, while the following day brought another death. Ten FEs set off at 06.10 to bomb Rumbeke aerodrome and, of the twenty 112lb bombs dropped, sixteen were seen to fall 'in the vicinity' of the target while four were unobserved. The formation was then attacked by eight Albatros scouts and, although one was brought down out of control by Lieutenant Hay's gunner, Private Allum, and another by the whole patrol, A6393 was badly hit. Lieutenant Stevens managed to bring it down in one piece on the British side of the lines near Watou but his observer had been shot through the chest and later died. He was 33 year-old Sergeant Albert John Clayton, a former labourer from Studley, Warwickshire, and the son of William and Harriett Clayton. A pre-war soldier, Albert had first enlisted for eight years with the Kings Royal Rifle Corps at Birmingham in January 1904, and was married to Ellen Smith on Christmas Day 1911. Following the outbreak of war, Clayton re-enlisted on 3 December 1914 but his return to the colours was clouded by tragedy when his wife Ellen died of pulmonary tuberculosis on 26 March 1915 while he, now a lance corporal, was at the front. Promoted to Sergeant in December that year, Clayton was wounded in action and hospitalised at Rouen the following July. He was interviewed for the RFC on 19 January 1917 and officially appointed as a sergeant aerial gunner on 28 April 1917, two days after his death – from which one can only assume that the military paper trail always moves slower than events. He is buried at Watou Churchyard near Poperinghe. The month that had cost the RFC so grievously that it would forever be remembered as 'Bloody April' was drawing to a close but there would be no let-up in pressure from the 'higher-ups' in their demands for continual operations. A memorandum from RFC headquarters to all brigades in France, dated 27 April 1917, underlined the requirements:

> The GOC wishes to impress on Brigadiers that in the area that is allotted to the Army for aerial work by GHQ, the RFC are responsible that no great change *[i.e. in the enemy's dispositions – author's comment]* can occur without it being known to the RFC Brigade concerned. The GOC has neither the wish nor the power to interfere in any way with the work ordered by the Army in the reconnaissance area allotted to it, but he looks to Brigadiers

to see that sufficient reconnaissance work is done to ensure that all hostile activity is immediately discovered and, when necessary, to suggest to their Army any reconnaissance or other work which appears desirable.

The word then was reconnaissance, reconnaissance and yet more reconnaissance; and it was not a job that could be done without casualties.

******

The squadron carried out two successful reconnaissances on 29 April but the main action came during a late afternoon bombing raid against Bissegham Dump. As the FEs were turning back towards the lines for the return trip, they were attacked by eight Albatros scouts that had been shadowing them. Five more German machines now joined the fray and, although hits were scored by the British, it was difficult to see whether any of the enemy machines were brought down. Smart and Lewis recorded in their Combat Report that 'at three-thousand feet we were still fighting with five hostile aircraft or more, who eventually left us when we crossed the lines at one-thousand feet'. They also mentioned that the 'pilot and observer of A6430 (Thayre and Cubbon) saw A6412 (Smart and Lewis) shoot one HA (hostile aeroplane) down just the other side of the lines. About 5.25pm a pilot of No.1 Squadron saw a HA crash in no man's land.' In addition, Thayre and Cubbon claimed a German machine shot down in flames, while Second Lieutenants R.E. Conder and Henry Neville claimed another out of control. The 20 Squadron Record Book noted that an observer of 53 Squadron had also reported seeing an opponent of Smart and Lewis crash. But there were British casualties too. Second Lieutenant Perry was shot in the thigh and Private Allum was slightly wounded but both men survived their crash-landing near Sanctuary Wood. Thayre and Cubbon had their machine badly shot up and landed at 42 Squadron, while Burns and Houghton in A6391 and Sergeant Attwater and Second Lieutenant Davies in A19 failed to return. Fortunately, all the missing men were still alive, albeit as prisoners of war. Sergeant Attwater and Second Lieutenant J.E. Davies (ex-1/8 London Regiment) had been shot down by Leutnant E. Weissner of Jasta 18, while Second Lieutenants V.L.A. Burns (ex-RFA) and D.L. Houghton (ex-Middlesex Regiment) were hit in the engine by Leutnant P. Strahle of the same Jasta and were also taken prisoner[5]. Both survived their captivity, though not without harm: by 1918, Attwater weighed just six stone and had become so ill that the Germans released him into the care of neutral Holland, where he spent the remainder of the war billeted in a house in The Hague. Late in 1918 his wife Anne was out shopping in Preston when she was suddenly accosted by a skinny, ragged looking soldier who threw his arms around her neck and kissed her fiercely. She threw her assailant off with some force and slapped him across the face. It was only when he cried out her name that she recognised this emaciated shadow of a man as her very own Sydney back from the war. They embraced again, and a new life beckoned[10].

Another bombing raid was launched against Bisseghem the following day, 30 April, but ended without casualties. This was despite A5143 having all its controls shot away and catching fire on crash-landing on the British side of the lines; Lieutenant Hay and Air Mechanic Sayers were unhurt. A newcomer experiencing his 'baptism of fire' on this occasion was pilot Lieutenant A.N. Solly, flying A1965. Second Lieutenant H.M. Coombs, from Newport on the Isle of Wight, was recorded as having been wounded in another skirmish, although the circumstances are unclear. He was repatriated to England for treatment and convalescence before finishing the war with 100 Squadron, for which service he received the D.F.C.

So 'Bloody April' ended. The Squadron had seen its fair share of the fighting and, by the end of the month, had lost seven men dead, nine wounded and four missing, the last-mentioned all being prisoners. In return, their pilots and observers had claimed nine combat victories over the German flyers, with one of these being taken prisoner. In addition, Captain Knowles and Lieutenant Gordon Davis had each been awarded the MC, and Lieutenant H.W. Soulby had received the French *Croix de Guerre*. Despite their losses, amounting to nearly half the squadron killed, wounded or taken prisoner, 20 Squadron had in fact been luckier than many other units. Throughout that dreadful month, the RFC and RNAS combined had lost 319 men and, in pursuance of their leaders' strictures to at all times maintain the offensive over enemy territory, three-quarters of these had fallen on the German side of the lines. The glaring inferiority of most British types of aircraft compared to the latest German machines was depressingly apparent to everyone but, until the new designs arrived in substantial numbers, they would just have to soldier on regardless. For the rest of the spring and throughout the coming summer, 20 Squadron's men would have to fight and sometimes die as best they could with their obsolete FE2Ds before they would finally receive the superb new two-seater Bristol F2B Fighter in replacement. And during the months before that happy day arrived, their old 'pushers' would still be found deep behind the German lines – in some cases inflicting quite surprising casualties on the enemy.

******

Notes

1. Combat Report.
2. not used.
3. AIR 1/167/15/156/2 '20 Squadron Record Book'.
4. *The Jasta Pilots* by N Franks, F Bailey & R Duiven.
5. The Jasta War Chronology by N Franks, F Bailey & R Duiven.
6. AIR 1/676/21/13/1872 'Battles of Arras, including preliminary operations, 1917'.
7. AIR 1/689/21/20/20 'History of 20 Squadron, list of enemy aircraft brought down'.
8. War Diary of MFJ-1.
9. AIR 1/167/15/156/2: Letter from D/103 R.F.A.
10. Memoir of Sydney Attwater, Imperial War Museum.

Chapter 11

Towards Messines – May 1917

While the fighting at Arras continued, the British were also planning a major offensive at Ypres, where the Germans had the advantage of occupying the higher ground that partly surrounded the salient and overlooked the British. The first part of the plan was to tunnel under the German-held Messines Ridge, to the south of Ypres, and blow it up with underground mines along with the Germans occupying it. This was being done with utmost secrecy and the continued fighting at Arras was a useful tool to distract the Germans' attention away from where the real threat lay. The airmen of 20 Squadron began the new month under orders to keep the Germans in the dark by attacking their balloon sites, mounting bombing raids at various places to keep them unsettled, and preventing their reconnaissance aircraft from crossing the trenches to the British side of lines.

Early on 1 May 1917, two FE2D flown by Lieutenant Cunnell and Second Lieutenant Wilkinson in A6431, accompanied by Second Lieutenant Dalziel and Lance Corporal Bradley in A6392, their aircraft laden with phosphorous bombs, took off from St. Marie Cappel on a north OP over Houthem, Roulers and Menin. Notes were made on enemy rail movements and the German balloon winch near Bousbecque was bombed. Vain attempts were made to reach three German machines circling Roulers at 16,000ft and three more they spotted heading west over Menin at 18,000ft. Then the two FEs attacked four enemy reconnaissance machines lower down over Menin. Dalziel and Bradley targeted an Albatros C-Type in the group, which was seen to crash near Messines. Their German victims were probably Unteroffizier Gottwald and Leutnant Hecxmann from FA 6, who were both killed over Ploegsteert Wood at 11.20 German Time[2]. A little over two hours later, Captains Thayre and Cubbon shot up an Albatros two-seater that crash-landed in fields north of Ypres, while in the afternoon more German balloon sites were bombed forcing the Germans to haul down one balloon and put it back in its container. A similar pattern was followed on 2 May. The only combat victory came when Captain Cunnell and Second Air Mechanic Sayers sent an Albatros scout into a vertical dive over Comines after an eight-strong bomb raid on Ledeghem dump. Although they were not able to watch its fate due to another scout attacking them, fellow pilot Lieutenant Harry Satchell reported the German as having gone down trailing a column of smoke[1].

The Germans were now launching ferocious counter-attacks at Arras and on 3 May 20 Squadron mounted three OPs in an attempt to locate German reinforcements and troop concentrations. There was little to report until Captain Thayre took exception to the German anti-aircraft gunners on the way back from Sainghin and decided to teach them a lesson. As 'Archie' burst all around him, he threw his aircraft into a spiral nose-dive and sideslip from 12,000ft pretending his aircraft had been hit. The Germans ceased fire as the FE fell, only for Thayre to bring it back under control again at 5,000ft and dive straight onto their positions, strafing the enemy gunners with machine-gun fire as he swept over their heads before turning for home again[3]. The German reaction to these sort of antics – in no way limited only to 20 Squadron's pilots – is recorded in a German Sixth Army report of that week:

> …when our anti-aircraft open fire the enemy formations twist and turn and fire their machine-guns as if they were in aerial combat; often in this way they succeed in bringing our anti-aircraft fire to an immediate halt[4]

The day's main event came with another bombing raid on Lichterveldt Station in the late afternoon, during which Thayre and Cubbon forced a German Albatros two-seater to land south of Roulers, before dropping their bombs over the target and engaging around twenty-five Albatros scouts over Moorslede. The two captains fought eighteen of the Germans all at once and shot down one Albatros that crashed near Moorslede at 17.20, followed by another that hit the ground five minutes later near Westroosebeke. Undaunted by the fact that they had now run out of ammunition, they took on another three scouts and fought them off with an automatic revolver, for which they were both awarded the Military Cross[1]. The other FEs were also heavily engaged and, by the time the German attack was driven off, off, Second Lieutenant Frank Babbage, a former civil engineer from Exmouth, and Air Mechanic First Class Bernard Aldred, who had previously served with the Royal Marines Light Infantry (RMLI), had sent down one Albatros, apparently out of control, while Second Lieutenants R.G. Dalziel and L.G. Fauvel had been badly shot-up and slightly wounded in A1935 but succeeded in making a safe crash-landing near Poperinghe. All the other FEs returned safely, exposing twelve reconnaissance photographs along the way. Even Major Mansfield flew a lone photographic reconnaissance over the lines during the afternoon, while Cunnell and Sayers were sent up in A6431 at 22.05 for a solo night bombing raid on Wervicq dump. There was almost no German anti-aircraft opposition to their successful foray and they returned safely an hour later. The next day, 4 May, was passed in similar fashion, with the highlight being a bombing raid against Château du Sars aerodrome that left four hangars in flames, while the following day's target was Poelcappelle railway station in an early raid that set off at 06.45.

The FEs were in the process of dropping their bombs when the 'Albatrii' arrived and caught A1942 completely by surprise. After the war, Second Lieutenant Leonard Bacon, a married 26-year-old former bank cashier who had previously served as a staff sergeant in 4 Territorial Battalion of the Hampshire Regiment, recounted his experiences in a report he made on the circumstances of his capture. In it, he told how he was hit in his right arm by the German's first burst and knew nothing else until he woke up on the ground surrounded by soldiers. His aerial gunner, Air Mechanic Second Class Gerald Worthing, lay dead a few feet away, shot through the head. Bacon lost consciousness again and, when he woke up three days later in a German field hospital at Staden, he found his right arm had been amputated above the elbow. Not long after, he was visited by the German who had shot him down, Walter Gottsch, who told him that his machine had landed in a tree and he was lucky to have survived. His less fortunate aerial gunner Worthing, a 26-year-old ex-collier from Herefordshire, is buried at the famous Tyne Cot cemetery.

Revenge for these losses came with the OP of five FEs that set out at 16.35, with Captains Thayre and Cubbon once again leading in A6430. According to Major Mansfield's later summary for the benefit of HQ[3], subsequently re-issued in an edited form as part of RFC Communiqué No.87, the formation had got up to about 8,000ft over Boisinghe when they were attacked half-heartedly by two Albatros two-seaters, joined by around twenty-five Albatros scouts, all coming from different directions. This started a full hour of fighting at altitudes between 11,000ft and 3,000ft. Thayre and Cubbon sent one plunging to earth over Poelcappelle with its wings breaking off as it fell, while Air Mechanic Second Class Cowell claimed his first victory when he sent another down smoking and out of control. His FE's engine failed immediately afterwards and the machine dropped down to 3,000ft before his pilot, Lieutenant Conder, managed to restart it – with one of the Germans still in pursuit. Fortunately, their predicament had been noticed by Lieutenant A.N. Solly and Air Mechanic C. Beminster, who dived down on the German, sending him into in a vertical dive around 1,000ft over Hollebeke. The FE A5147 of Second Lieutenants Heseltine and Kydd was set alight just after they had sent an Albatros diving away with a cloud of smoke pouring from it. Their plight was spotted by Thayre and Cubbon who, having only just set another Albatros alight, dived onto their assailant and shot it down to crash close to Houthem. They then managed to get their own stricken machine back across the lines to a safe crash landing near Bailleul. Two more victories were claimed: one by Solly and Beminster, in which a burst from Beminster over the top wing sent a German fighter down in flames, and the other by Babbage and Aldred who shot up yet another Albatros and saw its tail break away before it crashed on the British side of the line.

After an hour of furious fighting, the FE crews were credited with having destroyed, disabled or put to flight eight enemy scouts without suffering a single human casualty themselves. However, the only recorded German casualty that can definitely be attributed to this action was that of VizeFeldwebel Peter Glasmacher of Jasta 8, who was killed in action in the St. Eloi and Zillebeke Lake area[2] on the British side of the lines. Since only Babbage's and Aldred's claim specifically referred to a German crashing on the British side, it might be fair to grant them the credit for Glasmacher's destruction. Two Jasta 18 pilots, Leutnant E. Weissner and VizeFeldwebel Flemming, were each credited with the destruction of an FE2 in the same area. However, the only British aircraft casualty was that of A5147, which was not a total loss and was flying again in July[2]. Like the Germans, RFC Headquarters took 20 Squadron's combat reports at face value on this occasion, and the British survivors must have felt a certain pride next morning when they learned of the congratulatory telegrams just received from their GOC Hugh Trenchard and from the GOC 2nd Army. To underline the High Command's satisfaction with the squadron, whose five slow FE2Ds had taken on twenty-five of the enemy, Captains Thayre and Cubbon were each awarded a bar to their Military Crosses.

Just two solo night bombing missions were flown the following day, 6 May, with Satchell and Second Lieutenant M. Tod bombing the Hellenes railway workshops at Lille, while Cunnell and Wilkinson attacked Lille's La Madelaine station and left two of the sheds on fire. On Monday, 8 May eight FEs were sent up to bomb Bissegham dump, after which they were attacked by twelve Albatros scouts while another six hung around nearby. Air Mechanic Aldred, flying with Second Lieutenant Frank Babbage again in A1935, claimed the only British victory by firing over the top wing as one of the German scouts came out of its dive and overshot the FE. Hit by their bullets, it dived away suddenly just a few feet in front of the FE and crashed southeast of Courtrai[1]. Lieutenant A.W. Martin and Private W.G. Blake failed to return in A5149 but fears for their safety were soon alleviated by a German 'courtesy message' dropped over the trenches. Their FE had been shot up by Walter von Bulow of Jasta 18 and was forced to land on his aerodrome at Halluin, where Martin suavely presented his captors with his visiting card as he was taken into captivity[5]. The FE was then repaired and adorned with black crosses by the Germans and used as a station 'hack' aircraft by all and sundry. (A 'hack' aircraft, it should perhaps be explained, was one used as a general runabout by a squadron; it was usually old, obsolete or captured.) The message also included news of the health of PoWs Second Lieutenants Davies, Burns and Houghton and Sergeant Attwater, along with sadder confirmation of the deaths, back in April, of Lieutenant H.R. Nicholson and Captain A.R. Johnston, who at the time had been only posted as missing[6]. These 'courtesy messages' did not constitute a one-way traffic, this one also requesting news of three missing German airmen. The RFC officer dealing with these appeals made a pencil note that a message had already been dropped on the German side concerning the death of one of them, noting too that a request had gone out to brigades asking for information on the other two German flyers. So it can be seen that, although the system was not publicly advertised at the time, it was carried out with the full knowledge and consent of the higher authorities on both sides.

******

On Wednesday, 9 May, a bombing raid against Courtrai goods station, which included newly promoted aerial gunner Sergeant Bernard Aldred, was attacked by seven Albatros scouts, led by a Halberstadt with a streamer on its tail. Second Lieutenants Howe's and Kydd's claim for two Albatros scouts sent down out of control was confirmed by some of the escorting Nieuport pilots, but the victories came at a price. FE A6429 was hit by anti-aircraft fire that fatally wounded observer Second Lieutenant Henry George Neville, who died at the nearby 2nd Canadian Casualty Clearing Station soon after his pilot E.J. Smart made a safe forced landing on the British side near Vlamertinghe. Henry was the 23-year-old son of London printing and lithography manufacturer George Neville and his wife Jane. Before enlisting at the Inns of Court OTC on 6 September 1915, he had studied for the Cloth with the Anglican Society of the Sacred Heart at Kelham Theological School, Nottinghamshire. Their members were committed to poverty, celibacy and obedience – the last of these virtues coming naturally enough to almost everyone required to serve on the Western Front, while the first two would most certainly have applied when not on leave. Neville is buried at Lijssenthoek Military Cemetery, near Poperinghe. Another casualty came in the late afternoon when Second Lieutenant H.R. Wilkinson was hit in the head by ground fire during an oblique photography mission over

'The Bluff' area southeast of Ypres. Lieutenant Harry Satchell immediately turned for home and landed at Bailleul where his observer was struck off the squadron's strength and rushed off to hospital. Later, an SOP that pin-pointed the flashes of German anti-aircraft guns located near Deulemont, about 500 yards northeast of Polygon Racecourse, was completed without incident marking the first patrol over the lines for Lieutenant Lee, Second Lieutenant Kirby and Sergeant Backhouse.

The following day brought two more victories. Lee and Beminster sent down two Albatros scouts in spinning nose-dives during a successful bombing raid against the German aerodrome at Reckem, just south of Courtrai. Two OPs in the afternoon included the regular reconnaissance and bombing any 'targets of opportunity'. The day's flying was completed by Lieutenant Solly and Private Beminster setting off alone in A6354 for a low reconnaissance over the Hooge area, where they pinpointed the locations of two German heavy artillery emplacements. Low-level reconnaissance was dangerous work, and their activities made such an impression on the British soldiers watching from the trenches that the commanding officer of 6 Wiltshire Regiment wrote to his Divisional HQ to sing their praises in a letter that was then passed on to 20 Squadron in order that the pilot might be congratulated.

To: H.Q. 19 Division   From: Major J.J. Tynan
                                          CO, 6th Wiltshire Reg.

Aeroplanes – own

One of our aeroplanes appeared over our lines last night at about 8.40pm, obviously to make a reconnaissance. The pilot behaved in a most daring manner. Although fired at from all quarters by 'Archies' and machine guns he took absolutely no notice and continued to circle and nose-dive in all directions. In my opinion he carried out a most daring and magnificent reconnaissance, and I would like to suggest that this airman be informed that all ranks in the Salient felt proud to think that such work, apparently by one Englishman, should be carried out with such bravery.

Bombing raids against the German aerodrome at Ramegnies-Chin and a German artillery position over the next two days, led to further casualties when Second Lieutenant H. Kirby and Sergeant T.E. Wait were captured after A23 was shot up by anti-aircraft fire and forced to land on the German side of the lines. The next real fight came on Sunday, 13 May when eight of the squadron's FE2s were attacked by between twenty and thirty enemy scouts, just after another bombing raid against Reckem aerodrome. Thayre and Cubbon added two more victories to their tally, sending one of them down in flames over Gheluvelt and another to crash near Zandwoorde. Irish aerial gunner John Cowell, flying with Lieutenant Scott, shot down a red two-seater that turned on its side and then nose-dived into the ground near Menin[1]. Solly and Beminster added to the toll by forcing another enemy scout to land near Zillebeke at map reference 28.I.23. But Second Lieutenant G.C. Heseltine, a married man from Southsea in Hampshire, who had previously served with 9 Battalion West Yorkshire Regiment, was shot through the back by Jasta 18's Paul Strahle and crash-landed on the British side, along with Lieutenant Lee and Private Lloyd, who had also had their FE badly shot-up but were unhurt. Heseltine eventually recovered enough to take up ground duties in 1918 and ended the war as an Acting Captain at the RAF Armaments School.

An overnight bombing raid on Gheluvelt station was carried out by Lieutenants Cunnell and Gilson in A6431 and Lieutenant Stevens and Second Lieutenant Kydd in A6393, followed on 15 May by two more FEs departing at 05.55 for a northern patrol, in which Solly and Beminster forced down a balloon and chased an Albatros two-seater back over its own lines. They then returned to the balloon site and bombed its winch, at which point they were attacked by six Albatros scouts and claimed two shot down: one seen to go out of control and the other to crash near Fort Carnot.

Once again the cost was high and Lieutenant Grout and Air Mechanic First Class Tyrell flying A6446, were captured after being hit in the engine and crash-landing near Lille. Even so, they had done their bit as, according to Grout's post-war report, they had managed to shoot down one of the enemy scouts first. Immediately after their capture, the luckless duo were paraded for the German propaganda cameras, and pictures of them and their wrecked machine were later displayed in the German magazine *Flugsport*. The pair were sent on to Inglemunster for questioning, following which they were separated and sent to different PoW camps. Lieutenant Edwin Grout, from Clapham in London, was a former naval officer who had transferred to the RFC in 1916. He had passed out at the Central Flying School on 24 April 1917 and was typical of the many casualties suffered by the RFC around this time: fresh from training and new to the front. His gunner, 24-year-old Alexander Tyrrell, was almost as new to aerial combat. A married man from Hanwell, Middlesex, he had been flying with the squadron in addition to his ground duties for barely a week when he was captured, having originally transferred to the RFC in August 1916 from 5 Reserve Battalion of the Gloucester Regiment.

Repatriated to England on 19 January 1919, Tyrell was re-united with his wife Kathleen and became a father and grandfather. His grandson Jamie now lives in Belfast[7].

No flying was possible for the next three days. Then on 19 May, a new observer, 22- years-old Second Lieutenant W.C. (Bill) Cambray, made his operational début flying with the squadron on four patrols and photo-reconnaissance missions over the Messines area in the build-up to the long campaign that would lead to Passchendaele. Cambray had first enlisted as a private in the Rifle Brigade on 4 September 1914 and was posted to France as a Lance Corporal in August 1915. News of his commission came through on 12 November that year, his twenty-first birthday, and after a posting back to England for officer training, he returned to France in July 1916 as a subaltern in 2 London Regiment, Royal Fusiliers in the Somme area. After taking part in a number of actions there, Cambray applied for the RFC and returned to England for observer training. Following his arrival at St. Marie Cappel, he got his first look at a FE2D and, over the months that followed, came to love it for its strength and flying characteristics, although it could hardly have been called graceful.

The squadron flew three separate southern patrols, each of two machines, on the morning of 20 May and, although they were fairly uneventful, they are worth noting for some other new faces that had arrived around the same time as Bill Cambray. New observer Second Lieutenant W.M.E. Chester flew with recently arrived pilot, Second Lieutenant W.P. Scott, in A6412 on the first patrol between 04.30 and 06.17, along with the more experienced Second Lieutenants E.J. Smart and T.A.M.S. Lewis in A6415, recording train movements around Lille. The second patrol was carried out by Lieutenant Hay and Bill Cambray in A6368 and new pilot Second Lieutenant J.H. Baring-Gould and Sergeant Aldred in A6466. Then at 07.00, new pilot Lieutenant Foster and aerial gunner Private C. Lloyd set off in A1965 accompanied by, Lieutenant R.A.P. Johns and Sergeant W. Backhouse in A6392. All returned safely.

The offensive patrol that set out at 08.20 was more eventful. The six FEs took on an equal number of Albatros scouts shortly after bombing the anti-aircraft battery at Polygon Wood racecourse and the supply dump at Langemark. Condor and Cowell in A6412 sent down one of the 'Albatrii' out of control, while Boucher and Birkett in A6415 sent down another in a spinning nose-dive. But A6413 was shot up and had to land at Bailleul, while A6444 suffered a seized engine and crashed near Cassel, killing Second Lieutenant Howe's aerial gunner, Lance Corporal '907' Roland Irvine Bradley. He had recently transferred to the RFC after originally going to France with 'A' Squadron of the

North Irish Horse in August 1914: he was later buried at Hazebrouk communal cemetery. One of five brothers, his parents were Mr and Mrs William Bradley, from Charlemont, County Tyrone, who had already seen tragedy when one of their sons, Frederick, a leading stoker, was killed when his submarine hit a mine[9]. Further bad news came that same day when A6457 was shot down over Hollebeke by German ace Leutnant Karl Schafer, commanding officer of Jasta 28, for his twenty-seventh victory: both 29-year-old Ontario born Lieutenant Albert C. Lee and his English gunner Air Mechanic First Class C. Beminster were captured[2, 8].

Several other patrols were flown during the day and over the next two days, but not until there was an improvement in the weather on Wednesday, 23 May did 20 Squadron see heavy fighting again. Captain White claimed an 'out of control' victory over one of the 'Albatrii' before having to force-land his badly shot-up machine at Abeele – where he was soon joined by Second Lieutenants W.P. Scott and E.B. Cogswell who landed A6357 in a similar condition. And FE A6466 came down near a British gun battery with its wounded pilot Second Lieutenant W. Howarth and his dead aerial gunner Frederick Bird. Sergeant 77646 Bird was the 24-year-old son of Thomas and Eliza Bird of Sidcup, Kent, and is buried at Vlamertinghe Military Cemetery. The one remaining FE flown by Lieutenants N. Boucher and N.M. Birkett came back alone.

That was only the start of the fighting that day, with even worse losses being suffered by the central OP that went up at 14.09. The four FEs were attacked by ten 'Albatrii' just after crossing the lines at Armentieres at 15.05 but continued their fight north along the salient for the next ten minutes. The 'Albatrii' attacked from close range, with one of them passing only fifty feet in front of Thayre's and Cubbon's machine. Both men opened fire and the enemy turned over and went down out of control before crashing near Zandwoorde. However, two FEs were lost: one went straight down in flames near Hollebeke, killing Second Lieutenants R.G. Masson and F.W. Evans, while the other looked like it was on fire but under control and still being attacked as it disappeared low down near Comines. Thayre and Cubbon tried to assist it by driving off the Albatros, which they claimed as an 'out of control' victory northeast of Ploegsteert[1] but it was to little avail as A6468 came down with Lieutenant R.A.P. Johns suffering severe burns to his hands, legs, face and neck. German soldiers rescued both crewmen from the burning wreck, but Sergeant Aldred died in hospital the following day while Johns survived his captivity and was repatriated on 6 January 1919. However, his burns had left him with serious disabilities and he resigned his commission in August 1919. He moved to India, where he died less than three years later at Adra on 26 October 1922. Two Jasta 28 pilots were credited with victories after the fight: Leutnant Karl Emil Schafer and Offizierstellvertreter M. Muller[5]. Schafer now counted seven FE2s among his twenty-eight victories – but this would be his last.

Second Lieutenant Robert Geoffrey Masson, 22-year-old son of Robert and Harriett Masson, of Ottawa, Ontario, served with the 156 Battalion Canadian infantry before transferring to the RFC in December 1916. He was following in the footsteps of his older brother Flight Sub-Lieutenant Donald Howe Masson, who was killed serving with the RNAS less than a month before Robert and who is buried at Dunkirk. Frederick Evans, from Muswell Hill, London, previously served with 21 Battalion the Middlesex Regiment and left wife Esther Cecilia Evans and a one-year-old daughter, Eileen Esther. Sergeant '77449' Bernard Aldred, a 21-year-old from Nottingham, had originally enlisted in the Royal Marines Light Infantry on 21 May 1915 and, after serving with the RMLI in France, had been awarded the Military Medal on 15 May 1917. But now, less than two weeks after his award, he had been shot through the stomach and, according to Lieutenant Johns, 'was worthy of special notice for gallant behaviour' in materially helping him to bring the aircraft safely to the ground despite his wounds. It is believed that the Germans originally buried the three men in Bousbecque Communal Cemetery but after the war their bodies were exhumed by the Imperial War Graves Commission and now lie alongside each other at the Pont-du-Hem Military Cemetery near Estaires, just yards from where the author's maternal grandfather and his pilot also lie. Second Lieutenant R.A.P. Johns, who came from Plymouth and was 24 when he was shot down, had previously served with Marlborough College OTC before being commissioned into the 20 Hussars at Colchester on 14 August 1914, transferring to the RFC in 1916. Another less serious casualty came the following afternoon when A6374 was badly shot-up and Second Lieutenant Scott was forced to make a crash-landing at Vlamertinghe, from which he escaped unhurt while his observer, Second Lieutenant Cogswell, from British Columbia, broke both legs.

Given the recent casualties, it was not surprising that 20 Squadron now began to send out larger patrols to face the 'Albatrii'. Thus the first so-called close offensive patrol ('COP') of Friday, 25 May went up eight-strong, which was just as well because, while noting canal traffic near Wervicq, it was attacked by two groups of Albatros scouts at 07.30. Conder and Cowell quickly sent one of these down in a spinning nose-dive that was credited as an 'out of control' victory, while Thayre and Cubbon added to their own tally by sending another down over Reckem with its right wing hanging off[1]. The enemy scouts temporarily dispersed but attacked again at 08.45, with Jasta 28 pilot Leutnant A. Hanko shooting Second Lieutenant J.H. Baring-Gold through the abdomen. Baring-Gould managed to get the FE down on the British side of the lines but his observer, Lieutenant C.A. Hoy, was injured in the resulting crash-landing. Meantime, Second Lieutenant R.G. Dalziel was severely wounded flying A3 while Lieutenant R.E. Johnson and Second Lieutenant L.G. Fauvel were both injured in a forced-landing after being shot-up in A6471, possibly by Leutnant S. Rohe of MFJ1. Fauvel was struck-off the BEF's strength but had 'done his bit'. After being awarded the Military Medal as Sergeant 2484 of the Yorkshire Dragoons Yeomanry, and having also been wounded twice while flying with 20 Squadron, he deserved a rest. Boucher and Birkett were also seriously shot-up in A6357 but came down safely at Bailleul. The one British victory claim coming from this later fight was from Thayre and Cubbon, who shot down an Albatros in flames near Wervicq[1]. The day's flying was brought to a close with an evening OP that saw new pilot Lieutenant Harry Luchford flying A6415 on his début patrol with Private Lloyd as his gunner. Luchford, a 23-year-old former bank clerk, from Bromley, Kent, had previously served with the Norfolk Regiment and the ASC. He would go on to become one of 20 Squadron's leading aces, although the only fighting he saw on this occasion was inconclusive.

******

Saturday, 26 May brought the squadron no fewer than six victory claims for no losses when Captain H. G. White led up a central OP of eight FEs escorted by ten Nieuports from 1 Squadron. At 10.45 the formation dived on fifteen Albatros scouts climbing towards them between Quesnoy and Comines, and made full use of their initial height advantage. Cunnell and Gilson latched onto the tail of one of them in A6431 and managed to stay there for 'a considerable time at about 30 yards range'. Both front guns were used and the Albatros finally went down out of control before being seen to crash by Second Lieutenant Conder, who was flying A6415 with his now customary observer, Air Mechanic Cowell[1]. Meanwhile, Harry Satchell and A.N. Jenks were also getting stuck into the 'Albatrii' in A6469, as Satchell later reported:

We dived to within a few yards of one H.A. After firing about 30 rounds the machine was seen to loop backwards, the pilot falling out. The pilot of 'A6393' (Lieutenant Stevens) saw this, and the machine was seen to crash by Second Lieutenant Conder (at 28.V.9). This machine had a bright red fuselage and tail.

The locations for the two crashed Germans given in the Squadron Record Book are map references 28.V.7 and 28.V.9 respectively, placing both victories in German-held territory just west and just east of Bas Warneton. However, there are no surviving records of any German Jasta casualties anywhere near the area on this date, so one can only assume that both pilots escaped the wreckage, with Satchell and Stevens both mistaking a falling part of one of the Albatros scouts for a falling pilot. Satchell and Jenks also reported sending down a second Albatros in a damaged condition although they did not see it crash. Three more 'out of control' victories were also claimed: one by White and Lewis in A-6412, the second by Boucher and Birkett in A6377 and the third by Condor and Cowell in A6415. Conder and Cowell scored again in the evening during a fight with eight Albatrosses at 12,000ft southeast of Ypres, getting a good burst into one from close range and watching it go down in a vertical dive before it burst into flames[1]. Shortly after this, Captain White was posted back to England, returning to France in 1918 with 29 Squadron, with which unit he scored another four victories flying SE5s.

The last five days of the month were similar, with 20 Squadron's flyers fending off more 'Albatrii' attacks as they went about their business of bombing and reconnoitring east of Ypres, and claiming five more victories in the process. The first of these was on 27 May when Solly and Kydd in A6354 drove down an Albatros to what looked like an emergency landing at 07.00[3], quickly followed by Thayre and Cubbon shooting down a two-seater that crashed and burst into flames near Gheluvelt[1]. The two scored again when they forced an Albatros scout to land on the southeast edge of Comines at 15.45, afterwards reporting that they had also seen what appeared to be a 'German Nieuport'. The most likely explanation is that they saw one of the new Siemens-Schuckert scouts that were being field tested at the front by the Germans.

The squadron's final two victories of the month came on 31 May when an evening patrol of eight FEs was attacked by two formations of five and twelve 'Albatrii' between Lille and Quesnoy. Cunnell and Cambray in A6430, destroyed one, the wings of which broke off on the way down, while Lieutenants Taylor and Lingard in A6413 claimed another, which fell in a vertical dive behind a wood near Korentje[1]. May had seen frenetic fighting – and June, it transpired, would bring no respite.

******

Notes

1. Combat Report.
2. *The Jasta War Chronology* by N Franks, F Bailey & R Duiven.
3. AIR 1/167/15/156/2 '20 Squadron Record Book'.
4. *The Red Baron Combat Wing*, P.92, by Peter Kilduff.
5. Paul Strahle's personal diary: *Cross & Cockade* Volume 11 No. 4, page 148.
6. AIR 1/435/15/273/11 – Messages Dropped by German Aircraft.
7. Information re Alexander Tyrell thanks to Jamie Tyrell.
8. *The Jasta Pilots* by N Franks, F Bailey & R Duiven.
9. Commonwealth War Graves Commission.

Chapter 12

Aces High – June 1917

Secrecy was just as important as tunnelling in the planning for the forthcoming Battle of Messines. Operations Orders issued by Second Army on 10 May 1917 constituted a deliberate attempt to mislead the Germans by stating that the objective of the Messines attack was a deception to 'enforce the enemy to withdraw reserves from the main (Vimy-Arras) battle-front'. The campaign, which began with a preliminary artillery bombardment on Thursday, 31 May 1917, would last five long months. The official name of the battle was 'Third Ypres' ... but it was doomed to be condemned by posterity as 'Passchendaele'.

The role of the fighter squadrons of the RFC, including 20 Squadron, was to prevent or seriously hamper German aerial reconnaissance by keeping their aircraft east of the German balloon line and preventing their scout aircraft from interfering with our own reconnaissance and bomber squadrons. If they were successful in these two goals, then the British artillery-spotting aircraft would be free to roam at will over the German trenches. At the same time, their German equivalents and the fighting Jastas would have to try to carry out their own tasks from a considerable distance, thereby limiting their efficiency. It was also hoped that the large numbers of British aircraft near the German balloon line would force the Germans to either keep their balloons on the ground or withdraw them still further east. In attempting to cover all possibilities, the Germans spread their air services all along the northern front from Ostend to Arras. The RFC also spread its resources; but given its overall numerical superiority, it was able to concentrate many of its units where it knew they would be most needed.

RFC HQ issued orders splitting the battlefront into north, central, and south sectors, patrolled by layers of British single-seat and two-seat fighting scouts, with the single-seaters operating at the higher altitudes while the two-seaters covered the lower. The central sector, east of the lines from Becelaere to Quesnoy, was given to 20 Squadron which was tasked with its usual three duties of reconnaissance, bombing and offensive patrols. In total, the RFC deployed more than 400 aircraft on the immediate battlefront, of which 170 were single-seat scouts. Facing them were a roughly equal number of German fighting scouts based along a longer front. So, although the British and German numbers appeared similar at first glance, there were fewer Jastas based in the immediate area of Messines than might be supposed. However, the German Sixth Army, covering the line from just south of Messines to Douai, had nine more Jastas, with some of these close enough to the Ypres Salient to intervene if needed. The difficulty for the RFC was that most of its aircraft, with the exception of the Sopwith Triplane, were seriously outclassed by the improved Albatros DIII and DV scouts equipping most of the German Jastas. The campaign would see 20 Squadron pitted against some of Germany's finest airmen and aeroplanes – yet even in its first two months would see the squadron leave five German aces and a number of other Jasta pilots killed or wounded.

******

The squadron flew three uneventful but successful reconnaissances on Friday, 1 June. The following day was very different. The first eight-strong patrol set off around 07.20 including squadron newcomer Second Lieutenant Richard Trevethan (or 'Trev' as he became known) flying A6480 with Air Mechanic Cowell as his gunner. Pilots usually used the FE2's gravity-fed reserve fuel tank on the aeroplane's top wing as they climbed up to their patrol height before switching to the pressure-operated main tank for the rest of the patrol when violent manoeuvres might lead to fuel starvation. This was the case at about 09.50 as they laboured for height over Gheluvelt, and had only reached 10,000ft when they were attacked.

Perhaps sensing his newness, three Albatrosses dived onto Trevethan's tail, but he immediately turned to face them and John Cowell's first burst of fire sent the leading German machine plummeting down. Then their own machine was hit, and the last the other patrol members thought they saw of A6480 was a trail of smoke and flames plunging earthwards as the Nieuports of 1 Squadron joined the fight and helped repel the attackers. The remaining FEs landed safely back at St. Marie Cappel between 10.15 and 10.20 to report Trevethan and Cowell's deaths and the successful conclusion of the reconnaissance, during which they had made detailed notes on German movements and exposed eighteen plates over 'the required area'. They were mistaken about one thing though. The 'flamer' they had seen had not been A6480 but the Albatros that Cowell had hit. Its fate was confirmed in a report from 236 Battery RFA, whose gunners saw it crash in flames northwest of Polygon Wood.

The then-unknown fate of Trevethan and Cowell was quite exceptional. A German bullet had penetrated their main petrol tank causing a loss of pressure and their engine to cut out[1]. But they were both alive and well after making a forced landing in a hollow in 'no-man's land' out of sight of the German trenches but a short way from the New Zealand trenches, where they took refuge. After two or three hours of unsuccessful attempts to telephone the squadron office, the two Britons sneaked back out to their aeroplane and discovered that the reserve tank still contained some petrol. So they switched over to it and started the engine – but the noise immediately attracted such a storm of German artillery fire that they switched it off again and returned to the trenches to plan their departure more carefully. The New Zealanders willingly helped them by bringing up some ammunition boxes to act as chocks for the FE's wheels and a couple of soldiers volunteered to hold onto the wings while they revved-up prior to take-off. Then Trevethan and Cowell crept back out to the machine with the soldiers. The engine was started, the makeshift chocks were pulled away, the soldiers let go of the wings… and the FE rumbled gently into the air in full view of the Germans!

When they landed back at St. Marie Cappel, Trevethan and Cowell were greeted as those who have come back from the dead, and it had most certainly been a most remarkable combat début for the 22-year-old Cornish officer. It was in keeping with his character, though, for although he was new to air fighting he was not new to war, having served as a lieutenant in the Lancashire Regiment both in France and at Gallipoli[1, 2]. Even so, he was especially lucky in having had the remarkable J.J. Cowell as his gunner: a Limerick-born former sapper who would go on to achieve much with 20 Squadron.

The squadron flew no less than seven assorted patrols, reconnaissance flights and bombing missions on Sunday, 3 June. Thayre and Cubbon were aloft in A6430 for a dawn reconnaissance over the lines at 04.16, while Stevens and Jenks led an eight-strong patrol that went up at 07.10 to patrol the Comines-Menin area. New pilot Second Lieutenant Stacey, flying A8480 with Private Benger as his observer, and new observer Second Lieutenant Tennant flying with Harry Luchford in A6384, were treated to a début skirmish when the patrol was attacked by about twelve Albatrosses. Second Lieutenant Robins was wounded by machine-gun fire flying A6413 but made a safe forced-landing with his gunner Private Lloyd near Locre. The enemy machines were then chased off without further casualties, two of them reportedly driven down in vertical nose-dives.

The following day was only noteworthy for including two more new pilots. Second Lieutenant Gardiner flew his first patrol in A6357 with Lieutenant Jenks as his observer while Second Lieutenant Marshall flew A6392 with Private Lloyd. Tuesday 5 June, however, was very different. Captains Thayre and Cubbon and Lieutenant Solly and Second Lieutenant Kydd went up in the dark at 02.30am to successfully photograph a British artillery bombardment in the Wytschaete area, and three hours after returning were airborne again with an eight-strong OP that was attacked at intervals by around fourteen Albatros scouts. Thayre and Cubbon shot down one that crashed on its back on Coucou aerodrome and another that force-landed northwest of Menin. Cunnell and Sayers in A6414 sent an Albatros down in flames over Wervicq. The morning had brought three victories but was only a prelude to the main event.

At 13.45, Lieutenant Harry Satchell and Second Lieutenant T.A.M.S. Lewis led a six-strong OP in A6469 that that was attacked by fifteen Albatros scouts at about 10,000ft over Becelaere. The German leader, whose Albatros was described as having a red fuselage, immediately got onto the tail of Sawden's and Madill's machine, A6384. Sawden was severely wounded and ran for the lines but Satchell and Lewis spotted the struggle and dived down behind the German and opened fire. There then began a classic fifteen-minute, one-on-one duel between the large, lumbering FE2 and the fast, nimble Albatros, with each aircraft twisting and turning without either getting the advantage. Eventually, the Albatros dived at them from behind – at which Satchell dramatically slowed his aircraft's speed so that the pair of them ended up side-by-side only 30 yards apart. Lewis fired a long and accurate burst that shot off all the Albatros's wings, and the fuselage plunged vertically to earth near Becelaere.

William Sawden managed to get his crippled FE back over the lines and made a forced landing near Ypres but died soon afterwards, while Satchell and Lewis and the others made their way safely back to St. Marie Cappel[1]. If they were upset that they had not managed to save Sawden, their sorrow was slightly eased a few days later by an intelligence extract that identified the fallen German flyer. He was the famous Richtofen trained ace Karl Emil Schafer, commander of Jasta 28, whose thirty victories included two against 20 Squadron. A celebrated 25-year-old recipient of the *Pour le Mérite* (an ancient Prussian medal that became known as 'The Blue Max'), Schafer's exploits had been eulogised in the German press, so his death was felt deeply all across the country. He was honoured with a state funeral attended by Manfred von Richtofen and Werner Voss[1, 3, 4, 5, 6]. So the RFC and 20 Squadron had been done a vital service by Lewis and Satchell: both 23-year-olds, the former from Edenbridge in Kent, and the latter a Rugby School pupil who had originally enlisted as a private in the Honourable Artillery Company infantry reserve on 21 September 1914.

William Sawden was the 26-year-old son of William and Emily Sawden, of Cottingham, East Yorkshire. He had worked as a clerk while serving with 5 Battalion East Yorkshire (Cyclists) Territorials from 1908 to 1913 and reached the rank of sergeant. He re-enlisted on the outbreak of war and was later commissioned into 1 East Riding Brigade, RGA before transferring to the RFC in July 1916, being posted to 20 Squadron from 20 October that year. Promoted to Lieutenant on 1 December 1916, he was wounded on 25 April 1917 but returned to the squadron after a brief spell in hospital. He is buried at Lijssenthoek.

It seems the Germans were still in a state of shock the following day, as 20 Squadron carried out patrols and bombing raids where the only opposition came from a British anti-aircraft battery. They hit the FE of Conder and Cowell, causing them to make a forced landing at Abeele, in which Conder's neck was seriously injured. This brought the former Bedfordshire chemistry student's flying career to an end. Conder spent the next six months recuperating before being sent on light duties work with the Examination Board at the Officer Cadet Brigade HQ at St. Leonards-on-Sea, Sussex. He remained there until after the Armistice as, although a medical board later passed him fit to fly, the authorities could not find a suitable replacement. He was finally discharged from the RAF in February 1919, having been credited with six victories during his service with 20 Squadron.

******

The big day, 7 June 1917, finally arrived. As 20 Squadron's pilots and observers waited for the dawn, they might have reflected on the success of 2 Brigade's fighter squadrons in keeping the Jastas away from the vital but vulnerable Corps Wing aeroplanes as they went about their art-obs' (artillery observation) and other work during the previous week. The Corps machines had observed or directed British artillery onto 231 German batteries and 225 trench bombardments, as well as making 716 zone calls to bring artillery fire down onto targets of opportunity. Despite this massive effort, they had not lost any aircraft to enemy fighters by midnight on 6 June[5]. As the clock ticked slowly past midnight that morning, Captain Cunnell and Sergeant Sayers took off in the darkness in A6393 to patrol a north-south line from the so-called (and now mined) 'Peckham Farm' west of Wytschaete, to the River Douve just two miles south. Because of poor visibility, they were not able to see the damage caused by the eight 20lb bombs they dropped; but the bombing was only intended to keep the German troops awake and leave them tired and irritable as dawn approached. Following their safe return, a thunderous, cataclysmic series of explosions at 03.10 lit up the horizon and skies over Messines as nineteen of the carefully laid British mines were detonated. In a few seconds of truly volcanic proportions, the Germans were not simply blasted from the face of the high ground but it seemed that the high ground itself had been blasted from the face of the earth. Less than a minute later, as the mud and other debris settled to the ground again, the human waves of British and Anzac infantry went over the top and forwards, sweeping almost unopposed across the devastated remains of the German defences.

Thayre and Cubbon led the first close offensive patrol of the day and returned at 06.00 to report that British troops had reached the eastern side of Messines and were in front of Wytschaete, that British tanks were moving up in front of Messines and that two German reconnaissance machines had been driven off. The next COP drove off two more enemy reconnaissance machines and returned around noon with reports that gave the British time to prepare for a counter-attack from German reinforcements packing the roads from Comines and Wervicq to the battlefront. The third patrol concentrated on bombing and strafing the enemy troops, transport and huts on the Comines-Wervicq road, with six direct hits being recorded on their return at around 13.15.

When Thayre's and Cubbon's eight-strong COP went up at 15.15, it would seem that the German Jasta pilots had recovered from the initial shock of dawn and were now up and angry. The patrol was reduced after one was hit by anti-aircraft fire and forced to land on the British side. Then, as the remaining FEs crossed the lines, the pilots and observers noted a smashed-up Martinsyde lying in the canal north of Deulemont, and on the main road nearby the wreckage of 45 Squadron's Sopwith One-and-a-half Strutter A8296 in which Lieutenant A.E.J. Dobson and Second Lieutenant G.A.H. Davies had both been killed, probably by ground fire[7].

The patrol then went on to force a German reconnaissance machine back over its own lines and drive down a balloon over Quesnoy with machine-gun fire. Troop and transport movements were noted as usual, and four Albatros scouts were spotted attacking a 6 Squadron RE 8 escorted by three of 45 Squadron's Sopwiths. The RE 8 was hit and shot down before the FEs could reach it, but they were in time to call the victorious Jasta pilot to account. Jasta 18's seven-victories ace Leutnant Ernst Weissner fell under a hail of bullets from Captain Cubbon's Lewis gun, his Albatros shedding its wings and plummeting to the ground just like Schafer's two days before[1, 8]. His victims in the RE 8 were 6 Squadron's Lieutenant A.J.E. Phillipo who was killed, and his observer Second Lieutenant F.V. Durkin who was captured. They were not the only ones to fall, with 20 Squadron's A6403 failing to return after being shot down by Leutnant S.G. Sachsenberg of MFJ-1 for his third victory of the day[9]. The pilot, 22-year-old Second Lieutenant Bernard S Marshall, MC, was killed but the Germans managed to extricate aerial gunner Private 11192 C. Lloyd from the wreckage and take him prisoner. If the details of Marshall's burial place were recorded by the Germans in the maelstrom of battle raging all around, they were soon lost again and the 22-year-old son of son of John and Helen Marshall, from Swansea, is remembered at the Arras Flying Services Memorial.

With Second Army's first objectives having all been taken by midday and a heavy German counter-attack having been beaten off in the afternoon, a fresh British attack took most of the Oosttaverne line. By evening the British had advanced about two miles depth along a seven to eight mile front[10]. Of even more importance from the RFC's point of view was the fact that their Corps machines had been able to carry out their vital artillery and contact patrol work almost unmolested by German fighters, losing just two RE 8s east of the lines during the day. The heaviest RFC casualties were borne by the fighter squadrons which lost no fewer than sixteen aeroplanes whose pilots were killed, captured or wounded while protecting the Corps machines.

The Messines attack had gone very well indeed, and an Order of the Day sent out to all regiments and units by Field Marshal Haig on Friday, 8 June was clearly designed to praise and encourage all those who had taken part. It was echoed by a congratulatory memorandum sent to 20 Squadron from Lieutenant Colonel G.B. Stoppard, commanding 11 Wing, in which he thanked the squadron's pilots and observers for their fine work over the weeks involving long flying hours and frequent fights against superior numbers. He also congratulated all the other ranks for their equally good efforts in keeping aircraft and guns serviceable and in keeping up a good supply of photographs for the intelligence branches.

******

Although a couple of 20 Squadron's crews had earlier managed to survive their aircraft being set alight in the air, they had been extremely lucky. More commonly, fire in the air meant a ghastly death, and this was amply illustrated on Friday, 8 June. Cunnell and Gilson were leading the squadron's first COP, bombing targets of opportunity in the Wervicq area, when it was attacked by more than twenty enemy scouts. As a patrol of 46 Squadron Sopwith Pups came diving towards the battle, Second Lieutenant Durrand and Sergeant Sayers in A1965 opened fire on one of the 'Albatrii' and sent it down in flames, its wings breaking away at around 5,000ft[1]. The unfortunate German pilot was 21-year-old VizeFeldwebel Franz Bucher of Jasta 30 and his death was witnessed not only by the patrol leaders but also by 46 Squadron's Arthur

Gould Lee, who wrote how the doomed German jumped from the blazing Albatros rather than be burned alive. He had no parachute, of course, and having seen such sights far too often by the time of the Armistice it is little wonder that Lee chose *No Parachute* as the title of his famous memoir. The second and third COPs were completed safely, made more rewarding by Thayre's and Cubbon's claim for destroying an enemy two-seater... but they would never report another one[3].

At 05.30 the following morning, the two captains set off at the head of another COP and, about half an hour into the mission, dived on a German two-seater that they chased down low and saw go into a vertical dive with smoke pouring from it. German anti-aircraft opened up as they pulled away from their victory and A6430 reared up suddenly before falling off on one wing into a final dive from which it never recovered, killing both men as it hit the ground. There was no time to dwell on the tragedy as a formation of enemy scouts appeared. Lieutenant Trevethan and Second Lieutenant M. Dudbridge in A6431 claimed an Albatros with a black fuselage and a white band around its centre that went down in flames[1]. But that was no compensation for the loss of two such respected and experienced flyers. Captain Thayre had been credited with no less than twenty combat victories during his career with 20 Squadron, nineteen of these while flying with Captain Cubbon. If their final two claims were also allowed, their total would have been 22. Their FE having fallen in the midst of the battle area, neither of their bodies was ever found and, like so many others with no known grave, their names are recorded on the Arras Flying Services Memorial.

Two more COPs were flown that day but the only air fight came at around 18.00. Nine enemy scouts and two two-seaters were engaged north of Wervicq and one of the two-seaters was shot down out of control by Lieutenants Bailey Strange and James Tennant in A6427. Former engineer 24-year-old Frank Stevens, from Bury St. Edmunds, was now appointed temporary captain and flight commander, while Sub-Lieutenant W.T. Gilson was posted back to England for pilot training.

The first patrol on 12 June brought tragedy when A6383 stalled and crashed on take-off. Pilot D.W. Stacey died of his injuries at the New Zealand hospital in France on 18 June and his observer W.R. Macaskill the day after that. A former mining engineer, 30-year-old Douglas William Stacey, who had crossed the continents from his native Bulawayo, Rhodesia, to serve the mother country, left a wife, Cecilia, and his parents John and Louisa. William Ross MacAskill, a 28-year-old Canadian, who described his former occupation as a 'merchant' and who had previously served with the Canadian 94 Regiment, also left a widow,

Eira, and his father E.G. MacAskill, of Cape Breton, Nova Scotia. Both men are buried at Hazebrouk.

The patrol, of course, continued without them, with the other flyers noting the usual balloons and road transport movements before depositing 20 bombs on Houthem dump. The second patrol set off at 11.05, first bombing the balloon winch at Comines and then the balloon shed south of Westroosebeke before being attacked by eight enemy scouts over Zandwoorde. All six FEs returned safely, claiming three more 'out of control' victories from the fight: by Solly and Kydd in A6354, by Richards and Wear in A6368 and by Luchford and Tennant in A6516. This was Solly's fifth victory, thus making him an 'ace', and counted as ex-bank clerk Harry Luchford's first. His second would come the following morning during a fight in the Quesnoy-Ploegsteert area. Thursday, 14 June brought a mid-morning skirmish between the patrol's six FEs and 22 German scouts that ended with Richards and Wear claiming another 'out of control' victory and all the FEs returning safely before midday. The patrol's progress had, like so many others, been eagerly watched by the ground troops, and Major Foster, the commanding officer of H Battery Anti-Aircraft, Royal Field Artillery, put pen to paper in a letter to Wing HQ. Mentioning the fights of 13 and 14 June that his battery had witnessed, he wrote:

It is very obvious to us from the ground that the enemy fighters do not like tackling the FE2Ds even when twice their strength, and at the end of a combat it is always the enemy who breaks off the fight by diving out of range. I cannot speak too highly of the wonderful zeal and pluck shown by the pilots and gunners of the FE2Ds and on behalf of this Battery I would like to express our whole hearted admiration for this very gallant squadron.[3]

The 'very gallant squadron' flew a total of seven assorted offensive patrols, line patrols and photographic missions on 15 June but, although the enemy were encountered several times, there were no decisive fights. The same applied the next day when once again the FEs were allowed to carry out their bombing and reconnaissance missions without interference, even though the enemy scouts were clearly in sight. As the 20 Squadron Record Book put it: 'Several formations of H.A. seen, including one of 12 and one of 6, north of Ypres and over Polygon Wood respectively, and engaged without decisive results as H.A. *would not fight*.'

The Recording Officer made a point of underlining the last three words of this entry, but was perhaps a little premature in doing so. For the last patrol of the day, a COP led by Solly and Kennard in A6354 did draw a reaction from the Germans. The patrol had taken thirty-six photographs east of Ypres and over the Comines canal and bombed enemy positions at Houthem, Comines and Racecourse Wood when about 25 Albatros scouts attacked. Although the FEs were quickly reinforced by two SPADs from 23 Squadron and a couple of Nieuports, it was still an unequal fight. Two Albatrosses were claimed shot down out of control by Second Lieutenant Gardiner and Private McLeod in A6572 and by Lieutenant Harrison and Private Potter in A5415. Gardiner was slightly wounded in the throat but made a successful forced landing near Ypres, while Solly had to force-land A6354 at 21 Squadron after Second Lieutenant Kennard was slightly wounded. The two 'out of control' victories were later confirmed by British anti-aircraft gunners[1], and surviving German records show VizeFeldwebel L von Raffay of Jasta 6 having been severely wounded in the fight while crediting him and Oberleutnant Dosstler with causing A6572 and A6354 to make their forced landings. In all, two FEs with wounded crews had made forced landings on the British side and one German pilot was severely wounded. Considering that the Germans outnumbered the combined FEs, SPADs and Nieuports by about three to one, this was a reasonable result.

******

The second week of June saw General Plumer's Second Army achieve virtually every objective it had been set, while the next stage meant moving the ground offensive's focus to the crucially important Gheluvelt Plateau, straddling the Ypres-Menin Road, and east and north from there towards Menin, Passchendaele, Staden and beyond. Among other things, this would involve the shifting of vast amounts of artillery, munitions and other supplies to the area, despite the fact that much of it still lay under the enemy's direct observation from the ridges that continued northeastwards from Messines to Passchendaele. The Gheluvelt Plateau would see some of the most bitter and drawn-out fighting of the campaign both on the ground and in the skies above it. The fact it all fell within 20 Squadron's area of operations meant that its men would have to provide continual reconnaissance and offensive patrols over the ground fighting. Sunday, 17 June provides a good example of the daily grind.

The usual early line patrol of two FE2Bs – Second Lieutenants Makepeace and Woodbridge in A846 accompanied by Second Lieutenants Hay and Lewis in A840 – returned safely after taking notes on fires burning behind the enemy lines and the locations of seven German balloons. Then, at 05.18, Satchell and Jenks led up six FE2Ds on a COP split into two formations of three each, the first led by Harry Satchell and the second led by Noel Boucher. Nearly two hours after take-off they were patrolling east of the lines over Polygon Wood when Boucher led his formation down on three German two-seaters engaged in artillery work. Richards and Wear, flying FE2D A6431 shot down one of them in flames, its fiery end north of Becelaere confirmed by watching British anti-aircraft gunners[1]. The Germans who died were probably Unteroffizier Severin Hornun and VizeFeldwebel Robert Neidhardt of Schasta 30b, who were both listed as killed at nearby Zonnebeke that day[11]. A little later, the patrol rescued a RE 8 being attacked by two German scouts before turning for home.

Boucher was up again when the day's last patrol was attacked southeast of Ypres at 20.30. As ten Albatros scouts came down on the FEs, the 20-year-old was shot in the stomach and A6469 caught fire. Despite his wound and the flames, Boucher got down on the British side of the lines where he and his observer were immediately rushed off to hospital. Alston and Chester sent an Albatros down to crash 'in the O.6 neighbourhood', which translates from the trench-map reference as being inside the German lines just northeast of Hollebeke, while Strange and Cambray took on two more 'Albatrii' in A6516 and sent one down to crash in the same area, with both crashes being witnessed by the ever-watchful H Battery anti-aircraft gunners[1]. Boucher's and Birkett's FE was claimed by Oberleutnant E. Dostler of Jasta 6, but both men recovered from their wounds and survived the war; with Noel Boucher spending the next three months in hospital before becoming an instructor. After the war, he became a solicitor and was commissioned again in the Second World War, this time into the Air Training Corps. He died in 1968 and in April 2006 his son Chris made a pilgrimage to France to his father's old aerodrome at St. Marie Cappel[12]. Lancashire born William Birkett, aged 32, had left for Canada before the war and lived at Moose Jaw, Saskatchewan. He transferred to the RFC from the Canadian Expeditionary Force but it is not known what became of him post-war.

******

The rest of June passed in similar fashion, with 20 Squadron's bombing and reconnaissance missions being carried out as if in scornful defiance of the Jasta pilots – even though the greatest German ace of them all, Manfred von Richtofen, had arrived in the area at the head of his 'flying circus'. The men of 20 Squadron first met him on 18 June when he shot down an RE 8, A4617 of 53 Squadron, despite the best efforts of a COP led by Solly and Cambray to intervene. The RE 8 crew, Lieutenant M.E. Newton and Second Lieutenant

H.M. Jackson, were both killed. Shortly afterwards, another RE 8 was saved by 20 Squadron's timely intervention in a brief fight that resulted in Solly being awarded an 'out of control' victory. Second Lieutenant Alston and Lieutenant Chester were injured making a forced landing during a thunderstorm on 19 June. The next day, two brave souls from Jasta 6, Oberleutnant E. Dostler and Leutnant E. Reiher, took advantage of the low clouds to cross the lines and shoot down two British balloons at 18.00. Their audacity was recorded in a brief note in the 20 Squadron Record Book. As if in retaliation, 20 Squadron sent out six FEs at 05.15 the following morning and attacked the German balloons at Comines and Quesnoy with phosphorous bombs; and although they missed, they did at least force the Germans to haul them down.

On 23 June, however, the German balloon-busters repeated their audacity by diving out of the clouds and downing three more of our balloons. Two 20 Squadron reconnaissances were carried out successfully but O.H.D. Vickers's aerial gunner, Private 200280 J.E. Macleod was killed by anti-aircraft fire during the second patrol. The 27-year-old aerial gunner, from Beauly, near Inverness, who had gone to France with 7 Battalion the Cameron Highlanders in February 1915, is buried at Bailleul. His pilot, Oliver Henry Douglas Vickers, was the 18-year-old Eton-educated son of Douglas Vickers, chairman of the now famous Vickers Aviation Company that produced the Vickers machine-gun and the Vickers FB5 'Gun-Bus' aeroplane that had taken on the Fokkers in 1915. After gaining his Royal Aero Club certificate (number 3293) at Hendon on 3 August 1916, he was commissioned on 5 March 1917, and had only recently arrived at 20 Squadron.

Two patrols on 24 June saw A6511 hit by anti-aircraft fire and Lieutenant McCall and Private Benger were injured in the resulting forced landing on the British side of the lines. Malcolm McCall, aged 20, was a recent arrival at 20 Squadron. The son of master baker Malcolm McCall and his wife Florence, from Ayr in Scotland, he had worked in locomotive and railway engineering before being commissioned into 5 Battalion the Royal Scots Fusiliers in November 1915. After active service in Egypt, he returned to England and transferred to the RFC in late April or early May before being posted to 20 Squadron in early June. Fortunately, neither he nor Private Benger had been seriously hurt in the forced landing and were soon back in action. Then, during the night, enemy bombers appeared over St. Marie Cappel and the 20 Squadron Record Book recorded that: 'Great damage (was) done.'

So passed the next few days, with 20 Squadron's patrols meeting little opposition and again finding that most German formations they encountered used their superior speed to avoid a fight. One can only wonder whether the recent losses of Karl Schafer and Ernst Weissner to FE crews had made the Jasta pilots wary; and if this was the case they were right to be so. A fight on Friday, 29 June underlined the message when 20 Squadron brought down another of their aces. Five FEs had just finished bombing targets around Houthem and Deulemont when a little after 13.00 they ran into fifteen of Jasta 8's Albatros scouts over Hollebeke. One of these came a bit too close and, after being fired on by the whole formation, went spinning down in flames. Shortly afterwards, Canadians Makepeace and Waddington hit another that went spinning down out of the fight, while Luchford and Kennard claimed a second Albatros shot down on fire minus its wings near Zonnebeke dump. After that, the 'Albatrii' backed off. Two Jasta 8 casualties commonly attributed to this fight were five-victories ace Leutnant Alfred Ulmer, who was killed, and 20 Squadron's old adversary Walter Gottsch, who was wounded for the second time. In addition to reconnaissance notes, ten photographs were taken of 'the required area' so that, all in all, it had been a very successful patrol, with the victorious Britons returning to St. Marie Cappel at 14.15. According to RFC communiqués, Lieutenant Joslyn and Private Potter, flying A6415, and Luchford and Kennard, flying A6516, both claimed and were awarded separate 'destroyed in flames' victories, while Makepeace and Waddington, flying A6498, were awarded an 'out of control' victory.

There was another fight during the late-afternoon patrol led by Satchell and Jenks in A6431. The patrol had bombed German positions at Racecourse Wood and Frezenberg when they attacked five enemy aircraft over Becelaere. The Germans quickly escaped but five minutes later the FEs were in action again. They attacked five enemy machines they spotted below them – despite there being another fifteen above – and Satchell and Jenks hit one that went down into the clouds out of control. The larger enemy formation then fell upon the FEs, and Vickers and Cowell in A6376 claimed an Albatros with a red fuselage while Patterson and Hoy in A6547 claimed another of the Germans that was seen to go down out of control shedding its wings on the way. However, due to thick clouds and poor visibility, none of these were seen to crash and it has been impossible to trace any related German casualties. It was not uncommon for enemy pilots to escape from a fight by feigning damage, and it may well be that Patterson and Hoy saw pieces falling off their opponent, although whether it was actually the wings that broke off remains questionable.

The weather brought the month's flying to an end after these two fights. It had been a month of mixed fortunes. At least three German aces – Karl Schafer, Ernst Weissner and Alfred Ulmer – had been killed by 20 Squadron's flyers. Walter Gottsch had been wounded again, and another twenty German machines had been claimed as destroyed or out of control. Set against that, the squadron had lost six dead and four wounded. The great movement of everything needed for the looming Third Ypres offensive was underway, but the whole of July would have to pass before everything was ready.

******

Notes

1.   Combat Report.
2.   'Notes on R.M. Trevethan' held in the Documents Archive at the Imperial War Museum and Combat Report by Trevethan and Cowell.
3.   AIR 1/167/15/156/2 '20 Squadron Record Book'.
4.   AIR 1/689/21/20/20 'History of 20 Squadron, list of enemy aircraft brought down'.
5.   *The War in the Air*, V4, H. A. Jones.
6.   *Popular Flying*, October 1933, page 380.
7.   *The Sky Their Battlefield* by Trevor Henshaw.
8.   'Who Downed the Aces in WW1' By N. Franks.
9.   *The Jasta War Chronology* by N Franks, F Bailey & R Duiven.
10. AIR/1/167/15/156/3: 2nd Army Intelligence Summary No.690 dated 8th June 1917.
11. Casualties of the German Air Service by N Franks, F Bailey & R Duiven.
12. Personal correspondence with Chris Boucher, and also thanks to Tony Grange Bennett of Cross and Cockade International.

Chapter 13

Aces Low – July 1917

Most of General Gough's Fifth Army dispositions east and northeast of Ypres were under the direct observation of the remaining enemy-held ridges, and mining beneath the ridges as at Messines was not possible as the shafts quickly became flooded due to the low water table. The best way to deal with the German artillery was to force it out of range further east. This job fell to the RFC who had to locate the enemy guns on the other side of the ridges so that our own artillery could carry out effective counter-battery work. All of 2 Brigade's squadrons were involved to some extent and, as the enemy artillery was pushed back, our own artillery moved forward to keep up the pressure.

This was extremely risky work for two-seater crews. Senior RFC officers at home in England seemed almost dismissive of ideas that might encourage morale among the volunteer non-commissioned aerial gunners, upon which the two-seater squadrons in France and Belgium were becoming increasingly reliant. This was again demonstrated when the idea of an 'air gunner' badge resurfaced. Perhaps symbolic of the high esteem with which the General Staff regarded these men, the OIC Aerial Gunners RFC was a mere Second Lieutenant: a certain W.T. Douglas. Lowly subaltern though he may have been, Douglas was genuinely concerned for the interests of the men and in June 1917 he wrote to the Air Board suggesting that all second class air mechanics who had passed the Hythe Course of Aerial Gunnery should be promoted to air mechanic first class and those of good conduct should be granted four days leave with free travel warrants every six months. Finally, he suggested that it was clear that they would very much appreciate being allowed to wear a distinctive trained air gunner's badge. Other army 'specialists' had such badges, he pointed out, and it would give them a sense of pride and achievement. In the middle of July he received a reply from Lieutenant-Colonel Basil Foster, who worked for the Director of Air Organisation. It was not encouraging:

In future, such air gunners who have qualified on the Observer's Course at Hythe, and who have performed eight trips overseas shall be entitled to wear the Observer's badge... I am to add that no other distinctive badge for Air Gunners will be sanctioned.

What constituted a 'trip' overseas was not defined, although it appears that the writer probably meant an attachment or tour of duty of some kind. The prospects of an air gunner surviving just one such tour or attachment were slim; while to survive eight would require extreme good luck. In addition, since very few 'other ranks' were at that time allowed to take the observers course, as opposed to the aerial gunnery course, it seems that the upper echelons in the RFC were against the idea of flying ORs being distinguished in any way unless they were pilots. As a way of getting round this, the CO at Hythe promptly awarded the observer badge to six air gunners who had made eight ferry trips overseas, and a furore erupted. Lieutenant Colonel Foster took up the ORs' cause with some gusto on this point and the granting of the observer badge to them and others making eight similar trips became official. But there was no change in policy over the idea of an aerial gunners badge, which was again refused – as illustrated in this extract from a letter from the Director of Air Organisation, probably from Foster. The reasons he gave were that 'tailoring labour and the state of the market for woven material absolutely prohibit this, and there is no point in proceeding further with this matter'[2].

The system for awarding the observer badge to qualified officers and NCOs was also under discussion. A pilot was awarded his wings when he qualified as a pilot, regardless of whether he had faced the enemy, but it was not the same for observers. While some senior officers believed the observer's badge should be a 'service badge' issued in the same way as a pilot's wings, others, including Hugh Trenchard, held that the half-wing should be regarded as a 'war service' badge' such as a wound stripe or bravery decoration. So on Trenchard's orders it became the rule that newly qualified observers were officially rated as 'probationary observers' until they had completed their six weeks at the front and had also won the agreement of their squadron commander to wear the observer wing. Fortunately, such regulations did not survive long after the war, and in the Second World War pilots, observers, navigators, air gunners and other aircrew were given their own distinctive badges on completion of their training[3].

When Harry Satchell and his flight took off at 11.30 on Monday, 2 July his men included qualified and unqualified observers and aerial gunners alike. Once across the lines, the patrol bombed Houthem dump and then spotted a cleared area of ground near Tenbrielen that the Germans immediately tried to hide under a smoke screen. However, the FEs served notice of their interest by dropping their remaining bombs into the smoke. Satchell and his men then began their painstaking photography and note taking and, in between times while supported by some of 1 Squadron's Nieuports, met up with various formations of enemy scouts and two-seaters. The fighting lasted about an hour. Satchell and Jenks attacked a red enemy machine that went down out of control emitting black smoke and was later seen in flames. 'Out of control' victories were claimed by Trevethan and Hoy in A6528, Lieutenant Joslyn and Private Potter in A6415, Second Lieutenant Burkett and Private Greener in A6547 and 1 Squadron's Sergeant Beadle. The British machines were outnumbered throughout the fight and, although badly shot-up and nearly out of ammunition, they all returned safely[4]. Three more patrols were flown that day including an oblique photography mission by Luchford and Second Lieutenant Kydd but there were no further combats.

On Tuesday, 3 July the squadron flew three more OPs. The only fighting fell to the flight of recently promoted Captain 'Inky' Stevens, flying A6516 with Second Lieutenant Kydd as his observer. In the late afternoon, the patrol of six FEs engaged five Albatros scouts near Becelaere – but this was a trap. As Stevens and Kydd shot down one of the Albatrosses out of control, ten more dived down on the FEs. Luchford and Tennant in A6547 shot down one that crashed near Hooge, while Vickers and Thompson in A6376 fired on an Albatros that went down out of control although, due to low mist, was not seen to crash[4]. The unequal odds were then relieved a bit as four DH4 bombers came to the FEs' aid. They arrived at a timely moment, and their willingness to mix it with a larger number of Albatros scouts was evidence of the bomber's versatility. The DH4 was probably the best British single-engine bomber of the war and was considerably faster than the FE2D. Highly manoeuvrable for its size, it was armed with from two to four machine-guns. The confidence this machine gave to its crews led some of its more aggressive pilots to tangle with enemy fighters even when they did not have to, and by the end of the war a number of them had become fighting aces in their own right. In contrast, the four patrols on Wednesday, 4 July did not involve any fighting, although Lingard was wounded by anti-aircraft shrapnel and Second Lieutenant Patterson and Lieutenant Waddington smashed up FE2D A6341 on landing after a later NOP.

Friday, 6 July brought the squadron a fight that sent shock waves throughout the German Air Service. At 09.50, Captain D.C. Cunnell and Second Lieutenant A.E. Woodbridge took off in A6512 with five other FEs. Around the same time, Germany's most celebrated air ace Rittmeister Manfred von Richtofen had taken to the air with most of his 'circus' of about thirty 'Albatrii'. Around 10.45 to 11.00, Richtofen spotted Captain Cunnell's formation bombing Houthem dump and immediately led his fighter group into an attack that the FEs met with a hail of fire. Richtofen later recalled that he had been amused by the British gunners opening fire at what he supposed was far too long a range – but how everything suddenly changed as a British bullet slammed against his head in a glancing, paralysing blow. He lost consciousness and his red Albatros fell suddenly towards earth. Finally, just 2,000ft above the ground Richtofen came round in time to make a safe forced-landing near some German soldiers. Meantime, the fight above continued fiercely over Comines, Warneton and Tenbrielen with the Germans making repeated attacks at very close quarters against the heavily outnumbered FEs until they were joined by four of Naval 10's Sopwith Triplanes led by Canadian ace Raymond Collishaw. Gradually the British fought their way back across the lines to safety, their only casualty being observer Lieutenant Stuart Trotter who was mortally wounded and died at 53 Casualty Clearing Station shortly after his pilot landed at Bailleul. The airmen in A6376 and A1963 landed at other aerodromes due to battle damage, but the remainder of Cunnell's patrol made it back to St. Marie Cappel[1].

Cunnell and Woodbridge claimed four German scouts shot down out of control, while Richards and Wear claimed one. However, some of them may have been those that followed Richtofen down to check whether he survived, and the 20 Squadron Record Book notes that none of them were seen to crash. As to the Navy: Collishaw reported that he had shot down one Albatros definitely out of control and another five that appeared to be out of control, and also that he saw an Albatros crash after it was shot down by another Sopwith Triplane. Flight Sub-Lieutenant Reid and Flight Lieutenant Alexander also claimed one and two Albatros scouts shot down out of control respectively. Despite Richtofen's pilots coming into very close range during the fight, it is quite remarkable that his elite 'circus' of around thirty 'Albatrii' had not been able to shoot down a single British aeroplane. The one man killed, Kent born Stuart Fowden Trotter, had served for five years in the Queens Westminster Regiment before emigrating to Winnipeg, Canada, to work as a fur trader. A 30-year-old married man, he joined the Active Militia (34 Fort Garry Horse) and in August 1916 enlisted with 9 (Reserve) Battalion Royal Canadians. Having volunteered for the RFC in 1917, he had been with 20 Squadron barely a month when he was killed. He left a wife, Dorothy, and he rests among many other former pilots and observers of his squadron at the military cemetery extension at Bailleul.

After his emergency landing near Wervicq, Richtofen was rushed semiconscious to hospital and was out of action for several weeks. Even after he had returned to duty, he continued to suffer sudden blinding headaches for the last few months of his life accompanied by a marked change in his temperament. The great ace now knew that he was mortal, and his change in mood was reflected in a remark he made while on leave. His mother recorded:

I found Manfred very changed. I think he had seen death too often. He needed to go to the dentist to have some small everyday treatment done, and I reminded him. He said quietly to himself, but I still heard it, 'There really is no point.'[5]

With all the FEs probably opening fire at the same time, it is almost impossible to be certain whose bullet it was that actually hit the great ace. But it may be that the British authorities actually got it right when they finally credited Albert Woodbridge with the deed. Given that he was the patrol leader's observer and that they may have been slightly nearer to the German machines and, in addition, that he and Cunnell claimed a total of four scouts shot down out of control, Woodbridge was as very plausible contender for the accolade. They counted as his first four combat victories, while Captain Cunnell's score now rose to eight due to British pilots also being credited with all their observers' victories. A second German casualty that may also have come about during this fight was that of Jasta 26's Leutnant F. Loerzer who was wounded in action, though the details are unclear.

In the late afternoon 'Inky' Stevens set out on his own patrol at 17.25 in A6516 along with five other FEs. After bombing Houthem dump and some enemy troops around Polygon Wood racecourse, they came up against around twenty enemy scouts over Comines. Stevens and Jenks opened fire with both guns and sent one of the Germans down out of control, which was confirmed by Luchford and Tennant. The patrol leaders then assisted McCall and Waddington in A6498 as they attacked an Albatros that went down in flames, to be recorded as McCall's first victory. Makepeace and Kennard also claimed an Albatros out of control while Luchford and Tennant claimed two. The fight was eagerly watched from the ground by British anti-aircraft crews, whose CO kept 11 Wing informed of its progress. The last report he sent, timed at 19.40, noted laconically:

The fight previously reported was continued at 6.40pm by 5 FE2Ds and 11 Albatros scouts and a Rumpler, and lasted until 7.25pm. The FEs kept well together, and several times drove the EA away. 2 FEs apparently ran out of ammunition and have gone home. The remaining 3 are still over the lines for Hun anti-aircraft practice. [All returned safely.]

Captain Stevens's COP in the early afternoon on Saturday, 7 July saw more action when they ran into two groups of five enemy scouts over Becelaere. After Richards and Wear in A6498 shot down one of them out of control, the others withdrew a little and eventually landed at Coucou. An evening patrol the same day ended differently. Four FEs met up with ten of Jasta 36's Albatrosses about 12,000ft over Wervicq led by Leutnant Walter von Bulow, an experienced fighter ace with sixteen victories to his name. A running fight lasting half-an-hour followed, with the FEs sticking closely together as they fought their way homewards. Joslyn and Potter in A6415 claimed one of the enemy machines out of control and Trevethan and Hoy in A6528 claimed another that burst into flames, although they were hit immediately afterwards but managed to get down safely at Bailleul. Sadly, A6498 did not return, giving Bulow another victory. The FE came down on the German side of the lines and, although Lieutenant Crafter was pulled from the wreckage alive, he died soon after, and Sergeant Backhouse was already dead. Jasta 36 pilot Heinrich Bongartz also put in a claim for a FE in the fight that probably reflects Trevethan and Hoy's forced landing at Bailleul in A6528.[6]

Born at Honor Oak Park, South London, in March 1893, James Crafter was single and had enlisted in August 1914, being recommended for a commission by his company commander a year later. His observer, Sergeant 65004 Walter Douglas Backhouse, had originally enlisted with the Army Service Corps on 23 October 1914 and came from Ramsgate in Kent. He was 23 and had been with the squadron for two months. He and his pilot are remembered on the Arras Flying Services Memorial. One other departure from the squadron that day, albeit in happier circumstances, was that of former milkman Sergeant 12315 E.H. Sayers, who was posted back to Home Establishment in England. He had been with the squadron since 1 March 1917, being credited with the destruction of at least two German scouts in early June 1917. Five days after his departure, he was awarded the French *Medaille Militaire*. Poor weather prevented active flying over the next three days, then in the evening of Wednesday, 11 July, Captain Cunnell and Lieutenant Bill shot down an Albatros scout in flames in the Menin-Wervicq area[1].

The following morning brought mixed fortunes. Captain Stevens's Central OP found itself powerless after attacking a new type of German two-seater. Victory should have been assured with odds of seven to one but their bullets seemed to have no effect on the German machine, which flew on as if nothing had happened. The 20 Squadron recording officer was probably correct in surmising that the enemy aircraft was armoured, as the Germans were now introducing dedicated armoured ground attack aircraft into service, such as their new AEG J1, Albatros J1 and Junkers J1 biplanes. The day got worse. At 15.35 Captain Cunnell set out at the head of four FEs. Just after 17.00, as he was pulling away after sending down an Albatros out of control over Menin, German anti-aircraft opened up and he was hit and killed by shrapnel. As the rest of the formation fought off the other German scouts, Cunnell's observer, Australian ex-civil engineer Albert Bill, managed to take over the controls of B1863 and somehow get back across the lines and make a successful crash-landing but was injured in the process. The 20 Squadron Record Book notes that the enemy was unusually persistent throughout this fight, although Vickers and Cowell in A6376 claimed an Albatros that crashed near Wervicq and another that went down apparently out of control, while Second Lieutenant Trevethan and Private Arkley claimed a third that burst into flames and crashed northwest of Zandwoorde.

An architect by profession, 23-year-old Norfolk farmer's son Douglas Cunnell had served two years with the Norfolk OTC before enlisting as a private in early September 1914, being promoted to sergeant just a few days later. Commissioned into 20 Battalion, Royal Fusiliers, he was appointed as a flying officer in the RFC on 24 November 1916. He was credited with nine combat victories – or ten if the 'out of control' Albatros of 12 July is included. He is buried at Bailleul.

The second half of July 1917 saw the RFC carry out its work so successfully that Douglas Haig remarked on it in his despatches, mentioning how 'the effective work of our airmen once more enabled our batteries to carry out successfully a methodical and comprehensive artillery programme'. Very little of the RFC's artillery observation work could have been accomplished without the help of the fighter squadrons, and 20 Squadron's FEs, charged with both reconnaissance and fighting, saw just as much action as any single-seat scout unit. However, where the scout pilots had a chance to break off or remain aloof from an action if they chose, the FE crews had no choice in the matter. Their aircraft were too slow to escape uneven odds, their only option being to stand and fight as best they could. Slow and cumbersome as the FE2D might have been, an 'ugly duckling' in Bill Cambray's words, it was still not easy meat for the Germans.

Tuesday, 17 July brought a particularly hard fight. It began at 09.45 when Lieutenant Solly's eight-strong distant offensive patrol (DOP) took on five Albatrosses east of Polygon Wood. The rush of FEs broke up the enemy formation, with some of them going down into spinning nose-dives before pulling out when out of machine-gun range. But one that had apparently been hit by Second Lieutenants Durrand and Thompson in A6548 kept on going down and was not seen to flatten out. Seven more 'Albatrii' then joined the fight, but six of 1 Squadron's Nieuports also dived in and their premier ace, Captain Fullard, claimed an Albatros out of control over Polygon Wood at 09.50. Around the same time, Hay and Tod in A6512 shot down an Albatros over Sanctuary Wood that was followed down by three DH5s and was seen to crash near the lines both by them and a forward British anti-aircraft battery[1, 7]. In a second round, some three-quarters of an hour later, 20 Squadron's FEs were joined by eight of 23 Squadron's SPADs and the Sopwith Triplanes of Naval 10's B Flight. Richards and Wear in A6448 then got behind an Albatros that was trying to escape towards Menin and sent it down out of control, closely pursued by a SPAD. A few moments later, they engaged another Albatros that spun down to crash at map reference 28.J.22.b, on the outskirts of Gheluvelt, at about 10.40[1].

Hectic though the above fights had been, they were just a prelude to the final rounds that came after Captain Stevens led up eight more FEs for another DOP just before 19.00. In the course of a massive hour-long dogfight ranging from Menin to Polygon Wood, German pilots from Jastas 6, 8, 11 and 36 found themselves up against 20 Squadron's FE2Ds, 70 Squadron's Sopwith Camels, 56 Squadron's SE5s, 1 Nieuports, Naval 10's Sopwith Triplanes and 32 Squadron's DH5s. Second Lieutenant Richards and Sergeant Cowell in A6448 accounted for three of the seven victories claimed by the FE crews. Their first victim crashed near Hopital Farm, just west of Comines (Sheet 28.P.33), their second went down just north of the River Lys close to Bousbecque (Sheet 28.Q.28) and their third went down in flames over the western half of Wervicq (Sheet 28.Q.25). Second Lieutenants Trevethan and Hoy in A6512 sent down another out of control, seen by Richards and Cowell to crash near Gheluwe. 'Out of control' claims were also put in by Captain Stevens and Second Lieutenant Cambray in A6516, by Luchford and Waddington in A6548 and by Beldham and Watt in A1865. One of the above claims might refer to Jasta 11's Leutnant K Meyer who was wounded in action[8].

There was little flying over the next two days. This was probably just as well as Richards and Cowell might well have been recovering after celebrating the news that Richards had been awarded the Military Cross for this and previous fights, and Sergeant Cowell had been awarded a bar to his Military Medal.

Friday, 20 July brought inconclusive fights. The 20 Squadron Record Book notes that Vickers and Cowell in A6376 claimed an Albatros out of control over Wervicq but were then forced to break off the action and land at Bailleul after being hit by anti-aircraft fire. Curiously though, Jasta 6's Leutnant H. Adam was subsequently granted a victory over a 20 Squadron FE west of the lines near Ypres at 07.40 that could only apply to the FE of Vickers and Cowell.

Still there was no let-up, and the following evening brought two more casualties when 25 Albatros scouts attacked Captain Stevens's patrol of eight FEs over the Menin area. One of them, A1865, broke off and escaped across the lines to a forced landing south of Ypres after Second Lieutenant Malcolm McCall was wounded in the face and his observer, Second Lieutenant Madill, was killed. The timely intervention of assorted SE5s, SPADs, Nieuports and DH5s prevented further casualties and allowed the remaining FEs to get away. Luchford and Waddington were subsequently credited with an Albatros sent down out of control over Menin, but it was little compensation for the loss of the popular 21-year-old Lieutenant Ralph Mackenzie Madill – generally known in the squadron as 'Mc Madill'. Ralph was the unmarried only son of the late Captain Frank Madill MP and Mrs Florence Madill, from Toronto, Canada. A former clerk, he had previously served with the 9 (Reserve) Battalion Canadian Infantry and, like so many others from his squadron, he is buried at Bailleul. Malcolm McCall's wound was serious; but after hospitalisation and a lengthy convalescence followed by service with Numbers 36 and 148 Home Defence squadrons in England, he eventually returned to 20 Squadron in mid-1918.

There was yet more fighting on Sunday, 22 July when a photo-reconnaissance patrol led by Captain Satchell was attacked by six Albatros scouts over Menin. These were beaten off after Lieutenant Joslyn and Private Potter in A6548 sent one of them down in flames, but a little later the FEs ran into another fifteen near Wervicq. Trevethan and Hoy in A6528 claimed a flamer, while Vickers and Cowell in A6376 claimed one out of control that went down on its back northeast of Wervicq. The rest of the Germans made off towards Courtrai. The FEs then linked up with ten Nieuports before returning to the Wervicq area and attacking twenty Albatros scouts that may or may not have been made up of the same two groups they had encountered earlier. In any event, according to the 20 Squadron Record Book, these Germans 'did not show as much spirit' as the earlier formations they had encountered. Captain Satchell and Lieutenant Jenks in A6512 managed to send one down out of control before the FEs were forced to turn for home with little ammunition left.

The past few days had seen 20 Squadron engaged in mass dogfights that often involved upwards of thirty or more aircraft. The level of German opposition had ruffled some feathers on the British side and 20 Squadron volunteered to provide the bait that would bring the Germans to heel. So at 18.15 on Friday, 27 July, eight of the squadron's FEs took off and headed east towards Menin, circling over the town until they attracted the attentions of a large number of

'Albatrii'. That achieved, the FEs turned back towards the trenches, luring the unsuspecting Germans some ten miles towards Polygon Wood where large numbers of British and French scouts were waiting in ambush at a higher altitude.

Of the original FEs, one had been forced to drop out with engine trouble. Another, A6512 flown by Burkett and Lewis, lagged behind the others due to a rough engine but was able to continue. This left A6512 vulnerable, however, and some of the Germans singled it out as an easy target. The remainder took on the other FEs that had deliberately abandoned their usual tactic of forming a 'defensive circle' and turned towards the rendezvous in their original formation so as to present a more enticing bait. In the meantime, Burkett and Lewis were having a hard time of it on their own, with Lewis jumping from one gun to the other in his efforts to beat off repeated attacks and getting a good burst into one Albatros that seemed to fall apart in the air. By this time, A6512 had been hit so badly that only the rudder worked properly, and Burkett was hit in the shoulder as he tried to run for the lines while the Germans continued to attack from all directions. Not long afterwards, Lewis was hit in his left knee and collapsed into the nacelle, where he took a long draught from the brandy flask he always carried and fitted a fresh drum of ammunition to his front gun before struggling to his feet to start firing again. Burkett threw the FE about as never before, swinging it round to allow Lewis to fire forwards at an Albatros that came straight at them firing continuously. That Albatros too fell away suddenly as if out of control and, with the stricken FE almost over the lines, the remaining enemy scouts turned away rather than cross the trenches; their fire replaced by that of the German anti-aircraft batteries.

Burkett was by now in no condition to take evasive action and, in any case, the 'Fee' was so badly damaged that it could scarcely fly in a straight line, so it was lucky that none of the German shells hit their target. Eventually Lewis recognised Bailleul aerodrome not far away and Burkett brought the machine down safely by careful blipping of the engine and some gentle rudder use. After stopping some distance from the hangars, the two wounded flyers sat back exhausted before they were able to gather enough strength to start waving their arms for help. When they were taken to the casualty clearing station at the edge of the aerodrome, it was found that a phosphorous bullet had hit Lewis. He must have been in agony and, brandy or not, it is a wonder he had managed to remain conscious all the way home.

The other FEs had also been having a hot time of it but successfully made it to the rendezvous at Polygon Wood where Naval 10's Sopwith Triplanes and 56 Squadron's SE5s dived down to the rescue. Over the 85 minutes that the fighting lasted, at varying heights between 7,000ft and 13,000ft, the FE crews claimed eleven enemy aircraft either destroyed or out of control, while the single-seat pilots claimed a further ten.

Second Lieutenant Makepeace and Private Pilbrow in A6548 were hailed as the undisputed stars of the main battle after first claiming a flamer over Menin and then two more Albatrosses that were reported as having crashed in and southwest of Polygon Wood. Luchford and Waddington in A1956 also claimed a flamer and one out of control over Menin, while Lieutenant Joslyn and Private Potter in A6415 sent one down with smoke pouring from it. Captain Stevens and Second Lieutenant Cambray hit two more, causing smoke to pour from one and clouds of steam to belch from the engine of the second. Trevethan and Hoy added to the total by claiming an Albatros out of control between Menin and Lille before all the FEs made it back to friendly aerodromes. Two of Burkett and Lewis's 'kills' were subsequently confirmed by the RFC: the first one which fell to pieces and a second that crashed east of Menin. They were still being cared for at the CCS a week later when they were told they had both been awarded the Military Cross for their exploits. Lewis's account of the fight mentions his pleasure not only at their own awards but also at those of the same medal to Lieutenant Trevethan and Second Lieutenants Cambray and Hoy, and of the Military Medal to Private Potter. Lewis and his pilot were finally hospitalised at Rouen, where Lewis's leg was amputated. However, he was cheered by a visit from his mother and his sister Charlotte, during which Burkett also visited – and met Lewis's sister for the first time. They fell in love and later married.

With more than fifty allied aircraft, some of them French, involved in the main combat, it is remarkable that only one was lost, the pilot being Flight Sub-Lieutenant G. Roach who was killed flying Sopwith Triplane N5492. Makepeace and Pilbrow, Luchford and Waddington and Naval 10's Raymond Collishaw and Flight Sub-Lieutenant Rees all made virtually identical claims for an Albatros destroyed over Menin, and this strongly suggests that the Germans should have suffered at least one fatality. Although the death of Jasta 33's Leutnant Fritz Vossen has also been attributed to the French ace Charles Guynemer, the lack of detailed records leaves the matter shrouded in the fog of war[8]. Another German loss that might tie in with this fight was that of Vizeflugmeister (aviation chief petty officer) Otto Brandt of MFJ-1, who was killed in action at 18.20 between Middlekerke and Westende, although again it is not clear who was responsible. The last of the fighting ended about 20.40; and although Burkett and Lewis had landed at Bailleul just after 19.00, the final word quite rightly came from Lewis's own hand when he bravely wrote: 'What a crowded hour of merry life!'[9]

The last four days of July were no different to the first twenty-seven. New pilot Second Lieutenant Cameron took part in an inconclusive early-morning skirmish on 28 July while flying the now tired FE2B A5514, with Private Greenner as his gunner in Captain Stevens's patrol, but the usual routine of noting enemy ground movements was not interrupted. A little later a patrol led by Lieutenants Trevethan and Hoy had to leave Second Lieutenants Beldham and Watt behind because their FE2D A5147 would not leave the ground. Not long after that, Second Lieutenant Harrison and Private Benger also dropped out due to engine trouble in A3. An entry in the Squadron Record Book noted: 'These machines were newly available from 1 Aircraft Depot and had not been properly inspected before being sent out again.' The tone was one of annoyance, and no doubt the Recording Officer was well aware that such sloppiness could cost lives. As it turned out, the patrol came back with three victory claims after a fight that started between Polygon Wood and Gheluvelt. Lieutenant Joslyn and Private Potter in A6429 claimed one hostile aircraft driven down out of control, while Trevethan and Hoy claimed another near Becelaere and Makepeace and Pilbrow claimed another at more-or-less the same place. The reconnaissance itself was a failure due to very bad visibility but had improved by evening, allowing an eight-strong patrol led by Satchell and Jenks in the now repaired A3 to take 69 photographs over the designated area. More skirmishing resulted in Satchell and Jenks claiming an enemy machine sent down out of control northeast of Tourcoing, and Vickers and Cowell claiming another east of Menin that they watched as it 'turned over and over all the way down'.

Bad weather prevented most flying on 29 and 30 July but cleared for Zero Hour by the following day – and the start of the 'Third Ypres' campaign. The British Fifth Army under General Gough was tasked with making the main advance while the British Second Army and the French First Army respectively were to advance to the south and northwest of 5 Army to protect its flanks. Zero Hour was set for 03.50. A few hours later, a COP of four machines that had set off at 08.45 reported enemy cavalry and artillery movements east of Ypres. This was followed by Second Lieutenants Vickers and Urquhart flying a lone reconnaissance over Comines. Second Lieutenants Beldham and Watt went up at 12.08 for a similar duty and also returned safely.

Beldham and Watt took off again at 14.32 in A1965 for their second lone reconnaissance of the area in an attempt to locate the German reserve troops. They were last sighted flying northeast over Polygon Wood towards Moorslede where, at 2,000ft, two Albatros scouts attacked them from behind a cloud, leaving Lieutenant Watt unconcious from a shot to the head. Despite the Canadian pilot's best efforts, the two scouts had soon riddled the FE and set it alight. Beldham was lucky to make a forced landing in which the FE was entirely burnt out and he and his wounded observer were taken prisoner[10]. Two German fliers, K. Wusthoff of Jasta 4 and 20 Squadron's old adversary Walter Gottsch of Jasta 8 were both credited with victories after the fight, having each claimed an FE2 shot down in the same immediate area at very similar times[4, 6]. However, one of these could well have been A6369 that got down safely at Bailleul despite being badly shot-up and with Second Lieutenant Woodbridge wounded. Meanwhile, the launch of the Grand Offensive in heavy rain had met with mixed results, with both air reconnaissance and artillery work hampered by the weather. Nonetheless, the German first line of defence from the River Lys in the south to Westhoek, just east of Ypres, had all been taken. Gains to the north included the German first and second line defences as far as Bixschoote. At the end of that momentous day, 20 Squadron's score had passed 200. Then the rain began in earnest.

******

Notes

1. Combat Report.
2. AIR/1/818/204/4/1306 – Air Gunners' Badges.
3. AIR 1/161/15/123/15 – Memorandum on the training of observers 1915 to 1918.
4. 20 Squadron Record Book.
5. *Richtofen*: BBC Documentary by Michael Davies, Hartswood Films, 1998.
6. *The Jasta War Chronology* by N. Franks, F. Bailey & R. Duiven.
7. RFC Communiqués.
8. My thanks to Russ Gannon.
9. Sources include: 'An Account of an Air Fight by a Formation of FE2Ds of No.20 Squadron Over Menin' by 2/Lieutenant T. A. M. Lewis, AIR/1/733/185/4 and '20 Squadron Record Book' held at the The National Archives Kew; 'Royal Flying Corps Communiqués 1917-1918' edited by Chaz Bowyer., *The Sky Their Battlefield* by T Henshaw, and 'The War in the Air' Volume 4 by Raleigh & Jones.
10. 'Report on Circumstances of Capture' by Lieutenant Charles Hayes Beldham following repatriation: WO 374/5419.

Chapter 14

Third Ypres – August 1917

The rain that began on 31 July continued over the next two weeks as the British ground offensive struggled and floundered against the mud and German counter-attacks. The weather also severely hampered air operations during the first few days in August, and may have been responsible for a casualty report showing that Lieutenant R.N.D. Earwaker suffered concussion in an aircraft accident on the first day of that month. Despite the weather, 20 Squadron did manage to fly a very few largely uneventful patrols during the first week of August. This provided a useful breaking-in period for the newest arrivals including new pilot 21-year-old Second Lieutenant Jack Boles, from Ontario, and new observers Second Lieutenants L.H. Gould, J. Cawley and Lieutenant Dimmock. The first serious contact with the enemy did not come until 8 August when another new observer, Lieutenant J.A. Hone, flew with Second Lieutenant Vickers on a six-strong COP that set off at 09.35 led by Trevethan and Hoy.

The patrol area covered Messines and the now fiercely contested Gheluvelt plateau area, and at 10.30 the FEs attacked ten to twelve Albatros DVs found stalking some RE 8s east of Messines. Taking a chance, Trevethan and Hoy dived in pursuit of one these and shot it down for his own tenth victory and his observer's eighth. Shortly afterwards, another group of ten or eleven Germans was found attacking a second flight of RE 8s, but these too were driven off after what Trevethan reported as, 'a half-hearted fight lasting for about fifteen minutes'. The FEs, now joined by a French SPAD and two Nieuports, moved on to tackle another five 'Abatrii' discovered strafing British infantry near Gheluve. Lieutenant Trevethan emptied a whole drum into one of these from his fixed gun and watched it dive upside down into a small wood south of the village before he headed for home ahead of the rest: out of ammunition, a bracing wire shot through and his propeller broken[1].

Gunner Arthur Owen, who had transferred to the RFC from the Royal Garrison Artillery, made his first trip over the lines flying with Second Lieutenant Maclean as part of an eight-strong DOP that set out at 07.35 on Thursday, 9 August. As the fighting for Glencorse Wood on the Gheluvelt plateau swung this way and that, four enemy machines were dispersed and sent packing towards Menin. After that, and having been joined by two SPADs, the FEs attacked four Albatros scouts north of Becelaere. One of these was driven down into the clouds by a SPAD, while Richards and Wear in B1890 sent down another completely out of control with their victory claim supported by Lieutenant Hoy and Second Lieutenant Cawley flying as observers in other FEs. Two DFW two-seaters were also attacked and driven back into their own territory before the formation safely returned after three hours[2]. Other recent arrivals at St. Marie Cappel were also listed as flying that day. These were new observers Second Lieutenant J.P.F. Adams and Second Lieutenant Richard Hill and aerial gunner Lieutenant Corporal W. Harrop. Their flights were uneventful, but later on the squadron claimed another victory when Captain Solly's and Lieutenant Hay's patrol of six FEs engaged around twenty Albatros scouts over Polygon Wood, with the patrol leaders claiming one of them shot down out of control.

The squadron's first patrol on 10 August having proved uneventful, Captain Solly led up the second patrol of eight FEs at 07.48. Two had to drop out with engine trouble, and the remaining six were attacked by two separate formations of 'Albatrii', totalling no fewer than 35 enemy scouts. Richards and Wear drove one of them down out of control over Polygon Wood at 08.40 while Solly and Cawley attacked two German two-seaters over Becelaere and sent one of them down in flames. Another Albatros was claimed out of control by the whole formation, having fired at it over their top wings as it passed overhead. It was last seen still going down out of control east of Tenbrielen, after which the six FEs returned safely to St. Marie Cappel[1]. Maintenance problems also plagued a lunchtime patrol led by Captain Stevens, with two more FEs returning with engine trouble, and also affected the evening patrol as new observer Second Lieutenant Skelton made his debut in A3, piloted by Second Lieutenant Makepeace.

Although 10 August had brought some fighting, the day's most significant event was the arrival at St. Marie Cappel of the first of 20 Squadron's new Bristol F2B fighters, serial number A7108. The new machine was a tractor engine biplane powered by a Rolls Royce Falcon II engine with the pilot and observer sitting back to back. With a maximum speed of 123mph, manoeuvrability as good as any fighter and a ceiling of around 20,000ft, the Bristol Fighter could be used much more offensively than the FE2D and was earning itself quite a reputation with those other squadrons already equipped with it. The following morning, Captain Solly and Lieutenant Hay took it up to see what it could do – but this ended in tragedy. According to Bill Cambray in a 1969 interview with *Flight Magazine*, the Bristol Fighter climbed up above St. Marie Cappel to 8,000ft and looped twice; at which point the wings folded back and broke away and the aircraft plunged to earth in a shattering crash that killed both men. Later investigations revealed that the ash-wood inter-plane struts had been hollowed out to save weight and, thus modified, could not withstand the stresses of some manoeuvres. But whatever doubts the accident induced in the watching pilots and observers, more Bristol fighters were delivered to 20 Squadron over the coming days and weeks and training on them began. It had not been an auspicious beginning, by any means, but it was not a true reflection of the aeroplane's qualities, and 20 Squadron would soon learn to use it to its fullest abilities. Aside from the Bristol Fighter's disastrous début at 20 Squadron, the rest of the day passed quietly enough. There were no air fights and the only other casualty came when Private A.M. Potter was slightly wounded by German anti-aircraft fire while flying as aerial gunner for Lieutenant Joslyn in A6376.

Arthur Norbury Solly, 23, was the son of Major Ernest Solly (RAMC) and Mrs Mary Solly, of Harrogate, Yorkshire. Enlisting at the beginning of the war on 16 September 1914 as a private in the Public Schools Battalion of the Royal Fusiliers, he was later commissioned into 4 Battalion the Manchester Regiment, from which he subsequently transferred to the RFC. His first posting had been as an observer with 23 Squadron in 1916, with which unit he had shot down two German aircraft before being sent for pilot training and then on to 20 Squadron. At the time of his death, he had been credited with shooting down a total of nine German aircraft including the two with 23 Squadron. His observer, 24-year-old Donald Yalden Hay, from Bromley, Kent, had previously served with the Wellington College OTC and Inns of Court OTC before being commissioned into 2/5 Battalion of the Royal West Kent Regiment. Both men were buried together in the same grave at Longuenesse Souvenir Cemetery in France, where they share a fitting epitaph on their headstone: 'Brothers in Arms'[3].

Sunday, 12 August began with 20 Squadron's DOP setting off at 07.50 led by Stevens and Cambray in A3. The patrol should have been of eight FEs but the continuing maintenance problems yet again meant one was left behind, this time with a faulty magneto. Forty-five plates were exposed over the designated area before the appearance of six Albatrosses led by Jasta 18's Paul Strahle. The 'Albatrii' made several attacks, and recent arrivals Second Lieutenants Boles and Cawley, flying A6548, made a very creditable start for a relatively new team. Cawley, who had come to the RFC via the Manchester Regiment, fired a whole drum into one of the attackers, sending it into two backward loops before plunging into the clouds completely out of control. Paul Strahle's diary recorded the plane being flown by Leutnant Runge received a number of hits but made it back to base[4]. Except for Joslyn's and Hone's machine being badly shot up by anti-aircraft fire, 20 Squadron's FEs returned unscathed. An evening patrol that set off at 19.12 included another new pilot, Second Lieutenant Burritt, who was flying A6375 with Private Greenner as his gunner. Visibility was fair and, after first making its way east over Wervicq, the patrol turned northwest and followed the lines up to and beyond Ypres, eventually drawing near enough to the coast to report two ships signalling each other. Six enemy scouts were seen in the distance but were too far off to engage.

The next day's first patrol was also uneventful, but not the second. Eight FEs set off for a DOP at 08.37, and once again the formation included a new face. This was Air Mechanic Second Class 106099 James McMechan, a former baker from Howick, Lancashire, who flew as aerial gunner for the A3 of Second Lieutenant Cameron. Durrand and Thompson had to drop out in A5147 at 09.00 after engine pressure trouble but the rest of the patrol reconnoitred over Lille and Quesnoy, taking seventy photographs for Intelligence. Three Albatrosses attacked at around 10.00, and Boles and Cawley dived on one of them in A6369. A quick burst of fire sent it diving into cloud cover, and almost simultaneously a hit-and-run burst of fire from another Albatros hit Cawley in the arm. Then the Germans made off and left Boles free to break away for a hurried return to base with his wounded observer. Another patrol of four FEs went out over the Lille area in the evening. The Germans were in the habit of using smoke-screens to hide their artillery batteries from British aircraft, but the FE crews spotted their gun flashes anyway and plotted their positions around Perenchies, among trees and fields defended by trenches and wire entanglements. Another gun battery was found southwest of Lille in a position close to the canal, south of Ancoisne in what is now an industrial estate. This was important work and, once the information had been passed on to the British gunners, it would be the Germans' turn to receive a bombardment. Ten enemy aircraft were seen but there was no fight and all the patrol members returned safely to St. Marie Cappel, where they no doubt helped to celebrate the newly announced award of the Military Cross to Second Lieutenant Makepeace.

Tuesday, 14 August brought a victory to Second Lieutenants Lee and Urquhart in B1891 when the six FEs that had set out at 08.45 were crossing the lines and spotted nearby British anti-aircraft fire aimed at a DFW two-seater heading back east. Second Lieutenant Lee swung his FE around, close enough to be opening fire as he did so, whereupon a short chase began. The German observer returned fire but the fight ended when the DFW tipped over and went down out of control as if the pilot had been hit. British anti-aircraft gunners later confirmed that they had seen it crash[1]. Schusta 4 (a German ground-support squadron) recorded two casualties that day, these being Unteroffiziers Podboil and Slater who were wounded and forced to land. However, a similar claim to Lieutenant Lee's was also submitted by 23 Squadron, so who really got who remains in doubt. After that, the patrol pressed on further into German-held territory, noting train movements and balloon dispositions near Roulers and canal movements near Wervicq before making a safe return to St. Marie Cappel.

******

As the intensity of the ground fighting increased, so also did that of the air fighting, and Wednesday, 15 August brought casualties. Six FEs had set out at 16.40 on a COP but after the two formations of three became separated in poor visibility, and the formation led by Joslyn and Adams in A6359 was spotted by a force of around twenty 'Albatrii' at 9,000ft southeast of Poelcappelle. A flight of 1 Squadron Nieuports led by Captain Fullard tried to keep the Germans from diving on the FEs but at least one of them got through and, according to Lieutenant Joslyn's Combat Report, it attacked FE2D A5152 killing Private Pilbrow. Joslyn and Adams dived on the German with both front guns firing and it went down, being seen by Captain Fullard to crash at sheet 28.D.5 Meanwhile Pilbrow's pilot, Second Lieutenant C.H. Cameron, made a successful forced landing near Dickebusch. Moments later, Joslyn and Adams noticed another Albatros fall out of control past their FE with smoke pouring from it. This was later credited to Captain Fullard. In the same action, FE2D A6500 was seen diving for the lines with smoke coming from the engine; it had been badly shot-up and Second Lieutenant J.M. McLean wounded, but he made it back across the lines to a successful forced landing just northwest of Ypres. However, his gunner Arthur Owen had been hit in the head by a German bullet and died shortly afterwards. Joslyn and Adams's engine had also been badly shot-up by now and they landed at 1 Squadron. Two German pilots were officially credited with victories after the fight: Jasta 10 commander Werner Voss, for a FE2D over Zillebeke See at 19.10 German Time for his 36th victory, and Jasta 24's Leutnant H. Kroll for a FE2D shot down north of Ypres at 18.55 German Time. In addition, Jasta 10's Unteroffizier Hermann Brettal was reported wounded in action near Moorslede at about the same time[5]. Because of the given location, Kroll's claim can probably be tied in with McLean and Owen in A6500, while that of Voss probably relates to A5152.

As to the dead: 26-year-old Chelsea resident Private 44340 Stanley Edward Pilbrow, MM, had originally served with the 22 Battalion of the Manchester Regiment and left a widow, Elsie. The son of Edward and Minnie Pilbrow, he is buried at 'The Huts' Cemetery, southwest of Ypres. Gunner Arthur Owen 35716, aged 23, was also a Londoner, from Camberwell. A former porter, he had originally enlisted on 19 July 1911 as a gunner in the Royal Garrison Artillery, serving in France from 25 September 1914 before joining the RFC on 10 July 1917. He left his parents, Henry and Elizabeth and four brothers, and is buried at Gwalia Cemetery, west of Ypres.

The following morning brought a renewed British ground offensive extending from Westhoek in the south to almost as far north of Ypres as Bixschoote, where the French took over the line. A solid advance in the northern sector saw the British establish themselves on a new line from St. Julien to a little east of Langemark. However, fierce German resistance further south limited the British advance to a few small gains on the western edge of Glencorse Wood and north of Westhoek. That day 20 Squadron flew two distant and two COPs the purpose of which was, as always, to look out for German reinforcements moving up, plot the map references of any other important military targets they saw, and keep the sky clear of German fighter and reconnaissance aircraft. This last duty was gradually becoming more difficult for the FE2D crews, not only because of the FEs' slow speed and obsolescence, but also because of the numbers of enemy scouts they were encountering. The importance of the British assaults around Ypres had not been lost on the German generals, and the number of fighting Jastas based there had now been further increased to eighteen. The five FEs of 20 Squadron's first DOP that day, accompanied by six of 1 Squadron's Nieuports and three SPADs, met up with some of them over the Zonnebeke-Passchendaele area around 09.00.

Vickers and Hone, flying A6376, drove down a black and white Albatros out of control and then attacked another that went down to crash northeast of Zonnebeke. Two 'Albatrii' were claimed by Richards and Wear in B1890 and Makepeace and Waddington in A3, while another attacked Taylor and Tod from behind but was driven down by Tod's return fire, nearly taking the FE's tail with it before it plunged down into the clouds[1]. The Germans then withdrew and the FE2Ds completed their reconnaissance before returning with reports on the enemy's balloon deployments and other dispositions. Shortly after their return, a three-strong COP led by Stevens and Cambray in A6516 came up against nine Albatross scouts over Menin around 11.40. In the short fight that followed, the FEs flown by Stevens and Cambray and Luchford and Tennant each shot down an enemy scout out of control. But Luchford was not able to put in his claim until the following day as, just after this, his machine took a direct hit from German anti-aircraft fire and he made a forced landing in the countryside near Vlamertinghe.

The second COP did not meet any aerial opposition and returned to report masses of German troops and transport moving up the road between Gheluwe and Gheluvelt, plus the co-ordinates of a new German gun emplacement just south of the Armentieres-Lille railway line due north of Premesques. Such information was vital to the ground troops, as was the report on heavy enemy rail and road transport movements in the areas of Ledeghem, Menin, Gheluwe and Courtrai brought back by the evening DOP of six FEs. This patrol was evidently considered of some importance and was given an escort of twelve 1 Squadron's Nieuports, which was probably just as well as it was opposed by around twenty 'Albatrii' over Courtrai that were soon joined by nine more sporting red noses and tails. Despite the odds, the 'Albatrii' were unable to make any inroads into the British formations and were driven off, with the Nieuport pilots later reporting they had seen at least one Albatros shot down out of control by an FE2D. However, the 20 Squadron Record Book noted that 'it is not known which machine drove down this EA', and the German's fate is unknown.

The following day, Friday, 17 August, brought a frantic fight and further casualties. At 08.10 Lieutenant Joslyn and Second Lieutenant Urquhart in B1891 led up a DOP of six FEs. Once across the lines, the FEs were carefully pinpointing the locations of enemy balloons over Lille, Quesnoy and Wervicq when eleven 'Albatrii' of Jasta 26 came down on them. Several of them latched onto the rearmost machine, A6376 crewed by Vickers and Hone, and forced them out of the formation. The unfortunate duo then found themselves under attack at close range from all directions, but kept up a running fight along a line from Wervicq to near Warneton, well south of Ypres. The rest of the British formation might well have come to their aid but for the arrival of another twenty 'Albatrii' that kept them heavily engaged, forcing them northwards towards St. Julien and away from Vickers and Hone. While Hone stood up and fired backwards over the top wing at one attacker, Vickers let fly with his fixed gun at another diving down on them from ahead and to the right. Hone's target broke off its attack and feinted down, in the now familiar 'out of control' routine, while Vickers's target swept down and under them barely ten feet away, its pilot either slumping down wounded or ducking to avoid the British bullets. Glancing down, the British crew saw the Albatros go into a spin but had no time to dwell on it as another attack came in. Hone fired off another burst over the top wing and then jumped down to grab his forward Lewis gun in time to fire a quick burst at yet another Albatros coming from the front. This one also broke off its attack and tried the 'out of control' manoeuvre even as Hone let fly at yet another Albatros, hitting it in the engine and causing part of its cowling to break off. The English flyers were certainly not escaping unscathed, however, their A6376 having been badly shot up and holed in its petrol tanks and oil tank, as well as having had its controls and undercarriage damaged. After sending a hurried burst of fire into yet another attacker, Vickers was no doubt heartily relieved when the Germans suddenly broke off their attack freeing him to make a rapid forced landing on the British side of the lines, just south of Ploegsteert Wood at map reference 28.U.27.c. Vickers suffered concussion in the landing[1].

As to the other FEs: they had been fighting hard too and, on returning to St. Marie Cappel, found that Joslyn and Urquhart were no longer with them. Ground troops reported seeing B1891 make a forced landing between the lines in the St. Julien area and for a while there was reason to hope they would soon be home. But no further news was heard from them, and by the day's end they had been reported missing and were later confirmed as dead. Canadian Harold Waddell Joslyn was a 23-year-old former teacher from Manitoba who had previously served with the 95 Saskatchewan Rifles and had come to Europe with the 32 Saskatchewan Battalion of the CEF. He had been credited with shooting down seven Albatros scouts in the period of less than three months he had been with the squadron. Also aged 23, Alexander Urquhart came from Inverness and was the son of John Urquhart, a former deputy sheriff's clerk, and Mary Urquhart. He had previously served in the Highland Light Infantry. Both are remembered on the Arras Flying Services Memorial.

After the fight, Vickers and Hone were credited with four 'out of control' victories, which critics of the British victory count system might question in the absence of other witnesses. What is even more questionable, though, is why Jasta 26 pilots Leutnant Dannhuber, Leutnant Drekman and VizeFelfwebel Kosmahl, along with Leutnant K. Deilman of Jasta 6 were each credited with shooting down a FE2 in the St. Julien area at 11.10 German Time. St. Julien is a long way from where Vickers and Hone force-landed and, as no other FEs were lost that day, all four claims can only refer to B1891 flown by Joslyn and Urquhart. Curiously, no German pilot seems to have a made a claim that fits Vickers's and Hone's FE, which might be interpreted as meaning that they knew they had escaped and were happy to let them go in the face of their determined defence[5, 6].

This was not the only fight of the day. A DOP that had been reduced to four from its original six due to more engine problems with the old FEs was attacked at 14.30 by seven Albatros scouts east of Houthem. The 20 Squadron Record Book states that 'the enemy machines fought with great determination and came to very close quarters' but were unable to make any headway against the FEs' determined defence. One 'whose pilot was seen to collapse and fall forward' was claimed as an out of control victory by Luchford and Tennant in B1897. More fighting accompanied the four-strong COP that set off at 18.30 and included new observer Second Lieutenant Flynn flying with Second Lieutenant Durrand in A6459. The patrol had been up for ninety minutes, and had already seen several small groups of enemy scouts driven off by 1 Naval Squadron's Sopwith Triplanes, when eight Albatrosses attacked from the direction of Polygon Wood. Second Lieutenant Makepeace and Gunner McMechan in B1897 sent down a red Albatros apparently out of control that was also fired on by Durrand and Flynn in A6456. As they did so, Second Lieutenants Taylor and Tod engaged another Albatros that banked around steeply above FE B1890 and allowed Tod to get a good burst into it that sent it down totally out of control for at least 4,000ft, according to some of the naval pilots. The remaining enemy machines sensibly broke off from the fight and dived for home as two SPADs and six more naval triplanes joined the fight.

When the FEs got back, it was to the news that a British anti-aircraft battery had reported seeing the red Albatros targeted by Makepeace and McMechan's crash behind enemy lines[1, 2]. It seems that the German pilot got away with it, however, for German records show no corresponding casualty that evening. Nonetheless, all the machines in the patrol had made it safely home with their reconnaissance reports, and the Germans had again been put to flight. There was no fighting the next day and the patrols took thirty-six photographs without interference, which was a useful experience for new observer Second Lieutenant Berry as he flew with Second Lieutenant Richards in A6359 that evening.

A morning patrol on Sunday, 19 August was uneventful except for its members getting their first airborne view of British troops using flame-throwers in action near Pilkem. Second Lieutenant Vickers dropped out of the second patrol a short while after take-off as he was still suffering from concussion. Then, at about 15.50, another six FEs went out on a photo-reconnaissance mission and had just taken twenty-five photographs over Wervicq when it was attacked by a similar number of Albatrosses. Second Lieutenant Boles and Lieutenant Corporal Harrop in A6359 claimed one Albatros out of control, and Simpson and Hill flying A6456 claimed another. But Australian Gallipoli veteran Cecil Richards and ex-Suffolk Regiment Second Lieutenant S.F. Thompson were both wounded prisoners of war after their FE took over eighty hits and came down east of Wervicq. Its fall was credited to Jasta 28 pilot Leutnant Ernst Hess for his ninth victory, the news being greeted with delight at German HQ. A signal to Kofl 4 from General von Hoeppner congratulated Jasta 28 for its victory over a FE squadron that for too long had succeeded in defending itself against all attacks and had enjoyed far too much freedom over German territory. Obsolete though the FE2Ds may have been, coming from the enemy this was praise of the highest order for their flyers. In doing their very best to protect the FEs with their equally obsolete Nieuport 17s, 1 Squadron had also lost an aircraft: B1683 flown by Second Lieutenant H.E.A. Waring, who was shot down and captured by Leutnant Max Muller, also of Jasta 28[5, 6, 7].

Monday, 20 August was quieter, with the next day passing in similar style except that Private Greenner was wounded in the leg in the course of a COP and hospitalised before being repatriated to England, marking the end of his service with 20 Squadron. Another departure was that of O.H.D. Vickers. Following his patrol he was medically examined and ordered home for a period of rest under medical supervision. Not yet nineteen, Vickers had been credited with no fewer than thirteen combat victories in the two months he had been with 20 Squadron. The after-effects of his concussion stayed with him for several months but he was eventually able to return to flying duties with other units before finishing the war as a captain.

Wet weather now set in for the remainder of the month, severely hampering operations on the ground and in the air. Although the soldiers made small local gains or consolidated their positions here and there, the next stage of the ground offensive was delayed until September. The RFC flew whenever conditions allowed and on 22 August 20 Squadron was able to compile a useful list of German artillery batteries at various locations that was passed on to Intelligence. Captain E.H. Johnston made his first appearance leading a COP early the next morning but an afternoon patrol led by Captain Satchell returned to report that the winds were so strong at 10,000ft that the FEs were actually being blown backwards. There was little in the way of fighting for 20 Squadron, which must have come as a welcome respite to the doubtless exhausted pilots and observers. It also enabled several new arrivals such as Lieutenant Kirkman and probationary aerial gunners Air Mechanics Bawley and Matthews to settle in without too many distractions.

******

Notes

1. Combat Report.
2. 20 Squadron record Book.
3. From an article by Bob Solly, originally published in the August 2002 edition of Soul Search, the journal of The Sole Society, and from the service records of both officers: WO 339/15352 for Solly and WO 374/32032 for Hay.
4. *Cross & Cockade* Volume 11 No. 4, and thanks to Russ Gannon.
5. The Jasta War Chronology by Norman Franks, et al.
6. *Cross & Cockade* Volume 11 No. 2.
7. *The Sky Their Battlefield* by Trevor Henshaw.

Chapter 15

Ugly Duckling Swan-Song – September 1917

The first half of September 1917 brought drier weather that allowed the British armies in the salient to regroup and prepare for a renewed offensive against the Germans still doggedly clinging on around the Ypres to Menin road. The ground troops were taking casualties but, in terms of the numbers of men involved, the RFC casualties were disproportionately higher. Thus September 1917 brought many more new faces to 20 Squadron as replacements for those lost in August – and saw some of them disappear again so quickly that the older hands scarcely had time to learn their names. Late September also saw the final departure of the faithful but hopelessly obsolete FE2Ds from St. Marie Cappel and their replacement with the long-awaited Bristol F2B Fighter. At the beginning of September half the squadron was still equipped with the FE2D, and the Squadron's casualties of early and mid-August were at least partly due to the fact that its 'Fees' were simply too old and slow to compete with the latest German scouts. It was inevitable that Major Mansfield would commit the new Bristol Fighters to the test as soon as enough crews were trained on them. The first two days of the month were noteworthy only for new pilot Second Lieutenant Chambers flying his first patrol and receiving his 'baptism of fire' on 2 September during an inconclusive brush with five Albatros scouts near Passchendaele.

On the morning of 3 September four Bristol Fighters set off led by Captain E.H. Johnston and Lieutenant Hone in Bristol F2B Fighter A7215 to escort four FE2Ds on a photo-reconnaissance mission. The other members of the first Bristol Fighter mission for 20 Squadron were Second Lieutenants Babbage and Hill in A7213, Lieutenant Kirkman and Second Lieutenant Berry in A7211 and Second Lieutenant Makepeace and Lieutenant Waddington in A7214. The FE2D formation was led by Captain Stevens and Lieutenant Cambray in A6516 accompanied by Lieutenants Trevethan and Hoy in A6456, Second Lieutenants Boles and Flynn in A6548 and Second Lieutenant Simpson and Air Mechanic 2nd Class Benger in A1897.

The comforts of the Bristol Fighter must have come as a revelation to pilots and observers alike. The higher cockpit walls and tractor-engine meant extra protection from the cold for the pilot, while the fast-firing synchronised Vickers machine-gun installed inside the engine cowling gave him plenty of 'punch'. For the observer too, long used to his draughty and precarious perch at the front of a FE2D, with no seatbelt and only the Lewis gun and the sides of the nacelle to cling onto during dogfight manoeuvres, this was luxury. His cockpit was fitted with a rudimentary seat, a circular Scarfe-ring gun-mounting on which the Lewis gun could be quickly and easily traversed in almost any direction and a basic control column to give him a fighting chance of a safe landing if the pilot was killed. It was a big step forward for everyone.

At about 10.10 the Bristol Fighters were flying behind and higher than the FEs when ten to fifteen Albatros scouts dived on the FE2Ds east of Wervicq. The Bristol Fighters then used their height advantage to dive on the 'Albatrii', and at the same time five Sopwith Pups of 46 Squadron's B Flight also came plunging into the fray. The odds had now been levelled, more-or-less, and in the ensuing dogfight Makepeace and Waddington shot down one of the 'Albatrii' in flames while 46 Squadron's Lieutenant V. Joske sent down another that was seen to crash. There is a strong possibility that one victim was Jasta 31's Unteroffizier Walter Koenig, who was recorded by the Germans as having fatally crashed at Tidietelhof following air combat that day[2, 3]. So 20 Squadron gained its first Bristol Fighter victory, although 46 Squadron with its brave but outdated Pups suffered two casualties. Lieutenant S.W. Williams was shot down and taken prisoner by Jasta 26's Leutnant O. Fruhner, while Lieutenant F.B. Barager was shot through the leg but managed to make it back over the lines to 23 Squadron's base at La Lovie[1,2,4]. The Germans having departed, the Bristol Fighters and FE2Ds resumed their patrol, locating an enemy artillery battery firing just north of Kruiseeke close to the Menin Road and exposing 48 priceless photographs over the 'counter-battery area'. There must have been great satisfaction at the outcome of the experiment following the safe return of all the FEs and Bristols. Not only had the Bristols (or 'Biffs' as they became known) scored a victory on their first patrol, they had also enabled the FEs to complete their vital reconnaissance.

Similar joint patrols were flown over the next two days and introduced more replacements to the squadron. Second Lieutenant Tomlin was flying FE2D A6456 with newly promoted Sergeant Benger as his observer while Harry Luchford carried Second Lieutenant Richard Hill as his observer for the first time during a patrol on 4 September. The mid-morning patrol on Wednesday, 5 September saw new observer Second Lieutenant V.R.S. White flying with Captain E.H. Johnston when, at 11.15 while counting trains and rolling stock, they were attacked by ten Albatrosses west of Lille. New Canadian pilot

Clairmarais Aerodrome from the air. The National Archives AIR 1/1078

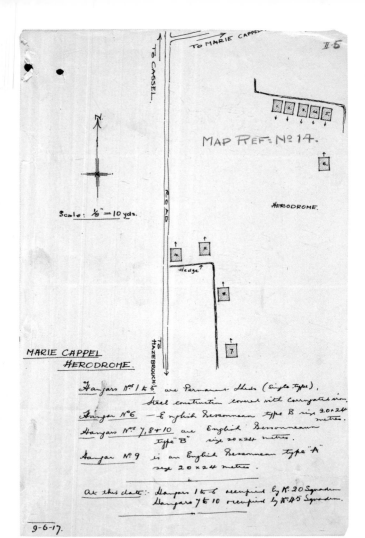

Sketch-map of Marie Cappel aerodrome.
The National Archives AIR 1/1078

FE2D 'A6516' presentation aircraft from the colony of Mauritius. The National Archives-AIR 1/168

The gunner's precarious position when attacked from behind in an FE2D.
The National Archives-AIR 1/168

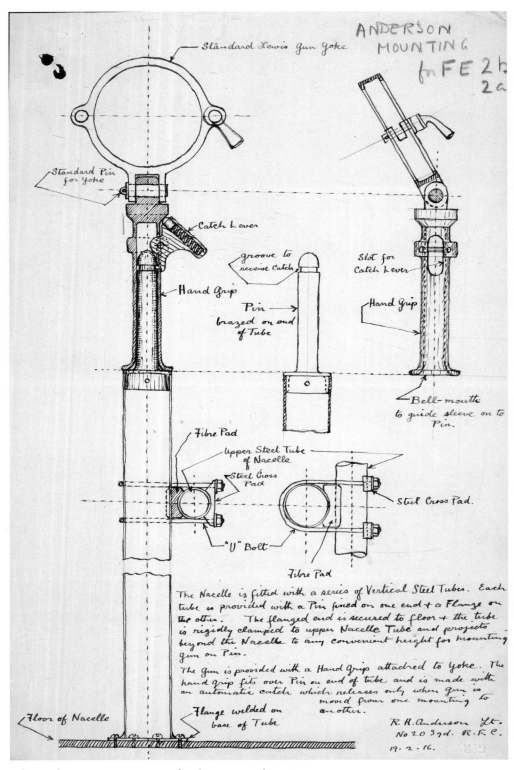

The Anderson Gun Mounting for the FE2B and FE2D. The National Archives AIR 1/867

The wreck of FE2 No. A1942 flown by Second Lieutenant Bacon who survived and Air Mechanic Worthing who was killed when it was downed on 05.05.1917. Photograph Courtesy of I. Simpson

Lieutenant Grout and Air Mechanic Tyrell taken after their capture.
Photograph courtesy of Jamie Tyrell

FE2Ds Line-up at St. Marie Cappel.
Photograph courtesy of Jamie Tyrell

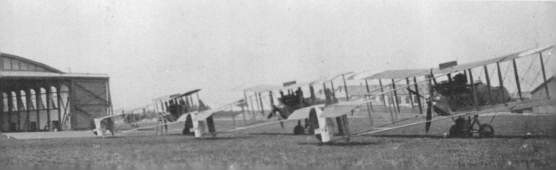

27/7/17.   Sender's No. P.244.

To :-
O.C., No. 20 Squadron, R.F.C.

———————————————————

        Congratulate you on your magnificent fight
tonight   AAA   The whole of the 9th Wing are
enthusiastic about it   AAA

        Message from :-
            GENERAL TRENCHARD, ADVANCED H.Q., R.F.C.

            - - - - - - - - - -

        The G.O.C.-in-C. awarded the following Honors
on this day :-
            Lieut.R.M.Trevethan.   Military Cross.
            2/Lt. W.C.Cambray.   Do.
            "   C.A.Hoy.   Do.
            Pte. Potter F.   Military Medal.

            - - - - - - - -

Hard fighting took place EAST of YPRES.

No. 20 Squadron fought magnificently throughout and lost no machines.

Further details will be issued in our next Communique No. 99.

===========

On the evening of the 27th, as reported in R.F.C. Communique No. 98, very heavy fighting took place, with the result that German aviators were totally beaten and driven East in all the big engagements. This was principally noticeable on the front of the Fourth Army and East of YPRES, where No. 20 Squadron took part in a fight between many types of our machines and about 20 Albatros Scouts. 2/Lt. Makepeace and Pte. Pilbrow dived on one, which fell in flames, and destroyed two others near Polygon Wood. Lts. Luchford and Waddington drove down one of their opponents out of control, and shot down another in flames. 2/Lts. Burkett and Lewis engaged one, which they shot down and which fell to pieces, and then destroyed a second. Lieut. Joslyn and 2/A.M. Potter, in one machine, and 2/Lt.Trevethan and Lt.Hoy, in another, each drove down one of the Albatros Scouts out of control.

RFC Communiqué re July 27, 1917. The National Archives AIR 1/167

On 21st September 1917 the Squadron having been requipped with Bristol Fighters, the last F.E.2d. was returned to No.1 aircraft Depot St Omer.

On first landing in France on 16th Jan. 1916 the Squadron was equipped with the F.E. 2b machine (120 H.P. Beardmore Engine) These were changed to F.E. 2d's in June 1916, the latter machine having a 250 h.p. Rolls Royce engine.

At the time, the F.E. 2d. was the finest two seater fighting machine in existence, and the Squadron soon won a reputation for hard and successful fighting against heavy odds.

The armament was 3 Lewis guns. One of which was fixed in the axis of the machine, and fired by the pilot, by a

'Bowden' cable, on the control lever.

The other two were fired by the observer; one to fire forwards and the other backwards over the top plane.

The principle duties of the Squadron on these machines were:

1. Offensive Patrols.
2. Photography and Reconnaissance
3. Bombing by Day & by Night.

Lieutenant Malcolm McCall.
Photograph courtesy of Courtesy Tom and Mark and Dee Arkell

Lieutenant Malcolm McCall in Full Flying Gear.
Photograph Courtesy of Tom and Mark McCall and Dee Arkell

Lieutenant Malcolm McCall's Bristol Fighter 'C951'.
Photograph courtesy of Tom and Mark McCall & Dee Arkell.

Lieutenant Malcolm McCall gathered these 20 Squadron signatures after the Armistice.

Photograph courtesy of Tom and Mark McCall and Dee Arkell

Lieutenant R.W. White.

Photograph Courtesy Major Les Donnithorne

Lieutenant R.W. White. The Mothers Cross, awarded by the Canadians.

Photograph courtesy Major Les Donnithorne.

Driver George Tester. The Author's Maternal Grandfather was killed on 28 September 1917 – RAS.

Lieutenant Tommy Colvill Jones.
Photograph Courtesy of Lorraine Colvill-Jones.

Captain Leslie Burbidge.
Photograph Courtesy of Simon Burbidge.

Lieutenant Noel Boucher.
Photograph courtesy of Chris Boucher.

Lieutenant James Tulloch in 1918.
Photograph courtesy of Sue Briggs.

Lieutenant D.G. Campbell's Bristol Fighter.
Photograph courtesy of Robert Campbell.

Lieutenant J.H. Colbert.
Photograph courtesy of John Colbert.

Bristol F2B Fighter 'B883' Shot Down on January 25 1918 in which Sergeant H.O. Smith died of wounds and Second Lieutenant Clemons was seriously wounded. Photograph courtesy of I. Simpson.

Captain H.P. Lale and Lieutenant W.H. Welsh in their Bristol Fighter.
Photograph courtesy of Luc Di Guglielmo

Captain H.P. Lale and Lieutenant W.H. Welsh pose in front of their Bristol Fighter.
Photograph courtesy of Luc Di Guglielmo.

Lieutenant D. Weston's Bristol F2FB, probably taken after the armistice.
Photograph courtesy of C. McDevitt.

Officers of 20 Squadron R.A.F. on 13 November 1918. Photograph courtesy of Luc Di Guglielmo from the estate of the Welsh Family.

Lieutenant E.B. Maule's German War Grave.
Photograph courtesy of the National Archives WO 339/16294

Lieutenant D.G. Campbell's Propeller Cross
Grave marker. Photograph courtesy of Robert Camp

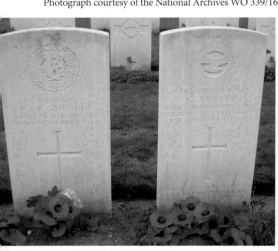

The War Graves of Driver G. Tester &
Captain J.S. Campbell lie at Pont du Hem
Military Cemetery – image was taken on
28.09.2017: the 100th Anniversary of their
deaths - RAS

War Grave of Sergeant
Tom Mottershead DCM,
VC at Bailleul – RAS

War Grave of Samuel
Catton. 20 Squadron's fi
combat fatality is buried
at Lijssenthoek – RAS

The Flying
Services Memorial
at Arras - RAS

Second Lieutenant W.R.A. Campbell was flying Bristol Fighter A7214 when his gunner, Air Mechanic Second Class Harrop was wounded in the leg by machine-gun fire, though this did not prevent Harrop shooting off one side of an Albatros scout's tail-plane a short while later. In the meantime, Makepeace and Waddington in A7203 drove down another Albatros out of control and the Germans broke off their attack[1]. In addition to Harrop, there was one other casualty: Sergeant Frank Potter suffered severe abdominal injuries when his pilot made a forced landing on the road near St. Marie Cappel after the engine failed, and he died on 11 September. A former warehouseman from Caterham, Surrey, Potter had originally enlisted in the Border Regiment on 1 January 1912 and had served in India, Egypt and France. He was 24 and is buried at Bailleul. Two more newcomers flew later in the day. Lieutenant Pilkington flew FE2D serial A3 with former 45 Squadron observer Lieutenant George Brook during a late afternoon northerly OP led by Captain Stevens, while Second Lieutenant Dandy was the observer in FE2D B1895 flown by Second Lieutenant Chambers in a simultaneous SOP led by Captain Satchell. The Germans kept their distance.

Just like 20 Squadron, the Germans also had a new fighter to try out, and 20 Squadron's flyers met up with it the following afternoon. At 15.35 on 6 September, during a northerly offensive patrol (NOP) of four FE2Ds led by Captain Stevens, the patrol was southeast of Boisinghe when it ran into five Albatros scouts led by an unusual-looking triplane: the new Fokker F1. Only two had been delivered to the front so far, one of which had been assigned to Manfred von Richtofen and the second to his friend and rival, Werner Voss. It was Voss whom 20 Squadron met now, and as soon as he got close to the 'Fees' the German ace latched onto the inexperienced Pilkington's tail and fired a savage burst that set B1895 alight and plunging to earth with the loss of both men. There was no time to avenge Pilkington and his observer Air Mechanic Second Class H.F. Matthews: for after another burst of fire that left Simpson and Wear struggling to get back over the lines with their propeller shot through, the Germans departed and left the stunned FE crews floundering in their wake[1, 2, 5]. The simultaneous SOP that included new observer Second Lieutenant Morris flying with Second Lieutenant Harrison in B1892 and new pilot Second Lieutenant Seward and Air Mechanic Second Class Townsend in A6359 was more fortunate with all its men returning safely.

John Oscar Pilkington, aged 25, the son of John and Sarah Pilkington from Port Erin, Isle of Man, had attended Liverpool's Facility of Engineering, after which he saw service with the King's Liverpool Regiment in Egypt and Salonika. A keen motorcyclist, he was the proud owner of a 'Rex' type motorcycle registration number MN103. Former motor lorry driver Air Mechanic Second Class 1712 Herbert Frederick Matthews had originally enlisted in August 1914 and was the 22-years-old son of Robert and Harriet Matthews, from Worthing, Sussex. Both men are buried at Bailleul.

A new sergeant pilot named Frank Johnson flew his first patrols on Sunday, 9 September in a photo-reconnaissance of six Bristol Fighters that set out at 12.45. Having already achieved four victories with 22 Squadron, he flew Bristol Fighter A7211 with Second Lieutenant Adams as his observer. His skills would not become apparent on this particular day, though, as he and another Bristol Fighter had to return early with engine problems. That left only four to carry on and, after exposing thirty-five plates of the required area, they ran into about twenty 'Albatrii' near Becelaere. Harry Luchford and Hill in A7215 fired a short burst into one of them, and when it quickly came back around onto their Bristol's tail, Richard Hill hit the attacker with another burst that made him fall from the fight to be credited as an 'out of control' victory[1]. The remaining 'Albatrii' then withdrew to the east, and the only damage recorded was to A7129 after Second Lieutenant Tomlin made a heavy landing and wrecked its undercarriage, and to A7203 flown by Second Lieutenants Boles and Berry which landed at Bailleul with its pressure gauge shot through. Two more photo-reconnaissences were successfully carried out in the late afternoon and evening, and another two the following day; while Tuesday, 11 September saw the squadron's patrols get into three more fights.

The first action came in the morning that day when six Bristol Fighters led by Captain Johnston were attacked by a Fokker Triplane leading a group of Albatrosses. The Triplane engaged Babbage and Skelton in A7193 and Skelton fired off at least one and a half drums at the Fokker before the Bristol's engine suddenly cut out for a few seconds as his pilot switched fuel tanks. This allowed the Triplane to force them out of the formation but they kept it at bay until they reached the safety of the lines[1]. Babbage got his revenge for the fright when he went up again later with Second Lieutenant Purvis as his observer. After noting the trains and rolling stock at Courtrai and some activity at the German aerodromes at Heule and Harlebeke, the six Bristol Fighters were attacked by about twenty-five 'Albatrii' over Menin. Purvis emptied a drum into one of the enemy scouts that immediately burst into flames, its fate confirmed by Lieutenant Dandy and Second Lieutenant Morris flying in other Bristol Fighters as the fight continued northwest above the Menin road.

Kirkman and Flynn in A7234 also reported getting an Albatros down in flames that they said crashed in fields just south of the Menin road east of Kruiseeke. Kirkman then swept low over their downed opponent while Flynn used his Lewis gun to spray the still burning wreck for good measure. The final tally also included 'out of control' claims from Makepeace and Waddington in A7214 and Luchford and Hill flying A7248. A footnote to Luchford's combat report noted that one of the Germans had been using a new kind of ammunition that left a twenty to thirty feet trail of smoke behind it before exploding in the air like a small shell[1]. Incendiary and explosive bullets had been introduced by both sides for attacking balloons and although international law prohibited their use against people, it was tacitly accepted that their use against aircraft was a different matter. The legal position remained in doubt throughout the war and, for this reason, many pilots on both sides using such ammunition carried written orders stating they were doing so primarily for balloon attack work. It may well be that one of the Germans also carried such orders.

In the last fight of the day, six FEs led by Captain Stevens were taking pictures over the counter-battery area when an enemy scout latched on to A6548 flown by Second Lieutenants Taylor and Brook below the rest of the formation. The result was inconclusive, with the Albatros going down as another 'out of control' after an exchange of fire at 25 yards range. This was counted as George Brook's fifth victory, the first four having been achieved with 45 Squadron. The day was not without tragedy, though, as Sergeant 332 W.H. Roberts stalled Bristol Fighter A7211 at the start of a practice formation flight and spun into the ground killing him and his observer, Second Lieutenant Albert Wear. Aged 21, William Roberts had worked as a motor fitter in London before joining the RFC shortly after its formation in 1912, qualifying as a pilot and being promoted to sergeant on 31 May 1917. Albert Wear was an accountant by profession and the son of a Middlesex clergyman. He had seen six months active service in France with the Royal Fusiliers before being commissioned into the RFC, and during his flying career as an observer had been credited with nine combat victories. Both men are buried at the nearby Longuenesse (St. Omer) Souvenir cemetery[5].

The next few days brought their moments of excitement but few casualties. On Thursday, 13 September the squadron found another task added to its duties when the mid-morning patrol led by Captain Johnston and Lieutenant Hone was ordered to drop propaganda leaflets over Menin and Comines while carrying out its reconnaissance work. Fortunately, the visibility was so bad that morning that they were able to complete the mission without seeing any enemy aircraft. Tomlin and Morris had a narrow escape the next day when they lost contact with their colleagues in the clouds and, on coming out into clearer skies, found themselves at only 4,000 feet directly over Lille. Three Albatros scouts and two DFW two-seaters immediately came after them, but Morris managed to drive down one of the two-seaters out of control as Tomlin got A7203 back into the clouds and streaked west before landing at Savy with his aileron controls shot away[1]. Saturday, 15 September saw new observer Second Lieutenant Green flying with Second Lieutenant Simpson in FE2D B1892 on a day of no combats except for the NOP that set out at 17.30 led by Harry Luchford. The patrol was opposed by several small formations of Albatros scouts, and Second Lieutenant Babbage had to bring his crippled Bristol Fighter down to a forced landing at 4 Squadron with observer Second Lieutenant J.E.L. Skelton shot through the lung. The only noteworthy event the following day was the appearance of new pilot Sergeant Hopper flying Bristol Fighter A7245 with Lieutenant Waddington as his observer. The next day, the *London Gazette* announced that Richard Trevethan had been awarded of the Military Cross, but the good news was overshadowed the day after when he was wounded in action and repatriated to England. His slow recovery prevented his return to the squadron.

******

Considering that the main business in September 1917 centred on the continuation of the Third Ypres campaign, it is surprising that General Haig and his staff became personally involved in questions about the internal organisation of the RFC. The point at issue was whether or not NCOs should be allowed to train as pilots, ignoring the fact that small numbers of NCOs had been flying as pilots from the earliest days of the war. However, someone had evidently raised doubts with General Haig as to whether they were suitable material for such a role. The matter having been brought to his attention, he wrote to the War Office on 6 September 1917, in the midst of the Third Ypres campaign, laying down the conditions under which he would find such a policy acceptable. Writing as if the suggestion of NCO pilots was something brand new instead of an already established fact, he stated that he would prefer to reserve his opinion as to 'the wisdom of adopting such a policy'. However, accepting that there were difficulties in obtaining enough officers for the role – and that the Germans seemed determined to kill them whenever they could – he did agree to adopt the measure as an experiment subject to the following rules:

a) Non-Commissioned Officer pilots should have a Pilots' Mess separate from the NCO messes of the rest of the squadron. This is done in both the French and German Armies.
b) Whatever establishment of such pilots is fixed, it must be introduced into a squadron at one time, and pilots should not be scattered through the Royal Flying Corps as they become available.

c) It will further be necessary for the training of WO and NCO pilots to be undertaken at home, as it cannot be undertaken in France.

d) If these conditions are accepted, I am prepared to receive Warrant Officer and Non-Commissioned Officers as pilots in the following proportions:

Corps Squadrons: One Flight of NCO pilots when these squadrons are raised to an establishment of 24 machines. This works out to be 25% in each of these squadrons.

Single-Seat Fighting Squadrons: It is doubtful to what extent, if at all, NCO pilots could be introduced in these squadrons, but I am prepared to try one flight of NCOs in six squadrons as an experiment. This works out to be 33% in each of these six squadrons.

Two-Seat Fighting Squadrons: I am similarly prepared to try one flight of NCO pilots in one squadron as an experiment, i.e. 33% of that squadron.

Two-Seater Day Bombing Squadrons: 50% NCO pilots. The proportion in these squadrons can, I consider, be higher as they manoeuvre in formation under a leader, who would be an officer, and individual action is reduced to a minimum.

I consider that all pilots in two-seater Night Bombing Squadrons must be officers.
(Signed) D. Haig"

While the idea of NCO pilots having their own mess facilities would allow them to mix together in their spare time, swapping yarns and learning from each-other's ideas and experiences without distractions, they could not share their experiences with the commissioned pilots except in more formal settings such as briefings. A more enlightened approach might have argued for all flyers sharing one Aircrew Mess regardless of rank – but that would have gone against the class barriers of the day. Some traditions die hard, and Haig's letter makes the real reasons for his caution plain. Officers and gentlemen were the sort of chaps who could think for themselves: Warrant Officers and NCOs, however loyal and dependable when shown the right lead, were clearly not! Considering all the other matters he had to contend with, the foregoing begs the question of why pilot selection should merit the personal consideration of a C-in-C who had never actually flown or had close command of flyers. Perhaps the kindest thing that can be said Douglas Haig's view is that it was somewhat irrelevant.

Notwithstanding Haig's opinions, both Sergeants Hopper and Johnson flew into action on the morning of 19 September as part of a patrol of five Bristol

Fighters led by Luchford and Hill to photograph German positions between Becelaere and Polygon Wood. With a new ground offensive planned for that area the following morning, the all-important photography had been entrusted to Taylor and Dandy in A7246. They were flying somewhat higher than the others in order to get the best shots and, as they did so, the formation was attacked by around twenty German scouts including two of the new Triplanes. Dandy had already taken eighteen photographs and was crouching down in his cockpit taking more when German bullets ripped through his cockpit and leg. As Taylor tried to evade the eight enemy scouts that appeared to have singled out A7246, Dandy abandoned his photography, struggled to his feet and kept up a hot fire on the pursuers bringing one down in flames and two out of control. Then just as Dandy's gun jammed, Taylor became aware that the Bristol's tail-plane had been so badly shot through it was almost severed from the fuselage. There was only one place to go and that was down. Skilfully handling his stricken fighter, Taylor dived just below the rest of the formation, which put up a wall of protective fire until the Germans withdrew. It seems that Taylor telephoned his combat report in from Choques, where they landed, as it is actually signed only by Major Mansfield, who took pains to point out in it that: 'Second Lieutenant Dandy was hit before he had a chance of opening fire. All his fighting therefore took place after he was wounded.' To which someone else – a staff officer at wing or brigade, one assumes – promptly appended the question: 'Why not?'[1]. In fact, Dandy's wound was sufficiently serious for the ex-sergeant from the King's Liverpool Regiment to be repatriated to England, where he remained until the end of the war after a medical board declared him permanently unfit for flying.

While all that was going on, two more commissioned pilots also appeared on the duty roster. Lieutenant Kirkpatrick flew A7193 with Second Lieutenant Berry in a morning Line Patrol led by Captain Stevens, while Captain J.S. Campbell flew his first uneventful patrol with Second Lieutenant Flynn as his observer in the late afternoon. John Santiago Campbell was the son of Scottish shipbuilder Archibald Jack Campbell and Catherine Crawford, and derived his unusual middle name from his birthplace in 1891 at a village near Bilbao in Spain. His father was working with Vickers Shipyard during this time and his job frequently took him to Spain where he was decorated by King Alfonso with the order of *La Cruz de la Merito Naval* in 1909. Captain Campbell was first commissioned in 9 Battalion the Argyll and Sutherland Highlanders at the age of 23 in October 1914 and was promoted to captain before he transferred to the RFC.

******

Zero hour for Second Army's attack around the Menin Road came at 05.40 on Thursday, 20 September, and RFC Headquarters had issued special instructions for the brigades and squadrons that would be involved. For operational reasons, the new battlefront had been divided into two sectors north and south of a line from Ypres to Tenbrielen to Quesnoy. Weather permitting, the Army Wing patrols were to operate in two layers at 10,000ft and 6,000ft. The northern patrols, covering the area where the heaviest fighting would take place, were to be double the strength of the southern patrols. In addition to this, single-seat scouts had been assigned to work over strictly specified areas attacking enemy infantry, artillery and ground transport while looking out for German reinforcements moving towards the fighting. Finally, more single-seat scouts were ordered to strafe the German aerodromes at Marcq, Bissegham and Heule while 20 Squadron was reserved for reconnaissance and photography as required[6].

The British Second and Fifth Armies attacked simultaneously at zero hour and 20 Squadron's first patrol went up at 07.44 comprising five FE2Ds led by Stevens and Cambray. The poor visibility of the early morning gradually gave way to clearer conditions but there were no decisive air fights above the fierce ground fighting taking place below, in which the British were largely achieving their objectives. Following numerous unsuccessful counter-attacks during the evening and overnight, the Germans redoubled their efforts on the next day with further heavy counter-attacks around Tower Hamlets, Polygon Wood and northeast of St. Julien. This brought a rush of air fighting and, following some skirmishes in the early morning, Kirkman and Flynn were lucky to return from a Special OP in Bristol Fighter B1110 with a bracing wire and the main tail-plane spar shot through. Sergeant Hopper and Second Lieutenant Morris were also shot up and had to land inside the British lines a little northwest of Hill 60.

In mid-morning, Captain Stevens led up the very last but not uneventful FE2D patrol that 20 Squadron would carry out. The FEs were escorted by four of the squadron's Bristol Fighters, including Kirkman and Flynn who had apparently shrugged off their earlier experiences and were flying A7141. Sergeant Johnson and Second Lieutenant Purvis had to return early in A7193 with a difficult gun jam while the remaining machines carried out the patrol and had a fight with about eighteen Albatrosses over Becelaere. It ended at about 11.30 when the German machines broke off and headed east after Kirkman and Flynn sent one down in a vertical dive pouring black smoke and Second Lieutenants Durrand and Jenks in B1892 sent another down out of control[1]. One new name on this patrol was Private Snoulton, flying as Lieutenant Kirkpatrick's gunner in Bristol Fighter A7214. Captain Johnston's flight set off for its second patrol in mid-afternoon, including new pilot Lieutenant Dalley carrying Richard Hill as his observer for Hill's second patrol of the day, while Sergeant Johnson carried Second Lieutenant Flynn on Flynn's third patrol of the day. It was a case of third time unlucky for Flynn as their Bristol Fighter A7228 suffered engine failure and crashed on approaching the aerodrome, slightly injuring both men.

Captain Campbell led up the last patrol of the day at 16.55 and this resulted in the loss of new pilot Second Lieutenant C.H.C. Woods and Second Lieutenant T.W. McLean in A7234 following a fight with seven enemy scouts near Wervicq. An Albatros that dived and zoomed to attack a Bristol Fighter was sent spinning down by Luchford and Cambray in A7248; but A7234 did not return. The likeliest German claimant for this would seem to be Offizierstellvertreter R. Weckbrodt of Jasta 26 who was credited with a British two-seater over Wervicq at 17.45 (Luchford and Cambray's 'out of control' claim having been timed at 17.50). Some other sources have credited the German victory to Leutnant F. Kieckhafer of Jasta 29, but as his claim was for a fight over Hooglede, northwest of Roulers, Weckbrodt's claim would seem to be correct. Woods and McLean were killed, and Luchford and Cambray's claim for an 'OOC' victory was of little consolation[2, 3,4].

Canadian Charles Halkett Carson Woods, a 22-year-old science student from Montreal, had previously served in the OTC and the Canadian Army Service Corps. He had been with 20 Squadron for just six days. His observer, 19-year-old former apprentice engineer Thomas William McLean, from Sunderland, had come straight into the RFC and had served as an observer with 45 Squadron from 29 July before it replaced its two-seat Sopwith 'Strutters' with single-seat Sopwith Camels. His family was by no means wealthy and the tragedy of his father's earlier death and now his own was compounded when Alicia, his mother, died on 7 January 1918 at the Workhouse Hospital in Sunderland. Neither of the flyers' bodies was recovered and both men are remembered at the Arras Flying Services memorial.

That brought the day's fighting to an end for 20 Squadron and a final farewell to its 'Faithful Fees' that Bill Cambray had so affectionately dubbed the 'Ugly Ducklings'. It is worth noting what the squadron's Recording Officer had to say of the event:

On 21 September 1917, the squadron having been re-equipped with Bristol Fighters, the last FE2D was returned to No.1 Aircraft Depot at St. Omer. On first landing in France on 16 January 1916 the squadron was equipped with the FE2B machine (120HP Beardmore engine). These were changed to FE2Ds in June 1916, the latter machine having a 250hp Rolls Royce engine. At the time the FE was the finest two-seater fighting machine in existence, and the squadron soon won a reputation for hard and successful fighting against heavy odds. The armament was three Lewis guns, one of which was fixed in the axis of the machine and fired by the pilot, by a 'Bowden' cable on the control lever. The other two were fired by the observer: one to fire forwards, and the other to fire backwards over the top plane. The principal duties of the squadron on these machines were Offensive Patrols, Photography and Reconnaissance and Bombing by day and by night.

The above is a brief enough epitaph on the passing of the aeroplane that had served 20 Squadron so long and faithfully; but what it lacks in length and poetry can perhaps be read between the lines: 'The finest two-seater fighting machine in existence' and 'hard and successful fighting against heavy odds' and 'Bombing by day and night'.

In the twenty-one months since its arrival in France, 20 Squadron had suffered heavy losses but its members had formed an affectionate trust with their ungainly aeroplanes and had pushed the fight deep into enemy territory day after day, month after month. Their reconnaissances had warned the British ground troops of impending German offensives and of reinforced German defences in advance of British attacks. In keeping with the rest of the Royal Flying Corps, each and every squadron casualty suffered in gaining this vital information had undoubtedly saved many times that number of British lives on the ground.

The FEs were fighter aircraft too. They had arrived in France when the 'Fokker Scourge' was at its height and British air operations in support of the army had become so difficult as to be almost impossible. The 'Fees' had met the Fokkers in combat and proved them wanting. Then having disposed of that problem, they had in turn found themselves somewhat outclassed by the new generation of German Fighting scouts: the fast and nimble Albatrosses and Halberstadts. In many of their fights the 'Fees' had been outnumbered two or three to one but had still held their own and inflicted casualties on the enemy. Most importantly, they had retained possession of the battlefield in the sky so that the British side always had up-to-date reconnaissance information about the Germans – while the Germans, it seems, were seldom permitted to gather a similar amount of such information for themselves. According to Norman Franks, author of numerous highly respected reference works on the First World War in the air, 20 Squadron had claimed a total of no less than 220 combat victories with the FE2B and FE2D. My own tally is slightly higher, at 223; but that is by the way. Had the squadron been equipped with any lesser machine – and there were plenty around – they could never have won the reputation they did. So the 'Fees' passed into 20 Squadron's history. The fast and manoeuvrable Bristol Fighter would prove an inspiring ally in the fourteen months of war remaining, and 20 Squadron would need that ally: for what was yet to come would be just as bloody, and sometimes bloodier still than what they had so far fought through.

******

Although 20 Squadron's pilots and observers were now competent at flying their new Bristol Fighters, many of them still had to learn the best way to use it in combat. Their most demanding examiner would be the enemy, and failure usually meant death. They would not just have to learn new tricks, they would also have to 'unlearn' some old ones. Patrols of several aircraft fighting as a team in tight formations or defensive circles relying on each man knowing and keeping his place would become a thing of the past. Although the patrol members would still be part of a team, the Bristol Fighter's speed and manoeuvrability would allow much more scope for individual initiative in a fight. The unit's most successful crews would be those who used their new mount's attributes to their fullest extent, which meant learning to fly and fight the aircraft as if it were a single-seat scout that could shoot backwards as well as forwards. The fighting roles of the pilot and observer in the FE2D would be almost reversed in the Bristol Fighter. For where the pilot's Lewis gun in the 'Fee' had been something of an afterthought, a secondary weapon occasionally brought into use while the observer did most of the shooting, Bristol Fighter pilots had to learn to use their own gun for the initial attack, and to break off afterwards in such a way as to allow their observers or gunners to exploit the situation.

The full potential of the new fighter was highlighted on Sunday, 23 September when new observer Captain English was flying with Lieutenant Kirkpatrick in A7214 on a late afternoon patrol that fought seven Albatros scouts over Lille. The Bristol Fighter formation got broken up in the failing light and its leader Captain Johnston began trailing the enemy scouts on his own, finally diving on them in a surprise attack that sent one down trailing smoke and which the British anti-aircraft H Battery recorded as having crashed just west of Houthem at 18.30[1]. Such actions would have been almost impossible in the FE2D, which was simply too slow to keep up with or launch surprise attacks on a formation of 'Albatrii', let alone make good its escape afterwards.

The next phase of the land campaign had been pencilled in for 26 September 1917, and 20 Squadron's machines were in the air continuously over the three days preceding it, carrying out the usual mix of reconnaissance and air fighting. The four patrols sent up at various times two days earlier included a new pilot and four new observer/air gunners. South African agriculturist and ex-trooper of 4 South Africa Horse, Second Lieutenant G.D. Jooste BSc (University of Minnesota), was the new pilot flying A7215 as part of the late-afternoon patrol. The new observers included Captain L. W. Burbidge, Captain J.E. Johnston, Lieutenant H. Henry – and the author's maternal grandfather, probationary aerial gunner Driver T2/10816 G.S. Tester. The only noteworthy incident was when Lieutenant Henry and Sergeant Hopper got lost in Bristol Fighter A7123 after becoming separated from the others, and a forced crash-landing at La Gorgue, near St. Marie Cappel, left the lieutenant with serious concussion that brought his 20 Squadron service to an abrupt end. Two days later he was sent back to England for lengthy convalescence. Sergeant Hopper was unhurt.

******

As a flight-commander, the Scottish ship-builder's son Captain J.S. Campbell had the privilege of choosing his regular observer or air gunner, and now chose to adopt 20 Squadron's newest gunner, Driver Tester, to fill the role. Whether this was due to Tester having a reputation as an excellent shot or was simply down to the fact that they could easily understand each-other's thick Scottish brogue will never be known; but they flew together from this point on. The 27-year-old son of a Kirkcaldy blacksmith, George Tester had enlisted as a horse transport driver in the Army Service Corps early in the war and served with 141 Field Ambulance. When his duties had brought him into contact with 20 Squadron he had answered the call for volunteer observer/gunners at a time of grim shortages. His motives probably included a desire for adventure and an end to the depressing routine of bringing back the dead and wounded from the trenches. But being married with a two-year-old daughter, he may also have considered the extra flying pay of four shillings for each day he spent in the air would be very useful to his family. So Driver Tester manned the Lewis gun of Captain Campbell's Bristol Fighter on the mid-morning SOP on Tuesday, 25 September. Road transport, balloon locations and fires were recorded over the Menin, Comines and Wervicq areas during the patrol – which dramatically included a fight with fifteen to twenty Albatros scouts that left B1116 so badly shot up so that Lieutenant Kirkpatrick was forced to land on the British side of the lines with his wounded observer, Captain English.

The early evening patrol was even more eventful. Luchford and Hill led up an NOP of six Bristols at 17.44 that were reduced to four after Second Lieutenants Boles and Berry returned early with a broken gun foresight and Second Lieutenant Morris became so airsick that Second Lieutenant Jooste took him back to base. At about 18.30, six Albatros scouts attacked the four Bristol Fighters over Becelaere and in the ensuing fight Luchford and Hill shot one down that crashed east of Gheluvelt. Second Lieutenant Harrison and Lieutenant White in B1126 got a second in flames in which the observer was credited with the victory. The other two Bristols – Sergeant Hopper and Captain Burbidge in B1111 and Lieutenant Dalley and Sergeant Benger in A7255 – shared one that they sent down out of control. Two German victims of the fight were 20 Squadron's arch-enemy Leutnant Walter Gottsch of Jasta 8, who having been responsible for so many of the squadron's casualties in the past had now been wounded by them for the third time. The other was Leutnant Rudolf Wendelmuth of the same unit who survived after his engine was hit and he had to make a forced-landing[2, 3,7]. British anti-aircraft gunners confirmed one of these victories, and the officer commanding 11 Wing, who was also watching from the ground, reported an enemy aeroplane bursting into flames in the direction of Becelaere at 18.30[1].

The following morning heralded the start of the next stage of the great offensive and once again the British onslaughts saw German retreats. The Australians took the remainder of Polygon Wood and the German trench line to the east of it while English troops took enemy strong points on both sides of the Wieltje-Gravenstafel road. As always, progress was slower along the Menin Road, but by the evening of 27 September the limited objectives planned for that area had been achieved. The Germans were not about to allow this to happen without attempting heavy counter-attacks, of course, and once again 20 Squadron was tasked with looking out for any signs of these so they could be met in time.

The first two patrols mounted on the 26 September were not opposed and, as enemy counter-attacks developed on the ground, a third patrol was ordered to set off at 15.50 in worsening weather. Captain E.H. Johnston and Lieutenant Hone in A7240 led their four-strong reconnaissance at only 4,000ft and particularly noted 'a great amount of MT [motor transport] and horse transport heading in the direction of Gheluwe on the Menin-Ypres road'. This indicated that either many German casualties or even whole units or supplies were being withdrawn from the fighting area. The squadron's recording officer made a note that the patrol was considered to have been most successful. Luchford and Hill then led out the last patrol in the late afternoon with two more new observers, Lieutenants Sanders and Rowan, flying with Chambers and Harrison respectively, although visibility was now so bad that no enemy aircraft or anything else of interest was seen. The day finally ended with Private 9035 C.M. Snoulton, who had flown as an aerial gunner with 20 Squadron after transferring from the Wiltshire Regiment, being temporarily struck off the squadron's strength on being admitted to hospital. It is not clear whether this was due to accident, illness or wounds.

Five more patrols were flown the following day, the first two being carried out without problems while the third brought three more victories to add to the tally. After taking fifteen photographs over the Moorslede area, the five Bristols were attacked by a dozen Albatros scouts. Lieutenants Dalley and Rowan in A7248 shot down one of these in flames while Second Lieutenant Durrand and Sergeant Benger in A7245 did likewise to another. Second Lieutenants Babbage and Purvis in A7255 then got a third out of control. All the Bristol Fighters returned safely, although Dalley and Rowan were lucky to make it back as their machine had been badly shot up, with all its wings, longerons and struts having being hit. The last two patrols passed without casualties.

Captain E.H. Johnston led the first patrol on Friday, 28 September with another new pilot, Second Lieutenant Slade, flying B1111 with Second Lieutenant Morris as his observer. There were no engagements and enemy ground movements appeared to be normal. Eight more Bristol Fighters took off at 11.40 and formed up as two formations of four. One formation was a NOP led by Captain Campbell and the other an SOP led by Kirkpatrick and Veacock. The two formations flew out over the Menin-Wervicq road together and began the usual photography, but they had only exposed ten plates when around twenty-five Albatros scouts came down on them. As the heavily outnumbered Bristol Fighters tried to fight their way home, Luchford and Hill managed to shoot down two of the Germans. Tomlin and Noble were shot down in flames in A7241 a little east of Hollebeke by Leutnant Joseph Veltjens of Jasta 18[2]. Captain Campbell and Driver Tester, flying A7210, were last seen still in combat between Menin and Wervicq and did not return. As the recording officer at St. Marie Cappel wrote tersely in the Squadron Record Book: 'Second Lieutenants Tomlin and Noble are dead. Captain Campbell and Driver Tester are missing.'

Educated in Sussex at Brighton's secondary school and technical college, 20-year-old Harry Francis Tomlin was born in New Malden, Surrey, the son of Harry Tomlin and his wife Alice Louise. Former teacher Harold Taylor Noble, aged 22, the son of Mr and Mrs F. R. Noble from Edmonton, Alberta, first enlisted with the Queen's Battery at Kingston, Ontario, on 9 January 1916 before transferring to HQ 9 Brigade Field Artillery on 1 February 1916. On applying for a commission, he stated that his first preference was to be an observer in the RFC and, unfortunately for him, got his wish being with the squadron just five days before he was killed. Both men are buried at Bailleul. As was usual in such cases, the CO or his appointee would immediately write to the dead or missing airmen's next of kin to inform them of what had happened, and in the case of George Tester, the author's maternal grandfather, the letter was written by the 2 Brigade chaplain and has been preserved by the family.

In the Field,
Sept. 29, 1917

Dear Mrs Tester,

I am writing to inform you that your husband of the 20th Squadron went up yesterday with Captain Campbell and his flight, and both of them have failed to return.

It does not necessarily follow that both of them have been killed, in fact we hope that they may have come down safely and are only prisoners in Germany. The flight went out yesterday morning right over the Hun lines and came across a large number of Hun machines which they at once engaged, and the machine your husband was in was brought down. It is very difficult for others to know what has happened, even to those nearest to him in the fight. One pilot tells us however that he thinks he saw their machine land under control. We do hope this is the case and that they are not even injured.

The officers and all of us are so very sorry for the unnecessary anxiety and suspense that will unfortunately follow until we hear from the Huns. But you may be sure that as soon as we hear news you shall know at once and we will do everything possible to get it as quickly as we can. It is difficult to know what to say, except do not give up hope. Your husband is a brave and splendid fellow and has done splendidly. If he happens to be a prisoner in Germany I don't think you need fear but that he will be well treated. Airmen seem to get special treatment.

If there is anything I can do please write to me c/o 2nd Brigade Headquarters, RFC, BEF. I shall only be too pleased to give you any information I can or to do anything for you that I can. I am so sorry for you,

Yours sincerely,
J W Wallace-Smyth
Chaplain 2nd Brigade RFC

George's wife, Isabella, and Captain Campbell's father, Archibald Campbell, exchanged letters in their efforts to find out whether their missing loved ones were dead or alive, and Campbell Senior used his influence in Spain to enlist the help of Signor Polo de Bernadi, the Spanish Ambassador in Berlin. No news was forthcoming until the end of February 1918 when both men's names were published in a German list of British airmen killed. They had been shot down by Leutnant Harald Auffahrt, of Jasta 18, and the Germans had buried them at Bousbecque. Isabella died three years later and the author's mother, named Mary, was adopted and raised by George's sister, Helen, who lived in South London with her English husband Gilbert Thorns. After the war, the Imperial War Graves Commission exhumed the two bodies and they now rest side-by-side at the Pont-du-Hem military cemetery near Estaires.

******

The squadron soldiered on regardless and, in keeping with Trenchard's policy, two replacement pilots arrived the following day, almost before their predecessors' beds had grown cold. Captain D.D. Walrond-Skinner came from the Monmouth Regiment, while 24-year-old Second Lieutenant David Mackay McGoun was from Montreal, Canada. At St. Marie Cappel there could be no time put aside to get over the loss of another four comrades. Captain Johnston led out the third patrol at 13.20, while Luchford and Hill led out the fourth of the day at 16.45, and Kirkpatrick and Veacock the fifth at the same time. All three patrols had fights but they were inconclusive and ninety-six good photographic plates were successfully exposed over the Army Counter Battery Area.

Sunday, 30 September saw the Germans counter-attacking with flame-throwers north of the Menin Road and 20 Squadron carrying out three more patrols. Captain E.H. Johnston led up the first patrol of four Bristols at 09.50, and they exposed a further seventy plates over the Army Counter Battery Area, reporting exceptionally heavy movements along the Roulers-Menin road. A second patrol of four Bristols led by Lieutenant Kirkman used a wide-angle camera to photograph an 'immense area' over and around Courtrai. When some enemy scouts attempted to climb up to them, the Bristols simply climbed higher still, to over 18,000ft and well beyond the reach of the Germans. Being able to do this must have given the British a great sense of satisfaction that would most certainly have outweighed any thoughts about the bitter cold at such a height. It was much better to be cold than to go down in flames! A third patrol of five Bristols led by Harry Luchford in B1122 also found signs of heavy road activity near Menin, but the enemy aircraft they saw kept a long way off.

******

Notes

1.   Combat Report.
2.   *The Jasta War Chronology* by Norman Franks, et al.
3.   My thanks to Russ Gannon.
4.   *The Sky Their Battlefield* by Trevor Henshaw.
5.   Personnel records: AIR 79, WO 339, and Casualty Report: AIR 1/968/204/5/1100.
6.   II Brigade Operations Order; AIR/1/931/204/5/927.
7.   20 Squadron Record Book.

Chapter 16

Passchendaele: October/November 1917

More than 150 valuable reconnaissance photographs had been taken over the last two days of September and on 1 October another eighteen were added. They had been specifically requested by Corps HQ and five Bristol Fighters led by Luchford and Hill engaged four 'Albatrii' over Roulers at 14.45 to cover Chambers and Berry as they raced B1125 back across the lines to drop them off. Luchford and Hill, flying B1122, then claimed an Albatros as shot down southeast of Roulers that may have been Leutnant E. Wendler of Jasta 17, who crashed after being wounded, although it also possible he fell in other fights[1,2,3,4]. The photographs safely delivered to the Belgian RFC HQ, Chambers and Berry rejoined the patrol later.

The following day brought two more fights at 15,000ft over the Moorslede-Roulers area, after four 'Biffs' were attacked by fifteen 'Albatrii'. The result was a measure of the fact that the Bristol Fighter pilots were now starting to use their new mounts to their full potential. Already aware that they could climb higher and faster than the Albatros, they now found they could also turn more tightly than the Albatros scouts at high altitude. This meant that an outnumbered but high-flying Bristol Fighter patrol could, unless caught unawares, stay above the enemy, choose when to fight, and then keep the advantage in the fight. This sort of performance was as good as any single-seater, let alone an aeroplane that had a rear gunner defending the tail[1, 4].

Rain and a strong southwesterly wind prevented flying on the morning of Wednesday, 3 October but improved enough for Lieutenant Kirkpatrick to lead up an SOP of five machines at 14.11. Thick clouds hampered the reconnaissance work but did not prevent the patrol diving on six Albatrosses they found 3,000ft below them over Wervicq. The enemy fled and, as they did so, Second Lieutenant A.G.V. Taylor, who was struggling to clear a stoppage in his Vickers gun, found himself alone in the sky with A7245 flown by McGoun and Veacock. The Two Bristol Fighters headed west together and, when they were somewhat north of Wervicq, the 'Albatrii' returned and attacked from out of the sun. Second Lieutenant Taylor's observer, Sergeant Benger, sent one of them down out of control[1] and the safe return of the two 'Biffs' brought the day's flying to an end.

With so much of the Third Ypres offensive having been delayed by continuous rain and almost impassable mud, it was clear to Sir Douglas Haig and his commanders that the most they could now hope to achieve before winter set in would be to extend the line of captured ridges to a point where they could be defended against counter-attacks. They settled on the already ruined village of Passchendaele. The only problem was getting there; but since doing anything else would leave many of the front-line troops in very exposed positions, a standstill until the following spring was not an option. So, albeit reluctantly because of the weather conditions, Haig decided to proceed with an attack on the 4 October. The main assaults were to go in against the ridges east of Zonnebeke, while limited attacks would also be made south of the Menin Road to consolidate the gains already been made there. Despite the rain and clouds that made most operational flying almost impossible, reconnaissance missions were essential to report on the British advance and any German counter-moves. So at 11.34 Harry Luchford led up a special reconnaissance of four Bristols in 'a blizzard of fine rain'. Flying at only 500ft, the Bristols swept over Polygon Wood and north to Zonnebeke Lake before turning southeast along the Dadizeele-Becelaere Road, where they spotted about 2,000 enemy troops marching west towards the fighting. Luchford immediately put out a wireless 'zone call' asking for an immediate artillery bombardment, and this was quickly answered by the heavy guns of the Anzac Corps pouring down a deluge of shells that shattered the enemy columns. The 20 Squadron recording officer made a special note that: 'The Wing Commander sent his congratulations to Lieutenant Luchford and his companions on the splendid results of this fine effort.'[4] As for the renewed ground offensive, General Haig was able to report in his dispatches that 'it was successful at all points', with German counter-attacks being beaten off yet again and our armies just a little closer to the end of the campaign.

Luchford was in action again the following morning when he led an NOP of four Bristol Fighters charging to the rescue of a flight of SE5As under attack from twenty Albatros scouts. The Germans were driven off after a short fight, but when the SE5A and Bristol Fighter formations regrouped they were each one aircraft short. Bristol Fighter B1133 was last seen losing height over Roulers before it was lost sight of in the clouds, having fallen to the guns of Leutnant E. Bohme of Jasta 2; its occupants, Captain D.D. Walrond-Skinner and Private F.J. Johns, managed to land and were taken prisoner. The missing 56 Squadron SE5 was that of Second Lieutenant C.H. Jeffs who was also a prisoner after being shot down by Oberleutnant Bruno Loerzer of Jasta 26[2]. The flyers of 56 Squadron appreciated the Bristol Fighters' timely intervention, and sent a thank-you telegram shortly afterwards.

The losses were somewhat compensated by two victory claims submitted later in the day. The first of these came after B1114 flown by Lieutenant Slade and Gunner Veale lost contact with Captain E.H. Johnston's SOP after a sudden storm caused them to drop far behind. Around 11.30, although they were still alone, they dived on three Albatros scouts over Ledeghem and Gunner Veale got a good burst into the centre one. Slade reported that he watched it fall all the way from 11,000ft to 1,000ft before he lost sight of it in low clouds. The other two Albatrosses dived away, probably having spotted the approach of the rest of the British patrol coming to Slade's and Veale's aid. More rain swept in however, and after losing their colleagues once again, Slade and Veale landed near Armentieres. Gunner Veale had done well – but the aftermath provided another example of the conditions under which the flying services fought. The ground temperature had been recorded as 52F that day (or about 11C). This was not particularly cold but, with an average temperature loss of about 2 degrees centigrade per 1,000ft of height and the wind–chill factor created by a 100-120 mph slipstream, the effect on the body was closer to minus 40F (which is also minus 40C). Regular flyers wrapped up well before setting out each day; but occasional gunners volunteering from the ranks would not always have been so well equipped with all the scarves, woollens and leathers that the officers possessed, and also may not have been so scrupulous in the application of whale fat and Vaseline to their faces before take-off. Whether it was lack of the preferred clothing or other precautions is not known, but Gunner Veale had suffered such severe facial frostbite that he was immediately admitted to hospital.

In a mid-afternoon patrol, five Bristols attacked twelve 'Albatrii' over Becelaere around 16.35. Captain E.H. Johnston and Lieutenant Hone in A7240 sent one of these spinning down and, along with other pilots, watched it fall all the way down to within a couple of hundred feet above the ground. His combat report pointed out that it looked as if it could not avoid crashing[1]. About ten minutes later, the patrol dived on a two-seater west of Ypres, the enemy diving into the clouds in order to escape. This was in vain, however, for on re-emerging from the clouds, the German machine found itself in the middle of a formation of 1 Squadron's Nieuports, and was promptly shot down in flames – to join two others claimed by the same squadron that day[3].

That brought to an end the day's action, tales of which must have given an instant insight of life at the front to new observer Second Lieutenant D. French, who had just been posted to 20 Squadron. Another recent arrival, pilot Tommy Colvill-Jones, was settling in well, and bad weather on 6 October gave him a chance to write to his family in Argentina. In his letter, he told his mother that new pilots usually dined in the HQ Mess for the first week or so in order to get to know the CO better, and that he thought Major Mansfield 'a very decent chap'. He also described how they lived in huts holding six officers each that were 'very nice and comfy', and how everyone liked the cinema that had been set up at St. Marie Cappel, supplied with films hired in the local town, which was probably Cassel[5]. The few patrols the flyers were able to carry out over the next two days brought another loss when Second Lieutenant W.D. Chambers and Lieutenant F. Berry were forced to land B1125 on the German side of the lines after engine failure during a fight on 8 October. A post-war report by Chambers stated that they had brought down an enemy machine before being forced to land, their capture coming on the very same day that 11 Wing Routine Orders announced that Francis Berry was now permitted to wear his lieutenant's badges pending notification of his promotion in the *London Gazette*.

At 05.20 on Tuesday, 9 October, 2nd Army's X Corps and I and II Anzac Corps attacked northwards from the Menin road across the ground on which now stands the famous Tyne Cot Cemetery, while Gough's 5th Army attacked in the Poelcappelle and Langemark area. Above them, 20 Squadron assisted the ground forces by flying four patrols over the battlefronts, although few enemy aircraft were seen until mid-afternoon when an NOP led by Luchford and Hill fought an indecisive engagement with twenty to thirty enemy scouts beyond the Roulers–Menin Road. An SOP brought an almost miraculous escape for Dalley and Brooke when A7269 took a direct hit from a shell that wrecked the Scarfe Mounting and passed clean through the fuselage without exploding. Robert Slade was not quite so lucky, though, taking shrapnel wounds in his arm while flying A7193. It seems that Harry Luchford and his four-strong NOP met a new opponent when, assisted by some SPADs and SE5s, they tangled with twelve German scouts over Moorslede on 11 October. Luchford shot down an Albatros in flames while his gunner, Sergeant Benger, got a second out of control. Another German aircraft, described as an 'Enemy Nieuport type', was claimed shot down out of control by Sergeant Frank Johnston and Lieutenant Sanders, and this was very likely the Pfalz DIII scout in which Jasta 10's Leutnant Gustav Bellen was reported severely wounded in combat in the same area. Bellen had one balloon victory credit at this time and would not get any more, as after hospitalisation he was declared permanently unfit for flying[1, 6].

In compliance with General Haig's policy of 'bite and hold' attacks, the first Battle of Passchendaele began at 05.25 the following morning, 12 October. It did not get far. Heavy rain and hail, allied with dogged German resistance, limited the advance to little more than 100 yards along the whole front despite heavy casualties. Unfailingly, 20 Squadron went up regardless, Captain Warden making his operational debut flying as Sergeant Hopper's observer during a morning patrol of five Bristols, during which the patrol made some useful observations of large German troop movements along the Menin road. A new pilot flying with a later patrol that went up at 11.56 was Second Lieutenant B. Starfield, while observer Lieutenant Wornum made his first operational sortie with Second Lieutenant Simpson as his pilot. By early afternoon, the clouds came down to 250ft forcing Harry Luchford to abandon the day's last patrol shortly after take-off. The bad weather continued throughout the following day as Tommy Colvill-Jones and L.H. Phelps flew their first mission across the lines. Further patrols were abandoned.

In addition to wind, rain and fighting, the first half of October had also brought a number of administrative and personnel changes not mentioned so far. The first news, and it was good news for some, came when 11 Wing Routine Orders relayed an announcement from the War Office stating that, from 2 April 1917, qualified officer observers actively and continuously employed in aerial observation duty, or on sick leave or who were qualified in their rank and grade on the date of their capture, would now receive the same level of continuous flying pay as pilots: an extra five shillings a day. Claims for periods prior to 2 April and from those not yet fully qualified would continue to be paid only for the days they actually flew, and those captured before 2 April or before they qualified would receive no extra pay from the day they ceased flying. This was followed a few days later by a *London Gazette* announcement that recently promoted Temporary Captain Harry Luchford and his now usual observer Second Lieutenant Richard Hill were each awarded the Military Cross. In addition to the above, Wing Routine Orders announced that Captain Burbidge and Lieutenant Rowan were now officially permitted to wear the observer's badge. Three aerial gunners were also posted to the squadron, these being qualified aerial gunner Air Mechanic Second Class 36564 J. McMechan and probationary aerial gunners Air Mechanics First Class 20024 M. Mather and 36233 H. Townsend. Bill Cambray and A.N. Jenks were posted back to England for Home Establishment duties after five months at the front, while Second Lieutenant R.S.V. Morris was admitted to hospital with concussion on 7 October. Second Lieutenant J.G.E. Green returned to the 10 Welsh Regiment after a brief attachment with 20 Squadron and Lieutenant Hone and Second Lieutenant Babbage were given two weeks leave.

Although heavy cloud persisted, the weather finally cleared enough for Captain Luchford to lead up a four-strong mid-morning photo-reconnaissance on Sunday, 14 October. Eight to ten Albatrosses came down on them from higher clouds and scattered the formation, forcing N.V. Harrison to run for the lines in a badly shot-up B1137. Hotly pursued by three 'Albatrii', he was very lucky to make it across to the British side and a successful crash-landing at 6 Squadron's aerodrome; but his observer John Percy Fitzherbert Adams was dead. A possibly unusual candidate for a fighting role, the 26-year-old son of Colonel Herbert and Mrs Emma Adams, from Exmouth, Devon, had been educated at Oxford and Durham universities before leaving for Canada where he was ordained as reverend and assistant curate at the Cathedral of Newfoundland. He returned to England following the outbreak of war and, after being commissioned into 11 Battalion Durham Light Infantry, was sent to France where he was wounded by shrapnel on 4 August 1916. Accepted into the RFC as a probationary observer on 25 May 1917, he had been with 20 Squadron only since mid-September and is buried at Lijssenthoek.

The following day, Monday, 15 October, brought another loss. As R.H. Kirkman and R.F. Hill left for two weeks leave, an SOP led by Captain A.G.V. Taylor ran into eight Albatros scouts north of Wervicq at 14.10. The clash resulted in two deaths: John Dalley, a married man who had previously served with 104 Rifles of the Indian Army and Leslie Gould, who was born in London but whose family now lived in Winnipeg, were killed near Becelaere, most likely by Jasta 36 pilot Leutnant H Hoyer. Their bodies were not found and both are remembered at the Arras Flying Services Memorial[1]. The 'out of control' victory over an Albatros claimed by Lieutenant Kirkpatrick and Second Lieutenant N. Couve in the same fight was of little comfort.

The day also brought the squadron a change in command. Major Mansfield was transferred to Home Establishment and Captain E.H. Johnston assumed temporary command of the squadron; an appointment that was soon made permanent and for which position he was promoted to Temporary Major. This marked real progress for the young South African, who had enlisted in 2 Imperial Light Horse in November 1914 for the German Southwest Africa Campaign. After being promoted to lance corporal, he was recommended for a commission in the Royal Flying Corps, and in August 1916 his appointment as a flight commander and temporary captain was announced in the *London Gazette*[7].

******

The four patrols that were carried out on 16 October completed their photography and reconnaissance tasks without interruption, but there was more fighting the following morning. German fighters were very active, and at about 08.40 Captain Taylor's patrol of five Bristols encountered nine Albatros scouts in the Houthulst-Zonnebeke area. Four of these swept down on B1114 flown by Second Lieutenant French, and Gunner Veale, who had now recovered from his frostbite, managed to shoot one down that was seen by his pilot to crash. Makepeace and Waddington then shot down another 'out of control' that was getting onto French's tail, and then a second that tried to get on their own tail[1]. But the other side of the coin came when Bristol Fighter A7271, crewed by acting flight commander Captain A.G.V. Taylor and Sergeant William Benger, went down in flames. Both men were rescued from the wreckage alive but later died from their wounds. Although he was born in England, with a mother living in Cornwall, Arthur Gilbert Vivian Taylor had come to the war from India, where he had served with the 41 'Dogras'. His observer, 22-year-old William Joseph Benger, from Epsom, Surrey, died two days before it was confirmed that he had been awarded the Military Medal for his previous exploits. Taylor and Benger had shot down almost a dozen German aircraft between them, with Taylor being credited with seven and Benger five. Neither Taylor nor Benger's bodies was found, and both are remembered at the Arras Flying Services Memorial. They were not the only casualties, however; Stanley Veacock, Lieutenant Kirkpatrick's observer in A7193, was shot through the abdomen and died shortly after landing. A 27-year-old married man, Veacock came from Hammersmith, London, and had served four years in the Territorials with 13 County of London Regiment before enlisting full-time with the 1 Sportsmen's Battalion of the Royal Fusiliers on 6 October 1914. He is buried at Hazebrouk. The likeliest German victors for this fight would seem to be Jasta 36's Leutnant Quandt accounting for A7271 and Leutnant Bongartz shooting-up A7193[2].

These losses were partly redressed when an SOP attacked four DFWs west of Menin at 09.25, with Second Lieutenants Durrand and Woodbridge in A7141 shooting one down that Captain Burbidge, observer in B1126 saw crash two miles north of Bousbecque[1]. Shortly afterwards at around 10.00, a photo-reconnaissance flight of four Bristols met up with six Albatrosses and two two-seaters over Dadizeele. Harry Luchford and Lieutenant White, flying B1138, shot down one that crashed near the village, while Lieutenant Jooste and Captain Johnston in A7256 got another in flames that was confirmed by Second Lieutenant Couve, observer in A7250, and by the men of H' Anti-Aircraft Battery who had watched the fight from a great distance[1].

There was more fighting for Harry Luchford during the first patrol on Thursday, 18 October when he rescued an RE 8 from three enemy scouts between Roulers and Houthulst, and drove one down to crash between Houthem and Tenbrichen at 08.45. Fifteen minutes later he attacked a DFW near Dadizeele and, after firing about 200 rounds into it from his front gun, manoeuvred to allow

V.R S. White to give it a further raking. The German pilot slumped lifelessly in his cockpit and Lieutenant Waddington flying in another Bristol confirmed its crash near Dadizeele[1]. Luchford had enjoyed a productive morning but he missed out on the afternoon's fight when he had to return early from the patrol after his trigger-bar snapped. The others went on without him, however, and after meeting seven Albatros scouts over Gheluvelt at 16.10, Tommy Colvill-Jones and Lieutenant Phelps in B1139 shot down one of them out of control, with British gunners confirming the victory after watching the fight from the trenches[1].

There was another fight on Saturday, 20 October. The four Bristol Fighters that went up at 07.27 took on a total of fifteen enemy scouts in different groups over Dadizeele at between 7,000ft and 12,000ft. After making five separate attacks, Second Lieutenant Boles and Lieutenant Rowan in A7240 managed to send down one of them out of control[1]. However, A7245 was badly shot up and its control wires subsequently gave way over 6 Squadron's aerodrome. The machine plunged into the ground, crushing Robert Slade's legs and concussing his observer G.B. Booth. The culprit in this case may well have been Jasta 18's Offizierstellvertreter Klein who claimed a DH4 (which was often confused with a Bristol Fighter) as damaged over this area at about the right time[2, 3].

With renewed land attacks planned for the following morning, 20 Squadron mounted at least two patrols on the Sunday. Haze and ground mists hindered the photographic reconnaissance that set out at 11.16, although the OP that set out at 14.30 did see some action. Harry Luchford led his flight down onto a group of seven Albatros scouts and two LVGs engaged in artillery spotting, and while Luchford attacked one of them, the rest of the patrol engaged the escorts. Luchford and White gave the LVG a heavy strafing from both guns, and its crash was witnessed by British ground troops[1]. The ground attacks carried out by the British on 22 October brought limited advances east of Poelcappelle and within the southern edge of Houthulst Forest, this being in the absence of air cover from 20 Squadron as the poor weather prevented any flying until early afternoon. Even when the Bristol Fighters did get airborne, including new arrival Captain Knight flying A7285 with Second Lieutenant Agelasto as his observer, they proved of little benefit to the ground troops as the weather made photography impossible. A second reconnaissance fared only slightly better by exposing 33 plates over ground that was barely visible. The weather really closed in after that and only the occasional patrol was sent up when conditions allowed.

The next air fight did not come until a full day after British and Canadian infantry had secured a small but significant hill south of Passchendaele and beat off the enemy's counter-attacks. Then, at 12.27 on 27 October, Durrand and

Woodbridge led up a reconnaissance of six Bristols over the Staden-Roulers-Menin area and shot down an Albatros that crashed approximately half-way between Wervicq and Comines (Sheet 28.P.36) at 13.15. Another Albatros was shot down out of control by McGoun and Couve in A7250 but they could not watch it down to the ground due to attacks by other enemy aircraft[1]. Later in the afternoon, Second Lieutenant Babbage's observer in B1104, Gunner McMechan, engaged one of two Albatros scouts that dived onto the Bristols from 'out of the high mist' and sent it falling out of control for several thousand feet before losing sight of it[1].

On Tuesday, 30 October, Canadian troops reached the outskirts of Passchendaele and beat off a succession of counter-attacks with the aid of some German machine-guns they had captured during earlier fighting. Other advances on the lower ground came to nothing in the impassable mud-swamps but the Canadian achievements had brought the campaign to within a hair's breadth of its end. The air fighting that accompanied the ground battle proved very interesting for Second Lieutenant Wilfrid Beaver as he made his first patrol east of the lines. Lacking the experience and local knowledge of his colleagues, Beaver lost his way in the heavy clouds and, on coming out of them, was attacked by two Albatrosses that shot his observer Private C.M. Snoulton through his thigh. Beaver ran for the lines and, having made it back in one piece, went up for another patrol, led by Captain Knight and Lieutenant Wornum, in which he again met the enemy. At 11.15 the four-strong formation engaged nine Albatros scouts at 11,000ft over Gheluvelt, during which Wornum's Scarfe-ring gun mounting was hit and damaged by an explosive shell. It was not put out of action, though, and Wornum was able to return fire and send the Albatros plunging a long way down apparently out of control. The patrol returned unscathed, which was a little fortunate perhaps, as in addition to having the still inexperienced Wilfrid Beaver in its number, it also included three newcomers: Lieutenants Noon and Wallis, flying as observers with Second Lieutenant French and Lieutenant Brander respectively, and new aerial gunner Air Mechanic Second Class Thomas flying with Tommy Colvill-Jones in B1122.

Yet more bad weather ensured there was little flying for 20 Squadron during the first few days of November; but in the meantime, the ground troops were preparing for the 'final push' that would bring the Third Ypres campaign to an end. The RFC would play its part – with crucial actions on 6 November as the ground battles moved rapidly towards their climax. That Tuesday dawned overcast with occasional showers, though far from cold at 52F, as the Canadians launched their assault at 06.00 and 20 Squadron's first patrol going up in the rain at 07.21. It returned two short. Second Lieutenant E.S. Brander and Air

Mechanic First Class A. Townsend in B1114 were badly shot up in a fight with German scouts but, although both wounded, managed to make a forced landing at 29 Squadron. The other missing crew had not been so lucky. According to the 20 Squadron Record Book, Second Lieutenant C.B. Simpson and J.H.W. Duggan in B1139 got lost in the clouds and were both dead, apparently brought down by anti-aircraft fire. Claude Battwell Simpson, 26, was a married South African who had been with 20 Squadron since June 1917. His observer Joseph Duggan was a 27-year-old single man, the son of the late John Thomas Duggan and Mrs R.A. Smith (formerly Duggan) of Redcliffe, Bristol. He had previously served with the Gloucestershire Regiment. Yet again, neither of the men's remains were found and they are both are remembered at the Arras Flying Services Memorial.

Passchendaele and the eastern crest beyond it fell three hours later. Despite the appalling casualty lists since the campaign began with the mining of the Messines Ridge back in June, Haig had finally achieved his minimum objectives. The Germans no longer held the high ground overlooking the salient, and it could be supposed that that this would make life much safer for everyone on the British side. It was also hoped the British gains would provide a good jumping-off line for future offensives. The Passchendaele campaign, however, would not officially end until 10 November.

On Thursday, 7 November, 20 Squadron carried out three unopposed patrols, while the following day brought three more victory claims. At 07.30 Captain Knight's NOP of nine Bristol Fighters got the better of five Albatros scouts when Lieutenant Hutchinson, Second Lieutenant Starfield's observer in A7255, fired about 200 rounds at the rearmost one and sent it into a steep dive earthwards from which it did not recover, its crash being witnessed by a British anti-aircraft battery[1]. An afternoon patrol brought a fortunate escape for Lieutenants Kirkpatrick and Brooke in A7193 after they became separated from their formation and were attacked by four Albatros scouts that pounced on them over Staden. One of the 'Albatrii' fell out of control and burst into flames after Brooke fired three drums into it at very close range, his victory claim confirmed by Lieutenant Kirkman and Captain Burbidge and by 'H' AA Battery RA.[1]. Half-an-hour later, British anti-aircraft fire alerted the patrol to five more Albatros scouts over Houthulst Forest, and one of these was promptly brought down and reported as crashed northeast of the forest by newly promoted Captain Durrand and Second Lieutenant Woodbridge in A7253[1]. Despite the clarity of the day's three combat reports, it appears that HQ downgraded the results somewhat; RFC Communiqué 113 crediting Starfield and Hutchinson with one enemy aircraft seen by ground observers to crash, while the other two crews, Kirkpatrick and Brooke and Durrand and Woodbridge, being credited only with 'driven down out of control' victories. There was no further fighting before night fell, thus ending 20 Squadron's last day of fighting in the Third Ypres campaign. There was little flying on 9 and 10 November, although Lieutenant Couve was injured and admitted to hospital after Lieutenant Kirkpatrick wrecked A7118 in a crash northeast of Ypres. Other than that, the last two days of the campaign mainly involved training flights for some of the many new pilots and observers who had arrived in the previous few weeks.

The list of new arrivals and departures was lengthy. New pilots posted in included Second Lieutenant R.F. Tattersall, Lieutenant L.S. Brander, Londoner Second Lieutenant Douglas Cooke and Second Lieutenant Wilfrid Beaver – the latter who, although born in Bristol, had emigrated to the USA some years earlier and returned to England when war broke out. New observers arriving over this period included Lieutenants L.H. Gould and A. Hutchinson, and Second Lieutenants C.J. Agelasto, J.H.W. Duggan, W.T.V. Harmer, F.O. Wallis and G. Noon. In addition, Lieutenant Wornum, Captain Warden, Captain J. E. Johnston and Canadian Lieutenant N.M. Sanders were all told they could now put up their observer wings. Among the other ranks, 71991 E.M. Veale was officially passed out as a qualified aerial gunner and was soon joined in this work by Corporal F. Archer who had originally joined the RFC as a carpenter and had just transferred in from 19 Squadron on re-classification as a qualified aerial gunner. Private 13010 B. Matthews of the Army Cyclist Corps also arrived at the squadron as a probationary aerial gunner.

Departures included Captain Burbidge and Lieutenant Kirkpatrick starting two weeks leave on the 20 November. On 27 October Lieutenant John Alfred Hone was medically boarded unfit for further front-line service and he was posted back to England for light duties and convalescence. Hone had served in Salonika before joining the RFC and had suffered a decline in his health that began when he contracted paratyphoid during RFC training in Egypt. The 22-year-old native of Tewkesbury, Gloucestershire, would not return to the squadron but after the war would apply himself to collecting all the squadron's surviving paperwork and laying the groundwork for an eventual history of 20 Squadron. The lists of personnel, combat victories and decorations and awards he compiled did not result in such a history at the time but, retained in the safe keeping of the National Archives at Kew, have been an invaluable aid to the author of this history. The squadron's recording officer, Second Lieutenant W.E.G. Bryant, who had come to the RFC from the Royal Fusiliers, was also on his way home; and the author also acknowledges that his detailed compilation of the 20 Squadron Record Book has, like Lieutenant Hone's notes, also proved of great value. Also posted home was Frank Babbage, who had been in France for more than six months and would now enjoy a brief leave before being posted to a flying school. Notable announcements in 11 Wing Routine Orders came on 27 October declaring that temporary Captain H.G.E. Luchford and Lieutenant V.R.S. White had each been awarded Bars to their Military Crosses, followed two weeks later by the announcement that Second Lieutenant Richard Hill had also been awarded a Bar to his Military Cross.

******

Notes

1.   Combat Report.
2.   *The Jasta War Chronology* by Norman Franks et al.
3.   Thanks to Russ Gannon.
4.   20 Squadron Record Book.
5.   Thanks to Lorraine Colvill-Jones.
6.   *Above the Lines* by N. Franks, F. Bailey & R. Duiven.
7.   My thanks to Michael Laidlaw.

Chapter 17

Winter War 1 – November/December 1917

E ven though the ground campaign had ended, continued air operations were still needed to spot any signs of a major German counter-offensive and to keep the Germans guessing as to what the British might do next. Thus, except for the limitations on flying imposed by the shorter days and worsening weather of the approaching winter, the war continued as usual. There were a considerable number of personnel changes, though, as replacement pilots and observers, most of them fresh from training, provided the numbers to allow some of the squadron's members to be granted leave, others to attend courses and two to be sent back to England for Home Establishment postings.

In addition to those already mentioned, two new pilot arrivals were Second Lieutenant S.A. Mowatt on 18 November and Second Lieutenant J.J. Gowing on the 30 November. Five new Lieutenant observers were also posted in on the 12 November. These were A.D. Keith (Canadian Local Forces) and J.D. Boyd (British Columbia Regiment), and Britishers S.T. Lyon (the Middlesex Regiment), F.B. Gloster (Army Service Corps) and L.R. Speakman (ASC). Second Lieutenant observers arriving at the squadron around the 30 November were H.S. Clements (ASC), H.G. Crowe (Royal Irish Regiment.) and H.E. Easton (London Regiment). Probationary Observer Lieutenants Phelps and Hutchinson were allowed to wear their Wings from 11 November, followed about a week later by Second Lieutenant Harmer. A new aerial gunner, Air Mechanic Garrick also arrived at this time.

There were also some new faces on the ground at St. Marie Cappel. Medical Officer Captain H.B. Porteous, RAMC (T) and his assistant Private 106391 H.J. Webb were posted in around the 20 November, followed two days later by the arrival of intelligence officer Second Lieutenant R.V. Oliver from the Border Regiment. Second Lieutenant Oliver took command of a new 20 Squadron intelligence section that comprised six other ranks posted in from 14 Wing. These included Sergeant 1530 W.J. Crabbe and Sappers 244271 J.E. Watts, 245951 D. Kennard and 245529 A. Brady, along with Private 240119 J. Burnes from the Border Regiment and Private 1311 T.E. Sudds from the Surrey Regiment. The main purpose of the intelligence branch at a reconnaissance squadron was to maintain the cameras to the highest standard and ensure that photographs were developed and printed as quickly as possible after a mission before they were sent on to the brigade for detailed analysis. As well as having overall control of this, it is also likely that the Intelligence Officer would have been involved in keeping the squadron's officers informed of new developments and military dispositions that were likely to affect them.

Second Lieutenant C.B. Stratton left the squadron on posting to Home Establishment on 19 November followed on 30 November by Captain Satchell, who had joined the Honourable Artillery Company in 1914 and had seen active service with the Royal Warwickshire Regiment. Also leaving the squadron for good was former armaments officer Lieutenant G.M.F. Prynne, who was returning to the Border Regiment. A lucky few got two weeks leave during the course of the month: starting with Second Lieutenants Jooste, Woodbridge and Purvis, then aerial gunner Private 13010 B. Matthews, followed by Captain Durrand and Lieutenant Rowan on and finally McGoun and Sanders. A temporary departure was that of Second Lieutenant C. Agelasto, who was admitted to hospital on 20 November through sickness and returned in late December. There were also two promotions: Captain Johnston was officially confirmed as the new Commanding Officer and promoted to major, while Second Lieutenant W. Durrand was confirmed as Temporary Captain and Flight Commander, a role he had been carrying out for several days.

******

Misty, murky weather prevented much being accomplished on 11 November, while slightly better conditions the next day brought a fight for the NOP that set off at 13.30 led by Captain Knight and Lieutenant Wornum. At about 14.45 they engaged seven Albatros scouts at 11,000ft over Wervicq: two being driven down out of control by the patrol leaders while another was sent down in similar condition by Second Lieutenants Boles and Wallis, flying A7253. Two of the three claims were allowed as 'decisive out of control' victories. The only other flying during the day included Major Johnston and Lieutenant Purvis carrying out a 'special mission' in mid-afternoon, and two crews practising with the Hythe Camera Gun: an invention that looked and handled like a Lewis gun but, instead of firing bullets, took photographs when the trigger was pulled.

The following afternoon, Tuesday, 13 November, brought a mid-afternoon fight at 10,000ft over Houthulst Forest in which eight of the squadron's Bristol Fighters, including Second Lieutenant Clark on his first patrol over the lines, fought a number of 'Albatrii'. Beaver and Agelasto dived B883 onto the tail of one and chased it down to 3,000ft, firing all the time until it crashed into the ground southeast of the forest where Second Lieutenant Starfield reported it caught fire. Lieutenant Kirkman's observer, Captain Burbidge, sent another down out of control after emptying three drums of ammunition into it during a second engagement about fifteen minutes later[1], while Second Lieutenant French and Noon got badly shot-up in A7164 and had to force-land at Reninghelst. The only patrol flown on Wednesday, 14 November almost ended in disaster when three of the four machines lost their bearings because of dense ground mists. Makepeace and Harmer were uninjured after making a forced landing near Estaires in B1155, but Air Mechanic First Class McMechan was admitted to hospital after Second Lieutenant Babbage wrecked A7223 when he force-landed near Hondeghen. McMechan was joined in the same hospital by Second Lieutenant Wallis after Second Lieutenant Clark similarly damaged B1114 in a forced landing near Morbecque. There was better luck the following day. Four Bristols on a photo-reconnaissance mission over the Lille-Menin-Courtrai area met up with five Albatros scouts over Moorslede. Makepeace and Harmer in A7193 pursued one of them as it tried to escape into clouds and shot it down out of control, their claim being confirmed by British anti-aircraft gunners[1].

The fair weather did not last long and there was little flying from 16 to 26 November, during which period six pilots and six observers and aerial gunners were sent on a gunnery course at the RFC Musketry Range at Berck-sur-Mer. There is no mention of any fighting in the 20 Squadron Record Book, but casualty reports for 18 November indicate that Second Lieutenant B Starfield was injured in a flying accident and that observers Second Lieutenant F.B. Wallis and Lieutenant L.H. Phelps were both wounded in action.

For 20 Squadron, the war did not resume in earnest until Tuesday, 27 November when six machines went up on a NOP in the afternoon but became separated in the low clouds and poor visibility. Colvill-Jones and Captain Speakman were alone at only 2,500ft over Westroosebeke when they were attacked by two German scouts that they described as 'enemy Nieuports' but which were most likely the new Pfalz DIIIs. Captain Speakman was able to fire a whole drum into one of the attackers that went down 'completely out of control', while the other Pfalz broke off and escaped. A possible German casualty might be Jasta 26's OfStv Otto Esswein who was wounded. The two victors then returned to St. Marie Cappel and made a safe landing despite B1122's aileron controls having been shot away.

The next day saw the squadron back in the familiar routine of photo-reconnaissance and offensive patrols; but there was no fighting until the following day when five machines on a N.O.P. met up with two enemy formations over Ypres at 10.52. French and Keith brought an Albatros scout down out of control over Moorslede, but shortly afterwards 2/Lt's E.V. Clark and G. Noon were flying just below the clouds when they were suddenly dived on and shot down in flames by three enemy machines that immediately climbed back up into the clouds. They had lasted less than three weeks. The enemy aircraft were identified as DFW two-seaters in the Squadron Record Book, but the vaguely similarly shaped Pfalz DIII is more likely as Jasta 36's Ltn Harry von Bulow-Bothkamp claimed a Bristol F2B shot down northeast of Moorslede at around 13.00[7].

Surrey-born Ernest Vaughan Clark, aged 24, came to the war from Port Elizabeth, South Africa, where he had served as a Sergeant in 'Prince Alfred's Guards' in August 1915. After being commissioned in the Royal Fusiliers, he was seriously wounded in the head and both legs in October 1916 and transferred to the RFC the following June. Gilbert Noon, a 21-year-old former schoolmaster, had studied at University College, Nottingham and was a cadet in Durham University OTC in 1915. Commissioned into 6 Battalion, the Sherwood Foresters, he left his lace-maker mother, Jane Noon; his father having already died. A few weeks later, as if to prove that chivalry could still exist despite all the death and carnage, a German aeroplane dropped a message over the British lines confirming the deaths of the two officers, and the news was passed on by the War Office to Ernest Clark's mother. However, it appears that the War Office felt it might not be a good thing for this German chivalry to be advertised, and the letter to Mrs Clark concluded that: 'The Military Secretary desires to add that under no circumstances whatever should the source of this information be divulged in any obituary or other notices inserted in the Press or elsewhere.'[2, 3, 4].

******

Poor weather on Saturday, 1 December limited 20 Squadron's flying to a few engine tests, with the veteran Harry Luchford taking up new observer Lieutenant Harold Easton on one of these. Easton was a 23-year-old who was wounded in France on 27 May 1915 while serving with the Queen Victoria's Rifles, and was subsequently commissioned in that regiment. Their acquaintance would be short-lived, however, as the next day a four-strong NOP led by Captains Luchford and J.E. Johnston in A7270 was bounced by nine Jasta 36 'Abatrii' after diving on an enemy two-seater southeast of Passchendaele. The Bristol Fighters were quickly reinforced by a patrol of 60 Squadron's SE5As and in the course of the melee Air Mechanic First Class Mather, flying with Second

Lieutenant Beaver in B883, emptied a Lewis drum into an Albatros that went down in a slow spin that the squadron pilots confirmed as having ended in a crash just south of Passchendaele[1]. The timely arrival of 60 Squadron enabled Captains Knight and Wornum in A7294 and Beaver and Mather to make a safe return to St. Marie Cappel, while Second Lieutenant Jones and Captain Speakman in B1122 made a forced landing in the countryside west of Ypres. But Luchford and Johnston failed to return at all after A7270 was brought down near Becelaere by Walter von Bulow[7]. German ground-troops rescued the wounded Captain Johnston from the Bristol's wreckage and sent him to hospital but Harry Luchford was already dead. The loss of the gutsy 23-year-old flight-commander was a bitter blow for 20 Squadron. The ex-bank clerk had been credited with 24 victories in the more than six months he had been with the squadron. Although the Germans probably buried him near where he fell, the site of his grave was lost in later ground fighting and he is remembered at the Arras Flying Services Memorial.

The day after that was almost a repeat of the previous action. The first and second patrols returned with little to report in the face of similar ground mists to those the day before but the third patrol brought more losses. The four-strong NOP that went up at 11.25 ran into opposition just after midday over Comines; and while Sergeant Johnson and Second Lieutenant Masding in A7214 drove down one of the enemy scouts out of control over Comines, A7141 was seen to crash near Hollebeke. It seems that relative newcomers Second Lieutenants W. Bevan and F.B. Gloster had been brought down by ground fire, and both would be honoured with a most unusual epilogue...

On 12 January 1918 Leutnant C. Mayweg, an officer in an unidentified German artillery regiment, was moved to write a letter to the RFC that was later dropped over the British lines; the wording of which suggests an attempt to comfort the bereaved families.

Much Respected Sir,   In the Field

12 January 1918

You will by now have learned that Lieut. Gloster did not return from his flight on 3rd December. As one of the few eyewitnesses of his fall I regard it as my duty as a comrade to give you details of his death. His machine was apparently damaged by heavy artillery fire, and I saw it fall headlong to earth, out of control. Hurrying up I found the two occupants dead. There were no external traces of injury, their peaceful smiling faces testified to a rapid and painless death. On Lieut. Gloster's body I found some private letters and photographs, one of a young girl was inscribed 'with fondest love from Baby'. I found nothing on his very youthful companion. As circumstances did not allow of the bodies being taken to the rear, they were buried on the spot where they fell. Their mutual grave lies in a neighbourhood which even in that fairly unquiet time was not much shot over by our opponents. Our Pioneers have put a cross over the grave with the inscription 'Here lies the English Flight Lieut. Gloster and his companion.'

If it is possible, and you would like it, I will endeavour to obtain a photograph of the machine which was taken shortly afterwards, and of the grave, in order to send them to you eventually.

In assuring you of my sympathy

I remain,

C. Mayweg

Lieutenant in an artillery regiment

Wilfrid Bevan, who was 20, came from Gowerton, Glamorgan and had been commissioned into the Artists Rifles. Frank Beresford Gloster was also 20 and a married man who had worked as a bank clerk in Parteen, Limerick, before being commissioned into the Army Service Corps. A copy of Leutnant Mayweg's letter was forwarded to the two airmen's' next of kin by the War Office, and a few months later Mrs Gloster received a package containing the possessions her dead husband had been carrying when he was killed. These had been returned to England by the Germans in yet another gallant gesture, and enclosed with them was the now standard request from the War Office that Mrs Gloster should not publicise the details. Unfortunately, despite all Leutnant Mayweg's efforts, continued fighting in the area over the following months obliterated the graves and, as with Harry Luchford, the two men's names are remembered at the Arras Flying Services Memorial[5].

******

December had begun badly; but the deteriorating winter weather and shorter days brought a gradual reduction in flying time that helped the squadron avoid heavy losses during the rest of the month. Tuesday, 4 December was spent on test and practice flights, while the following day brought four victory claims and a bravery decoration. Two flights of five Bristols took off at 08.00 for a NOP led by Captain Babbage (who had replaced Harry Luchford as Flight Commander) and Lieutenant Wornum in A7250. After meeting the enemy at 09.25 over Dadizeele, Sergeant Johnson and Captain Hedley in A7144 shot down an Albatros out of control. After becoming separated from the others, Second Lieutenant Beaver and Air Mechanic First Class Mather attacked a German two-seater in B883 and sent it 'spinning down quite out of control', although it was not seen to crash[1]. A third claim came from Lieutenant Kirkpatrick and Second Lieutenant Harmer after Harmer emptied a Lewis drum into an Albatros that dived on them from out of the sun, and then watched it from A7299 as it turned over and over before crashing into the ground and bursting into flames south of Dadizeele[1].

The Bristol Fighters returned safely at 09.50; and less than three hours later three of the crews – Second Lieutenant Beaver and Air Mechanic First Class Mather in B883, Lieutenant Kirkman and Captain Burbidge in A7298, and Sergeant Hopper and Captain Warden in A7250 – went up again at 12.19 on a photo-reconnaissance mission. After exposing eighteen plates at 15,000ft over Oostnieuwkerke they engaged five Albatros scouts, three of which attacked A7250: shooting Sergeant Hopper in his arm and damaging his engine and controls. Despite this Hopper managed to evade their continuing attacks and made it back across the lines to a forced-landing approximately halfway between Pilkem and Ypres. Captain Warden was uninjured, and his recommendation that Sergeant Hopper be decorated was accepted and confirmed in a citation published in the *London Gazette* on 28 March 1918 for the award of the Distinguished Conduct Medal for conspicuous gallantry and devotion to duty. As well as mentioning the incident above, the citation concluded with the words: 'Lately he shot down two enemy planes completely out of control, and throughout he has shown the greatest vigour, determination and courage.' The fight also bought another victory: an Albatros scout shot down out of control by Kirkman and Burbidge and confirmed by Wilfrid Beaver. The last patrol of the day was a four-strong photo-reconnaissance that returned safely at 15.22 after taking forty photographs of the required area without meeting opposition.

The weather over the next few days limited 20 Squadron's activities to just a handful of uneventful but useful OPs and reconnaissance missions. But clearer skies on Monday, 10 December brought another victory – and loss. Lieutenant Kirkman and Captain Burbidge led up a five-strong NOP that engaged an equal number of Albatros scouts escorting two two-seaters near Staden. Sergeant Johnson and Captain Hedley in 7144 attacked one of the 'Albatrii' with the front gun and followed it down to the ground where it crashed and turned over[1]. But A7299 was hit by German anti-aircraft fire; and although the observer, Second Lieutenant W.T.V. Harmer managed to bring the machine down in one piece, suffering a broken leg in the process, his pilot was already dead. He was 26-year-old John Crichton Kirkpatrick, who had attended Glasgow University where he made Lance Corporal in the OTC before being commissioned into 11 Scottish Rifles in November 1914. After being wounded by bullets in both legs on 26 October 1916, he transferred to the RFC and joined 20 Squadron in mid-September 1917. He is buried at Lijssenthoek Military Cemetery.

Alternating periods of good and bad weather now brought a spell of relatively peaceful routine to the squadron that lasted until 22 December. This allowed many of the new intake of pilots and observers to settle in and hone their skills in relative safety while some of the older hands got leave. New pilots arriving during the first half of the month of December included Sergeant 4407 O. Schorah, Second Lieutenant A.L. Pemberton, Lieutenant D. Leigh-Pemberton of the Grenadier Guards, Second Lieutenant R. J. Gosse, D. Weston and Sergeant H.O. Smith. Two new Canadian pilots were also posted in: Major J.A. Dennistoun as Flight Commander and Second Lieutenant D.G. Campbell. Major Dennistoun was from Winnipeg, and had previously served with the Manitoba Regiment and later as a flight commander with 39 Squadron in England, while his brother John Romeyn Dennistoun, had served with 7 Squadron until he was shot down and killed on 4 May 1916. Duncan Gordon Campbell came from Montreal and had also served with the Canadian Local Forces. His older brother Archie was serving as a doctor in the Canadian Army Medical Corps[6]. There were also some new faces in the rear cockpits: Canadian Lieutenant N.W. Taylor was followed by Lieutenant J.H. Stream (Lincolnshire Regiment) and Second Lieutenants W.H. Nash and D.H. Prosser (both from the General List). They were followed on 16 December by Second Lieutenant J.H. Behrens, who had previously served with the West Yorkshire Regiment, and at the end of the month by Second Lieutenants Walter Noble (Essex Regiment) and James Scaramanga and F.D. Miller, both from the General List. Around the same time, Captain Hedley and Second Lieutenant Masding were authorised to wear their observer wings, and aerial gunners Corporal Mann of the Honourable Artillery Company and Gunner A.S. Ackling of the Machine Gun Corps also arrived. On the ground, Captain C. Woodhill who had formerly served in the North Hampshire Yeomanry (Territorials) was posted in as a new intelligence officer, and Second Lieutenant S.A. Mowatt was hospitalised after falling ill and was then repatriated to Canada.

Other movements included Second Lieutenant L. Lindup transferring to 20 Squadron on temporary attachment from 70 Squadron, before being granted leave from 30 December to 13 January 1918, and Equipment Officer Lieutenant G.P. Achurch leaving for Home Establishment on 30 December.

One last curious movement was that of Second Lieutenant N.V. Harrison, who was listed in Wing Routine Orders as leaving for Home Establishment on 1 December – and returning two weeks later. Whether his posting to HE was simply temporary or he should have been shown as being on leave, or whether he did not want a HE posting and kicked up a lot of fuss will probably never be known. Others were leaving the squadron for good. Captain A.A. Knight, Lieutenant M.N. Waddington and Second Lieutenant R.V. Tattersall left for HE during the first week of December, and Flight-Sergeant Ray transferred out of the squadron on 12 December. Finally, in a continuation of the process started in November, those flyers that had not yet done so were sent on the air-gunnery refresher course at Berck-sur-Mer.

******

The weather finally improved on 22 December and an OP of seven Bristol Fighters met up with seven enemy scouts, including two 'enemy Nieuports' or Pfalz scouts at 11,000ft over Roulers. Sergeant Johnston and Captain Hedley, in A7144, then 'engaged about five enemy aircraft at fifty yards. The pilot dived, firing at one enemy aircraft and putting about sixty rounds into it, causing it to go down completely out of control. About ten minutes later, two more enemy aircraft attacked A7144. The observer fired about eighty rounds into one of these at point-blank range. It then burst into flames and fell to earth at Sheet 28.E.4.d and was seen by the observer to be burning on the ground. In the course of the fight, one of the enemy aircraft got below the Bristol formation, at which A7255, with Second Lieutenant Makepeace and Lieutenant Brooke, then dived and fired about ninety rounds into it. This E.A. then went into a spin, which turned into a vertical dive. It was followed down to 3,000ft and was seen by Makepeace to crash.[1]. Frank Johnston and Captain Hedley were credited with one enemy aircraft destroyed in flames and one out of control, making Sergeant Johnson's ninth and tenth victories and Hedley's third and fourth, while Second Lieutenant Makepeace was for some reason only credited with an 'out of control'. The only casualty was observer Lieutenant N.M. Sanders, who was wounded.

The 20 Squadron Record Book for 1917 contains just a few entries for the last week of the year. On Christmas Day newly arrived pilot Captain Steele flew with Second Lieutenant Clemons in A7193 during a morning patrol led by the recently promoted Captain Kirkman, following which Captain Steele and Lieutenant Stream in C4825 led an afternoon Reserve Patrol made up almost entirely of relative newcomers. These included Second Lieutenants D.J. Weston and M.S. Dougall in B1157, Second Lieutenant Jones and Private Matthews in A7256 and Sergeant Smith and Second Lieutenant Prosser in B883. With so many new faces in the formation, it is just as well that visibility was poor and no enemy aircraft were seen. One more uneventful patrol was recorded on 28 December and apparently brought the year's flying to an end. The squadron's victory score now stood at 300; and high though that was it would be more than doubled in 1918 as the air war reached unprecedented levels of ferocity.

******

Notes

1. Combat Report.
2. WO 339/41693: Officer's Record of Service.
3. *Above the Lines* by N. Franks, F. Bailey & R. Guest; Grub Street Press.
4. Russ Gannon's database of aerial combats.
5. WO 339/1413: Officer's Record of Service.
6. Thanks to Robert Campbell.
7. *The Jasta War Chronology* by N. Franks et al.

Chapter 18

Winter War 2 – January/February 1918

The allied generals, well aware of Russia's collapse and the massive number of German troops now being released from there, rightly anticipated a big German offensive against the Western Front before American intervention became decisive. The only question was when and where that would happen, so the air services were now called upon to discover that vital information. The airmen of 20 Squadron once again found themselves in the thick of the action in 1918. It was a year that brought almost daily air fights – and in late March the unexpected requirement to add low-flying ground attack work to their repertoire.

At 15.45 on Thursday, January 3 Wilfrid Beaver and H.E. Easton, flying B883 with four other Bristol Fighters, dived on an Albatros two-seater northeast of Moorslede. Beaver opened fire with his front gun and watched the Albatros go down out of control before it crashed into the ground and burst into flames. His victory was confirmed by Jooste and Masding in A7294, the possible German casualty being Schusta 23's Unteroffizier Postel who was reported wounded in action in air combat over the Ypres sector[1, 2]. The following day, R.M. Makepeace and Captain Hedley and four other Bristols fought eight Albatros scouts over Menin, five of which particularly targeted Hedley's A7255. Hedley fired about fifty rounds into the nearest one at only thirty yards range and it immediately turned over and went down completely out of control. The remainder came in for a second attack but Captain Hedley kept them at bay with his Lewis gun until it jammed due to a broken extractor, at which point Makepeace very sensibly spun down out of the fight before racing off home to report what turned out to be his last victory with 20 Squadron. On 20 January he was promoted to Captain and Flight Commander and transferred to 11 Squadron after achieving sixteen combat victories.[1]. A third victory, also of the 'out of control' variety, came at about 12.10 on Sunday, 6 January when Beaver and Easton were over Houthulst Forest and attacked three Albatros two-seaters below them. Beaver got into close range and fired about 200 rounds into one of the Germans; but although he watched the two-seater plunge earthwards out of control for a long way, four Albatros scouts came diving into the fight and he was unable to see if it crashed[1].

There were a number of personnel movements in the first half of January. Second Lieutenant Behrens rejoined his former unit, the West Yorkshire Regiment on 4 January, and Second Lieutenant N.V. Harrison was promoted to acting Captain and Flight Commander to replace Captain W.D. Durrand M.C. on his posting to Home Establishment the following Monday. The same day, Second Lieutenants Dougall and Boles left for England on two weeks leave, while Major Dennistoun and Lieutenant Speakman departed for temporary duty at Biggin Hill, to be followed there on 12 January by R.M. Makepeace. New pilot Second Lieutenant D. Latimer had arrived on 5 January, and a new probationary aerial gunner at St. Marie Cappel was Air Mechanic '67051' F. Deighton, who had transferred to the squadron from the 2 Balloon Wing. Another new arrival on 10 January was Lieutenant A. T. Packham, taking over as Recording Officer, while Captain C.R. Steele left the squadron two days later on being posted to Home Establishment.

The next fight came on Sunday, 13 January. Tommy Colvill-Jones and H.G. Crowe were up in B1122 with nine others when they spotted a German two-seater at 5,000ft north of Moorslede. This was despatched with 150 rounds from the pilot's gun, and both pilot and observer watched it crash into the ground on the northern outskirts of Moorslede[1]. This was Colvill-Jones's third victory since arriving at the squadron and the first for Henry Crowe. Although flying was still something of a novelty for the Dubliner, fighting was certainly not. Crowe first joined up in 1915, and while at Sandhurst had his interest in the RFC kindled by a lecture from a visiting squadron commander, reinforced by a visit to the RAE at Farnborough. Commissioned into the Royal Irish Regiment in July 1916, Crowe was in France with its 6 Battalion by September. The regiment was based in the Wytschaete-Messines line until April 1917, during which time his interest in the RFC was rekindled by a visit to 1 Squadron at Bailleul, and by the pre-Messines battle training he received at Acquin in April and May 1917. Here, as he later wrote, he rehearsed his part in the coming battle 'on a piece of land which was topographically similar to the Wytschaete-Messines ridge, and on which enemy trenches were marked in white tape in accordance with the latest air photographs.' This was followed by an officers' conference at which he met one of the reconnaissance pilots, after which he applied for the RFC. Crowe later wrote that 20 Squadron's observers 'had to learn the front by heart and pass a test in this before the "wing" was granted.' He also recorded how each observer had his own guns and spare parts, and took a special pride in freedom from stoppages. 'Morale was excellent,' he wrote, 'and everyone was full of praise for the Bristol Fighter[3].'

The first losses of 1918 came on 19 January during an OP over the Roulers area led by Captain Harrison and Lieutenant Noel in C4617. The patrol engaged four Albatros scouts at 9,000ft southwest of Roulers, and Harrison and Noel claimed one of these that went down out of control until it disappeared into the clouds below in a slow spin[1]. But Starfield and Hutchinson, flying A7193, became separated from the others and were last seen over Wytschaete, later falling to the guns of Oberleutnant, Bruno Loerzer of Jasta 26 for his twentieth combat victory[4]. Both Baron (Baron is his first name) Starfield from Johannesburg and Ambrose Hutchinson from Rock Ferry in Cheshire were killed and are buried at Larch Wood (Railway cutting) cemetery. A later patrol brought some kind of revenge when Tommy Colvill-Jones and L.H. Phelps shot down an Albatros DV out of control east of Moorslede. The day was also marked by Lieutenant Kirkman's promotion to Temporary Captain and Flight Commander.

Just after 11.00 on Tuesday, 22 January 1918 the squadron's eleven-strong OP was attacked by twenty Albatros scouts at around 12,000ft west of Roulers. H.G. Crowe fired off about one-and-a-half drums into one of the attackers and sent it down 'completely out of control' before his pilot D.G. Cooke fired on another Albatros that also went down out of control. Second Lieutenant McGoun and Lieutenant J.H. Stream reported that they later saw one of the two 'Albatrii' burning on the ground[1]. At about the same time, Captain Kirkman and Air Mechanic First Class McMechan in B1156 were dived on by another Albatros, and Kirkman made a quick left-hand climbing turn to follow it around as it swept down below them before firing about 100 rounds into it. McMechan reported that it went down in a series of stalls and nose-dives but did not see if it crashed[1]. The fourth British victory was recorded by Sergeant H.O. Smith, flying B883, who was diving on one of the enemy scouts when another came diving down behind them but was forced to turn away by observer Second Lieutenant Agelasto's fire. As it turned, Sergeant Smith swung the Bristol around and got behind it, getting in a 'good burst' from close range that sent it falling out of control, watched all the way down by Second Lieutenant Jooste until it hit the ground[1].

Once again there had been a cost. The crew of C4825, Second Lieutenant A.R. Paul and his aerial gunner Corporal A. Mann, failed to return after being shot down by Leutnant K. Gallwitz of Jasta 2. Corporal Mann was dead and was buried close to the scene but A.R. Paul was still alive and the Germans attempted to have him sent to their hospital at Roulers. However, the young officer died en-route from a double fracture of the skull and another to his left thigh and was buried in the German military cemetery at Beveren. There was originally some confusion as to whether it was Corporal Mann or A.R. Paul who was buried there, but this was finally settled in March 1920 when the grave was exhumed and his mother identified Paul's remains. In the years that followed the war, the IWGC relocated many of the British war dead to the new British war cemeteries, with the result that A.R. Paul, from St Helen's, Lancashire, found his final resting place at Harlebeke New British Cemetery. Sadly, the remains of 23-year-old Corporal 3567 Albert Mann, who came from Tooting, London, and had served with the HAC before the RFC, were not found after the war and he is remembered at the Arras Flying Services Memorial[2, 4,].

Another hectic fight came on 25 January, following which three Bristol Fighter crews were credited with individual victories over what, with hindsight, appears to have been just one Albatros during a ten-strong patrol that fought about the same number of 'Albatrii' at 12,500ft over Courtemarck. Two of the enemy dived on B883 flown by Sergeant Smith and Second Lieutenant Clemons and were in turn attacked by three other Bristol Fighters flown by Captain Kirkman and Lieutenant Keith in B1156, Sergeant Johnson and Second Lieutenant Prosser in C4640 and D.J. Weston and Walter Noble flying B1177. One of the two German scouts attacking B883 then lost its wings under the three Bristol Fighters' combined fire, and each of the three Bristol crews then claimed the unfortunate German as separate combat victories. Their combat reports are very similar, with 60 Squadron's Captain Soden supporting Kirkman and Keith's claim, Colvill-Jones and Phelps in B1122 supporting Sergeant Johnson and Second Lieutenant Prosser's claim, and a British anti-aircraft battery that of David Weston and Walter Noble. Weston's combat report also noted that immediately after this he attacked a second Albatros that went down in a spin that quickly developed into a straight dive at tremendous speed with no attempt to flatten out. Around the same time, Lieutenant D. Leigh-Pemberton also reported sending down an Albatros out of control that may well refer to the same aircraft reported as Weston and Noble's second claim. The Bristol Fighters' almost certain victim in the Albatros that broke up in the air was VizeFeldwebel H. Werner of Jasta 7, who was killed in action in the immediate area at about that time.

A few minutes later, at about 12.40 over the Roulers area, McGoun and Agelasto dived on an Albatros scout in C4836 and then pulled out, turned, and fired on another coming from the side. This one went up into a side stall before falling away out of control, and was watched all the way down by Lieutenant Phelps in another Bristol Fighter, who reported seeing it crash into the ground at trench map reference 20.W.3.c. The Germans continued their attack, and after Agelasto fired a whole drum into one that was only about twenty yards away, it went over on its side and into a slow spin that was seen by Lieutenant Boyd, the observer in C4617[1]. In all then, 20 Squadron's pilots made a total of seven claims reporting four 'Albatrii' destroyed and three out of control for what was only one certain German loss. In fairness, though, it is also possible that one or more other Albatros pilots might have received enough damage to send them down as if out of control, or even to a crash-landing.

But what of Sergeant Smith and Second Lieutenant Clemons in B883? The attempts to rescue them had failed. Both men were very seriously injured after making a bad crash-landing east of the lines near Courtemarck, where German soldiers rescued them from the wreckage and sent them to hospital. Second Lieutenant H.S. Clemons eventually recovered and survived his captivity but his pilot was less fortunate. Despite being transferred to Hamburg for treatment, Sergeant Smith eventually died in hospital on 15 July 1918 and is buried at Hamburg Cemetery. The victory over B883 was credited to Leutnant C. Degelow of Jasta 7[4]. A former plumber's mate from Lavender Hill in Battersea, Sergeant Pilot 328 Herbert Oliver Smith MM first enlisted for boy service in August 1909 and was classified as a Second Class Air Mechanic in the Royal Flying Corps in 1912. He went to France as part of the early RFC's initial contingent in August 1914 and was promoted to sergeant before returning to England on 18 January 1915. He returned to France for a second tour from 6 November 1915 to 28 May 1916, after which he was posted back to England for pilot training. He qualified as a first class pilot at the end of September 1917 and arrived at 20 Squadron in early December 1917, by which time his award of the Military Medal for his previous service had been announced in the *London Gazette* of 28 September 1917. He was 24.

It had been a frantic fight but, although each of the Bristol crews' claims were independently verified by third parties, it should have been obvious that at least three of them referred to the same enemy aircraft. The fact that each crew was granted an individual victory in RFC Communiqué Number 124 begs the question of whether the claims were deliberately exaggerated at a higher level. However, as the RFC generally credited an individual victory to every pilot involved in the destruction of a German aircraft, it can also be argued that they were simply following the usual procedures. As to the 'out of control' claims: it had been known for a long time that German pilots favoured the spin or dive to safety when the going got too hot, but the British High Command still regarded such 'scaring away' of the enemy as a victory. The problem facing modern historians is how to distinguish today between the 'out of control' victories where the enemy had simply run away, and the 'out of control' victories where the enemy had actually been shot down. Except in a very few cases, the answer is, sadly, that the lack of surviving German records for damaged or destroyed aircraft, as opposed to records of killed and wounded pilots, means that in the majority of cases we cannot reliably distinguish between them. The only certain conclusion that can be drawn is that regardless of whether the enemy was actually shot down or ran away, he was most certainly 'vanquished' or 'beaten' in that particular fight. So it was a 'victory', of sorts.

Another victory claim came on 28 January when Tommy Colvill-Jones and Lieutenant Phelps, flying B1122, brought down an Albatros DV out of control northwest of Westroosebeke at 13.50[1]. The final claims for the month came just before 14.30 two days later when Lieutenant Rex George Bennett and Air Mechanic First Class Matthews were attacked by two Albatrosses near Ghistelles but were rescued by McGoun and Agelasto in C4836. Bennett and Matthews were credited with getting one Albatros out of control, while McGoun and Agelasto claimed the second as having crashed in a wood just west of Zeldegham at trench map reference 12.P.10 after they poured 300 rounds into it from both guns[1]. Rex Bennett, aged 29, had only arrived at the squadron five days earlier so enjoyed a lucky escape. Another new arrival was pilot Second Lieutenant L.P. Roberts on 23 January; and one final highlight for January was the award of the Belgian *Croix de Guerre* to Second Lieutenant R.C. Purvis and Air Mechanic First Class 56564 J. McMechan.

******

By the end of January 1918 it was becoming clearer from intelligence reports that the coming German offensive would be directed primarily against the British front rather than the French one. General Trenchard issued a memorandum entitled 'The Employment of the Royal Flying Corps in Defence' in which he repeated the need for observers to make careful notes on enemy construction of new railways and sidings, roads, dumps, aerodromes, camps and gun positions that might indicate where any attack or feint might develop. He also instructed that all available aircraft were to bomb and strafe enemy reinforcements about a mile behind the battle line, and to attack enemy detraining and debussing points and also their most advanced troops. The effect of this was calculated to encourage and cheer the hard-pressed defenders as much as to dismay and confuse their attackers. They were also to engage any enemy aircraft they encountered, the memorandum concluding:

'The successful performance of the role of the Royal Flying Corps in defence must primarily depend on its ability to gain and maintain the ascendancy in the air. This can only be done by attacking and defeating the enemy's air forces.

The action of the Royal Flying Corps must, therefore, always remain offensive, even when the Army, during a period of preparation for offensive operations, is standing temporarily on the defensive.'

******

So the attrition continued. At 12.45 on Sunday, 3 February Beaver and Easton dived B1156 onto an Albatros DV between Menin and Roulers, Beaver firing about 150 rounds into it from close range so that it fell out of control before bursting into flames close to the ground[1]. The identity of the German pilot remains unknown, but it is known that an eight-strong patrol of Jasta 27 was involved in several fights over the area around this time and that a later patrol mounted by the Jasta was sent up only six-strong[2]. The next day saw even heavier fighting. Colvill-Jones and Captain Hedley started well by destroying a German observation balloon northwest of Dadizeele at trench map reference 28.K.5.c at 10.55. But at 12.20 German time Second Lieutenants Gosse and Miller were brought down over Poelcappelle, the pilot wounded and his observer killed. A former irrigation engineer in India's United Provinces 32-year-old Frederick Miller, originally from Shoreham, Sussex, is buried at Lijssenthoek Military Cemetery. The German victor most often credited with this succss is Leutnant K. Menckhoff of Jasta 3, although other sources indicate that his claim refers to an SE5 during a fight with 60 Squadron[2, 4].

In later fighting, Rex Bennett and Air Mechanic First Class Mather shot down one Albatros scout out of control and a second in flames over the Menin-Roulers road at 14.15, while Captain Cooke and Second Lieutenant Agelasto claimed an Albatros DV shot down out of control over Roulers at about the same time. Two more Albatros DVs were claimed shot down out of control at 14.15 over the Menin-Roulers road by Lieutenant E. Lindup and Second Lieutenant Dougall, and by David Weston and Walter Noble. Ten minutes later Beaver and Easton claimed another out of control over the town of Roulers. Twenty minutes after that, Second Lieutenant Roberts and Lieutenant Farquharton-Roberts engaged an Albatros scout in C4617 southeast of Houthulst Forest, with Farquharton-Roberts firing about 100 rounds into it at close range causing it, too, to fall away out of control[1]. Once again, the identities of the German pilots remain shrouded in the fog of war, and it is possible that the squadron's 'out of control' claims near Roulers may all refer to the same aircraft. In addition to their balloon, Colvill-Jones and Hedley had also claimed an Albatros destroyed in the fight – the seventh and last victory that the Argentine-born pilot would claim with 20 Squadron before he was promoted and transferred to 48 Squadron as a flight commander. So the day ended with 20 Squadron having claimed eight enemy aircraft and a balloon shot down for the loss of one observer killed and a pilot wounded. This was followed the next day by four more 'out of control' victories when twelve of 20 Squadron's Bristol Fighters attacked four Albatros scouts over Roulers at 11.20. These were awarded, two to each crew, to Beaver and Easton and Cooke and Agelasto[1]. Following this, Agelasto was posted back to England on Home Establishment, having been with the squadron since June 1917.

As to the British claims, it had not been a completely one-sided fight, as D.G. Campbell and W.H. Nash had a lucky escape when they had to crash-land A7255 near Combeke after getting badly shot-up. This seems to tie in with a claim by Offizierstellvertreter O. Esswein of Jasta 26 for a Bristol Fighter forced to land in the Moorslede area, and highlights another confusing aspect of the claims debate. The place names used by the British did not always coincide with those used by the Germans for the same location, and this is further complicated by the fact that many Belgian towns and villages had their names or the spelling of them changed after the war. For example, what was then known as Ypres is now spelled Ieper, and Combeke should today be identified as Krombeke.

High winds, mist and rain meant there very little flying possible until the afternoon of 15 February but that did not affect the usual personnel movements. Aerial Gunners M. Mather and E. Deighton were promoted to corporal with effect from 7 February and, along with Corporal Archer, were re-mustered as qualified observers from the same date, while Air Mechanic E. Veale was promoted to corporal and observer a week later. Second Lieutenants Walter Noble, J.J. Scaramanga and D. H. Prosser were all authorised to wear their observer badges from 13 February, and H. E. Easton six days later. The same day, Air Mechanics B. Matthews and D. Scott were posted back to England on Home Establishment along with Captain Burbidge, and Second Lieutenants R.C. Purvis and J.L. Boles on 21 and 23 February. Among those granted some leave during the month were A.L. Pemberton, L.H. Phelps, D.J. Weston, J.D. Boyd, R.J. Gosse and H.G. Crowe. The 'other ranks' were not left out and Corporal W. Foster got leave from 20 February to 6 March, and Corporal Deighton from 27 February to 13 March. Three new photographic staff were also transferred into the squadron from 19 February: these being Air Mechanics F. Simpson, W. Harvey and E. Bullett. When flying resumed, Beaver and Easton gained another victory at 11.40 on 16 February, their combat report simply noting the enemy aircraft as a 'two-seater' shot down out of control over Menin, to which their CO promptly added the question 'type?' to suggest they should have noted this.

The following day, the Bristol Fighters again went up twelve-strong, and at about 11.20 engaged ten Pfalz and six Albatros scouts at 10,000ft over Passchendaele and Moorslede. As the fight began, three Germans dived on B1177. One of them came as close as fifteen yards and Captain Hedley emptied a whole Lewis drum into it, sending it plunging down out of control. The other two Germans undershot the Bristol Fighter, and Sergeant Johnson quickly dived on one of them from behind and fired about 100 rounds into it, after which it fell earthwards and crashed. The fight had brought the Bristol Fighter down to about 2,000ft, and as Sergeant Johnson turned towards the lines Captain Hedley noted the position of the crashed German at map reference 28.E.9.c., placing it on the northwest outskirts of Moorslede[1].

Second Lieutenant Lindup and Corporal Mather in C4641 attacked a Pfalz scout over Westroosebeke that fell away with dense smoke pouring out behind. They were unable to watch its fall but it was observed by Beaver and Easton, who had also dived on it in B1122, and reported that it hit the ground and burst into flames near the village[1]. Three other 20 Squadron crews were also credited with 'out of control' victories. R.G. Bennett and Corporal F. Archer crewing C4604 watched their victim fall spinning earthwards 'obviously out of control … until lost sight of against a background of houses'[1]. Second Lieutenants McGoun and Masding in C4826 were also unable to observe the fate of the Pfalz they sent down out of control as they came under further attack[1]. The last claim was from Laurie Roberts and Walter Noble in B1209 who sent down one of the Germans completely out of control with dense smoke issuing from its tail. They too were unable to see its final fate as they were still under attack, and were compelled to break off the fight and make for the lines in B1209 after their radiator was shot through. It had been an interesting outing for Walter Noble, as he usually flew with David Weston and was less than comfortable flying with relative newcomer Laurie Roberts while his usual pilot was on leave. But Roberts had acquitted himself well. Although his machine had been badly shot up, the Germans broke off their pursuit just as he crossed the lines and the engine failed. There was no choice but to make a forced landing in a clearing among the huts and buildings in the rear lines, and Noble was injured when he was thrown out of the machine as it overturned. His reward was six weeks sick leave after the two men phoned in their combat reports to Major Johnston[1, 5].

The last ten days of the month brought one more victory claim and three more deaths. D.G. Campbell and J.H. Stream were killed on Tuesday, 19 February after being shot down in flames by Unteroffizier Otto Esswein of Jasta 26[4]. Revenge came two days later when Rex Bennett and Corporal Veale were on patrol in C4604 with seven other Bristol Fighters and dived on two German two-seaters they spotted at 8,000ft over Comines. Bennett opened fire with his front gun and sent one of them down to crash, confirmed both by Major Sanday of 19 Squadron and by British anti-aircraft gunners as having occurred at map reference 36.I.29, a little southwest of the village of Premesques[1]. The third death came when Laurie Roberts was killed in a flying accident near St. Marie Cappel in Bristol Fighter C4617 on 23 February.

Of those dead, Duncan Gordon Campbell, the 27-year-old son of Duncan and Helen Bickerdike Campbell, of Montreal, had originally served with the Canadian artillery, while 18-year-old John Harvey Stream, from Grimsby, had been first commissioned into the Lincolnshire Regiment. Both men were buried at Lijssenthoek, with Campbell's grave initially being marked by a Cross made from an aircraft propeller[6]. Laurie Roberts, aged 20, was the son of John and Janet Roberts of Callander, Perthshire, and is buried at Longuenesse St. Omer Cemetery. Captain R.K. Kirkman, who had been awarded the Military Cross on 5 February, was then given the task of presiding over the court of enquiry into Roberts's accident.

******

Notes

1. Combat Report.
2. My thanks to Russ Gannon.
3. AIR/1/2390/228/11/134: Flt Lieutenant H.G. Crowe, M.C.: Presentation to the RAF Staff College.
4. *The Jasta War Chronology* by N. Franks, F. Bailey & R. Guest; Grub Street Press.
5. *With a Bristol Fighter Squadron* by Walter Noble.
6. Thanks to Robert Campbell.

Chapter 19

Backs to the Wall – March/April 1918

Although the month began quietly, fighting on 9 March brought the squadron three more 'out of control' victories. These were noteworthy for the fact that two of them were claimed by a relative newcomer, and that led to his observer receiving a gallantry award. A 19-year-old Londoner, Lieutenant Leslie H.T. Capel, had arrived at 20 Squadron in mid-February on transfer from 60 Squadron, with which unit he had flown SE5As for just under three weeks. He was up at 08.00 that day in B1191 carrying Corporal Mather as his observer on a reserve patrol of five machines when they engaged twelve enemy scouts at 11,000ft over the Menin-Comines area. Capel and Mather became isolated from their formation in the early stages and, for the next fifteen minutes, fought off attack after attack by several 'Albatrii'. As Capel threw his aircraft around the sky to evade the German bullets, Corporal Mather used up all his ammunition defending their tail and shooting down two of the enemy before they were helped by Cooke and Scaramanga, who got a third Albatros out of control. As the German onslaught eased the Bristol Fighters crossed safely back over the British lines. The fate of the three Germans who 'retired' from the fight was not confirmed, as the fast-paced air combat and heavy ground mists made it impossible to watch them down to the ground and, although British AA gunners reported hearing the fight above them, they could not see anything[1]. Capel's combat report made it clear that Corporal Mather held off the enemy while he concentrated on the flying, and Major Johnston was sufficiently impressed by his account that he recommended Mather for a decoration. On 1 May 1918 the *London Gazette* announced he would receive the DCM

The month's first casualty came on 13 March when six 'Biffs' patrolling at 15,000ft over Houthem were attacked by nine Pfalz scouts. Corporal Archer was flying as Lieutenant Lindup's observer in B1191 and claimed one Pfalz that went down streaming smoke while Second Lieutenants Latimer and Scaramanga in C4615, claimed another. One German pilot almost certainly involved was Jasta 7's Leutnant Paul Lotz, as his commander Josef Jacobs recorded in his diary that he returned with his Albatros badly damaged by a

Bristol Fighter[1, 2]. However, 20-year-old observer, Second Lieutenant D.E. Stevens, had been shot and killed, although his casualty report lacks even the most basic details of who he was flying with or how and when he was hit. The son of Henry and Dora Stevens, from Liverpool, the young officer had come to the RFC via the Manchester Regiment and is buried at Longuenesse (St. Omer) Souvenir Cemetery.

******

Operation Michael

Apart from general warnings that the Germans seemed to be planning a major offensive somewhere on the British front, there was no obvious indication of the whereabouts. Thursday, 21 March 1918 brought more dense fog and mist across the Somme front through which there suddenly came a massive German bombardment: the prelude to the German Spring Offensive, code-named Operation Michael. Then the storm broke as a tidal wave of specially trained German shock troops led the main thrust, closely followed by regular infantry that drove an ever-deepening wedge between the outnumbered and out-gunned British Third and Fifth Armies. The crisis worsened dramatically over the next few days and, with the German armies thrusting many miles beyond the original trench-lines, the British desperately threw every available aircraft into the battle in continuous headlong ground-strafing attacks against the invaders. There was also strong evidence that the enemy might soon launch a second offensive further north in the Ypres Salient and, because of this threat, there was no let-up in the pace of events for 20 Squadron.

On Saturday, 23 March, Captains Kirkman and Hedley led a ten-strong OP in B1156 that attacked seven Albatros DVs at 12.10. Kirkman dived on one that went down burning over Wervicq, while a few minutes later Beaver and Easton dived B1114 and fired on an Albatros that had become separated from its formation and crashed south of Roncq. Watching it all the way down to the ground almost cost the two men their lives, though, as they were suddenly surprised by another nine 'Albatrii' plunging down on them, and only managed to escape by spinning down with their engine full on[1]. This was followed by another engagement at 12.45 when the patrol met ten more 'Albatrii' east of Menin. Kirkman first attacked one of them with his front gun and then manoeuvred to allow Captain Hedley to empty a drum into it from the Lewis gun. The Albatros went down in a spin, came out of it, and then went down apparently out of control, its fall confirmed by Corporal Mather in B1122[1].

In the meantime, the situation in the Somme had become so desperate that many pilots there were flying five or more ground-attack missions a day, bombing and machine-gunning every target that presented itself in accordance with Trenchard's exhortation that: 'All risks must be taken.' Those pilots who survived the hail of German small arms fire and repeated fighter attacks were now so exhausted that reinforcements became imperative, and 20 Squadron was instructed to send a flight down to Bruay each morning to assist 10 Wing in repelling the German advance. They were in action almost immediately. A large force of enemy troops had been reported massing west of Bapaume on Third Army's front and the target was considered so important that all the squadrons in 1 Brigade and four squadrons from 2 Brigade were ordered to attack it. Laden with all the bombs and ammunition they could carry, they flew south towards the main battlefront in the Bapaume area. There they began the first of the squadron's almost continuous ground-strafing attacks on the Germans. Their fortitude and resilience in this battle – together with all their other support for ground troops on the Western Front and their later post-war army co-operation over the Khyber Pass – would be taken into account when in 1937 King George VI authorised the official 20 Squadron crest incorporating an eagle with a sabre clutched in its talons, approaching from out of the sun.

On 26 March the first of 20 Squadron's patrols dropped twenty-four 25lb bombs and strafed enemy troops in the open with machine-gun fire, while the second patrol bombed enemy troops on the Irels - Grevillers road and the Bapaume-Le Sars road, and machine-gunned troops and transport on the Bapaume-Bilmcourt road and the Grevillers-Achiet-Le Petit road from low altitude. The trench-bound stalemate of the last few years had suddenly turned into a war of manoeuvre with soldiers fighting at close quarters for every individual hedge, field, copse and barn across the fast-moving battlefront. Pilots and observers had to fly low enough to see the differences in the soldiers' uniforms before dropping their bombs or opening up with their machine-guns and, in doing so, faced the perils of intense ground fire as well as attacks by higher flying German fighter scouts. The dangers of such work were quickly made clear when, Lieutenant Leigh-Pemberton was wounded by ground fire during the early afternoon attacks and wrecked B1196 in a forced landing near Albert. His observer, Captain N.W. Taylor, was uninjured. In the meantime, the same crews who had seen action in the morning (Captain Jooste and Lieutenant Phelps, Captain Kirkman and Captain Hedley, Lieutenants Bennett and Boyd and Lieutenants Purcell and Jones) shot-up German troops moving along various roads in the area. Nearly everyone involved flew at least two or three sorties that first day.

Neither, despite strong winds, low clouds and poor visibility, was there any rest the following day. Carrying four 25lb bombs apiece, five Bristol Fighters set out together on a low OP, before splitting up to attack individual ground targets wherever they could be found. Captain Jooste and Lieutenant Masding bombed troops and transport near Morlancourt before strafing more German troops around the village of Chingues, while David Weston and Captain Godfrey in one Bristol Fighter and, Lieutenants Harmer and McHattie in another, concentrated their efforts on bombing and strafing runs around the village of Bray. Captain Beaver and Corporal Deighton were attacked by an Albatros as they strafed German troops on the Albert-Bapaume road, but were rescued by the prompt intervention of two Sopwith Camels of 4 Squadron, Australian Flying Corps. Lieutenants Bennett and Noel in C4641 dived on an Albatros they spotted while they were bombing troops near Cappy, but the German promptly swung around to reverse the attack. It quickly developed into a minute's dog-fighting before Noel was able to fire a crippling burst into the enemy machine from his Lewis gun. The Albatros sideslipped suddenly and crashed into the river Somme[1].

While this was going on, patrol leaders Captains Kirkman and Hedley were having a rather different experience in B1156 as they strafed troops and transport near Bray sur Somme. They were attacked by an Albatros, believed to be flown by Jasta 2's Leutnant K Gallwitz[2], who riddled both their petrol tanks with machine gun fire. Captain Hedley took him on and, after the war, reported that he thought he had brought the German down. But the Bristol Fighter's damaged engine cut out while still over enemy territory, and the furthest Captain Kirkman could glide the aircraft from such a low height was to a forced landing barely twenty yards in front of the Germans' leading infantry wave. The German soldiers immediately opened fire and only stopped when the two captains abandoned the aircraft and surrendered themselves and their aircraft intact. It was another loss that 20 Squadron could ill afford; especially since Kirkman had been credited with bringing down eight enemy aircraft and Hedley eleven, with two of the victories being shared between them.

What little was left of the ruined town of Albert fell to the oncoming Germans the following day. Two more enemy scouts were claimed by 20 Squadron's flyers as they bombed and strafed all and any road and rail targets they could find. In the first sortie, between 08.30 and 09.00, seven Bristol Fighters attacked targets on the railway north of Albert and on the roads in Orvillers and between Albert and Bapaume. Lindup and Crowe used up over 500 rounds of ammunition fighting off three Fokker Triplanes, and one of these went down out of control. But the other two kept up the attack and shot up their controls so badly that they were lucky to survive an emergency landing on the British side of the ever-moving lines[1]. This may well have been the incident Crowe recalled in a personal memoir, now held at the National Archives, in which he was forced to land after taking a hit in the radiator but repaired the damage overnight with help from the mechanic of a Whippet tank. He also wrote how staff officers were trying to re-form the retreating soldiers and get them to dig in, many of whom were desperate for food and drink[3].

Meanwhile, two Pfalz scouts dived on Bennett and Boyd in C4641 as they were bombing troops near La Boiselle and, after Boyd fired about forty rounds at point-blank range into one of them, the German pilot slumped forward in his seat and the Pfalz went down in a vertical dive. Once again, though, the sheer pace of action and low drifting clouds meant they could not see if it crashed[1]. As if that were not enough, Rex Bennett was airborne again at 11.00 strafing German motor transport east of Cappy, while at around 15.10 three other crews from the morning patrol were attacking German troops massed in a field on the Albert-Bapaume Road near Boiselle. While this was, to put it mildly, an exciting time for 20 Squadron's established flyers it was also a very frustrating time for its latest arrivals.

Having transferred to the RFC from the West Yorkshire Regiment in September 1917, new pilot Victor Groom arrived at St. Marie Cappel three days before the start of the German offensive. There, to his intense frustration, he found that there were no spare aircraft for new pilots to practice on and he would not be not allowed to join the fight until he had done some practice flights. While the battle raged in the air and on the ground, Groom was effectively grounded: 'studying maps of the patrol area and silhouettes of enemy aircraft and hoping for a chance to fly'.[4] Another new pilot, who no doubt shared his feelings, was Lieutenant John Henry Colbert, posted into the squadron on 29 March. Born in Colombo, Ceylon, in 1894, Colbert had trained as an engineer and draughtsman in Bath and was described as being a very practical and exceptionally good pilot. Just like Victor Groom, his desire to quickly prove his flying tutors right was frustrated by the lack of spare aircraft, and air operations that were hampered by rain showers, mists and low clouds as well as the enemy. The truth was that no machines could be spared for training flights at such a critical time, and had the new pilots been immediately committed to the fighting it is doubtful they would have survived.

Second Lieutenant R.B.T. Hedges and Lieutenant A.G. Harlock were wounded on 1 April after being shot down in flames at 09.58 by German

Anti-Aircraft near Pypegale, while Major Dennistoun and Second Lieutenant Crowe escaped injury in the late afternoon after also being hit by ground fire that forced them to land near Wulverghem. Trying to halt the German ground offensive was not 20 Squadron's only responsibility though. For even as some of its flyers fought the Germans over the Somme, others had to cover the Ypres front with some of them covering both areas in the same day. Captain Jooste and Lieutenant Masding were granted this dubious honour on Sunday, 4 April, when they claimed the squadron's first combat victory of the month during a late-morning photographic patrol in A7294 over Passchendaele. This was one of two Albatros scouts they attacked around 11.00 that fell away out of control before crashing into the ground as its companion escaped to the east[1]. They barely had time to return to St. Marie Cappel and swallow some lunch before the afternoon found them flying ground attack missions for 10 Wing along with four other Bristol Fighters.

So the fighting continued until a combination of dogged resistance on the ground, the straightening of the British line in front of Amiens and the continual harassment of the advancing German columns from the air finally ground the enemy offensive to a halt on Friday, 5 April. Operation Michael had brought Germany to within a whisker of winning the war. So low had the British aircraft of all types flown in their desperate efforts to stop the enemy flood that a German prisoner reported that his officer had been killed after being hit by the landing wheels of a Sopwith Camel[5]. The object lesson as to the direction tactical air power would follow in the future was not lost on Haig and his generals during the remaining months of the war, which saw the RFC's successor, the RAF, repeatedly called upon to provide similar close support to our ground forces. Unfortunately, successive British post-war governments and air staffs forgot these crucial lessons all too quickly in the twenty years of peace that followed – while other less well-intentioned leaders took them to heart and taught them to the allies in reverse in 1940.

Even without the German land offensive, April 1918 would still have gone down in history. For on the first of that month, the Royal Flying Corps and the Royal Naval Air Service were formally bound together as one service, and the Royal Air Force came into being. It was indeed a historic day, for this was the first truly independent Air Force in the world. Although created to operate in conjunction with both the Royal Navy and the Army, it had its own command structure and was entirely independent of both. In the long term, the creation of the RAF would have momentous and favourable consequences for British history, but on the day of its creation the change was scarcely noticed by the men who, in the midst of their desperate daily fights, now became its founder members. Many of them later wrote that even by the end of the war the only noticeable change was the new uniform sported by recently arrived recruits.

******

Operation Georgette

On 7 April 1918 German artillery began a two-day bombardment of British positions around the Ypres salient and, two days later, German storm troopers attacked through the fog and mist. The second phase of the German Spring Offensive had begun, with the aim of seizing Ypres and its surrounding areas and then capturing the Channel ports and cutting off supplies to the British Army, hastening the end of the war in Germany's favour. Part of the plan involved seizing the three prominent hills that rise up from the Flanders plains in a fifteen-mile line from east to west: Mount Kemmel, Mont des Cats and Mount Cassel, the last named overlooking 20 Squadron's aerodrome at St. Marie Cappel. Then they could take the railway junction at nearby Hazebrouk, to be followed by all the ridges the British had so hardly won the previous summer and other major strategic points. The first thrust of the German attack fell around Laventie, close to the 1915 battleground of Neuve Chapelle. It was here, in earlier battles amid the ruins of Port Arthur, that Edmund Blunden drew the inspiration for so much of his fine war poetry and his autobiographical memoir *Undertones of War*. Once again the fighting was desperate, and the evidence of four years of death and destruction can be seen today at the beautiful Indian War Memorial at Port Arthur and in the numerous nearby British cemeteries such as Pont du Hem and Euston Post, whose gravestones span almost every month of all four years of war. Also, close by, is a Portuguese Military Cemetery commemorating the many that died on the first day of the offensive while the supporting British divisions were also badly mauled and forced to fall back. The town of Estaires fell the same day, and worse was to follow on 10 April with the capture of Armentieres closely followed by that of Messines, reversing Plumer's triumph of the previous June. Within two days, the general situation had become so desperate all along the River Lys front that the normally taciturn and laconic C-in-C Douglas Haig appealed to his men the next day in words that left no-one in any doubt at all of just how much was at stake. 'Every position must be held to the last man' he ordered, 'There must be no retirement. With our backs to the wall…each one of us must fight on to the end.'

The day Haig made that appeal brought mixed fortunes for 20 Squadron. Lieutenant Capel and Corporal Deighton were climbing back up after bombing and strafing the advancing German troops near Laventie when they saw an enemy two-seater a little below them just south of Armentieres. Capel closed in and circled around the target while Corporal Deighton opened fire with the Lewis gun. After the first burst of only thirty-five rounds, the German machine fell away as if out of control before it crash-landed in a field north of Bois Grenier at trench map reference 36.H.24.a[1]. But Canadian pilot Major Dennistoun, who had been lucky on 1 April, was less so today when he was again hit by ground fire and forced to land near Neuve Eglise, where German artillery destroyed B1275, seriously wounding both him and and Lieutenant Scaramanga and putting them out of action for two months.

Walter Noble had now returned to the squadron after his convalescence and on 12 April went up in a six-strong patrol ordered to reconnoitre the German forces pushing ferociously towards Bailleul and Hazebrouk. Four of the machines flew top cover for the other two, including that of Noble who was to carry out the observing and photography. In the course of this, as Noble recorded in his book *With A Bristol Fighter Squadron*, the patrol was punctuated by two-way exchanges of fire between them and the enemy ground troops. Enemy aircraft were also about: Lieutenant A.L. Pemberton and Corporal F. Archer failed to return in B1257 and were prisoners of war after being shot down by German anti-aircraft unit K. Flak 7, with Pemberton being wounded[2].

Noble wrote that every man was sent up on at least four missions that day; then, as evening approached, it was realised that the enemy had advanced to within artillery range of St. Marie Cappel and orders came through to evacuate the aerodrome. In the gathering darkness, the Bristol Fighters hurriedly took to the air to fly west to a safer refuge at Boisdinghem, in a venture that became something of a disaster. H.G. Crowe was highly critical of RFC Headquarters' lack of foresight:

> The decision to retreat from St. Marie Cappel to Boisdinghem was made so late in the afternoon that night flying was necessary. Few, if any, of the pilots had flown by night before and not one of the aircraft had any night flying equipment fitted. Only one aeroplane got to Boisdinghem and landed without flares. The unit at Boisdinghem would not put out flares as it was afraid of attracting the attention of night bombers. The rest of 20 Squadron landed or crashed at Clairmarais or St. Omer aerodromes, in company with one or two other squadrons who were also retreating. If the order to retire had reached units an hour earlier, the disorganisation, loss of aircraft, and casualties to personnel would have been avoided. It took several days for the squadron to collect and to be of use as a fighting unit.[3]

Two pilots were injured in the night landings and at least three machines, including Noble's, were wrecked. So it may probably be assumed that Crowe's sentiments were widely shared.

Continuing poor weather and the repair or replacement of the machines that had been damaged in the squadron's move reduced the effectiveness of what little flying the squadron was able to carry out over the next few days. The blood and tears of the previous summer's Third Ypres campaign were reduced to bitter waste as the British abandoned Passchendaele and fell back to the defence of Ypres. Somehow over the days that followed, through a combination of bloody-minded British obstinacy and the hurried arrival of French reinforcements, the line was more or less held. As with Operation Michael, the German advance ground to a halt and Ypres, Hazebrouk and the Channel ports were saved.

On Wednesday, 17 April, recent squadron arrivals Captains T.P. Middleton and F. Godfrey in C4699 brought down two Albatros DVs: one destroyed and the other out of control. These claims are probably reflected in a diary entry written by Jasta 57's commander, Paul Strahle, who recorded that Leutnant J. Jensen had to make a forced landing at an advanced landing ground after claiming a DH4 (which was often misidentified by the Germans for the Bristol Fighter) shot down at Petit sec Bois at 1500 German Time. Jensen's claim seems to have been in error though, as no Bristol Fighter or DH4 losses were recorded in the area that day[2,6,7,8,9].

On Sunday, 21 April at around 11.00, an OP of six Bristols engaged nine Albatros scouts flying below them north of Wervicq. Cooke and Crowe, in B4749, opened fire on one that immediately fell out of control and went on falling until they and Beaver and Noel, in B1114, lost sight of it against the background of houses. With scrupulous honesty Cooke and Crowe's account of their fight ended with the words: 'It was not actually seen to crash.' They also reported how Latimer and Noel in B1232 had fired 150 rounds into another Albatros that had also gone down, obviously out of control until lost to sight: its retirement or demise also being confirmed by Lieutenant Jones in B1279[1]. At 19.35 on 25 April, Captain Beaver and Corporal Mather in C817 added another victory to the squadron's tally when they attacked five Albatros scouts at 8,000ft over Ploegsteert Wood. Beaver fired a long burst into one of them and watched it crash and burn just north of the wood, while the remainder of the enemy were driven off after Corporal Mather fired a few rounds from his Lewis gun[1].

While all this was going on, Victor Groom was getting to grips with squadron life and training. Having received almost no high altitude or formation flying training in England, he was not at first allowed to take part in offensive patrols but was sent out with other new pilots and observers on two or three line patrols of around three aircraft led by an experienced pilot. The crews of each aircraft were arranged so that the novice was accompanied by an experienced observer or vice versa. The line patrols were carried out at height just over the German side of the lines so as to acclimatise the new men to high altitude flying, where the thin air would soon winkle out those who lacked the necessary physical endurance. It also gave the new men a chance to experience enemy flak while practising the simultaneous functions of keeping position, noting their geographical location and watching out for enemy aircraft. Groom also mentioned that he had received no previous instruction on the use of the Bristol Fighter's 'compensator' or 'altitude control', and that it was some time before he learned how to use it properly. It is perhaps a sad comment on the flying training standards of the time that such an important matter should have been overlooked. As an aircraft climbed to ever higher altitudes, the air sucked into the carburettor would become thinner and thinner while the fuel flow remained the same – resulting in an increasingly rich mixture that led to a general loss of power. The compensator or altitude control remedied this problem by allowing the pilot to reduce the petrol flow at high altitudes without affecting the flow of air into the mixture, so that the engine would run more efficiently. The mechanics of it took the form of a second lever mounted next to the throttle lever, while a device that coupled the compensator to the throttle prevented the engine being accidentally starved of fuel if it was throttled right back while the mixture was still very lean[4, 10].

So April 1918 drew to a close as RAF Communiqué Number Two announced the award of Military Crosses to William Beaver, Ernest Lindup and Robert Leigh-Pemberton. It also brought the usual round of personnel movements: though perhaps not as many as in some previous months as the people at HQ were probably snowed under given the level of fighting. Probationary observers J. Tulloch and W. Jacklin arrived at the squadron on 25 April and new pilot Lieutenant E.A. Magee arrived three days later. Four days after that, Wilfrid Beaver was promoted to Captain to replace Captain G.H. Jooste, who left the squadron for a Home Establishment role on 2 May.

Notes

1. Combat report.
2. Russ Gannon's database of WW1 Aerial Combats.
3. AIR 1/2390/228/11/134: FLieutenant Lieutenant H.G. Crowe, M.C.: Presentation to the RAF Staff College.
4. AIR 1/2389/Victor Groom, Service Experiences 1918 and 1920/21.
5. *The War in the Air* by H.A. Jones.
6. AIR/1/168/15/156/7: 20 Squadron Records of Decisive Combats – Pilots.
7. AIR/1/1580/204/81/52: 2nd Brigade RFC list of E.A. brought down by unit.
8. *The Jasta War Chronology* by N. Franks et al
9. *The Sky their Battlefield* by Trevor Henshaw.
10. 'The Claudel-Hobson Carburettor Models RAF, Z. & H.C.7., for Aero Engines: Instruction manual', published February 1918: Courtesy of 'RAF Louvert' member at theaerodrome.com.

Chapter 20

Aerial Combat Crescendo – May 1918

The start of May saw the arrival of two new pilots with an interesting family history. They were American brothers Second Lieutenants Paul and August Iaccaci, whose unusual surname was inherited from their much travelled French-born father, Auguste Florian. His surname had originally been the Hungarian 'Jacassy' but he adapted the spelling to the Italianised version 'Jaccaci' while living in Florence with his mother – and then Americanised it to 'Iaccaci' after emigrating to the USA. Auguste Iaccaci was a noted decorative artist and art dealer who included Theodore Roosevelt and Mark Twain among his friends. In December 1888, he married Mabel Thomas Thayer, daughter of a Massachusetts minister, in Dresden, Germany, and their first son, Paul, was born on 26 July 1890, followed by August on 6 June 1893. The marriage did not last, however, and when it broke up a few years later the brothers were separated. Paul went to Massachusetts with his mother, while August went to France with his father. When August was later sent back to the United States to finish his education, the brothers were reunited, and both joined the New York National Guard. Serving together in Texas during the Mexican Border campaign, their unit's return to New York brought only the frustrations of camp routine occasionally broken by manoeuvres. Their impatience to get to the real war in Europe soon led to the brothers sneaking across the border into Canada where they volunteered as pilots in the Royal Flying Corps. After their training in Canada, they arrived at Boisdinghem on 25 April 1918. They were the first of five Americans to fly with 20 Squadron, although the other three would not arrive until June and would fly as members of the American Army Air Service on attachment to 20 Squadron RAF instead of being actual members of the RAF.

The Iaccaci brothers made their first practice flights with the squadron on 2 May, the same day as the first flight of another newcomer: Second Lieutenant Brodie Wilson, who joined the squadron as an observer. All three men would all see a great deal of action in the months ahead; in fact, so much that the retelling of it almost becomes repetitious.

Brodie Wilson, aged 25, the son of Reverend H.E. Wilson, of Little Billing in Northampton, had studied at Oxford from 1912 to 1914. Originally enlisting as a private in 18 Battalion, Royal Fusiliers, he was soon commissioned into the London Regiment and served in France from November 1915 until he joined the RFC in December 1917. Over time, his skills in French and photography would make him a valued member of the squadron, while the meticulous manner in which he kept his log-book would provide posterity with a most illuminating insight into the life of an observer flying in France in 1918[3]. The 'Notes for Reports' he made at the very beginning of his logbook, before he had made any patrols, illustrate his thoroughness:

1. Begin message with:
    (i)   Time of flight
    (ii) Rough limits of flight
    (iii) Average height e.g. Address to….C.P. 10 am to 11.30 am, Zonnebeke to Meteren, 500 – 1,000 ft. A.A. [Anti-Aircraft Activity].
2. In reporting points as being in British or German hands, state time: e.g. 'Our men in Neuve Eglise 10.15A.M.'
3. In reporting general situation put in rough limits of observation: e.g. 'No movement observed in enemy forward areas Menin to Neuve Eglise.'
4. If possible, report information consecutively from N. to S., or vice versa, but this is not essential.
5. In reporting our troops visible at certain points, put in if this in the front line or not: e.g. 'Our men seen S23, front line." Or "Our men seen S16 apparently in support.'
    Note: Some reports have stated: 'Men seen at…..' This is valueless. It is essential to give opinion as to whether British or German.
6. In some cases when the situation is very obscure, in reporting artillery ambiguous terms are used and it is difficult to say whether guns are firing from the given point or the guns are shelling the given point. This must be made clear: e.g. Our guns firing from T6" or "Our guns shelling T6.
7. In reporting on transport movement on roads, if possible, give main direction of movement: e.g. Much movement on Fletre – Meteren Road, mostly Westwards.
8. The word 'retirement' should only be used if it is absolutely certain the front line is falling back. Parties of men dribbling to the rear do not necessarily mean a retirement. They may only be wounded.

There was little chance for Brodie actually to practice all these techniques when he went up for his first patrol with Lieutenant J.M. Purcell in Bristol Fighter 1279 on 2 May, as low clouds and mist made observations impossible. However, the weather having improved overnight, he and Purcell went up next morning on a near squadron-strength patrol of eleven machines for another venture over the lines. This brought Brodie his first taste of air fighting when Purcell dived on one of several Albatros scouts they encountered in the Ploegsteert Wood-La Touquet area and, although a front gun jam meant it got away, other patrol members were luckier. Captains Middleton and Godfrey in C4699 destroyed an Albatros DV south of Ploegsteert Wood at 10.55 and then sent down another out of control over La Touquet a few moments later, while Captain Beaver and Captain N.W. Taylor flying C817 destroyed another Albatros DV over Gheluvelt at 11.05[4, 5, 6]. In a later fight, Cooke and Crowe flying C4749 shot down a Fokker Triplane in flames southeast of Hollebeke at 17.20[4, 6], followed by an Albatros out of control southeast of Ypres ten minutes later[6]. There were no casualties but Lieutenant F.E. Boulton and Corporal W.H. Foster had to make a forced-landing at Wormhoudt with their fuel tank shot through[4, 7].

Second Lieutenants Victor Groom and Ernest Hardcastle were now flying full patrols with the others, and Groom described how patrols consisted of six, nine or twelve aircraft sub-divided into flights of three aircraft. When the patrol consisted of twelve aircraft, the fourth sub-formation flew slightly in rear and about 2,000ft above the main formation, and remained above and behind when the rest of the formation was engaging the enemy in order to prevent reinforcements joining in. If the rear formation was attacked they could quickly dive down to rejoin the main formation, Groom concluded[8].

The weather closed in again for the next two days, allowing new pilot Lieutenant J.E.L. Sugden and new observer Sergeant M. Samson to settle in. The next fight for 20 Squadron came on 8 May as a morning patrol of eleven Bristol Fighters patrolled via Cassel and Wormhoudt to Poperinghe and Ypres, bombing Messines and Wervicq en-route before engaging a mixed formation of Albatros scouts and Fokker Triplanes. Middleton and Godfrey were again flying C4699 and destroyed an Albatros DV southeast of Bailleul at 08.45 and a Fokker Triplane east of Dranoutre at 09.30. The highlight for Brodie Wilson, though, was that Purcell started teaching him how to fly the Bristol Fighter on the return trip[3,4,5].

Early afternoon saw Latimer and Noel bring down an Albatros DV in flames southeast of Wervicq at 13.20, making the squadron's third victim of the day[4,5]. But this was only the start, as the two men also took part in a later patrol that saw them claim a Triplane hat-trick after shooting down one Fokker in flames between Comines and Wervicq at 16.40 quickly followed by two more out of control. Captain Cooke and H.G. Crowe also claimed a Triplane they reported having crashed between Comines and Wervicq that possibly duplicated one of the claims from Latimer and Noel, while Groom and Hardcastle claimed their first victory as a team by setting a Triplane alight northwest of Wervicq at 16.45. This brought the squadron's tally to eight for the day, of which Latimer and Noel had accounted for four. One of the two 'flamers' claimed was quite possibly Jasta 27's Leutnant H. Muller who was reported killed in action near Ypres that afternoon[5,9,10]. Purcell's and Wilson's attempts to gain their first victory were thwarted when Purcell's gun jammed again as they dived after a Triplane that Brodie Wilson's shooting had forced into a spin.

The following morning 'parallel lines of fleecy cloud' on the British side of the lines and thicker layers on the German side prevented effective reconnaissance but cleared enough by lunch-time for Wilfrid Beaver and Sergeant Deighton to destroy an Albatros DV at 13.30 over the Warneton-Comines area[4,5]. In the same fight, Canadian pilot William Thomson and Second Lieutenant G.H. Kemp in C4851 brought down another Albatros DV between Comines and Wervicq for Thomson's first victory[4,5]. In a later patrol, Lieutenants L.M. Price and A. Mills brought down a Triplane in flames west of Lille at 16.50, possibly from Jasta 27, while Lieutenant D.E. Smith and Probationer F.J. Ralph in C4851 destroyed another southwest of Merris at about the same time[4,5,7,9]. Ralph was wounded but was back in action two weeks later.

Brodie Wilson evidently revelled in the experience of flying, his logbook recording the beauty of the white billowy clouds at 9,000 to 10,000ft on 12 May – then how, after dropping their 112lb bomb on Armentieres, they dived through the clouds and came home low over Poperinghe and Cassel in some very bumpy air. Two days later he was treated to a brief morning flight with Major Johnston in which they photographed Boisdinghem from the air. Then at 17.25 he set off with Purcell and eight other machines on another OP. Latimer and Noel claimed an Albatros destroyed near Wervicq at 18.45 as Thomson and Kemp shot down another that killed Leutnant Erich Weiss when his Albatros DV fell on the British side near Dickebusch. The remains of his aircraft were given the captured designation G/2/8. Five minutes later the next to fall was Albatros DV 5161/17 in which Jasta 51's Unteroffizier Friedrich-Karl Florian was taken prisoner at Zillebeke after being shot down by Latimer and Noel for their second that day. His captured aircraft was given the next designation number G/2/9. The following morning, German soldiers recovered the bodies of Offizierstellvertreter Wolski and VizeFeldwebel Warschumm, also from Jasta 51, on the German side of the lines near Zillebeke Lake. As there do not seem to be any corresponding British claims for that morning, it seems most likely that they had both been killed the previous evening. The location matches and may well be a confirmation of Groom's and Hardcastle's claims for a DV destroyed three miles east of Zillebeke Lake at 18.45 or Latimer's and Noel's first claim for the DV destroyed in the Wervicq area at 18.45[1, 3, 4, 5, 6, 8, 10]. Purcell and Wilson saw more fighting the following morning, 15 May, when they engaged eight or nine Triplanes and Albatros scouts, one Triplane being shot down in pieces by Latimer and Noel between Comines and Wervicq at around 10.25[3,4]. In a later fight, Rex Bennett and P.G. Jones claimed two Albatros DVs shot down out of control over Wervicq at 11.15 and Boulton and Holman claimed a Pfalz crashed northwest of Lille at 11.25[4, 6].

******

The first fifteen days of May had seen 20 Squadron's men claim twenty-five combat victories, of which at least five can be linked to definite German losses. Purcell and Wilson had also come close to becoming casualties on 15 May when a howitzer shell aimed at ground troops narrowly missed them at 16,000ft over Lille, Brodie noting in his logbook that he actually saw it pass them as it reached its zenith before falling to earth. Such sightings were not uncommon and presented yet another threat as the airmen carried out their already perilous duties. The first fifteen days had gone well but the next day brought losses when Boulton and Holman failed to return in B1232 from a midday patrol. Last seen leaving the patrol at around 12.30, both men had been captured and Holman was wounded. Since no German pilots seem to have claimed their machine, it seems most likely that they were brought down by ground fire[3,7]. Employed as a joiner in peacetime, 23-year-old Frederick Edward Boulton, from Croydon, Surrey, was one of the rare breed of RFC officers who had been promoted from the ranks. Educated at Christchurch school in Croydon, he first enlisted in the RFC at Farnborough on 9 November 1914 and was promoted to Corporal on 1 May 1916. After graduating as a pilot with 10 Reserve Squadron on 16 August 1916, he was promoted to sergeant before gaining his commission in the RFC with effect from 11 February 1918. He had been with 20 Squadron since mid-April 1918. His observer, 25-year-old Herbert Holman, from Kilburn, London, had worked as a secretary in civilian life and joined the Artists Rifles (28 Battalion, the London Regiment) on 27 August 1917, from which he was discharged to a commission in the RFC on 19 January 1918.

A later patrol that day brought some compensation when, just after bombing Menin aerodrome, Sergeant Deighton, flying with David Weston, shot down an Albatros trying to get under their tail and reported it crashed into the canal bank near Wervicq[4]. The next day, Cooke and Hardcastle claimed an Albatros DV brought down out of control over Armentieres at 08.15, while Thomson and Kemp in C859 claimed two more DVs over Armentieres at about the same time: the first one crashed between Armentieres and Lille and the second out of control. Lieutenants V.E. Groom and S.H.P. Masding then shot down another out of control near Armentieres[4, 5,6].

Saturday, 18 May 1918 brought 20 Squadron's combat victory total past 400 – a sure sign of the squadron's success. At about 07.00, according to Brodie Wilson, a morning patrol that had just bombed Wervicq ran into around thirty enemy scouts and left one of them crashed on a roof-top in Comines after being shot down by Latimer and Noel. The same team then claimed a Pfalz destroyed northeast of Nieppe Forest at 11.40 and another out of control over Merville five minutes later, bringing their day's tally to three. In the same fight, Thomson and Kemp claimed a Pfalz out of control south of Merville at 11.40, while another was claimed as destroyed by J.H. Colbert and R.W. Turner at 11.40 over Neuf Berquin, a small hamlet not far from Estaires. Two more claims were submitted for a Triplane shot down out of control southwest of Nieppe by Paul Iaccaci and his air gunner Arthur Newland and for a Pfalz out of control over Merville by Price and Mills[4, 5]. The only British casualty was Corporal W.H. Foster who was seriously wounded. He was taken to hospital after his pilot Lieutenant T.W. Williamson landed at Aire.

Sunday, 19 May was not exactly restful either. Brodie Wilson's flight took off at 09.15 to escort some SE5As on a balloon attack and was assailed by a twenty-strong force of Pfalz scouts and Fokker Triplanes south of Vieux Berquin at about 10.25. As Captain Cooke put it: 'C4749 dived on one EA (Pfalz) and after firing sixty rounds the machine was seen to go down burning with clouds of smoke issuing from it. Another EA then got under our tail. The observer, after firing thirty rounds, saw this EA going down out of control, and it was observed to crash at Laventie by Lieutenant W.M. Thomson.'[1]. Weston and Deighton's first claim involved a report that is fairly similar to that of Captain Cooke, and it is quite possible that they shot at the same Pfalz, but as Weston continued: 'The observer fired about 150 rounds into a second EA. The left side of this EA burst into flames and the EA went down in a slow spin, still burning. The observer fired about sixty rounds into a third EA which went down in a vertical dive and was seen to crash just north of Frelinghem cross-roads.'[1,4]. August Iaccaci manoeuvred C859 to allow Air Mechanic First Class Newland 'to fire on one EA underneath in a climbing turn. Observer emptied one magazine at close range and the EA spun down, leaving behind a trail of smoke, and was seen to crash just to the left of the road south of Vieux Berquin at map reference 36.a.e.23.d.'[1]. Fifteen minutes later his brother Paul and Sergeant W. Samson dived C856 onto one of the Triplanes and 'the pilot was able to get in a good burst of about 25 shots at about 25 yard.' Paul quickly cleared a gun jam but, before he could fire again, the Triplane went down in a vertical dive to about 4,000ft, then another dive before it flattened out upside down and crashed at trench map sheet 36.A.R.2, which is near Merville. As if to prove the value of the trans-Atlantic connection once and for all, Canadian W.M. Thomson and his English observer G.H. Kemp in C483 dived on one of the Pfalz scouts and Thomson fired about 150 rounds into it from the front gun before giving Kemp the chance to fire another three Lewis drums into it. The Pfalz then plunged away and crashed into a house near Estaires. The day's final claim came from Captains Middleton and Godfrey for a Pfalz scout shot down out of control east of Zillebeke. All the Bristol Fighters then returned safely to base at around 11.30. However, the similarities in the descriptions and locations of some of these victory claims suggest that several crews claimed the same German aeroplanes in the speed and confusion of the fight.

Following an afternoon patrol in which the Germans were conspicuous only by their absence, Brodie Wilson and Purcell and Noel went off by tender to collect a new Bristol Fighter that was flown back by Purcell and Noel. Brodie Wilson returned via Norvent Fontes in order to visit the Cadarts, a French family who owned the farm where he had spent Christmas in 1915. Further on he passed the Second Army shell dump near Aire which had been bombed the previous night, and marvelled at the 40ft-wide bomb craters and the fact that some shells had been blown two miles from the dump!

Purcell and Wilson 'only' flew one mission on 20 May as, according to Wilson, 'we have supplied the Army with more photographic information than they can handle'. But it was an interesting flight. Despite Bristol Fighter 873 only being able to manage 17,000 revs, the patrol first bombed Lomme Aerodrome before going on to drop their remaining bombs on an ammunition dump in retaliation for the German raid on Aire. This second attack seems to have been quite successful, with Brodie Wilson noting four large explosions and 'masses of red flames and high columns of smoke.' The return trip was also interesting, in that their low-revving engine meant they could not get above 14,000ft and they made an easier target for 'Archie' than usual. Passing over Wervicq, they were hit by a piece of shrapnel that took a two-inch chunk out of the leading edge of the right front inter-plane strut.

At 11.30 Latimer and Noel were on patrol near Moorseele when they dived on seven enemy machines, believed to be from Jasta 7[(9)]. Latimer became separated from the others during the attack and, while looking around to try to locate them, dived on the leader of three more enemy machines immediately below. Firing from about 150 yards with the front gun, Latimer pulled out at only ten yards range, at which point the German scout went down vertically pouring smoke before bursting into flames. Latimer relates what happened next:

> As I pulled out of the dive one of the EA dived on our tail. The observer fired about sixty rounds at 30 yards range and the EA went down completely out of control and was seen to crash in a field a little NE of Moorseele. After this I found two of our formation, and when over Comines, a third machine joined us from out of the sun. My observer thought it was another of our formation as it kept with us for four or five minutes. It then came slightly out of the sun and we were astounded to find it was an Albatros scout. The enemy pilot seemed to realise his mistake at about the same time as he suddenly dived towards Menin. We immediately dived after him, firing, but without apparent result. He went on down, and as the visibility was so perfect we could see him trying to land on Coucou aerodrome. He apparently overshot it and landed in a field [sheet 28.Q.18.5.8.] and turned over on his back.[1].

This was turning into a spectacular month for 20 Squadron, and German losses in April 1918 of about 500 men rose to nearly 700 in May. Although it is true that this total also includes deaths from illness, accidents and other causes than air combat, a trend was starting to appear that underlined the scale of the continuing fighting around Ypres.

******

Brodie Wilson flew two bombing raids against Comines on 21 May but it was a morning OP that saw the real action. The 'Biffs' dived on seven enemy scouts about 3,000ft below, Thomson and Kemp firing about 200 rounds into an Albatros DV that immediately caught fire and went down near Warneton[1]. This was followed by three fights on 22 May. At 07.05 Captain Middleton and Lieutenant Mills were flying C856 on a twelve-strong OP between Wytschaete and St. Eloi when they attacked three enemy two-seaters. Mills fired two drums downward at the leading German machine and then Middleton dived on it and fired another 250 rounds into it from the front gun. The German two-seater then crashed into the ground between Wytschaete and St. Eloi[1, 3, 6]. Later, August Iaccaci and Air Mechanic First Class Newland claimed a two-seater destroyed over Bailleul at 12.20 for August's second victory[5].

The evening patrol of eight Bristols set off at 17.50 and was reduced to seven when Magee's machine developed a fault and he had to make a forced landing in a field near St. Omer[3]. The remaining Bristols went on to bomb Comines and at 18.40 engaged seven German scouts at 15,000ft over Warneton in the last fight of the day. Brodie Wilson was flying with August Iaccaci on this occasion and related that, although he was only able to fire three rounds at a Triplane that tried to attack them from behind before his gun jammed, it was enough to make it break off its attack. Brodie then fixed the gun jam, caused by a double feed, but immediately afterwards got another caused by a broken return spring. Lieutenant Mills, who was flying as Lieutenant Thomson's observer in C843, sent an Albatros spinning slowly downwards after firing about eighty rounds into it and, although it was not seen to crash, its fall as an 'out of control' victory was confirmed by patrol leader Captain Beaver[1, 5, 6]. According to 20 Squadron's Record of Decisive Combats, a claim by Victor Groom for a Fokker Triplane was also approved[6].

Adverse weather meant there was little to report over the next few days apart from on 24 May when two new NCO observers, Sergeant Mechanics W. Barter and W. O'Neill, were posted in, and on 26 May when observer Second Lieutenant W. Jacklin was wounded by ground fire. Monday, 27 May was more productive, though, and marked a red-letter day for the industrious Captain Beaver when a hat-trick was scored during a twelve-strong OP that dived on nine enemy Triplanes and Albatros scouts from 12,000ft at around 11.25. Beaver, in C889, sent one of these down to crash northeast of Armentieres. After continuing northeast for a few minutes, the patrol dived on another Triplane formation, four of which immediately got onto Beaver's tail. Sergeant Deighton was on the ball, however, and sent one of them down out of control before opening fire on another with a long burst that caused it to crash northeast of Perenchies. But by this time, Beaver had lost the rest of the formation, the observer had run out of ammunition, their Bristol Fighter was badly shot up and it was only with great difficulty that the remaining EA were shaken off.[1] On the return trip, August Iaccaci and Air Mechanic Newland were attacked by eight Pfalz scouts over Neuve Eglise. Newland fired a full Lewis drum into one of them, which was seen to go down vertically trailing heavy smoke about three miles southwest of Neuve Eglise. Their combat report also carries a footnote signed by Major Johnston and the 11 Wing adjutant: 'Confirmed by French AA to have crashed'[1, 4, 5]. That did not quite spell the end of the day's fighting, though. Following an evening bombing raid on Armentieres, Sergeant A. Starsfield had to make a forced landing in B1193 near Clairmarais after 19-year-old observer James Tulloch was wounded in the leg by a Fokker Triplane. Tulloch was of a modest background: the son of plasterer the late John Tulloch and dressmaker Mary Urwin Jackson, from Gateshead, he had studied as an undergraduate teacher at Bede College, Durham, before joining-up. He never sufficiently recovered from his wound to be able to rejoin the squadron but did survive the war. He became an assistant schoolmaster, was married to Jane Brown in 1925, but sadly died in 1934[12].

On the morning of Tuesday, 28 May, after Major Johnston had told him he could now put up his observer's wing, Brodie Wilson flew with T.C. Traill, who had served as a Royal Navy midshipman in the Dardanelles before transferring to the RFC. The pair were on another bombing mission over Armentieres, during which they drove off two German scouts that tried to get under their tail. However, Rex Bennett and G.C.T. Salter failed to return in C4763 and were reported as having last been seen near Neuf Berquin at 10.30. Leutnant K. Baier of Jasta 18 claimed a Bristol Fighter shot down at La Gorgue at 11.20 German Time[10] and, although this was ten minutes earlier than the last sighting of Bennett and Salter, there can be little doubt about Baier's claim. Their Bristol Fighter was the only one lost or claimed destroyed during that day and Neuf Berquin and La Gorgue are scarcely a mile apart. Sadly though, neither could shed any further light on the question as they were dead. Bennett, of Hanwell, London, who had been credited with nine victories, and Salter, a Scarborough doctor's son awarded the Military Cross during earlier service with the East Yorkshire Regiment, are both remembered at the Arras flying Services memorial.

Having returned from an uneventful but useful low reconnaissance over the salient at 11.11 the following morning, Purcell and Wilson set off again six hours later on another OP. Led by Captain Beaver and Sergeant Deighton in C889, the mission involved photography, reconnaissance, bombing, artillery work and the now inevitable air fighting – which came when the twelve Bristol Fighters dived on a formation of four Triplanes and four Albatros scouts over Armentieres. Captain Beaver and Sergeant Deighton shot up a Triplane that rolled over and crashed near the river at Bac Sur Maur[1]. Three 'out of control' claims were also submitted after the fight: the first from Middleton and Mills for an Albatros DV out of control at 18.30[6] and the second from Thomson and Kemp for another DV over the same area[5, 6]. The third claim was from Traill and Jones for one of five Fokker Triplanes that attacked them from under their tail west of Armentieres after they became separated from the main formation.

In a personal memoir held by the Imperial War Museum,[13] Traill recounts how Percy Jones shot down one of the Triplanes out of control as it stood on its tail and strafed them from below and behind. Moments later Jones miscalculated his line of fire at the others, due to his gun barrel being six inches lower than his gun-sights – and in doing so, shot away the Bristol Fighter's starboard longeron. German bullets then hit the remaining three longerons. When Jones's gun-mounting jammed, Traill turned on the Germans – but saw that his own tailplane and rudder had been almost completely shot away and 'seemed to be following us in a sort of spiral'. Most of the Germans scattered as he opened fire with the front gun but one continued his attack. Jones managed to free his gun-mounting enough to drive him off with a burst in his general direction before the pair escaped back over the lines. Even then their ordeal was not quite over as they ran out of petrol shortly afterwards and had to glide most of the way back to Boisdinghem, where they finally crashed 100 yards short of the aerodrome. Both Traill and Jones were slightly injured and their aircraft was a write-off [5, 6, 13].

There was a change of pilot for Brodie Wilson on Thursday, 30 May when he flew two patrols with Lieutenant Colbert, a 23-year-old whose flying instructor had regarded him as a quite exceptional pilot. The air was so clear that morning that the cliffs of England were clearly visible in the distance as they gained height, after which they bombed a railway level-crossing east of Armentieres and made notes on German motor transport columns between Lille and Armentieres. They flew their second patrol in the late afternoon and, after noting that the fire their bombing had caused the previous evening was still burning, they dropped some more bombs to fuel the flames. Road, rail and canal movements were diligently recorded until 17.20, at which point their formation dived on a mixed force of nine Fokker Triplanes, Pfalz and Albatros scouts over Lille. Captain Middleton fired on an Albatros scout at 50 yards range, putting about 250 rounds into it before it turned over and he watched it crash on the canal northwest of Lille. As he led the patrol back towards the lines, he attacked another seven Pfalz scouts and his observer sent one down to crash near Wez Macquart. At the same time, Weston and Noble shot down another close to the canal by the Citadel in Lille, Captain Middleton confirming its fall. Colbert and Wilson came under fire several times and had a close call when a close 'Archie' burst near the centre section, its fragments only just missing the aileron control wire and leaving a 2½ inch chunk of shrapnel lodged in the top wing [3].

If the preceding days had been busy, 31 May was frenetic with the squadron submitting thirteen victory claims. The first action came at 07.30 during a ten-strong patrol that fought around fifteen Albatros and Pfalz scouts over Estaires. Two of them targeted C4604 piloted by Lieutenant Capel with probationary observer Ralph. When Capel put the Bristol Fighter into a continuous right-hand turn to evade them, Ralph engaged both with his Lewis gun and hit one that 'dived vertically into the ground just north of Laventie'. Ten minutes later Middleton and Mills shot down a Pfalz that crashed between Armentieres and

Estaires, while Colbert and Wilson attacked four Germans that were on another Bristol Fighter's tail and sent one down that was seen by Captain Middleton to crash to crash east of Estaires[3,4]. Paul Iaccaci and Air Mechanic Newland in B1122 got a Pfalz that crashed in flames east of Merville, quickly followed by an Albatros scout that went into a vertical dive but flattened out just before it crashed or crash-landed on the canal bank south of Merville[1,4]. Paul's brother August, who was flying C4762 with newly-arrived observer Sergeant D. Malpas, completed his family's tally that morning by sending down an Albatros out of control southwest of Armentieres. Another 'out of control' victory was claimed by Weston and Noble for an Albatros DV sent down over Estaires[5,6].

The morning's fight had brought seven combat victories for the squadron – and the evening patrol closely rivalled it. Ten hours later, Colbert and Wilson were back in action over Armentieres, but this time Colbert was flying with Lieutenant Mills as his observer while Brodie Wilson had Lieutenant Sugden as his pilot. According to Brodie Wilson, the Germans had laid a trap and, when the Bristol Fighters dived on a small group of enemy scouts below them, another twenty or more Germans came diving down on the Bristols. Incredibly, in the ensuing fight, six of their attackers were claimed destroyed or shot down out of control. Colbert and Mills claimed a Pfalz in flames[1,6], Ernest Lindup and Sergeant Deighton in C850 claimed a Pfalz destroyed south of Armentieres[6], and Thomson and Kemp claimed a Pfalz destroyed over Bois Grenier at 18.50 followed by an Albatros out of control over Armentieres just five minutes later[5,6]. August Iaccaci and Second Lieutenant Hardcastle shot one down out of control just north of Comines and Paul Iaccaci and Air Mechanic Melbourne claimed an Albatros in similar condition northwest of Armentieres[6]. Sugden and Wilson did not make any claims but were lucky to survive after Brodie's gun jammed while three Germans were attacking them. It was only Sugden's quick thinking that saved them as he S-banked and spun down before fleeing west with his nose down. When they got back, they found they had had one bullet through their left top main plane, another through its leading edge, one more through the rib of the bottom centre-section, and one right through the front section of the undercarriage. Their Bristol Fighter then had to be dismantled for repair[3].

It had been a day that summed up the entire month, during which 20 Squadron's flyers had claimed no less than 75 combat victories. It was also the month that saw H.G. Crowe complete his service with 20 Squadron. Shot down no less than six times in eleven days during the ferocious fighting, he now 'retired to England through No.24 General Hospital, Etaples'.[14]. There were also some more new faces in the squadron. Lieutenant A. Campbell had been posted in as a pilot on 26 May and NCO observer Sergeant Mechanic J. Helsby arrived the next day. They were followed on 28 May by probationary observers J. Ross and R. J. Gregory, and by new pilot Second Lieutenant A. J. McAllister the day after. Purcell was sent on two weeks leave on 31 May, while recently announced awards included the Military Cross to D. Latimer and a Bar to the Military Cross for T.C. Noel.

******

Notes

1. Combat report.
2. Author's correspondence with Mrs Hope Thayer, and *Over the Front* magazine, Volume17.1, article by Dennis Gordon.
3. Brodie Wilson's Observer's Logbook held the R.A.F. Museum, Hendon.
4. R.A.F. Communiqués.
5. *Above the Trenches* by N. Franks et al.
6. AIR/1/168/15/156/7: 20 Squadron Records of Decisive Combats – Pilots.
7. *The Sky Their Battlefield* by T. Henshaw, Grub Street Press.
8. AIR/1/2389: Victor Groom, Service Experiences, 1918 and 1920/21.
9. Russ Gannon's database of aerial combats.
10. *The Jasta War Chronology* by N. Franks et al.
11. Casualties of the German Air Service by Norman Franks, Frank Bailey and Rick Duiven.
12. Descendants of J. Tulloch.
13. Personal papers of Air vice Marshall T.C. Traill, Imperial War Museum.
14. AIR/1/2390/228/11/134: Flt Lt. H.G. Crowe, M.C.: Presentation to the R.A.F. Staff College.

Chapter 21

A New Fokker – June 1918

Germany's efforts to force a final victory before American intervention became decisive continued throughout June. More assaults against the French on the River Aisne and River Matz ended in failure and left the Germans armies weak and disillusioned. So too in the air: the advantages the Germans had previously held of better aircraft and better trained pilots were being steadily stripped away by a relentless allied offensive carried out by ever-increasing numbers of new and effective planes and squadrons. One year previously, the RFC had struggled to hold the line with obsolete aircraft flown by half-trained replacement pilots and observers. Now though, allied aircraft such as the Bristol Fighter, the Sopwith Camel, the SE5A and the French SPAD XIII were good enough to hold their own in most circumstances, while new pilots and observers were benefiting from longer and better training programmes. The increase in allied production meant higher numbers in the air, which in turn meant that many offensive patrols could now be carried out by whole squadrons that were frequently reinforced by similar size patrols from other squadrons. Contemporary combat reports point to an increasing number of fights in which the British outnumbered the Germans. The German Air Service was now fighting against odds it could no longer realistically hope to hold at bay, let alone overcome – although they tried very hard.

******

The first day of June brought Canadian pilot William Thomson his thirteenth combat victory; but it came at a heavy price. At 06.30 that morning, eight of 20 Squadron's Bristol Fighters fought nine of Jasta 7's Pfalz DIIIs over Comines, with Thomson and Kemp cut off from the main formation by four of the enemy scouts. They turned at bay in C843, and Thomson used his Vickers gun to send one Pfalz down to crash just before Kemp brought down another. But even as they watched their second victim going down, a lone Albatros scout dived on them from behind and loosed off a fatal burst that hit and killed Kemp. Thomson threw the Bristol into a spinning dive with the Albatros in hot pursuit and, when he got down to 2,000ft, came out of the spin and swung the Bristol around to face the Albatros and successfully drive it off[1, 5]. It was a cruel blow. The two men had become close friends after flying together for nearly a month and all bar one of Thomson's victories had so far been shared with Kemp. The usually cheerful young Canadian was hit hard by the loss and, as Brodie Wilson remarked in his log book, he became very quiet afterwards, hardly speaking a word. A Londoner, George Kemp had transferred to the RAF from the Durham Light Infantry. He was buried the following morning at Longuenesse, St. Omer, with most of the squadron in attendance.

In the same engagement, Traill and Jones had also been badly shot about in C4749, leaving Traill soaked in petrol, the engine stopped and the joystick partly stuck. Expecting they would crash, Jones dropped his gun over the British reserve trenches. Happily, however, when he helped Traill by pulling on his own emergency joystick, they managed to flatten out and make a safe landing on the British side near Dickebusch, getting back to the squadron that evening[2, 3]. Their machine was claimed shot down by Jasta 7 commander Josef Jacobs[4] whose unit recorded that Unteroffizier Kroeger was wounded in what was probably the same fight. Elsewhere in the fight, Groom and Hardcastle in C4764 claimed a Pfalz that crashed into the ground just north of Comines under Groom's gun and another under Hardcastle's gun that crashed northwest of the town[1]. Latimer and Noel were also busy in C892, with Noel bringing down a third Pfalz that crashed into a railway[1,4, 6]. Another OP set out at 10.13 and when it ran into trouble near Armentieres, August Iaccaci and Sergeant O'Neill shot down a Pfalz DIII out of control north of Merville[7, 8].

Bad weather proved the most dangerous enemy on 3 June, almost causing a serious 'friendly fire' incident that could easily have ended in further tragedy. Near-impenetrable clouds upset a planned rendezvous with a SE5A patrol, and two of the SE5A pilots had a narrow escape when the Bristol Fighters mistook them for Germans in the murk and dived to attack them. Luckily though, the Bristol Fighter pilots realised their mistake just in time and no shots were fired[2].

******

The absorption of the RFC and RNAS into the new Royal Air Force on 1 April meant that the former RNAS units had to be re-numbered to avoid confusion with RFC squadrons having the same number. This was done by adding 200 to the RNAS squadron number, so that 1 and 2 Squadrons RNAS respectively thus became 201 and 202 Squadrons RAF, and so on throughout the service. So when Colbert and Wilson and others were sent up at 09.10 on 5 June to escort some of 210 Squadron's Sopwith Camels on a balloon attack, they were actually flying alongside the former 'Naval 10' that had so bravely come to 20 Squadron's rescue with their Sopwith Triplanes a year earlier, when A.E. Woodbridge had shot down and wounded the famous Red Baron. This mission was also a success, and two balloons were destroyed by 210's Lieutenants A.L. Jones and E. Swale, although two other Camel pilots were wounded in a fight with German scouts afterwards. While that was going on, another more amusing case of mistaken identity occurred when an unknown two-seater joined the Bristol Fighter formation, flying peacefully along with them until the British pilots suddenly realised that it bore big black crosses on its wings and fuselage! The German pilot seems to have realised his mistake at the same time, and quickly dived to safety[2]. A later patrol that set off at 16.25 had a less amusing tale to tell when it returned with two of its aircraft missing. Both B1114 and C817 were last seen over Armentieres at around 17.40 just before they were attacked by some of Jasta 52's Pfalz DIIIs. Lieutenant J.E.W. Sugden and Sergeant W. O'Neill were both captured after they were shot down by ViceFeldwebel H. Juhnke. Also captured were Lieutenants Magee and Gregory when their aircraft collided with a Pfalz flown by ViceFelwebel P. Reimann, who was killed[4, 9].

Colbert and Wilson dropped a message bag over the German side between Armentieres and Lille on 6 June, informing the Germans as to the condition of three of their own flyers who had been captured. They returned safely. The following day's work included an early twelve-strong OP during which Brodie watched the sun rise on their way to bomb Armentieres before recording rail movements over Lille, Laventie and Bailleul. This was followed by a road trip to the aircraft depot at St. Omer, where Traill and Thomson had orders to collect Bristol Fighters, C938 and C987, to replace those lost the previous day. On their flight back, they enjoyed a mock battle before flying another OP in the afternoon. When they returned, it was to the news that William Thomson had been awarded the Military Cross and that Sergeant Deighton was getting the Distinguished Conduct Medal. Two new pilots also enjoying the celebrations were Lieutenants B.T. Davidson and H.C. McCreary who were officially posted to the squadron on 5 June 1918. Three more American pilots joined the squadron on attachment from the USAAS on 7 June: Earl W. Sweeney from Lafayette, Indiana; Clare (spelled Clair in some records) R. Oberst from Sandusky County, Ohio, and George H. Zellers from Lancaster, Pennsylvania. All three had graduated from the Ohio State School of Military Aeronautics in mid-1917 which is where they probably first met. Only two would return to their homes[11].

The next day, Saturday, 8 June, brought an inconclusive skirmish with some Triplanes near Comines from which August Iaccaci and Victor Groom brought their machines back riddled with bullets. Later on, Brodie Wilson experienced his own version of what he clearly felt to be a quite unnecessary close call. He and Traill, with Dennis Latimer in another Bristol Fighter, went up for firing practice on the aircraft silhouette placed in the floods near Clairmarais Forest. On the return trip, keeping very tight formation, there was nearly a collision when Traill failed to notice Latimer making an unexpected manoeuvre, the disaster only being avoided when Wilson punched him in his back just in time. Brodie later wrote that he thought close flying dangerous and foolish, adding that Traill had flown dangerously low over the army camp on the St. Omer road and had carried out a flying exhibition, including loops and dives, during which they nearly crashed. As if that was not enough, Traill had then hedgehopped and contour-chased all the way back to Boisdinghem before Brodie was finally able to alight from the machine and find some peace and quiet[2]. The day ended with Middleton and Godfrey claiming two Pfalz Scouts, one of them a 'flamer', southeast of Comines, while Arthur Newland, flying with August Iaccaci in C892, celebrated his promotion to corporal by getting another near Wervicq that was seen to stall and go into a vertical dive before crashing near the railway at about 17.20[1, 7].

On the morning of Sunday 9 June, an eight-strong 20 Squadron patrol met a mixed formation of around sixteen Albatros, Pfalz and Fokker DV11 biplanes at 8,000ft over Comines. This was the first time they had met the new Fokker in combat and, in doing so, they were facing what was probably the best single-seat scout produced in large quantities by any country in the Great War. It was especially remarkable in that its design removed the need for the unsightly, drag-inducing external bracing and control wires that were an unavoidable feature of other First World War aircraft. It was fast and highly manoeuvrable with an excellent rate of climb, and had the ability to point its nose upwards at a high angle and 'hang on its propeller' long enough to effectively rake the entire length of an enemy's underbelly. But Groom thought the Bristol Fighter matched it well, noting in his memoir, that the rear gun was particularly useful in deterring Fokker DVIIs from 'hanging on their props' and shooting up at their belly, as all the Bristol pilot had to do was go into a climbing turn while his observer shot down at the enemy. A well-flown Bristol Fighter was worth two of the enemy, he concluded[12]. On this occasion, though, the encounter brought no British losses. William Thomson claimed a Pfalz DIII destroyed between Comines and Houthem at 08.45 while Latimer and Noel in C892 claimed another destroyed over Comines half-an-hour later, its left wings breaking off as it fell[1].

A patrol on 12 June gave Brodie Wilson the opportunity to drop a copy of *Lloyds Magazine* to the hospital nurses at Cassel where Captain Beaver was being treated for scabies. This kindly mission brought Wilson up to a landmark 100 hours operational flying with 20 Squadron. Having been in action for a full month, he was almost an 'old hand'. With his early keenness now no doubt slightly moderated by the realities of war, he would probably not have minded too much the following evening when he and Colbert had to pull out of another mission with more carburettor problems. Captains Middleton and Godfrey and the main formation pushed on eastwards and at 19.10 they attacked three 'Albatrii' and sent one down to crash a little to the east of Zillebeke Lake[1]. Wilfrid Beaver was released from hospital the following morning and, going straight back to war flying, claimed his nineteenth victory by bringing down an Albatros DV out of control northwest of Armentieres, while another went to Paul Iaccaci and Walter Noble in B1122[7, 8]. Beaver's release from the hospital was premature, however, and he was re-admitted after catching a chill. His six months at the squadron having evidently taken its toll, he was taken off operations a week later and returned to England on Home Establishment duties[2].

Refreshed by his recent leave, J.M. Purcell reclaimed Brodie as his regular observer for an early fifteen-strong patrol on 15 June that did not go exactly to plan. Immediately after bombing Armentieres, Captain Middleton turned back for the lines and, as nobody had seen him signal new orders, Purcell and Wilson and some others turned to follow him. Eventually however, Middleton signalled to them that he had engine trouble and that they should continue the patrol. While this group searched for the rest of their colleagues, they were attacked over Halluin by what Brodie Wilson described as 'umpteen Huns'. Their Bristol Fighter trailing behind the others with engine problems, Purcell and Wilson struggled back last – quite a feat with six enemy aircraft on and under their tail. Wilson managed to keep them at bay by firing a total of 400 rounds in repeated bursts before his gun jammed with a broken extractor. When he tried to free the stoppage, his trigger finger poked through a hole in his glove and got frost-bitten. Fortunately, the Germans broke off their pursuit when they crossed the lines and, after they had glided gently home, Brodie Wilson found damage to the fabric and right-hand longeron. It had been a narrow escape; but the purpose of the OP had never been far from their minds and, despite the fighting, they were still able to report the time and locations of ten trains seen behind the lines and of canal barge movements in Halluin, Menin and Comines[2].

******

The second half of June was not unlike the first: a series of hair-raising encounters and narrow escapes that brought the squadron another twenty victories but, providentially, no further casualties. On 16 June Lieutenant D.E. Smith and Second Lieutenant J. Hills were bringing up the rear of an eleven-strong evening patrol over Comines when they shot down one of two Pfalz scouts attacking a Bristol Fighter. The Pfalz took hits from both of Smith's and Hills's guns before spinning slowly down to crash just south of Comines at 19.15, its fate being confirmed by Sergeant Samson, the observer in C980[1, 7].

Twelve hours later, a fifteen-strong morning patrol led by Captain Latimer and Lieutenant Noel in C987 engaged several small groups of enemy scouts in a series of fights. In the first of these, August Iaccaci and Arthur Newland dived C892 on a Pfalz scout that crashed near Houthem while Price and Hardcastle in C4672, fired three drums into another Pfalz that crashed northwest of Armentieres. A little later the patrol was attacked by eight more Pfalz over Menin and Lieutenant Capel and Sergeant Deighton in C4604 sent one spinning down out of control, followed by another that went down to crash northeast of Gheluvelt at about 07.40. There was more to come. The fifteen Bristol Fighters now turned northwards and, in approaching the lines from the east, attacked a small group of Fokker DVIIs north of Ypres. Latimer and Noel, aided by Thomson and Ralph in C843, fired on one that went spinning down until it was lost in the ground haze, with the men of anti-aircraft U Battery reporting they too saw it going down and that it looked certain to crash. The final scrap came at 07.55 when the Bristols flew back over Menin and attacked another eight Pfalz. Most of these quickly spun away to safety but two that had been flying higher than the rest were left behind. Paul Iaccaci, flying B1122 with Walter Noble as his observer, was able to get within 50 yards of one of them and fire about fifty rounds, sending the German down in a steep dive. They and others in the patrol watched it descend until it crashed at Sheet 28.Q.11.c: a little southeast of Gheluwe. The whole patrol then returned safely, another six claims added to the tally[1,5,7].

Low clouds and frequent rain hampered operations over the following week, but had cleared enough by 07.30 on Sunday 23 June for Lieutenant Capel to claim his final victory with 20 Squadron while flying C4604 over Laventie with Sergeant Deighton in a fifteen-strong patrol. Twelve Pfalz scouts dived onto the rearmost formation of Bristols and, as Capel forced one of them to spin away, Sergeant Deighton fired at another coming up under their tail that dropped away in a vertical dive with bits of the plane breaking off before it eventually went down in several pieces. The identity of the luckless German remains a mystery, although one would not have expected him to survive such an event. However, if the fight was against Jasta 43 – who recorded a fight with two-seaters at about the same time – it is worth noting that Leutnant Wernicke was forced to land with a shot–up engine: although that does not really fit the description of an aircraft that went down in several pieces[1, 6].

The next big fight came three days later, although it brought no real results. After attacking a German two–seater head–on, a sharp cracking noise made Brodie glance behind to find himself staring down the twin Spandau barrels of a Pfalz scout barely 40 yards away. He returned fire and it rolled away out of the fight, while 'Archie' opened up with a vengeance and three shells burst in front of their nose as two more Pfalz attacked from behind. When they got back, they found that some of the German two–seater's bullets had passed through the centre section main spar, rear spar and trailing edge and had left Purcell's cap cut up by with splinters. It had been another lucky escape for the pair. One victory claim was submitted after the fight, by Paul Iaccaci and Francis Ralph for a Pfalz DIII brought down out of control over Armentieres at 19.00[2, 7].

The following day Brodie Wilson noted a new type of British 'Archie', the bursts of which 'looked like little white balloons'. The same evening also brought him another 'friendly fire' incident after Purcell dived on some red–tailed machines that appeared to be trying to get under his own tail. He opened fire – but it was as well that he missed for they were Sopwith Dolphins. Although red was such a common feature and likely identifier of German aircraft, an unidentified Dolphin squadron had chosen to paint its own aircraft tails red for a while. Whether it was discretion or higher authority that stepped in is not known but the experiment was short–lived and the Dolphins' tails were soon repainted olive drab. Purcell's confusion was also understandable given the fact that the Dolphin was quite a new type on the Western Front, recognition not being helped by its decidedly unfamiliar shape that included a very large nose, a flat–sided fuselage and back–staggered wings.

******

The last day of June proved slightly more eventful when Purcell and Brodie took up Bristol fighter 873 at 14.15, on a two–strong patrol with Lieutenants Sweeney and Boothroyd. After seeing off four Pfalz scouts that escaped towards the east, they were themselves 'bounced' by two Fokker DVIIs; but Brodie hit one of them in the engine after which both Germans broke off the fight. Having just completed their own patrol, they were not involved in the evening OP led by Middleton and Godfrey, although one can get a fairly full description of what occurred by combining Captain Middleton's detailed combat report and Brodie Wilson's account of his own later conversation with T.C. Traill.

The fourteen-strong patrol was flying at about 10,000ft near Comines when they encountered half-a-dozen Fokker DVIIs led by an all-black Fokker Triplane that almost certainly belonged to Jasta 7's ace commander Josef Jacobs. Middleton and Godfrey dived on the black Triplane and, after both pilot and observer had fired a total of around 300 rounds into it, they saw it roll over and dive into the ground east of Comines at about 19.30, its crash also being witnessed by T.C. Traill. It would have been a famous deed had they killed Jacobs – but perhaps they had not. So what had really happened? In this case, it is not what was written down that provides a possible clue but what was not written. Jacobs kept a daily diary recording his exploits but unusually made no entry at all on 30 June. It was out of character, and it has been suggested that, after surviving a serious crash-landing in the countryside followed by a long walk home, he had little enthusiasm for writing[6].

This was not the only incident, though. A short while later, the Bristol Fighters dived on another eight German scouts flying at around 5,000ft. Middleton and Godfrey used both guns to attack a Pfalz that spun and dived downwards until it crashed just west of Wervicq. August Iaccaci and Sergeant Newland in C892 then attacked another Pfalz that crashed near the canal west of Halluin, while Latimer and Noel in C987 also attacked one that they reported broke up in the air after Noel fired about 200 rounds into it at close range from his double Lewis guns. Weston and Noble in B1307 claimed another Pfalz that Middleton confirmed he saw crash near Wervicq, and then shot two more down, both out of control, between Wervicq and Comines, giving them a hat trick. Another Pfalz was brought down by the joint efforts of Lale and Hardcastle in A8716 and McAllister and Robinson in C980. Lale fired first but a gun jam made him zoom upwards again to allow Hardcastle to empty three Lewis drums at the enemy before it dived away, closely followed by McAllister and Robinson who kept on firing until it crashed northwest of Menin. One German unit involved in the fighting was Jasta 20, and VizeFeldwebel Soltau's logbook records that the tail of his new Fokker DVII 626/18 was so shot-up that it took four days to repair[1,5,6, 6a].

Traill and Jones enjoyed a rather different adventure to the others. Having shot down an Albatros out of control, they lost the rest of the formation and found themselves alone at 2,000ft north of Comines with their petrol tank pierced by anti-aircraft fire, both guns jammed and a Pfalz shooting them up from behind at only 25 yards range. A lot of ground fire was still coming up at them and, as Traill ducked around the cockpit expecting to be hit at any moment, salvation appeared in the unlikely shape of a cumbersome Armstrong-Whitworth Ack-8 that attacked and drove off the Pfalz. Traill and Jones headed for home but lack of petrol forced them to land in a field near Clairmarais. In so doing, they carried away a barbed-wire fence, collided with one of a herd of cows and crashed and wrote off C938. They were unhurt but no sooner had they struggled free from the wreckage than the dead cow's angry owners, a mother and daughter, ran up and began screaming abuse at them for killing their cow – for the loss of which animal, Traill records, the family were later reimbursed by the British Army. Both men eventually made it back to base, but not until after they had been reported missing[1,2,3]. Brodie Wilson's summary also mentions that 'Scottie shot the tail off one Hun, which came off as he was spinning', which most likely refers to the Pfalz that broke up in the air after being shot at by Latimer and Noel, as Middleton's report also mentions its tail breaking away. 'Scottie' was ex-Etonian Tom Noel's nickname as, although he was born in Rutland, he had first been commissioned in 1 Battalion the King's Own Scottish Borderers, with which regiment he had been awarded the MC in September 1917. The mounting of twin Lewis guns in his Bristol Fighter was not limited to his aircraft alone, but neither was it universal. It would seem from what records remain that the choice of single or double guns in the rear cockpit was something that individual crews decided for themselves: some preferring the extra punch while others regarded the extra weight as a liability.

Apart from heavy fighting, the month had also seen the usual personnel changes. Probationary observers J. Hills, C.G. Boothroyd and A.S. Draisey were posted in from 6 June and T.V. Robinson arrived a week later along with qualified NCO observer Sergeant Mechanic J.D. Summers. Wilfrid Beaver's promotion to captain was confirmed on 9 June. A new pilot in the squadron was Second Lieutenant H.W. 'Slops' Heslop, posted in on 15 June. Sergeant Cormack and Corporals Foster, Melbourne and Newland were all regraded from aerial gunner to qualified observer during the third week of June. Captain Middleton's award of the newly introduced Distinguished Flying Cross was published in Wing Routine Orders on 12 June, and William Thomson and Sergeant Deighton got leave from 24 June to 9 July.

******

Notes

1. Combat Report.
2. Brodie Wilson's Flying Logbook.
3. Personal papers of Air vice Marshall T.C. Traill, Imperial War Museum.
4. *The Jasta War Chronology* by N. Franks et al.
5. R.A.F. Communiqués.
6. Russ Gannon's Database of WW1 Air Combats.
6a. Vfw Soltau's Logbook courtesy of Thorsten Pietsch via Russ Gannon.
7. AIR/1/168/15/156/7: 20 Squadron Records of Decisive Combats – Pilots.
8. *Above the Trenches* by N. Franks et al.
9. *The Sky their Battlefield* by Trevor Henshaw.
10. *The War in the Air*, Vol. VI by H.A. Jones.
11. Details of these three airmen thanks to Bradley Damon.
12. V. Groom's personal memoir held by the Imperial War Museum.

******

Chapter 22

Turning Point – July 1918

The fifteen-strong 20 Squadron OP that set out at 07.17 on Monday 1 July was not seriously molested as it bombed Bousbecque and noted enemy ground movements. Brodie Wilson drove off two Fokker DVIIs that approached them over Armentieres but, after firing five drums, found so much wrong with the sixth that he dropped it through the camera hole in the faint hope it might hit a German soldier. In other patrols, Lieutenant F.G. Harlock and Second Lieutenant A.S. Draisey claimed a Fokker Triplane falling out of control to Draisey's gun northwest of Tourcoing, then at 18.45 Latimer and Noel claimed a Fokker Triplane out of control over Menin[2, 6].

At 08.40 on the next day, a nine-strong OP was patrolling near Gheluvelt, the two flights staggered at 16,000ft and 12,000ft respectively, when some Pfalz scouts dived on the lower formation and lured the upper one into diving down to attack them. Then the Germans sprang their trap and six to ten Fokker DVIIs came diving onto them from an even greater height. Lieutenant Traill and Second Lieutenant P.G. Jones shot up a Fokker that was attacking another Bristol Fighter and other patrol members reported it caught fire on the way down. They then attacked a Pfalz that went spiralling down under Jones's fire. Turning towards Traill to signal that it was doomed cost Jones his life as another Fokker swooped down from behind and a hail of German bullets tore through the Bristol Fighter's aileron controls, a landing wire and shattered Traill's windscreen while a piece of debris banged into his left elbow. Then the Fokker broke away and, as Traill turned for the lines, he glanced back and saw Jones slumped across his gun and realised that he was dead. He landed the stricken aircraft safely at St. Marie Cappel, despite the damaged undercarriage collapsing as he did so, and once down found that Jones had been hit in the stomach by an explosive bullet that had made an 'awful mess' of him, as Brodie Wilson later wrote.[1,2,3,8,10]

Meantime, the fight raged on. One of the Fokkers dived from behind on Lieutenant Sweeney and Second Lieutenant Boothroyd in C843 and came firing through a hail of Boothroyd's bullets to as close as 20 yards, before suddenly plunging away in a vertical dive to crash between Dadizeele and

Gheluwe[1, 7]. Another victory was claimed by Lieutenants Weston and Noble in B1168 after they fired about 200 rounds into a Fokker from close range and saw it crash between Gheluwe and Menin at 08.45, its destruction confirmed by Tom Noel[1, 7]. The final claim came from Lieutenant D.E. Smith and Second Lieutenant J. Hills who sent a Pfalz down out of control southwest of Ypres[2, 6]. But the cost was heavy. In addition to Percy Jones being killed, 20 Squadron had lost two more aircraft and their crews. These were D8090 flown by Lieutenant H.C. McCreary and Sergeant W.J.H. Barter, and C850 flown by Lieutenant B.T. Davidson and Sergeant J. Helsby, the latter going down in flames. All four men were dead, the German victories going to Leutnant D. Collin for shooting up Traill's aircraft and killing Jones, and Leutnant F. Piechulek of Jasta 56 and Leutnant J. Schafer of Jasta 16 getting the others[2].

Percy Griffith Jones, a 29-year-old from Mold in North Wales, had previously served in the Royal Engineers. He was buried at St. Omer the following morning with most of the squadron in attendance. Canadian Bryce Thomas Davidson the 25-year-old only son of Douglas and Mary Davidson of Mimico Beach, Ontario, was a married law student living in Toronto when he enlisted. His observer, 19-year-old Sergeant 51777 Joseph Helsby, was the son of George and Ellen Helsby, of St Helens, Lancashire, and had first served with the Lancashire Fusiliers before transferring to the RAF, being promoted to sergeant on qualifying as an observer. Both men are buried at Menin Road South Military Cemetery, Ypres. Harry Charles McCreary was the 21-year-old son of shipping agent Albert Edward McCreary and his wife Helene. Born and educated in Southend, Essex, he had originally enlisted as an air mechanic in the RNAS before being commissioned and sent for pilot training. His observer, Sergeant 231124 William Barter, aged 27, was also an ex-RNAS man. He had been a leather worker in his native Southwark, South London, before enlisting in June 1917, and had qualified as an observer on 6 May 1918. Both are buried at Harlebeke New British Cemetery.

Traill's personal memoir provides a final footnote to a very grim day. The blow to his left arm had first made him think he had been wounded but he realised this was not so as he flew back to St. Marie Cappel and having just lost Jones, he felt disappointed. The fear and tension of war flying preyed on everyone's nerves and, after realising he not been wounded, he frankly wrote that to have been wounded would have been an easy way out of the constant fear of burning. It would also serve to sustain 'whatever it is that holds a man in the line – fear of being recognised as one who will leave his comrades to carry the can; the knowledge that you will have to live with yourself afterwards.' He raised the question of morale again a little later in his memoir, by mentioning how some men turned to alcohol, including one crew who not only needed a stiff drink before taking off but also took a bottle with them. That crew's fears were finally ended when they suffered a fatal accident. But such men, Traill went on, were braver and better than the types who got out of a fight as quickly as possible and tried to cover themselves in glory by bragging about an enemy aircraft they had supposedly destroyed while far away from the real fighting. 'It was usually such types,' he wrote, 'who at the end of a fight were the furthest west and nearest home.'[10]

There was some slight relief for Brodie Wilson the following morning when, after attending Percy Jones's funeral, he visited Lady Millicent, Duchess of Sutherland, for tea. The duchess was a strong-minded lady renowned for her relief work in Belgium during the early part of the war when she created what became known as the Millicent Sutherland Ambulance. She and her staff were in the Ypres sector now, and this would not be his only visit.

******

A patrol of three Bristol Fighters that set out at 10.27 on 4 July returned to Boisdinghem about two hours later to the sight of a crashed Bristol Fighter lying close to the aerodrome. The crew, Second Lieutenants McAllister and Robinson, had been doing target practice and were climbing on the turn when the engine failed and their machine nose-dived into the ground. Allan James McAllister was killed on impact. Aged 23 and a former car salesman in Canada, he was the son of John and Mary McAllister, of Quebec. Thomas Robinson, a married farmer from Cockermouth, Cumberland, died on the way to hospital. Their funeral was held at Longuenesse the following day.

At least the Reaper seemed even-handed, for a later patrol brought a hat-trick to Lieutenant Paul Iaccaci and Second Lieutenant R.W. Turner. Just after bombing Gheluvelt at 16.40 their flight became separated from the rest of the formation and met a number of Albatros scouts at an altitude of about 16,500ft. Iaccaci managed to get alongside one that was trying to out-climb the Bristols, and Second Lieutenant R. W. Turner fired 100 rounds into it at point-blank range, causing it to fall away and crash just west of Veldhoek. This may well have been FlugMeister Clements Kahler of SFS2, who survived a crash-landing near Thourout, which is only four miles west of Veldhoek. As Iaccaci and Turner fought their way home, helped by some Sopwith Camels that intervened, they engaged a second Albatros that fell out of control after it tried to attack them from behind. They then claimed a third that plunged away in a vertical dive before crashing into the ground close to the railway northeast of Zillebeke Lake. Kahler's SFS2 comrade Leutnant Theodor Lodemann was subsequently reported killed near Ypres, which may tie in with this stage of the fight[1, 2, 3, 4]. The next few days passed in the usual manner but without fights or casualties. A highlight on Tuesday, 9 July 1918 was the announcement that Sergeant Deighton had been awarded the Distinguished Conduct Medal.

There was more fighting the following day. At 07.45 Brodie Wilson's flight set off for a bombing raid on Warneton but had to take a roundabout route via Roulers and Menin in the face of repeated German attacks, during which Brodie and his pilot were forced out of the formation. Purcell had just managed to get above two German scouts when Brodie heard a cracking noise and was alerted to a third German attacking them from the right front. Having lost the rest of the formation, they had little choice but to run for the lines, chased all the way by a determined Fokker pilot who kept under their tail, making it impossible for Wilson to get a decent shot at him. The German broke off his attacks when they reached the trenches, though, and they made it safely back at 10.06. In the meantime, the rest of the patrol was fighting off repeated attacks, and at around 09.20 Paul Iaccaci's D8919 was assailed by five Fokkers at 16,000ft, which also forced him out of the formation. As the Fokkers attacked from front and behind, R.W. Turner signalled Paul that he could not change his ammunition drums because his hands were frozen. Paul dived the aircraft down to a warmer altitude of 6,000ft, where Turner managed to replace the ammunition drum and fire a burst into a Fokker that had followed them down. The German aircraft turned over and dived into the ground just east of Zillebeke Lake. Its pilot may well have been Jasta 56's Leutnant Oberstadt who was wounded in action[1, 2, 3,4].

Friday 12 July produced another hazard for Purcell and Wilson when they flew a low reconnaissance. They were accompanied by new arrival, George Randall, who had recently qualified as a pilot having previously been an observer with 3 Squadron, and American pilot, First Lieutenant Sweeney. The crews suddenly found themselves under fire from German field guns near Mount Kemmel as well as the usual rifle and machine-gun fire, so quickly climbed out of reach. Brodie Wilson had an easier time of it; having been given the afternoon off, he made the most of it by going into town to draw his pay before visiting the Millicent Sutherland Ambulance to take tea with a certain Sister Bridget.

There was no serious fighting the following day but it did bring three more gallantry awards when Weston, Noble and Godfrey were all awarded the DFC. The day after that, Latimer and Noel were credited with sending down a Fokker DVII out of control southeast of Ypres at 09.00 assisted by August Iaccaci and R.W. Turner and the rest of the patrol[5,6,7].

******

The Germans now pushed their war beyond the point of no return when, on 15 July, they launched what was to become known as the Second Battle of the Marne. It failed and left the German army in a state of near terminal exhaustion. German victory was now impossible unless the allies suddenly decided they could fight no longer. With troops and equipment flooding into Europe from across the Atlantic, and British and Empire arms production and military training having reached a peak, there was not the faintest chance that this would happen. But to those in the trenches and on the seas and in the air, the news of the new German offensive against the French, would have come as still further proof that the war would go on forever.

It was, of course, business as usual for 20 Squadron's airmen, and some would be lucky, others would be less so. One of the lucky ones, after a fashion, was Sergeant Deighton. Although he had the misfortune to be seriously injured in a flying accident on 15 July, it led to his repatriation to England where he survived the war. The same day also brought some light relief for Alfred Mills and Brodie Wilson when, after they had returned from a bombing raid on Estaires, Major Johnston took them out in his car for a picnic with some of the nurses from the Millicent Sutherland Ambulance. It must have gone well as the nurses then agreed to visit the squadron for tea on 18 July.

Following an uneventful morning patrol the next day, Brodie Wilson went swimming in the afternoon, and met and chatted with Colonel Lord Henry Scott who commanded the 20,000 labour troops in the area. The usual patrols and reconnaissances over the ensuing days passed without major incident, and the next fight came at 08.45 on Friday, 19 July. A nine-strong patrol attacked a group of Fokker DVIIs and a Triplane flying 1,000ft below them over Comines. Latimer and Noel dived onto one DVII in C987 and fired one hundred rounds into it at very close range. It crashed in a field[1]. Meantime, Lieutenant Thomson and Sergeant Summers dived to 7,000ft in C843 and came up against another four Triplanes as they turned west. In Thomson's words: 'One EA flew straight at the pilot, each pilot firing all the while.' The enemy aircraft then passed under the Bristol and, the pilot turning, allowed his observer to open fire at the EA at 10 yards range. It fell out of control and crashed south of Gheluvelt[1]. What Thomson and Summers may not have known was that some of 74 Squadron's SE5As had also joined the fight, which was almost certainly against Jastas 7 and 20, and that the first Triplane they had seen was most likely that German ace Josef Jacobs, a *Pour le Mérite* holder with a score of twenty-three victories. He had apparently spun down to their height under attack from 74 Squadron's Lieutenant L.A. Richards, who also claimed him as 'out of control'. Jacobs quickly regained control, however, and raced off eastwards at treetop height before climbing back up and shooting down 74 Squadron's American pilot Lieutenant A.M. Roberts, who was taken prisoner. The Triplane that Thomson and Summers thought they shot down must have been one of the others making a forced landing, as the Germans admitted no casualties in the area that day[1, 2, 4, 5, 7].

Brodie Wilson chatted with Lord Henry Scott again that evening while out swimming, and learned from him that the French had advanced ten kilometres after counter-attacking from Thierry to Soissons and were now threatening the German lines of communication. On the other hand, the infantry and artillery reinforcements being brought up on both sides in the Ypres Salient lent credence to the rumours of an imminent new German offensive in 20 Squadron's own backyard – and were actually true. The Germans were set to launch their attack at any time in the next two or three days. But it never came. The French successes Lord Scott had spoken of had set alarm bells ringing in the German High Command; the Ypres attack was hurriedly called off and the troops supplied for it were rushed to the south. Brodie would not be reporting on the German withdrawal, though, as he was about to go on leave[8, 9].

******

The next few days passed uneventfully until 20.00 on the evening of Wednesday, 24 July when a nearly squadron-strength patrol of fifteen Bristols fought several groups of Fokkers over Comines. Lieutenants Price and Mills dived on four of them in C4672 and, after Mills fired about 200 rounds into one of them from his twin Lewis guns, the German machine dived away and broke into pieces in the air about 2,000ft below[1,3]. At the same time, Lieutenant Colbert and Second Lieutenant Turner side-slipped under the Bristol formation and attacked two Fokkers below them, with Colbert firing 200 rounds into one that then spun slowly down to crash to earth three miles north of Comines[1, 5]. Fifteen minutes later Lieutenants Randall and Learmond were bringing up the rear of the formation in D8086 at 16,000ft over Wervicq when five Fokker DVIIs swooped on them and Learmond shot one of them down out of control. Although neither he nor his pilot was able to watch it to the ground, recently promoted Captain T.C. Traill confirmed having seen it crash north of Wervicq[1, 3]. Thus, the fighting ended with 20 Squadron claiming another three Fokkers destroyed. The German unit's identity is confirmed by the fact that Sergeants H.D. Aldridge and M.S. Samson failed to return in C4604 after losing their fight with OberLeutnant H.E. Gandert of Jasta 51, although both fortunately survived as prisoners of war. Jasta 51 also suffered, losing both

Unteroffizer Kurt Hoffmann and VizeFeldwebel Kurt Beinecke killed. The location given for their demise in *The Jasta War Chronology* is Pont Ronge, but this may well be a misspelling of Pont Rouge which is quite close to a likely flight-path from Armentieres to Comines and Wervicq, so may well tie in with two of 20 Squadron's victory claims[2, 7]. Twelve hours later, at around 08.55 the next day, Captain Traill was flying with observer Lieutenant R. Gordon-Bennett on a bombing raid to Menin when their formation was attacked by around twenty German scouts. Some Camels joined in on the British side but were not able to save Lieutenant Shearer and Sergeant Malpas from being shot down and killed by Jasta 16's fifteen-victories ace, Leutnant Friedrich Ritter von Roth. As Shearer and Malpas fell, their comrades claimed another four victories. One claim as 'destroyed' was by Lieutenant Thomson and Sergeant Summers, a second by Captain Lale and Second Lieutenant Ralph, while a third was shared by the whole patrol. An 'out of control' victory was also credited to Lieutenant D.E. Smith and Second Lieutenant J. Hills, although some records suggest that they should have been awarded two[2, 4, 7].

Lieutenant Frederick James Shearer, from Edinburgh, was the 22-year-old son of Mrs Mary Shearer and the late James Shearer. A former civil servant, he originally enlisted with the Argyll and Sutherland Highlanders at Edinburgh on 19 May 1915 and served in France as a lance-corporal until 17 March 1917 when he returned to England on being accepted for officer training. He was commissioned into the RFC as a temporary second lieutenant with effect from 26 September 1917. Sergeant 100024 Donald Malpas was the 18-year-old son of Frederick William and Eleanor Malpas, of Helmshore, Manchester, and had been with 20 Squadron since May 1918 after enlisting in October 1917. The news of Malpas's death hit Captain Traill particularly hard as they had flown together several times after P.G. Jones was killed. Perhaps unusually for an officer referring to a non-com, he wrote that he was 'sorry to lose Malpas; he was so steady and a good friend'.[10] The last three words are telling. Given the class-conscious norms of the day, where except in the course of their duties officers and other ranks were kept strictly apart in a kind of social apartheid, such an epitaph amounted to the highest praise possible. Both men are buried at Dadizeele New British Cemetery.

Another well regarded 'back-seat' NCO flyer, Sergeant John J. Cowell, was mentioned earlier in this narrative when in 1917 he came to 20 Squadron as an air mechanic. From that lowly start he had quickly gone on to make a considerable name for himself by shooting down fifteen enemy aircraft in a very few months and winning a DCM, MM and bar along the way. In late summer of 1917 he was posted back to England for pilot training and in late July 1918 he returned to 20 Squadron as a qualified pilot. At 07.00 on 29 July he set out on what seems to have been his first patrol as a pilot, flying E2471 with Corporal Charles Hill as his gunner. At 07.50 his patrol of twelve Bristol Fighters dived on four enemy scouts that were quickly joined by another twelve, including some Pfalz scouts painted black with blue tails. Cowell and Hill were attacked by three of the enemy, Corporal Hill firing at each of them before concentrating on one Fokker DVII that he sent down completely out of control northwest of Wervicq. It was recorded as Cowell's sixteenth and his own first victory[1]. Elsewhere in the fight, Captains Middleton and Godfrey in C951 shot down an enemy machine that turned over and went down in a slow spin before crashing just south of Gheluwe[1]. Traill and Gordon-Bennett attacked another that went down in a vertical dive and disappeared into the mist at about 4,000ft. One of the Germans then attempted to attack Colbert and Turner from below but Turner got in a burst of about 150 rounds, after which the enemy machine spun away and crashed northwest of Wervicq[1]. The fight the next day proved much grimmer.

At 19.25 that Thursday evening, an OP of fifteen Bristol Fighters patrolling a line over Armentieres, Bailleul and Ypres was attacked at 13,000ft north of Armentieres. Two groups of Fokker DVIIs and Fokker Triplanes, some of them described as having bright yellow wings and blue tails, attacked the Bristol Fighters from the front and rear and were soon joined by more. Lieutenant Purcell and probationary observer Second Lieutenant Hills dived D7897 onto a Fokker that was attacking Sergeant Cowell and Corporal Hill but were just too late to save them as E2471 burst into flames and fell from the fight. So the young Irishman's magnificent career came to a grisly end along with that of his equally young observer; the victory going to Jasta 56 ace Leutnant Franz Piechulek. Lieutenant Paul Iaccaci and Second Lieutenant Edwards rushed nose to nose with a German scout that suddenly broke away and glided down before hitting the ground northeast of Bailleul[1], while four more Fokkers latched onto the tail of C904 flown by American First Lieutenant George Zellers and Sergeant Cormack. Their machine too fell away in flames and, as it descended, Zellers climbed out onto the wing and Cormack lay astride the engine cowling in an effort to avoid the flames. Zellers managed to bring the burning machine down under control to within 200ft of the ground – but at that point it broke into pieces, and both men fell to their deaths. The German victor was Jasta16 ace, Ritter Friedrich von Roth[2, 7, 8].

On the credit side, 20 Squadron's men claimed four combat victories. Groom and Hardcastle claimed two 'flamers', while Sergeant Summers, flying as Lieutenant Shell's observer in C4718, claimed another in flames after firing

500 rounds into it before he ran out of ammunition[1]. The last victory of the fight went to Lieutenant Strachan and probationary observer Penrose in B1168 after Penrose shot down one of three Fokkers attacking them and saw it fall away completely out of control, although continuous attacks from the others prevented him from watching it to the ground[1]. That the fight finished with four Germans apparently shot down might have seemed like fair compensation for the loss of two Bristol Fighters but records suggest that only one of the British claims was probably correct with Jasta 16's Unteroffizier W Meyer listed as wounded in action. As to the 'flamers' claimed by the British crews, the sad likelihood is that these were mistaken glimpses seen from high above of the falling remains of the two Bristol Fighters that were lost[3, 4, 5, 7].

First Lieutenant George Zellers, attached to the RAF from the American Army Air Service, came from Pennsylvania and is buried in Flanders Field Cemetery, while 19-year-old Sergeant 317109 John Cormack, from Edinburgh, rests at Hagle Dump Cemetery, near Ypres. Sergeant 78171 J.J. Cowell DCM, MM and Bar, married and a native of Limerick, Ireland, found his final resting place at Longuenesse (St. Omer) Souvenir Cemetery. Corporal 2767 Charles William Hill, from Birmingham, is buried at Klein-Vierstraat Cemetery. That Cowell and Hill were buried in different cemeteries suggests that at least one of them chose a quicker end by jumping from the burning aircraft. Friday, 31 July brought another loss when Oberleutnant Harald Auffahrt, formerly of Jasta 18 but now with Jasta 29, brought down C859 over Vieux Berquin. Fortunately Lieutenant Shell and Sergeant Summers survived the experience and the war as prisoners.

June and July 1917 had seen 20 Squadron's men claim no fewer than sixty-five combat victories, bringing the running total to well over 500. The fact that so few of their victims can be definitely identified almost a hundred years after the event should not be allowed to detract from their accomplishments. The war in the air was not won by the side achieving the highest number of combat 'kills', as they are known today, although it appears that the Germans may well have accomplished that. It was actually won by the side that controlled the air above and behind the battlefronts: and 'control of the air' means being able to continue to carry out the vast majority of bombing and reconnaissance missions regardless of losses. Weight of numbers meant the British and French could do that but the Germans could not. Hard-pressed 20 Squadron and other fighting units accepting heavy casualties allowed our bombers, reconnaissance aircraft and artillery machines to carry out their vital work at a cost of what were, put bluntly, 'acceptable losses'. The Germans, on the other hand, hardly ever succeeded in turning back our patrols despite the casualties they inflicted.

It was the sacrifices of the British airmen who stoically faced becoming a part of that dreadful casualty list that made this situation possible.

During those two months, 20 Squadron had lost fourteen dead, six captured and three wounded or injured – and the war was still far from won. But Germany's final gambles on the ground had cost it over three-quarters of a million men killed or wounded. Very large numbers of these fell under massive artillery bombardments directed from the air, while no small number of others fell to bombing and ground-strafing attacks. The once proud would-be European superpower no longer had the men, equipment or industrial capability to repair those losses. From now on it would be the Germans who were on the defensive.

******

Notes

1. Combat Report.
2. *The Jasta War Chronology* by N. Franks et al.
3. AIR/1/168/15/156/6: 20 Squadron Records of Decisive Combats – Observers and Aerial Gunners.
4. R.A.F. Communiqués.
5. AIR/1/168/15/156/7: 20 Squadron Records of Decisive Combats – Pilots.
6. *Above the Trenches* by N. Franks et al.
7. Russ Gannon's Database of WW1 Air Combats.
8. Brodie Wilson, Observer's Logbook.
9. *The War in the Air*, Vol. VI by H.A. Jones.
10. Personal papers of Air vice Marshall T.C. Traill, Imperial War Museum.

Chapter 23

Amiens – August 1918

With their unsuccessful offensives now ended, August 1918 found the Germans completely on the defensive. Many of their units based around the Ypres Salient were now being moved south in an effort to counter any allied offensives there, while the British were now planning a major attack at Amiens. This meant that 20 Squadron's encounters with hostile aircraft became fewer and their days passed by with a mixture of almost completely unopposed offensive patrols and reconnaissance missions. The only casualties during the first ten days of the month came on 2 August when Lieutenants J.J. Quinn and K. Penrose were both wounded and forced to land on our side of the lines. Brodie Wilson was now back from leave and passed some of the time visiting other squadrons. On 8 August he tried out Lieutenant Price's twin Lewis guns for the first time when he and Purcell borrowed his aircraft for an OP. This was followed in the afternoon by the rather unusual experience of co-operating with an American infantry attack near Norbecourt by dropping messages and firing flares to indicate the American advanced positions. Some highlights Brodie recorded on 9 August consisted of an unopposed bombing raid against Menin, during which he noted being treated to some of the most beautiful cloud scenery he had ever seen. He also wrote of the squadron's pleasure at Dennis Latimer, Paul Iaccaci, Victor Groom and Ernest Hardcastle each being awarded the Distinguished Flying Cross – and that 20 Squadron was now top of the Wing for destroying enemy aircraft.

Sunday, 11 August brought a less usual mission. At 12.18 that afternoon, Captain Lale and Second Lieutenant J. Hills, flying E2467, led a near squadron-strength force of sixteen Bristol Fighters to harass the German communications system around Courtrai. Escorted by no fewer than three squadrons of SE5As, they crossed the lines at 8,000ft and headed north towards Houthulst Forest before diving down towards Courtrai, where they attacked the trains and rolling stock from 400ft. Brodie Wilson noted that he could feel and hear the bomb bursts as they made direct hits on a locomotive and a building that was blown 'sky high' and that afterwards the Bristol Fighters gave the area a thorough ground strafing. Wilson wrote how this sent German soldiers, cows and horses running and stampeding in all directions. Captain Lale had soon destroyed a nearby German balloon[1] and, shortly afterwards, Lieutenant Sweeney and Second Lieutenant C.G. Boothroyd, flying C987 with C Flight at the rear of the formation, did the same to another in a field south of Heule. A third balloon was destroyed by Captain F.J. Davies and Lieutenant R.G. Robertson flying 29 Squadron's SE5As. The raid had been carefully planned to achieve maximum effect with minimum British casualties and included arrangements for British artillery to engage all the known enemy anti-aircraft batteries within range. The result was that 20 Squadron suffered no casualties at all, Wilson attributing this to the good organisation and leadership that carried them through[1, 4, 7]. The next day saw the return of Malcolm McCall to the squadron following convalescence and Home Defence postings after he was wounded in July 1917. Other than that, there was little to report from the squadron, while far to the south the British Army consolidated its new positions after the successful Australian-Canadian offensive at Amiens.

On Tuesday, 13 August, Brodie Wilson's note-taking and navigational skills were put to the test when Major Johnston decided personally to lead a nine-strong afternoon OP and chose him as his observer. Immediately after the patrol had bombed Comines, Wilson set about making his meticulous notes: recording three trains with rolling stock and four barges seen in Comines, another train with rolling stock seen in Warneton, eight barges at Quesnoy, eight trains with rolling stock in the sidings at Lille and another two at Quesnoy and Perenchies. His reward for this was to be chosen for a second patrol with Major Johnston that set out at 17.56, barely two-and-a-half hours after they had returned from the first, and during which he noticed a German scout lurking in the sun to the west. Soon after the British machines had bombed Comines railway sidings for the second time, another German machine attacked Harlock and Draisey, who were lagging behind the main formation. The 'Hun in the sun' that Wilson had noticed earlier now dived down onto his tail but was easily kept at bay and, as he later dismissively wrote of it, never came within 500 yards. As for Harlock and Draisey: after missing with his first burst, the German began to shadow them from about 200 yards range. Draisey took very careful aim and, despite the long range, used only one drum from his Lewis gun before the Fokker suddenly fell away as if out of control. Harlock followed the German down, perhaps suspecting a ruse, but was finally convinced of Draisey's accuracy when the Fokker crashed into the ground near Quesnoy[1, 5]. All the patrol returned safely but Brodie Wilson was not entirely satisfied with the situation. In his view, the fact that they carried 112lb bombs on almost every mission meant that they were nearly always slower and lower than their opponents. If fighting enemy aircraft was their main job, he wrote, they would do better without the bombs that prevented them getting above the enemy. But if bombing was the main role, they would be better off not to linger over the trench lines as it gave the Germans plenty of time to gain altitude. These were fair points, and it may have seemed to the men that the powers-that-be wanted to get as much as they possibly could out of everyone all the time – both fighting and bombing – without having considered the practicalities.

The fine but hazy evening skies of Wednesday, 14 August brought 20 Squadron's first serious air-fight of the month. This came when Captain Lale and Second Lieutenant Ralph led a nine-strong OP which, at 17,000ft over Dadizeele, met a mixed formation of Fokker DVIIs that sported pink and yellow tails, plus Pfalz scouts painted green with red tails. Lieutenants Thomson and McKenzie in E2154 dived on a Fokker, firing until it fell away smoking and crashed near Dadizeele. Meanwhile, Lale and Ralph dived on another German and, when Lale's gun jammed at the crucial moment, he turned the Bristol to give his observer a better chance. Ralph opened up with his double Lewis guns at about 100 yards range, seeing the German machine apparently descend out of control for about 4,000ft before more German attacks made further observation impossible. Captain Latimer and Sergeant Newland dived on a Pfalz in D7993 and, after Latimer had fired about 200 rounds into it, Sergeant Newland watched it go down to crash near Dadizeele. Newland then spotted another Pfalz stalling about 40 yards below and fired about 150 rounds into it that sent it down to crash near its comrade. Randall and Learmond in D8086 were also in the fight and, after spinning down for a while to avoid an attack, came out of the spin and saw a Pfalz just beneath them. Randall immediately dived on it and, after he had fired about 150 rounds, the German machine turned over and spun down slowly. Once again, however, the pressures of the fight meant they could not watch it down to the ground. A little later, Thomson and McKenzie shot up a blue two-seater that fell away 'completely out of control' but were unable to see if it crashed, as other Germans resumed the assault. However, their attack may well have been successful as two German reconnaissance flyers were reported killed over Menin that day: VizeFeldwebel H. Schlink and Feldwebel P. Schroer of FA250 (A)[1, 2, 6].

When the Bristol Fighters reformed after the fight they found that C987 was missing. Pilot David Smith had fallen to the guns of Leutnant Schramm of Jasta 56 for his first victory[2]. After originally being buried by the Germans in the 'Cemetery of Honour' near Roeselare, his remains were later re-interred at the famous Tyne Cot Cemetery near Ypres by the Imperial War Graves Commission. Dundee-born David Esplin Smith was the son of Mungo and

Rebecca Smith, then living in Cambridge, Massachusetts, USA. David had worked as an apprentice to a chartered accountant before joining up in early 1917. A six-victory veteran, he was just 19 years old when he was killed. His observer, Second Lieutenant John Hills, from Bath, survived the crash and was taken prisoner.

The following morning, a nine-strong OP was nearing its end when, at 07.10 over Gheluvelt, its members engaged seven Fokker DVIIs painted with black and white stripes coming southeast from Ypres at around 9,000ft. Thomson and McKenzie quickly got on the tail of one of them and opened fire at 50 yards, causing the Fokker to go down in a steep dive and crash near Becelaere in sight of other members of the patrol who confirmed seeing it smoking on the ground[1]. The Bristol Fighters then turned southwest and at about 07.30 recrossed the lines at the end of their patrol, only for E2155 suddenly to turn back over the German lines. Lieutenant W.H. Markham had spotted a German balloon just west of Comines and, judging that the enemy gunners would be occupied keeping an eye on the main formation to their west, he manoeuvred his Bristol to approach the balloon from the east with the sun behind him. He then swept down on the unsuspecting target and opened fire at only 60 yards range, sending the balloon down in a cloud of smoke and flames as the German gunners opened up with a storm of vengeful anti-aircraft fire. Some of this came just too close and, when Markham finally brought his riddled Bristol Fighter home, his leg carried the souvenirs of a chunk of shrapnel and a German bullet. Having spent most of his flying service as an instructor in England, Markham had been with 20 Squadron only a brief while after engineering his transfer to France. It proved a short-lived posting, with this his only victory as, after being taken to the Casualty Clearing Station at St. Omer, he was sent back to England and was not passed fit to return to war flying before the Armistice[1, 4, 5]. Another balloon was successfully attacked west of Roulers during a later patrol led by Captain Traill, its observer escaping by parachute.

The evening of 21 August saw 20 Squadron's score mount up again. At 19.10, having just bombed the railway junction at Comines, they engaged around fifteen enemy scouts at 10,000ft over Menin. Lale and Ralph dived on a Pfalz whose right wings crumpled under their fire before it fell to the ground northeast of Gheluwe. A minute later, Lale dived on an Albatros scout and saw it fall away out of control after a burst of 100 rounds, although he could not watch it to the ground as they were attacked from above by seven Fokker DVIIs. Ralph opened fire on the nearest with a burst from his double Lewis guns and it turned over and fell away to crash west of the Menin-Roulers railway. Captain Latimer and Sergeant Newland in D7993 then found themselves flying head-on at a Pfalz scout, firing all the time until this machine too fell suddenly out of control before crashing just northwest of Ledeghem at map reference 28.L.1. Shortly after this, Newland, ever alert to the danger from below, spotted another Pfalz under their tail. He fired about 200 rounds into it that caused it to go down in a steep dive and crash northwest of Gheluwe at map reference 28.K.38. A fifth German was shot down by Colbert and Edwards in E1258 and a sixth was credited to the whole patrol[1, 4].

Things did not go so well the following morning when Captain Latimer took up a patrol at 07.30 and led them east towards Menin. He was flying D7993 again with his usual observer Tom Noel and, according to George Randall's combat report, the twelve Bristols were at 19,000ft over Comines at about 08.40 when between twenty-five and thirty enemy scouts attacked from all directions. Four of these came at Randall's Bristol E2158 but Newland kept up a steady fire on one until his bullets sent it down to hit the ground east of Comines[1]. But Latimer and Noel failed to return. A British anti-aircraft unit subsequently reported seeing a Bristol Fighter 'putting up a stout fight' against three Fokkers and a LVG two-seater before landing under control on the enemy side of the lines near Westroosebeke. Latimer was taken prisoner but 20-year-old Tom Noel was dead, the German victory going to Leutnant Willi Nebgen of Jasta 7[2]. Captain Latimer MC had been credited with no less than twenty-eight combat victories and Tom Noel MC and Bar had closely rivalled him with twenty-seven. The ex-Eton son of Cecil and Edith Noel, of Cottesmore in Rutland, is buried at Perth Cemetery (China Wall), Ypres.

Patrols continued as normal up to and including 25 August. The Squadron Intelligence officer, Lieutenant R.V. Oliver, had asked the crews to keep a particular eye open for fires behind the enemy lines that might signify the start of a 'scorched earth' policy prior to a wide-scale withdrawal to new positions. A number of fires were duly spotted and reported by Brodie Wilson on 23 August during an otherwise uneventful afternoon patrol. The next morning Brodie had a new pilot during the nine-strong OP, as Purcell had been taken off operational flying pending his transfer back to England and a Home Establishment post. Getting used to a new and inexperienced pilot could be a stressful period for an experienced observer (and vice-versa, for that matter), Brodie later recording that although he found 20-year-old Glaswegian Lieutenant James Nicolson to be a good flyer, he also thought him a little rash. After bombing Comines, his new pilot circled over the target to watch the bomb bursts and in doing so dropped behind the main formation which, in Brodie's words, left them 'cold meat for any Huns'. Fortunately, no German aircraft appeared and, after their safe return, he warned Nicolson never to do it again.

The heavy fighting that followed the British offensive at Amiens led to the RAF squadrons based in the area taking severe casualties as they supported the ground troops. Particularly mauled was 48 Squadron during a German bombing raid that night that left two pilots dead, thirteen pilots and observers wounded and ten Bristol Fighters destroyed. Indefatigable 20 Squadron was ordered south to take its place, which meant transferring from 2 Brigade to 5 Brigade. The flyers and ground crews set out for their new home at Vignacourt, about ten miles northwest of Amiens, on Monday, 26 August. There was no time to make proper preparations for the move. Purcell's transfer home having been delayed by events, he flew to Vignacourt with Wilson, his cockpit cluttered up with two suitcases, two Lewis guns, ammunition and one of the squadron's pets – a cat or dog named 'Ginger'. All the aircraft arrived safely except for one that made a forced-landing near Hesdin, and the pilots and observers hurriedly set about settling in as quickly as possible as their first operation, a reconnaissance, was scheduled for dawn next day. The main ground fighting at this time was happening further north where the Canadians and the British 51 Division were advancing steadily east of Arras.

In the meantime, 20 Squadron's men flew as many reconnaissance and offensive patrols over their own area as could usefully be made in the wet and cloudy conditions that prevailed, with Wilson flying at least once every day and twice on 29 August. His first patrol that day was spent tracking German railway movements and, during the second between 18.00 and 19.45 in very dark skies, he and Nicolson were surprised by five Fokker DVIIs that suddenly came at them from out of the mist over Matigny, only to disappear again just as quickly after a brief exchange of fire.

The next day brought a different kind of thrill when Wilson and Nicolson went up for a mock dog-fight with Captain Colbert and Lieutenant Gordon-Bennett, who were testing a new type of observer's safety-belt harness. The practice fight soon turned into a stunting exhibition including diving, sideslipping, looping, rolling and spinning before they finished their display with combat manoeuvres such as Immelman turns and falling-leafs. It must have presented a thrilling sight to any Tommies watching from the ground and was a great example of what the Bristol Fighter was capable of. However, there was rather less showing off after an otherwise uneventful evening patrol came to a slightly inglorious end when Nicolson broke their aircraft's propeller and rudder on landing. This, as Brodie Wilson made clear, was not due to Nicolson's poor flying but to their being unfamiliar with the sunken road that divided 20 Squadron's part of the aerodrome from that of 80 Squadron, which was equipped with Sopwith Camels.

******

Notes

1. Combat Report.
2. *The Jasta War Chronology* by N. Franks et al.
3. AIR/1/168/15/156/6: 20 Squadron Records of Decisive Combats – Observers and Aerial Gunners.
4. R.A.F. Communiqués.
5. AIR/1/168/15/156/7: 20 Squadron Records of Decisive Combats – Pilots.
6. *Above the Trenches* by N. Franks et al.
7. Brodie Wilson, Observer's Logbook.

Chapter 24

The Somme – September 1918

The first casualty for 20 Squadron since their move came on Monday, 2 September when observer Sergeant 57658 L.F. Bradshaw was wounded in the neck by anti-aircraft fragments during the evening patrol. The following day, John Colbert was posted back to England on Home Establishment and Lieutenant Sweeney transferred out of the squadron to one belonging to the United States Air Service[2]. The vicious ground fighting around Peronne was reflected in the air when in the late afternoon Captain Lale and Francis Ralph led up a late afternoon OP of nine Bristol Fighters over Havrincourt Wood in E2181.

At 17.45 they came up against a mixed formation of twenty Pfalz and Fokker DVII scouts from Jastas 5 and 36, and Lale led the Bristols under the enemy formation. Ralph got a long burst into one of the enemy machines that promptly went down out of control, but it was his last ever victory as moments later he was hit and killed by a burst of fire from Jasta 5's Leutnant Vollbracht, or possibly Ostv Mai[1,2,4,5]. As Captain Lale broke off the action and made for home, Randall and Learmond sent down another German scout out of control while Paul Iaccaci spiralled E2470 slowly upwards allowing Lieutenant Mills to fire down at an Albatros that came up from below them. It was seen last falling earthwards with pieces of its tail breaking away[1]. Paul Iaccaci's fellow-American, Lieutenant C.R. Oberst, and his English observer, R. Gordon-Bennett, closed with three Pfalz scouts in D7915. Gordon-Bennett fired a drum into the nearest that caused its top left wing to break away as it fell, spinning out of sight just as another Pfalz flew across their front. Oberst dived after it and opened fire at point-blank range. But although it went down in a very steep dive, they could not watch it to the ground as their own aircraft had been badly shot up and they were forced to disengage. Oberst just managed to get the machine back over the lines before the engine seized up and they were forced to land in the countryside[1,2].

Bristol B1344 did not return from the fight: Second Lieutenants Washington and Penrose were both dead after being shot down by Leutnant T. Quandt of Jasta 36 for his fourteenth victory[3]. There were also two German casualties that may tie in with this fight. Jasta 5's Offizierstellvertreter Mai was listed as wounded and Jasta 36's Wilhelm Skworz was killed in action at Abancourt, which is not far from the area over which the fight raged and might reflect Oberst's claim. 'Who got who' remains as elusive a quest as it has always been, and the only thing that is really certain is that it had been a grim beginning to a month that aviation historians would later dub 'Black September".

William Frederick Washington was born on 2 October 1898 at Chingford, Essex, the son of Frederick and Florence Washington of Sanderstead, Surrey. William worked as a clerk in London's Cannon Street until February 1917 when he enlisted, qualifying as a Bristol Fighter pilot in July 1918 and was posted to 20 Squadron. His observer Keith Penrose had been with 20 Squadron for about the same time. Born in Transvaal on 1 November 1897, the son of Mr and Mrs F.W. Penrose, he had studied engineering for 18 months at Potchefstroom College, Capetown, and reached the rank of sergeant-major in the OTC before enlisting in the RFC on 9 May 1917. Both men are buried at Lebucquiere Communal Cemetery Extension near Bapaume. Francis James Ralph, 25-year-old son of John and Charlotte Ralph, was educated at Newtons Secondary School, Leicester, before becoming a draughtsman A married man, he first enlisted in the Army Service Corps on 4 December 1915, and six months later on 1 June 1916 his wife, Emma Kate, gave birth to their only child. The couple named their new home in the Leicestershire village of Tur Langton, near Kibworth, 'Doreen Cottage' after their baby. After training at Reading, Hythe and Romney, he was commissioned as a temporary second lieutenant in the RFC with effect from 12 February 1918. The award of his DFC was announced in the *London Gazette* of 2 November 1918 and he is buried at Villers-Bretoneux Military Cemetery near Amiens.

Nicolson and Wilson flew two OPs on Wednesday, 4 September and at 11.25 came back from the first to report large-scale German motor transport movements heading eastwards. This, as Brodie Wilson rightly deduced, was in preparation for a further German withdrawal. When he returned from his evening patrol at 19.45, it was to report on the many fires the Germans had started on their own side of the lines to destroy anything and everything they could not take with them that might be of use to the pursuing British forces. In fact, the German retreat would go all the way back to the position they had held in early 1917 along the Hindenburg line, with all its formidable defences. But unlike the situation in spring 1917, this was not merely a tactical withdrawal. This time the German Army was close to final defeat.

The following morning Nicolson and Wilson had to drop out of an OP led by Victor Groom as their Bristol Fighter could not keep up with it; but the return trip was not completely uneventful as they spotted a high-flying German reconnaissance aeroplane. Their efforts to bring it down proved fruitless, however, as it quickly turned east and escaped when they got within 4,000ft of it. Coming down lower again, they exchanged greetings with the nurses of a hospital train before landing safely at Vignacourt at 12.20. Three hours later, they were in the air once more as part of a six-strong formation led by Captain Lale and Lieutenant Edwards in E2467 that was attacked from out the clouds by eleven Fokker DVIIs. Lale immediately turned towards the enemy formation and Edwards's third burst of fire found its mark so that what seemed to be the leader's Fokker 'broke up in the air, pieces falling from it as it went down'.[1,5] Randall and Learmond also scored after engaging a Fokker that had dived under a Bristol on their left, the German going down trailing smoke in a vertical dive after receiving two full drums of bullets from Learmond's gun[6]. Lieutenants A.R.H. Campbell and C.G. Russell were then attacked from below in E2512 but Russell shot their opponent down in a vertical dive that developed into a spin before they lost sight of it[1].

On Friday, 6 September, Lale and Edwards in E2181 led a patrol of nine Bristols which, after bombing Roisel, were attacked from above by seven Fokker DVIIs southeast of Cambrai at 08.30. Sergeant Newland, who was flying with August Iaccaci in E2213, fired two drums at one of these from 100 yards range, sending it down in a slow spin before it was lost sight of in the mist and smoke near the ground[1,5,6]. Paul Iaccaci and Lieutenant Mills fired at another Fokker that was seen to crash and burst into flames between the Cambrai Railway and the Peronne Road[1,6]. The remaining Fokkers made off, allowing Lale to re-form the patrol and lead it south, where they linked up with three formations of D.H.4s, Sopwith Dolphins and SE5As near St. Quentin. As they did so, thirty to forty Fokker DVIIs dived on the Dolphins and Lale quickly opened fire on one that passed 30 yards in front of him, sending it down in flames. Edwards then opened up with his twin Lewis guns on another Fokker 40 yards to their left, and this too burst into flames before falling into St. Quentin town centre[1,5,6]. Lieutenant Mills engaged another Fokker that he reported fell to pieces in the air, and Sergeant Newland emptied half a drum into a DVII that suddenly fell away in a dive and was seen to crash northeast of St. Quentin close to the St. Quentin Canal. Sub-Lieutenant A.B.D. Campbell and Second Lieutenant D.M. Calderwood fired at another Fokker which was last seen still spinning down a great distance below. Pencil notes at the bottom of the combat report show six enemy machines being credited: five crashed and one out of control[1,5,6]. The fight had brought August and Paul Iaccaci's scores to twelve and seventeen respectively – and proved to be Paul's last with 20 Squadron, as two days later he was promoted to captain and posted to 48 Squadron as a flight commander. There could have been a further victory in the afternoon when Captain Middleton, at the head of a five-strong patrol that had just bombed Roisel, attacked a German scout that was strafing the British balloon line. But as Brodie Wilson observed, two new pilots in the formation masked Middleton's aim and the German got away.

The following morning's patrol was uneventful apart from bombing St. Quentin Railway Station and Nicolson and Wilson later swooping low over the British hospital train mentioned earlier to drop a copy of *Tatler* magazine that was picked up by the nurses. Then, in the evening, Captain Lale fired a good burst into a Fokker that stalled and went down to crash northeast of St. Quentin; although he was prevented from downing another when the belt of his Vickers gun broke[1,2].

******

The British armies in the Somme area now rested and consolidated while air patrols continued despite rain and storms. On 15 September the mid-morning patrol that set off at 10.20 was at 16,000ft en-route to bomb Busigny when it was attacked by three formations of Fokker DVIIs and Pfalz scouts that were described as having a mixture of tail markings – some white, some yellow, and some with black and white stripes. The Germans came at them from various heights and three Fokkers got onto the tail of E2213 flown by August Iaccaci and Sergeant Newland. But Newland, now also using twin Lewis guns, shot one down that crashed and burst into flames near the main road south of Lesdins. August Iaccaci then dived on another and, after firing 100 rounds into it from close range, saw it go down almost vertically and hit the ground near the railway south of Morcourt. Lieutenant Strachan and Second Lieutenant Calderwood in C951 shot down another that crashed near Omissy and one more that fell away out of control. Patrol leaders Thomson and Edwards were attacked from below and from the side in E2154, and it may well be that they engaged the same machines shot down by Strachan and Calderwood, as they too claimed one that crashed near Omissy and another out of control[1,5,6,7]. Two more out of control claims were also put in. One was from Lieutenants N.S. Boulton and G.W. Pearce in E2493[1, 5] and the other from Sub-Lieutenant A.B.D. Campbell and Sergeant Winch in E5816, just after Sergeant Winch was hit in the leg[1,5,6]. The Germans also broke off the fight but the result was not a clean sweep for 20 Squadron. Lieutenant Francis E. Finch, from Manchester and Second Lieutenant C.G. Russell failed to return in E2512, and were captured after being shot down by Leutnant U. Neckel of Jasta 6[3, 4].

A second raid on Busigny in the afternoon brought more losses. D7939 was brought down by heavy anti-aircraft fire near Epehy, and Sub-Lieutenant A.B.D. Campbell and Sergeant T.A. Stac were taken prisoner. Nonetheless, the patrol returned with honours even after Middleton and Mills in E2470 shot down a Hanover two-seater in flames at 17.50 southeast of St. Quentin and their victory was confirmed by Malcolm McCall flying D7915[1]. German records confirm that VizeFeldwebel Wilhelm Lubrecht and his observer Leutnant Seydholdt of FA 245 (A) were shot down near St. Quentin that day, with Lubrecht killed and his observer severely wounded[4].

Five more victories were claimed after a fight at 08.15 the next day, Saturday 16 September, when Thomson and Edwards led nine Bristols in an attack on about a dozen silver-grey Fokker DVIIs at 10,000ft over St. Quentin. Another eight Fokkers dived down to join the fight but were themselves surprised by a formation of 23 Squadron's Sopwith Dolphins that came plunging down on them from higher still. Thomson and Edwards, again flying E2154, dived on a Fokker that they sent down to crash near the trenches north of St. Quentin, while Strachan and Calderwood shot up another that fell out of control – receiving another 100 rounds from Edwards's guns as it passed. Strachan and Calderwood watched it down until it crashed northwest of St. Quentin. Edwards now spotted a third Fokker that was attacking a Bristol Fighter and, after firing 200 rounds into it, watched it turn over and over on its way down to crash near St. Quentin, as confirmed by Lieutenant Boulton flying E2493. August Iaccaci and Sergeant Newland then found themselves directly under another Fokker and Newland emptied a whole drum into its belly before it fell away and crashed to the west of Lesdin in a cloud of dust and smoke[5]. Nicolson and Wilson dived D7951 onto another Fokker, firing continuously as it fell spinning towards the ground, but were unable to confirm its fate as they came under further attack. Out of control victories were also claimed by Lieutenant H.E. Johnston and Second Lieutenant E.S.W. Harvey in E4718 and by Lieutenant N.S. Boulton and Sergeant Dodds in E2467. A note on the Combat Report records that three crashed and two out of control victories were awarded[1,5,6]. Pilots of 23 Squadron also claimed four victories but it may well be that one or more of these unwittingly duplicate some of 20 Squadron's claims.

There was one other fight that day when Captain Traill and Lieutenant Gordon-Bennett. intercepted a Rumpler. Traill's first burst produced a stream of black smoke but then his gun jammed. The resourceful pilot then flew under the Rumpler so that Bennett could fire forwards and upwards into it over the top wing, causing the German observer to fall down inside his cockpit as if killed or wounded. Bennett now ran out of ammunition and, with Traill's gun still jammed, they were more than happy when a Sopwith Camel dived in to help out. They were less happy when, after a few seconds flying close behind the Rumpler without firing, the Camel pilot pulled off to one side and started hammering at the breeches of his guns, which had obviously also jammed. There was nothing for it but to let the Rumpler go, and the identity of its dead or wounded observer remains unknown[8].

Moving forward in the wake of the Fourth Army, 20 Squadron made another move on 16 September: this time to the old German aerodrome at Suzanne. Poorly filled-in shell holes and trenches made landing tricky, causing D7951 to suffer a broken undercarriage and propeller. Nicolson and Wilson were not injured in the mishap but Nicolson was less lucky in the evening when the engine of the new machine he was bringing in from Vignacourt failed and he cut his eye in a bad landing among the shell holes. Because of Nicolson's accident, Brodie Wilson flew with Lieutenant Strachan on 18 September in a nine-strong low patrol that set out at 17.30 and resulted in their machine (C951) suffering heavy damage from anti-aircraft fire, although neither man was hurt[2].

George Randall was forced to drop out of a patrol with engine trouble on 20 September and the remainder of the patrol, now led by Traill and Bennett, continued without him. At 10.00 they met up with twelve Fokkers east of St. Quentin and a strong westerly gale made retreat difficult. A half-hour dogfight developed during which the Fokkers were reinforced by another ten just before some of 84 Squadron's SE5As joined in. Harlock and Draisey fired on one Fokker in E2258 at very close range, after which it dived into the ground near Mesnil. They then went to the rescue of another Bristol under attack from five Fokkers but were just too late to save it from a fiery end. It was E2158, and both Andrew Strachan and David Calderwood were killed. Draisey then emptied two drums into the nearest Fokker in range, and this fell away to join the Bristol in its fiery descent and even the score. The other Bristol crews claimed five more. Lieutenant Boulton and Sergeant Mitchell attacked one in E2493 that they reported crashed northeast of St. Quentin. Malcolm McCall and Clement Boothroyd, flying D7915, claimed one that Boothroyd sent down to crash east of the river at Longchamps and another they sent down out of control. Meanwhile, Middleton and Mills had just sent a Fokker down to crash between Rouvroy and the railway when they were themselves set upon by four more. Mills opened fire on one that dived in to very close range, and it was seen to crash near the Neuville light railway. Lieutenants Walters and Kirkpatrick completed the tally by claiming two 'out of controls'[1,5,7]. Three further claims were also made by 84 Squadron.

On the German side, Jasta 5 made two claims: one by Oberleutnant Schmitt and other by Unteroffizier Leicht. It is also possible that Leutnant H. Bohning of Jasta 79 was wounded in this fight: for although published sources say this happened in a combat with DH9s, there do not seem to be any corresponding claims from DH9 crews, and the two aircraft types were often confused by the Germans[4]. On a more mundane note, Brodie Wilson later flew a half-hour trip to Vignacourt 'to take the washing' and in so doing achieved the distinction of having flown over 300 hours at the front.

Andrew Strachan, aged 22, from Shawlands, Glasgow, had worked as an apprentice mechanical engineer before the war. The son of James Strachan, he served with the infantry for three years during which he qualified as a first class signaller before transferring to the then RFC in October 1917. His observer David Miller Calderwood, 25, was born in Greenock, Scotland, but emigrated to Canada where he worked as grain buyer in Winnipeg before enlisting in December 1914 and serving with the Canadian 8 Infantry Brigade in France. He too qualified as a first class signaller before transferring to the RAF. Both men are remembered at the Arras Flying Services Memorial.

Nicolson and Wilson flew two more patrols on the 21 and 22 September, followed the next day by a test flight and display over the aerodrome that included loops, spins, falling-leafs and Immelman turns (a dog-fight tactic named after the German pilot Max Immelmann). They then went up with the evening patrol of nine Bristols led by Randall and Hackett. Randall was flying E2568 at 12,000ft near St. Quentin when he spotted two Fokker DVIIs below them and dived into the attack – but they were probably decoys. As soon as the patrol was committed to the attack, it was itself attacked from north and south by another twenty Fokkers of various colours. One of them made the mistake of soaring across the top of E2213 flown by Boulton and Edwards, who immediately opened fire with his double guns from only 30 yards range causing the enemy machine to break into pieces in the air. Edwards then lowered his sights onto another Fokker coming up under their tail and sent it down in flames. Boulton and Edwards noticed a Bristol Fighter bursting into flames under attack by two more Fokkers but had no chance to go to its aid as Edwards opened fire on another nearby German and saw it going down out of control. Lieutenants Kiernander and Boothroyd in E2340 intercepted another Fokker as it was diving on a Bristol and fired one-and-a-half drums into it. Harlock and Draisey in E2252 followed it down and confirmed that it crashed in flames two miles east of St. Quentin. Four more Fokkers attacked E2467 flown by Lieutenant Britton and Sergeant Dodds but Dodds fired forty rounds into the nearest at point-blank range and it went over on its side before crashing west of Rouvroy, their victory later being confirmed by Lieutenant Johnston flying E2181. A little later, Britton dived on another Fokker, firing until his gun jammed, causing the German to stall and fall away in a slow spin until they lost sight of it[1, 6].

Brodie Wilson was unable to comment on the fight in his wonderfully detailed logbook afterwards, for it was, very sadly, he and James Nicolson who had gone down in the burning Bristol Fighter and they were both dead. Two Jasta 24 pilots each claimed a victory over a Bristol in the fight, and it seems that both were credited: these being VizeFelwebel K. Ungewitter and Unteroffizer F. Altemeier[1, 2, 3]. Thomas Traill and Brodie Wilson having become close friends, it fell to Traill to write to Wilson's parents afterwards. Brodie's sister Maude then replied saying that her parents were still hoping for good news as the official information was that Brodie was only 'missing' and might yet be a prisoner. But Traill knew this hope was in vain and, in seeking to put Brodie's family out their misery as gently as possible, he wrote back telling Maude that he knew there could be no hope because of the circumstances. Taking the strain for all the family, Maude replied again, saying she 'thought it best to leave that scrap of hope for the old people'. Her brother is buried at Grand Seraucourt British Cemetery, southwest of St. Quentin[8]. His legacy is his observer's log-book, safe in the keeping of the RAF Museum at Hendon, which has provided the author with a wealth of material on his and 20 Squadron's daily activities in 1918. His untimely death in action just weeks from the end of his tour with the squadron was one of the war's many great tragedies. James Nicolson's remains were never found and he is remembered at the Arras Flying Services Memorial – suggesting that either he or Brodie may have jumped from the burning aeroplane.

******

The war ground on without mercy. The next day, Tuesday 24 September, saw more fighting and the Bristol Fighter crews claimed four more Fokkers in a clash that began just after they had bombed Busigny at about 16.00. Traill and Gordon-Bennett in E2252 quickly got one of the Fokkers out of control. Captain Hooper and Lieutenant Edwards in E2536 then engaged one and Edwards put 200 rounds into it from his double Lewis guns before it was seen to crash southeast of St. Quentin. Randall and Hackett dived on another in E2470 and followed it down, firing all the time until it crashed vertically into the ground south of Clery around 16.40. They followed up by sending another spinning down into the clouds apparently out of control[1,5,6]. This was also the day on which William McKenzie Thomson (or 'MckThomson' as other pilots referred to him) was sent back to Canada on leave. Having achieved twenty-six victories and been awarded the MC, the *London Gazette* would announce on 2 November 1918 his award of the DFC. He survived the war and died in the 1990s.

At 18.15 the next day, Hooper and Edwards in E2536 led nine Bristol Fighters in a clash with between fifteen and twenty silver-grey DVIIs northeast of St. Quentin. Hooper fired only twenty rounds at one Fokker at close range before it went down to a crash witnessed by two other Bristol Fighter pilots. Edwards, meantime, occupied himself by firing 100 rounds into another that went down in flames, and then fired on yet another that he reported crashed east of Bellinglise. Traill and Gordon-Bennett were also busy in E2252, diving on a Fokker that Captain Hooper confirmed seeing in flames. But moments later Gordon-Bennett was hit in the leg by an explosive bullet, possibly from Leutnant von Braun of Jasta 79, and Traill hastily turned for home. Harlock and Draisey, flying E2340, opened fire on a Fokker immediately above them that immediately spun down to crash near Magny. A few seconds later Harlock got within 50 yards of yet another and shot it down to crash near Lehancourt. In the meantime, Malcolm McCall manoeuvred his Bristol Fighter E2568 so that Boothroyd was able to pour one-and--half Lewis drums into a Fokker just below and behind them that they reported crashed at Estrees at 18.30, its end being witnessed by Lieutenant Edwards in E2536. The final claim was from Lieutenants S. Walters and T. Kirkpatrick in E2337 after Walters fired into a Fokker that dived away pouring smoke but whose fate could not be confirmed. A possible German casualty was Jasta 79's Gefreiter Franz Wagner who was killed in action flying Fokker DVII 4631/18[1, 4, 5, 6, 7].

Inevitably, the fighting could not continue at this pace without 20 Squadron taking yet more casualties, and the following day Second Lieutenants L.G. Smith and E.S. Harvey were shot down near St. Quentin. Both were killed. Edward Sandell Harvey, aged 21, had been educated at Kings School, Worcester, where he had served in the OTC before joining the London Regiment as a Territorial in October 1913. Commissioned as a temporary second lieutenant in the RASC, he served in France with his corps until 13 December 1917, after which he transferred to the RFC for observer training and was appointed a second lieutenant in that role with effect from 15 April 1917. He is buried at Honnechy British Cemetery. His pilot, Leslie George Smith, was also 21. The son of Sidney and Kate Smith, of Earlsdon, Coventry, he had studied engineering in the city before enlisting. He is buried at Gouzeaucourt New British Cemetery.

Two more casualties quickly followed on Friday 27 September 1918. Captain Burbidge had now returned to 20 Squadron from Home Establishment and, as Traill was now without an observer following Gordon-Bennett's wounding, they teamed up together. Traill later wrote of his new observer that Burbidge was not very good mechanically but was full of courage and very good with his twin Lewis guns[8]. Their first patrol together found them leading a patrol of nine Bristol Fighters over St Quentin where they attacked a dozen multi-coloured Fokker DVIIs that were quickly reinforced by another five. McCall and Boothroyd claimed one of them destroyed west of Bernot at 10.30, while Harlock and Draisey scored their seventh victory by bringing down another northeast of Marcy at about the same time. August Iaccaci and Sergeant Newland flying E2213 claimed one that crashed south of Fontaine and a second out of control north of Bernot[1]. This brought August Iaccaci's tally to seventeen to match his brother. However, Bristol F2B E2566 flown Lieutenant F.E. Turner and Second Lieutenant C.E. Clarke failed to return; both men were dead, their loss being attributed to Jasta 24's VizeFeldwebel Altemeier[1, 3, 5, 6].

A former building contractor's clerk in Nottingham, 21-year-old Frederick Turner had first enlisted in the West Yorkshire Regiment and qualified as an Infantry Bombing Instructor before transferring to the RAF. He is buried at Ruyaulcourt Military Cemetery. His observer, 18-year-old Charles Edward Clarke, from Wallasey, Cheshire, shared his pilot's civilian background in that he too had been employed as an apprentice building contractor before being commissioned into the RAF on 6 September 1918. He is buried at Grand Seraucourt Cemetery.

August Iaccaci returned safely, and like his brother Paul, was promoted to Captain and posted to 48 Squadron as a flight commander shortly after. Wounded in the eye a few days later, he was sent back to England on 2 October, enabling both he and his brother to survive the war, with Paul living into the 1960s.

'Black September' was drawing to its end and at 05.50 on Sunday, 29 September the British Fourth Army launched a major assault against the Hindenburg Line between Bellenglise and Vendhuille. Orders had been issued by 22 Wing that continual reconnaissance was urgently required of the battle area and the rear areas, and that it must be carried out at altitudes low enough for all road activities to be seen and reported to guard against surprise counter-attacks. These orders brought 20 Squadron its last big fight of the month when, at 10.20 that morning, Captain Hooper and Lieutenant Edwards led a nine-strong OP at 12,000ft heading south from Cambrai. Just north of St. Quentin, they attacked six Fokkers that were almost immediately joined by another fourteen. The German machines were described as being painted mostly dark blue or black with one top plane in greenish camouflage and the bottom plane black with a white diagonal line from the leading edge of the wing-tip to the trailing edge near the fuselage. Hooper dived E2536 onto the nearest and fired about fifty rounds into it causing it to turn over and over before it settled into a slow spin, after which they lost sight of it. Edwards then opened fire with his double guns at a Fokker to their right that they followed down until they saw it crash. Then he took on another that appeared only about 50 yards away at the top of a zoom and fired about fifty rounds into it. It was not seen to crash but, as Edwards reported: 'The enemy pilot fell forward in his cockpit, apparently hit or killed, and the machine went into a vertical nose dive at once. Lieutenant Walters, flying next to Captain Hooper, also saw this happen.' Traill and Burbidge in E2370 shot up another Fokker as it attacked a Bristol Fighter, and the German went down with pieces of its left wing breaking off after Burbidge fired two drums into it. Meantime, Walters and Kirkpatrick fired at a Fokker in E2470 that was in a stall about 100 yards away, and McCall and Boothroyd followed it down as it fell away in alternate side-slips before it hit the ground near Levergies. Another Fokker now dived on them but it seems the German's guns jammed as they saw no tracers come from them. McCall then brought his aeroplane alongside about 30 yards away and Boothroyd fired a long burst into it that caused it to fall and crash near Lehancourt, their claim being supported by an 80 Squadron patrol that had joined in[1]. It had been another desperate fight, and it had brought more losses. Boulton and Case failed to return in E2561 and were both were dead after being shot down by Jasta 24's Unteroffizier F. Altemeier[1, 3, 5, 6].

Nicholson Stuart Boulton, the 19-year-old son of J.P. Boulton of Westbury, Wiltshire, had studied at Clarence School, Weston Super Mare. Appointed as a second lieutenant with effect from 5 July 1917, he had been credited with six combat victories. His observer, Charles Henry Case, was the 21-year-old son of a jeweller from Widnes, Cheshire. Having enlisted in the Lancashire Regiment and been promoted to corporal, he was commissioned into the Manchester Regiment, with which he served in France from October 1917 until mid-June 1918 when he transferred to the RAF. Boulton's body, still in his wrecked Bristol Fighter, was not found until 3 October close to the St. Quentin Canal southeast of Lehaucourt, and he was initially buried close by. It seems that Charles Case must have jumped from the falling aircraft and landed some way from where it crashed as his body was not found until December 1918 near Levergies as the battlefields were being cleared. He was first buried in the local cemetery but after the creation of the Imperial War Graves Commission both his and Boulton's remains were exhumed and re-interred so that Nicholas Boulton now rests at Bellicourt British Cemetery while his observer lies in Uplands Cemetery, Magny La Fosse.[9]

******

Notes

1. Combat Report.
2. Brodie Wilson: Observer's Flying Logbook.
3. *The Jasta War Chronology* by Norman Franks, Frank Bailey & Rick Duiven.
4.   Russ Gannon's Database of WW1 Air Combats.
5. AIR/1/168/15/156/7: 20 Squadron Records of Decisive Combats – Pilots.
6. AIR/1/168/15/156/6: 20 Squadron Records of Decisive Combats – Observers and Aerial Gunners.
7. R.A.F. Communiqués.
8. Personal papers of Air vice Marshall T.C. Traill, Imperial War Museum.
9. AIR 76 R.A.F. Officers Service Records & "I Don't Want To Be A Sunbeam" by Harry Jones.

Chapter 25

To the Bitter End – October/November 1918

The British land assault continued over the next two days, with the Germans finally being forced to evacuate Vendhuille and withdraw over the canal. Further north, British and Belgian forces advanced steadily east from Ypres against slowly retiring enemy forces that knew they had no hope of reinforcements from the hard-pressed south where the Hindenburg line had now been broken and the German army faced catastrophe.

The first day of October very nearly saw Traill and Burbidge become casualties. While leading the squadron's dawn patrol on a northerly course just east of the lines, they noticed a group of German scouts flying parallel to them some distance to the east. The two captains watched the enemy carefully for signs of attack and, while they were so absorbed, three Fokker DVIIs smashed through their formation from the north-northwest in a nearly head-on and possibly pre-planned surprise attack that left them reeling. One of the German pilots fired a short but accurate burst into the patrol leader's Bristol Fighter that tore holes through the fuselage and through the rear petrol tank directly below Traill. Burbidge opened fire as the German swept past and behind them and, when the Fokker went down suddenly as if hit, Traill quickly broke off and got back across the lines. The pair then made a hurried forced landing on a nearby British cavalry exercise ground where the officers they met treated them both to large measures of whisky. Later on, in a display of his considerable inventive skills in the 'make do and mend' department, Traill patched up the holed petrol tank with dollops of strong muddy clay. After pumping up the pressure to check that the mud-patch was good enough, he got Burbidge to hold it in place as volunteer cavalry troopers pulled the propeller to start the engine. The engine started up immediately and the pair took off for home. Although their combat report does not seem to have survived the years, the 20 Squadron book of 'Decisive Combats – Pilots' shows they were credited with an 'out of control' victory over the Fokker that Burbidge hit. They had been very lucky, though, and Traill's memoir held at the Imperial War Museum gives the Germans full credit for their dash and cunning: 'They went through our formation like a dose of salt,' he wrote[7].

On Thursday, 3 October, a nine-strong patrol led by Horace Lale and George Learmond in E2588 surprised a formation of seven Fokker DVIIs 2,000ft below them over Fresnoy by diving onto them from out of the sun. Lale closed the range to 30 yards, firing continuously at one until the it fell away in a steep dive and began to spin. Pulling out of the dive, Lale now tried to get into position to attack another Fokker but in doing so lost sight of the first so that its end could only be guessed at. In the meantime, Lieutenant Britton and Sergeant Dodds, who were flying lower than the remainder of the formation, closed with two nearby Fokkers whose pilots had evidently not seen them. Dodds emptied two drums from his twin Lewis guns into one of them, causing its right wings to fold back and break away it as it fell to earth near Fontaine. Harlock and Kydd then dived E2338 onto another Fokker and fired into it without pause until it spun into the ground near Mericourt, its nose embedded in the earth and its tail sticking up into the air like a tombstone[1, 2, 3]. Lale's patrol returned without loss.

As the ground troops advanced below, 20 Squadron carried out numerous OPs aimed at protecting British aircraft employed in close reconnaissance and contact patrol work, and single-seat scouts in low ground strafing. Thus many of the squadron's final casualties came while trying to protect others. Captain Hubert Dinwoodie MC had been posted into 20 Squadron as an observer from 26 September 1918. The 22-year-old son of Mr G. Dinwoodie, of Bournemouth, Hubert had been awarded the Military Cross while serving in France with 3 Dorsets in 1916. Having been with the squadron less than two weeks, he attended a concert at 205 Squadron on the evening of 5 October, the programme for which is still kept by his great-nephew Mark Vincent. But the following day his career with 20 Squadron was cut short when he took a bullet wound during an air fight. His pilot in A2404, 20-year-old Canadian Second Lieutenant Angus McHardy, made a successful forced landing in the countryside – but in such an obscure location that both men were reported missing before they could contact the squadron, resulting in their relatives being sent 'missing in action' telegrams that were later corrected. Dinwoodie was packed off to the French hospital at Chartres on 8 October, and from there to Rouen for two weeks before being invalided back to England where he spent the remainder of the war and the next four months at Tidworth Military Hospital. Years later he would see more action when, despite continual problems resulting from his injuries, he was recalled to the RAF in 1939. He became involved in the establishment of the RAF Bomb Disposal Service and was posted to Germany in 1945 where he again made his mark. Sent to Lubeck in 1946 following an explosion at the Baltic port, he defused eleven very unstable German bombs that threatened to set off more explosions that would have obliterated the dockyard area and caused countless casualties. Hubert Dinwoodie was awarded the George Cross for this outstanding heroism[4].

On 8 October the British launched a further land offensive stretching from Cambrai to Sequehart, just north of St. Quentin. The accompanying air fights saw Frank Ely and John McBride both killed at around 16.30 when their Bristol Fighter E2420 was shot down over Brancourt by Unteroffizier Altemeier of Jasta 24[5]. If it was any consolation, the land forces were once again successful and the Germans were in retreat. Frank Wayman Ely, the 22-year-old son of George and Ann Ely, from Cottenham, Cambridgeshire, worked as a fitter and turner before he enlisted as a sapper in the Royal Engineers in April 1915. Commissioned in October 1917 while serving in France, he was appointed as a Flying Officer (Pilot) on 28 March 1918. John Gordon McBride was the 25-year-old son of John and Jane McBride, from Aberdeen, where his father worked as a wine and spirits merchant. A former clerk, he had seen action with 2 Battalion the Gordon Highlanders during the Battle of the Somme in 1916 and was wounded by shrapnel at Beaumont Hamel on 23 November. He was commissioned into 3 Battalion of the Gloucester Regiment in December 1917 and transferred to the RAF the following April, arriving at 20 Squadron only in September. Their bodies were never found and they are both remembered at the Arras Flying Services Memorial.

Low clouds and rain restricted operational flying over the next two weeks, although events were moving fast on the ground as, by 9 October, allied troops entered the western end of Le Cateau. The bad weather provided something of a respite for 20 Squadron, whose men were not involved in any further serious fighting until 23 October when 20 Squadron was tasked with bombing the important railway junction at Aulnoye. As the fifteen Bristol Fighters led by Lale and Boothroyd were photographing the effects of the attack, they spotted about fifteen Fokkers to the west barring their route home over the Foret de Mormal and a fight developed. C.G. Boothroyd opened fire on one of the enemy as it passed beneath his and Captain Lale's machine and the Fokker was seen to crash near Noyelles at 15.10. Minutes later, Captain Lale poured more than 300 rounds into a second Fokker that fell spinning from the fight and crashed in the forest east of Preux. A third was shot down by Lieutenant R.H. Tapp and Second Lieutenant W.H. Welsh in E2588. Welsh had fired 100 rounds into it from his twin Lewis guns at point-blank range, the dramatic effect of which was that: 'The enemy machine folded up and broke into pieces as it fell[1].' Another Fokker attacked Lieutenant A.C.T. Perkins M.C. and Second Lieutenant D.M. Lapraik in 2337 but Lapraik kept up a steady and accurate fire until it spun away earthwards and crashed west of Aulnoye. The final claim came when the Bristols were heading for home and Captain Traill and Captain Burbidge in E2403 noticed a lone Fokker following the formation. Burbidge took careful aim and opened fire on it at long range, not stopping until it went into a spin and crashed west of Aulnoye[1, 2, 3,6].

The formation then crossed back over the lines minus E2470, which was last seen low down over Aulnoye. Then as Traill and Burbidge were 'cruising gently home in the quiet air of the evening… there was a crash and everything went for six'. As Traill looked up, he saw the wreckage of another Bristol Fighter rolling over and under him that went on spinning down 'very fast and flat, like an ash key [the winged fuit of an ash tree] in the winter'. Part of Traill's right wings and an aileron then broke away and his machine immediately went into steep spiral to the left. Although Traill managed to keep some control, the damage was such that he could not fly the Bristol properly and it kept going into spins. Captain Burbidge bravely clambered out onto the opposite wing to restore the Bristol's equilibrium – and there he stayed until Traill was able to sideslip the machine onto the ground at the aerodrome, and Burbidge being ejected from the wing and landing face first on the grass[1, 7]. Captain Burbidge was taken to Number 59 Casualty Clearing Station with a broken nose and cut tongue and from there transferred to Number 8 General Hospital at Rouen on 26 October before being repatriated to Tidworth Military Hospital in England the following day. Although he was posted back to the squadron on 11 December, he was soon back in hospital as a result of infections and was not pronounced fully fit for service again until February 1919. After serving with other squadrons, he took up a new career as a shipbroker in Bilbao, Spain[10]. The news that he and Captain Traill were to be decorated with the DFC for their achievement in bringing their aircraft home would have come as a welcome relief during his convalescence, the awards being announced in the *London Gazette* on 7 February 1919. After the war, Captain Traill remained in the RAF and went on to become an air vice marshal.

There were, however, no decorations for the crew of Bristol Fighter E2590 with which they had collided. Its pilot, Canadian Lieutenant Francis Roy Goodearle, was killed and his observer, Lieutenant A. McBride was injured when their aircraft crashed. The 23–year–old unmarried son of Humphrey James Goodearle, of Kingston, Ontario, had studied economics at the citys's Queen's University and was originally commissioned as a lieutenant in 80 Battalion CEF in January 1916. He transferred to the RFC in March 1917 and, although during training he was described as being good in the air, a track record of poor landings delayed his transfer to France for over a year. He is buried at Awoingt British Cemetery, about three kilometres southeast of Cambrai.

As to the missing Bristol Fighter E2470: Lieutenant H.L. Pennal and Sergeant George Aitken were also dead. Howard Pennal, aged 23, was the son of Toronto residents F.G. and A.A. Pennal, who later moved to Minneapolis, USA. Howard had worked in various occupations in Saskatchewan and Montreal before enlisting. He received his flying training in Canada and the USA and completed training at the School of Aero-gunnery at Camp Hicks, Texas. Sergeant 175333 George Aitken, aged 18, was the son of George and Barbara Aitken, of Balmedie, Aberdeenshire, and worked as a gardener before joining the RAF on 3 May 1918. They are both buried at Leval Communal Cemetery, Nord. The German victory over E2470 was claimed by Leutnant J. Jensen of Jasta 57, whose unit also reported VizeFeldwebel Emil Hanzog and VizeFeldwebel Alfred Nauwerk as having been killed at Bantigny, which is just north of Cambrai and about thirty kilometres west of Preux[5]. There is good reason to believe that the two events were linked: the fighting having begun west of Aulnoye, the battle moved westwards over Noyelles, with Bantigny and Jasta 57's base at Aniche lying either side of this route. So it is quite feasible that Hanzog and Nauwerk were victims of the same fight in which their Jasta 57 comrade Leutnant Jenson claimed his victory over Lieutenant Pennal and Sergeant Aitken.

Two days later, on Friday, 25 October, 20 Squadron moved to Iris Farm as the German Army continued its retreat in the face of the relentless allied advances. The end was coming – and the German Air Service now flung itself at the British formations with near-suicidal desperation. Heavily outnumbered everywhere, the Germans sent their fighter Jastas into the attack in groups up to fifty-strong in an effort to achieve fleetingly effective control over particularly crucial areas of the battlefield. Massed air battles were commonplace, and 30 October saw the RAF engaged in more air fighting than any other day of the war.

At around midday, twelve Bristols of 20 Squadron attacked nine Fokker DVIIs south of Avesnes, with Lale and Boothroyd in E2407 sending one down to crash northeast of Boulogne. Second Lieutenant Tapp found himself pursued by seven Fokkers after breaking off the fight due to engine trouble but Lieutenant Welsh kept up such an accurate defensive fire that all but one soon gave up the chase. This Fokker pursued them down to 2,000ft, at which point Tapp pulled out of his dive and Welsh opened fire with his Lewis guns at what was now point-blank range. The Fokker fell away suddenly and crashed into the ground near La Croix[1]. In a second patrol later in the afternoon, nine Bristols led by

Captain Traill were patrolling over Aulnoye at 15.30 when they attacked twelve Fokker DVIIs east of the town.Second Lieutenant A. McHardy and Lieutenant W.A. Rodger were attacked in E2419 from below and behind by one Fokker, but Rodger returned its fire and the German machine turned over and went down in a slow spiral. Some SE5As now dived into the fight and the Germans were driven off. It is interesting to note that even at this late stage in the war, 'out of control' victories were still being counted as 'decisive combats' by HQ, as a pencil footnote at the bottom of McHardy's combat report clearly states: 'Decisive, out of control'[1,2,3]. On Friday, 1 November, 20 Squadron's midday OP again ran into the enemy over the Foret de Mormal and, in the melee that followed, F6116 was last seen going down in a steep dive over the forest. It did not return and Lieutenant Segrave and Second Lieutenant Kidd had both been killed. Philip Segrave, a former motor engineer, was the unmarried son of Mrs C. Segrave of Walton, Liverpool. After twice being wounded in action in 1915 and 1917 while serving as Private 3457 with 10 (Scottish) Battalion of the Kings Liverpool Regiment, he transferred to the RFC but had not been long with 20 Squadron. James Forrest Kidd was the 20-year-old son of George Kidd, a newspaper publishing clerk in Edinburgh. James had enlisted on 15 March 1915 as Private 3174 in 2/9 Battalion of The Royal Scots. Promoted to corporal within his unit, he was later appointed a Second Lieutenant in the 6 Kings Royal Rifle Corps before transferring to the RAF. He too had not been with the squadron very long, and both men are buried at Pont-Sur-Sambre Communal Cemetery.

Two days later, on 3 November, again over the Foret de Mormal, four Bristols were attacked from above and behind by no less than seventeen Fokker DVIIs, most of them being a dark green colour with lighter coloured tails. Randall and Learmond in E2492 shot down one of them a mile southwest of Berlaimont, while Lieutenant A.E. Johnston and Second Lieutenant W.N. Dawkes fired several long bursts at close range into a Fokker that was attacking another Bristol Fighter. The Fokker then turned over on its back and fell completely out of control, its descent being witnessed by Lieutenants H.J. Gye and S.B.P. de Moyse Bucknall in F4436[1,2]. Both victories were approved and the combat reports countersigned by Captain Lale. Qualified observer Sergeant Mechanic W. Gibson was wounded in action two days later, though details of his injury are not recorded.

With the war now hurtling towards its final conclusion, it might have been hoped that Gibson would be the squadron's last casualty. But despite the hopelessness of the German position, fighting continued without respite. At 11.30 on 9 November, Randall and Learmond were leading a patrol of nine

Bristol Fighters when they went to the assistance of some British photographic machines being attacked by ten Fokker DVIIs over Beaumont. Randall dived on a Fokker described as having black and white checks on its wing tips and tail, firing 300 rounds into it at a range of only 80 yards. His combat report described how: 'The Fokker turned over on its back and went down with dark smoke issuing from it. It was watched down to 6,000 feet still out of control [and] Captain Gardiner, leader of patrol of 211 Squadron, confirms this EA as being out of control near the ground.' The combat report was accordingly annotated as 'Decisive OOC'[1, 2].

That same day also saw Captain Traill make his last foray across the lines before the Armistice in an escort to some DH9 bombers. He was flying 'Slops' Heslop's Bristol Fighter on this occasion and noted how good the aircraft felt, remarking in his memoir that 'any machinery of his has to run like a sewing machine'. No Germans were seen and the patrol returned safely, with Traill looking forward to the rostered leave he would begin the following day. Yet, as the day drew to a close, everything was locking into place for the final tragedy to unfold, made all the more poignant by its timing...

Sunday, 10 November 1918 dawned like any other day of the war. At 08.30 Captain Hooper and Lieutenant McKenzie were escorting some DH9s in E2407 when they met up with four 'silvery-green' Fokker DVIIs over Charleroi. They dived on one of these, firing at it and seeing it go down completely out of control, still turning over and over when several thousand feet below. Its fall was witnessed by four other Bristol Fighter pilots and, once again, the combat report was marked up as 'decisive'[1]. Captain Traill was probably saying his farewells as Captain Hooper's flight returned but did not actually leave for Boulogne until three or four hours later – after watching Lieutenant Randall's later OP return two aircraft short.

At 11.30 that morning, Randall's patrol of eight Bristol Fighters had engaged seven Fokker DVIIs attacking a formation of DH9s over Charleroi. Randall and Learmond in E2429 claimed two Fokkers shot down in the opening stages of the fight, with one destroyed just west of Loverval and the second in flames. But four more DVIIs now joined the battle and, although Second Lieutenants F.H. Solomon and A.D. Sinclair shot one down that crashed in a wood south of Charleroi, and Heslop and Hackett brought down another that crashed southwest of Charleroi, there were also losses[1,2,3,6]. McHardy and Rodger in F6195 had gone down with its crew and both were dead. Second Lieutenant Alexander McHardy, aged 20, described by Traill as 'a big, quiet Canadian backwoodsman and a splendid man', was the 20-year-old son of Alexander and Isabel McHardy of MacLennan's Mountain, Nova Scotia. His observer,

25-year-old Second Lieutenant William Alexander Rodger was the son of William and Helen Rodger, who had emigrated from Edinburgh to Canada before the war. After originally enlisting in the Manitoba Regiment, he had transferred to the RAF in July 1918, arriving at 20 Squadron in early October. Both men are buried at Tournai Communal Cemetery, Allied Extension. The second loss of that morning's encounter with the Fokkers was F4421, shot down by Lieutenant H.V. Freden of Jasta 50. The Bristol Fighter's crew of two had differing fates. Sergeant 99859 Richard Dodds, a former clerk from Sheffield, was so severely wounded that he died soon afterwards and is buried at Vogenee Communal Cemetery, against the east wall. More fortunate was Lieutenant E.A.C. Britton, who survived and was marched off towards captivity, though it it would prove only a short march for him. Britton was nicknamed 'Babs', because he was so small and youthful looking, which is why some local people were able to help him to escape by disguising him in women's clothing. Once dressed that way, he quickly made his way to the British lines[8].

As for the dead: what made their fate even more tragic is that their families back in Canada and England would soon be celebrating the end of the fighting – and their loved ones' survival. It might be a whole day or more before their hopes would be heart-breakingly shattered by a military telegram.

Thus it was that 20 Squadron, possibly the highest scoring and certainly one of the most decorated aerial fighting units of the Great War, came to suffer what were probably the RAF's last combat fatalities over the Western Front. Four other RAF flyers are known to have died on 10 November 1918: two Sopwith Camel pilots of 46 Squadron were killed in an accidental collision, the pilot of a 210 Squadron Camel failed to return after last being seen over Mons at 09.10, and the observer of a 211 Squadron DH9 bomber was killed when his aircraft was shot down by anti-aircraft fire over Charleroi after setting out at 09.45. Although the evidence is not absolute, the times of departure of these four being earlier than that of 20 Squadron's men, it may be assumed that their deaths occurred before those of McHardy, Rodger and Dodds. As far as is known, the RAF's very last fatality from any cause in the Great War was Captain D.R.G. Mackay DFC., a DH4 pilot of 55 Squadron, who died of wounds as a prisoner of war on Armistice Day after being shot down during a bombing raid some time on 10 November. His observer survived.

Despite the Armistice coming into effect at 11 o'clock on 11 November 1918, patrols were still necessary to ensure the Germans did not breach any of the Armistice terms, which meant that aircrews and ground staff were kept almost as busy as they had been during the fighting. There are no surviving records of 20 Squadron's day-to-day activities for the rest of 1918 but casualty reports show that an end to the fighting did not automatically mean an end to danger. On 3 December 1918, the squadron moved from Iris Farm to Ossogne, where a flying accident brought two more deaths. Second Lieutnant Sydney Booth, a married man from Beckenham, Kent, and 32-year-old Corporal Mechanic 78179 Richard Moors, also married, from Oldham, Lancashire, are both buried at Charleroi Communal Cemetery. They are not alone there. Sergeant Major Bertie Billing was still keeping a stern and efficient eye on the ground crews when the Armistice came, and continued to do so until 8 February 1919 when he fell victim to the great influenza epidemic then sweeping across Europe. The influenza rapidly developed into bronchial pneumonia and he died on 16 February 1919, aged 29. Nearly six months later, his widow Hilda was informed that, in addition to Bertie having been awarded the Meritorious Service Medal, his services had been further recognised when he was mentioned in dispatches on 11 July that year. He too is buried at Charleroi, as is Aircraftman First Class 5245 F. Herriott[9], from Brighton, who died on 23 February 1919, probably also from influenza.

More than 600 men had flown with 20 Squadron on the Western Front during the war, of which 128 had been killed, almost the same number wounded and around 60 taken prisoner: an overall casualty rate of around 50 per cent. When the squadron left for the Northwest Frontier of India in June 1919 and remained in the Far East until after the Second World War, it seems its superb record went with them.

Heroic 20 Squadron became almost invisible to the general public, along with most of the other two-seater squadrons of the Great War, while it was the single-seat fighter units and their aces that grabbed the headlines and the glory. But the valiant flyers of the squadron awarded the royal emblem of the 'winged sabre' deserved much better than to be left forgotten and unlamented except in the family trees of their descendants and in the researches of a small number of enthusiasts and historians. They had braved all, with many paying the ultimate price, while serving in what was arguably the highest scoring British air force unit of the war. Their enduring legacy is that their often monotonous, always dangerous and sometimes terrifying reconnaissance work saved many times their number of British lives on the ground by providing vital intelligence to the generals. Their courage and skill in air combat truly epitomised the legendary 'offensive spirit' of the RFC and RAF.

My maternal grandfather, Driver George Tester, was killed within a week of joining 20 Squadron, and it was his death that first led me, nearly twenty years ago, to start looking into the squadron's fine record. Hence this First World War history of 20 Squadron, in tribute to the fallen and all the others who served in it to remind us of the words inscribed on the entrance Stone of Remembrance of so many British and Commonwealth War Cemeteries across the world, so that lest we forget:

"Their Name Liveth Forevermore"

******

Notes

1. Combat Report.
2. AIR/1/168/15/156/7: 20 Squadron Records of Decisive Combats – Pilots.
3. AIR/1/168/15/156/6: 20 Squadron Records of Decisive Combats – Observers and Aerial Gunners.
4. Thanks to Mark Vincent, and www.rafweb.org/GC_holders.htm.
5. *The Jasta War Chronology* by Norman Franks, Frank Bailey & Rick Duiven.
6. RAF Communiqués.
7. Personal papers of Air vice Marshall T.C. Traill, Imperial War Museum.
8. *Above The Trenches* by Christopher Shores, Norman Franks & Russell Guest, and officer's service record - WO 339 files at National Archives, Kew.
9. Commonwealth War Graves Commission.
10. Thanks to Simon Burbidge.

Nominal Roll Officers and Men
Who Flew with 20 Squadron

In alphabetical order

Names	Rank	Grade	Dates	Casualties
Ackling A S, 72535	Pte	AG	Jan – May 1918	
Adams J P F	2/Lt.	Obs	Aug – Oct 1917	Killed 14.10.1917
Agelasto C J	2/Lt.	Obs	Sept-Feb. 1917/18	
Aitken George, 175333	Sgt	Obs	Sept '18 – 23.10.18	Killed 23.10.1918
Aked H L G	Lt.	Obs	April/May 1916	
Alchin G	Lt.	Pilot	Nov 1916	
Alder S	Lt.	Pilot	Sept-Jan 1916/17	
Aldred B 77449	Sgt	AG	Jan –May 1917	Killed 24.04.1917
Aldridge H D, 7044	Sgt	Pilot	July 1917	
Alexander H, 6640	1/A.M.	AG	Sept – Nov. 1916	
Allcock W J	2/Lt.	Pilot	Sept.'15 - Jan '16	
Allum T E, P10708	Pte	AG.	Mar-Apr 1917	
Alston C R	2/Lt.	Pilot	June 1917	
Anderson R H	Lt.	Pilot	Jan-Mar 1916	
Anderson W	2/Lt.	Pilot	Jan-Mar 1917	
Archer A E C	2/Lt.	Pilot	Sept-Dec 1915	
Arkley	Pte	AG	July 1917	
Attwater S	Sgt	Pilot	Jan-Apr 1917	
Babbage F F	Captain	Pilot	May-Oct 1917	
Bacon L G	2/Lt.	Pilot	Feb-May 1917	
Backhouse W 65004	Sgt	AG	May-July 1917	Killed 07.07.1917
Baring-Gould J H	2/Lt.	Pilot	May 1917	
Barker R Raymond	2/Lt.	Pilot	Dates Unknown	
Barter W J H, 231124	Sgt	Obs	May-July 1918	Killed 02.07.1917
Bawley	2/A.M.	AG	Aug. 1917	
Beaver W	Captain	Pilot	Oct-Jun 1917/18	
Behrens H	2/Lt.	Obs	Dec-Jan 1917/18	
Beldham C H	Lt.	Pilot	July 1917	
Beminster C	2/A.M.	AG	May 1917	
P/DM/2/154352'				
Benger W J 88288	Sgt	AG	May-Oct 1917	Killed 17.10.1917

Names	Rank	Grade	Dates	Casualties
Bennett Rex G.	Lt.	Pilot	Jan-May 1918	Killed 28.05.1918
Berridge F.D.	Captain	Pilot	?	
Berry F H	2/Lt.	Obs	Apr-Oct 1917	
Bevan W	2/Lt.	Pilot	Nov-Dec 1917	Killed 03.12.1917
Bickersteth J R	Lt.	Obs	Jun-July 1917	
Bidder	1/AM	AG	Feb. 1916	
Bill A.G.	Lt.	Obs	Jun-July 1917	
Billing F	Lt.	Obs	Jan-Aug 1916	
Birch S 4174	Sgt	AG	Sept-Nov 1916	
Birch W E	2/Lt.	Pilot	May-July 1916	
Bird F 77646	Sgt	AG	May 1917	Killed 23.05.1917
Birkett N M	Lt.	Obs	May-June1917	
Blackwood J	Captain	Pilot	May-Apr 1916/17	
Blakes W G '1128'	Private	AG	May 1917	
Blatherwick R	Captain	Pilot	June-July 1916	
Blithoe	Captain	Obs	Jan. 1917	
Boles J L	2/Lt.	Pilot	Aug-Feb 1917/18	
Booth G B	Lt.	Obs	Oct 1917	
Booth S E	2/Lt.	Pilot	Nov-Dec 1918	Killed 03.12.1918
Booth	1/AM	AG	Feb – Oct 1917	
Boothroyd C G	2/Lt.	Obs	June-Nov 1918	
Boucher N	Lt.	Pilot	May-June 1917	
Boulton F E	Lt.	Pilot	Apr-May 1918	
Boulton N S	Lt.	Pilot	Sept. 1918	Killed 29.09.1918
Boyd	Sgt	AG	Feb. 1917	
Boyd J D	Lt.	Obs	Nov-Apr 1917/18	
Bradley R A	Captain	Pilot	Aug-Sept 1915	
Bradley R I 907	L. Cpl	AG	Apr-May 1917	Killed 20.05.1918
Bradshaw L F 57658	Sgt	Obs?	Sept. 1918	
Brander L S	Lt.	Pilot	Oct-Nov 1917	
Briggs A W	2/Lt.	Pilot	Sept – Oct 1915	
Britton E A C	Lt.	Pilot	Sept-Nov 1918	
Bronskill F H	2/Lt.	Obs	Dec-Feb 1916/17	
Brooke G A	2/Lt.	Obs	Sept. 1917	
Bucknell S P B	Lt.	Obs	Nov 1918	
Burbidge L W	Captain	Obs	Sept-Oct 1918	
Burdett A B	Captain	Pilot	Sept 1915	
Burkett E T W	2/Lt.	Pilot	June-July 1917	
Burns V L A	2/Lt.	Pilot	March 1917	
Burritt W A	2/Lt.	Pilot	Aug-Sept 1917	
Cahill	2/AM	AG	Jan. 1917	
Calderwood D W	2/Lt.	Obs	July-Sept 1918	Killed 20.09.1918

Names	Rank	Grade	Dates	Casualties
Callander G G	2/Lt.	Pilot	July–Oct. 1916	
Cambray W C	2/Lt.	Obs	May–Oct 1917	
Cameron C H	2/Lt.	Pilot	July–Oct 1917	
Campbell A	Lt.	Pilot	May–June 1918	
Campbell A B D	Sub/Lt.	Pilot	Sept. 1918	
Campbell A R H	Lt.	Pilot	Sept. 1918	
Campbell D Gordon	Lt.	Pilot	Dec–Feb 1917/18	Killed 19.02.1918
Campbell J S	Captain	Pilot	Sept. 1917	Killed 28.09.1917
Campbell L	2/Lt.	Pilot	Dec–Mar 1917/18	
Campbell W K	Lt.	Pilot	Dec–Jan 1915/16	
Campbell W R A	Lt.	Pilot	Aug–Sept 1917	
Capel L H T	2/Lt.	Pilot	Feb 1918	
Carbert C M	Captain	Obs	Dec–Feb 1916/17	Killed 01.02.1917
Carson W F	2/Lt.	Pilot	Aug 1918	
Case C H	2/Lt.	Obs	Jun–Sept 1918	Killed 29.09.1918
Caton N N	2/Lt.	Obs	May–June 1916	
Catton S 3994	2/AM	AG	Apr 1916	Killed 29.04.1916
Cawley J	2/Lt.	Obs	Aug 1917	
Chambers W D	Lt.	Pilot	Sept–Oct 1917	
Champion H F	Lt.	Obs	Jan–Feb 1916	
Chancellor G E	2/Lt.	Obs	Jan–July 1916	Killed 09.07.1916
Chester W M E	2/Lt.	Obs	May–June 1917	
Clarke A S	Lt.	Pilot	1915?	
Clark E V	2/Lt.	Pilot	Nov 1917	Killed 29.11.1917
Clarke C E	2/Lt.	Obs	Sept 1918	Killed 27.09.1918
Clayton A J 5781	Sgt	AG	Apr. 1917	Killed 26.04.1917
Clemons H S	2/Lt.	Obs	Nov–Jan 1917/18	
Cobbold E F N	Lt.	Pilot	Sept 1915	
Cobbold F R C	Lt.	Obs	Nov–Feb 1916/17	
Cogswell E B	2/Lt.	Obs	May 1917	
Colbert J H	Lt.	Pilot	Mar–Sept 1918	
Cole-Hamilton C W	Lt.	Pilot	Oct–Apr 1915/16	
Coles	1/AM	AG	Jan. 1917	
Collins	Sgt	Pilot	Jan. 1917	
Collinson	1/AM	AG	Jan. 1917	
Colvill Jones Thomas	Lt.	Pilot	Oct – May 1917/18	
Condor R E	2/Lt.	Pilot	Apr–June 1917	
Cooke D G	Captain	Pilot	Oct–May 1917/18	
Coombes H M	2/Lt.	Pilot	Mar–Apr 1917	
Cormack J D 16814	Sgt	Obs	May–July 1918	Killed 30.07.1918
Courtney F F	2/Lt.	Pilot	Oct 1916	
Couve N	2/Lt.	Obs	Oct–Nov 1917	

Names	Rank	Grade	Dates	Casualties
Coward	Cpl	AG	July 1917	
Cowell J J 78171	Sgt	Pilot	May-July 1917/18	Killed 30.07.1918
Cox C J 290	F/Sgt	Pilot	Oct-Jan 1916/17	
Crafter J	Lt.	Pilot	June-July 1917	Killed 07.07.1917
Croft	L. Cpl	AG	May 1917	
Crowe H G	2/Lt.	Obs	Nov-May 1917/18	
Cubbon F.R.	Captain	Obs	Apr-June 1917	Killed 09.06.1917
Cunnell D.C.	Captain	Pilot	Dec-July 1916/17	Killed 12.07.1917
Dabbs D H	2/Lt.	Pilot	Apr-Sept 1916	
Dalley J P	Lt.	Pilot	Sept-Oct 1917	Killed 15.10.1917
Dalziel R G	2/Lt.	Pilot	Apr-May 1917	
Dandy H	2/Lt.	Obs	Sept. 1917	
Davidson B T	Lt.	Pilot	June-July 1918	Killed 02.07.1917
Davies D H Saunders	2/Lt.	Pilot	July 1916	
Davies J E	2/Lt.	Obs	Apr 1917	
Davies H S	2/Lt.	Obs	May 1917	
Davis, C Gordon-	Captain	Pilot	Sept 1916	
Dawkes W H	2/Lt.	Obs	Nov 1918	
Dearing F 9882	1/AM	AG	Sept 1916	Killed 26.09.1916
Deighton E A 67051	Sgt	Obs	Jan-July 1918	
Dennis G N	Lt.	Obs	Aug-Mar 1916/17	
Dennistoun J A	Major	Pilot	Dec-Apr 1917/18	
Deuchar A G	Captain	Pilot	Sept. 1916	
Dewar A	2/Lt.	Obs	June-Sept 1916	
Dewson	2/A.M.	AG	Dec. 1917	
Dickinson A H	2/Lt.	Obs	Jan-June 1916	
Dicksee H	2/Lt.	Obs	Oct 1916	
Dimmock	2/Lt.	Obs	Aug 1917	
Dinwoodie A	Captain	Obs	Sept-Oct 1918	
Dixon R M	2/Lt.	Obs	Sept. 1916	
Dodds R S 9985	Sgt	Obs	Aug-Nov 1918	Killed 10.11.1918
Dougall N S	Lt.	Obs	Dec. 1917	
Dowling B L	2/Lt.	Pilot	July-Sept 1916	
Drabble C F	2/Lt.	Obs	Dec–Aug 1916/17	
Draisey A S	2/Lt.	Obs	June-Nov 1918	
Dudbridge M	2/Lt.	Obs	May-June 1917	
Duff A I F	Captain	Obs	Dec- Mar 1915/16	
Duggan J H W	2/Lt.	Obs	June-Nov 1917	Killed 06.11.1917
Durrand W	Captain	Pilot	June-Jan 1917/18	
Earwaker R N D	Lt.	Obs	July-Aug 1917	
Easton H E	2/Lt.	Obs	Nov-Mar 1917/18	
Edgerton-Johnson R	Lt.	Pilot	Jan-May 1917	

Names	Rank	Grade	Dates	Casualties
Edwards H L	2/Lt.	Obs	July–Oct 1918	
Eglington D C	Lt.	Obs		
Ely F W	Lt.	Pilot	Oct. 1918	Killed 08.10.1918
English A A	Captain	Obs	Sept. 1917	
Evans FW	Lt.	Obs	May 1917	Killed 23.05.1917
Exley G A	2/Lt.	Obs	Jan–Aug 1916	
Farquharson– Roberts M	Lt.	Obs	Feb 1918	
Fauvel L G	2/Lt.	Obs	Jan–May 1917	
Findlay W F	2/Lt.	Obs	Aug 1916	
Finch F E	2/Lt.	Pilot	Sept. 1918	
Flynn J P	Lt.	Obs	Aug–Sept. 1917	
Forbes E W	Captain	Obs	Jan–May 1916	
Fordred H J	2/Lt.	Obs	Jan–Mar 1917	
Foster	2/Lt.	Pilot	May 1917	
Foster W H 1040808	Cpl	Obs	Apr–May 1918	
Francis A H	Lt.	Pilot	May 1916	
Francis J W	2/Lt.	Pilot	Aug–Jan 1916/17	
French D	2/Lt.	Pilot	Sept–Feb 1917/18	
Fuller C D	2/Lt.	Pilot	Sept – Dec 1915	
Gardiner P J	2/Lt.	Pilot	June 1917	
Garrick	2/A.M.	AG	Nov 1917	
Garveys-Gadd G A	2/Lt.	Pilot	Sept.1915	
Gawthrop	Cpl	AG	Apr 1916	
Gayford D B	2/Lt.	Obs	Jan–Mar 1916	
Gibbon J T	2/Lt.	Obs	Oct–Feb 1916/17	Killed 06.02.1917
Gibson W 176662	Sgt	AG	Nov 1918	
Gilson W T	Sub/Lt.	Obs	Nov–June 1916/17	
Gloster F B	2/Lt.	Obs	Nov–Dec1917	Killed 03.12.1917
Godfrey F.	Captain	Obs	06.03.18 –	
Golding H M	2/Lt.	Obs	Sept 16 – 29.01.17	
Goodearle F R	Lt.	Pilot	Sept–Oct 1918	Killed 23.10.1918
Gordon C N	2/Lt.	Pilot	July 1918	
Gordon-Bennett R	Lt.	Obs	July –Sept 1918	
Gosse R J	2/Lt.	Pilot	Dec–Mar 1917/18	
Gould J	2/Lt.	Pilot	May 1917	
Gould L H	Lt.	Obs	Aug–Oct 1917	Killed 15.10.1917
Gower W E	Lt.	Obs	Jan 1917	
Gowing J J	2/Lt.	Pilot	Nov.–Dec 1917	
Grantham V M.	2/Lt.	Pilot	Sept – Oct 1915	
Graves E P	Captain	Pilot	Jan–May 1916	
Gray	1/A.M.	AG	Jan 1917	

Names	Rank	Grade	Dates	Casualties
Green J G	2/Lt.	Obs	Sept 17 – 07.10.17	
Green W C	2/Lt.	Obs	Sept 1917	
Greener H 68	Private	AG	Jan-Aug 1917	
Gregory R J	2/Lt.	Obs	May-June 1918	
Groom V E	2/Lt.	Pilot	Mar-Sept 1918	
Grout E J	Sub.Lt.	Pilot	May 1917	
Gye H J	Lt.	Pilot	Nov 1918	
Hackett J	Lt.	Obs	Sept 1918	
Hallworth	1/AM	AG	Jan 1917	
Hamilton H J	2/Lt.	Obs	Apr-Sept 1916	
Hampson H N	2/Lt.	Obs	Feb-Apr 1917	Killed 08.04.1917
Hardcastle E	2/Lt.	Obs	Apr-July 1918	
Harlock F G	Lt.	Pilot	May-Oct 1918	
Harmer R H	2/Lt.	Pilot	Feb-Apr 1918	
Harmer W T V	2/Lt.	Obs	Oct-Dec 1917	
Harris	Cpl	AG	Jan 1917	
Harrison N V	Captain	Pilot	June-Mar 1917/18	
Harrop W P/49486	2/AM	AG	Aug-Sept 1917	
Hart	Sgt	AG	Jan 1917	
Hartney H E	Captain	Pilot	June-Feb 1916/17	
Harvey E S	Lt.	Obs	June-Sept 1918	Killed 26.09.1918
Hay D Y	Lt.	Pilot	Apr-Aug 1917	Killed 11.08.1917
Hedges R B T	2/Lt.	Pilot	Mar-Apr 1918	
Hedley J H	Captain	Obs	Nov-Mar 1917/18	
Helsby J P/3422'	Sgt	Obs	May-July 1918	Killed 02.07.1917
Hemsworth G W	2/Lt.	Pilot	Feb-Mar 1918	
Henry H	Lt.	Obs	Sept 1917	
Heseltine G.C.	2/Lt.	Pilot	Apr-May 1917	
Heslop H W	2/Lt.	Pilot	June 1918	
Heywood J R	Lt.	Pilot	Jan-Mar 1916	
Hill C W 2767	Cpl	AG	July 1918	Killed 30.07.1918
Hill R F	2/Lt.	Obs	July-Oct 1917	
Hills J	2/Lt.	Obs	June-Aug 1918	
Hodder	1/AM	AG	May 1916	
Hofferman N	2/Lt.	Obs	May 1917	
Holgate P B	Lt.	Pilot	Mar-May 1918	
Holland W E	2/Lt.	Pilot	Pre Jan 1916?	
Holman H G	2/Lt.	Obs	Apr-May 1918	
Holmes	1/AM	AG	Jan 1917	
Hone J A	Lt.	Obs	Aug-Oct 1917	
Hook	Cpl	AG	Jan 1917	
Hooper G H	Captain	Pilot	Sept-Nov 1918	

Names	Rank	Grade	Dates	Casualties
Hopper 2015	Sgt	Pilot	Oct-Dec 1917	
Horlock A G	Lt.	Obs	Mar-Apr 1918	
Horner	1/AM	AG	Jan 1917	
Houghton D L	2/Lt.	Obs	Mar-Apr 1917	
Howarth W	2/Lt.	Pilot	May 1917	
Howe H B	2/Lt.	Pilot	May 1917	
Howett J R	Captain	Pilot	Sept-Mar 1915/16	
Hoy C A	Lt.	Obs	May 1917	
Hughes S C	1/AM	AG	June 1916	
Hume R	Lt.	Obs	Apr-May 1917	Killed 06.04.1917
Hutchinson A	Lt.	Obs	Oct-Jan 1917/18	Killed 19.01.1918
Illsley	1/AM	AG	Jan 1917	
Iaccaci A T	Lt.	Pilot	Apr-Sept 1918	
Iaccaci P T	Lt.	Pilot	Apr-Sept 1918	
Jacklin W	2/Lt.	Obs	Apr-May 1918	
James C E H	Captain	Pilot	Jan-May 1916	
Jefferson L H	Lt.	Obs	Sept 1916	
Jenks A N	Lt.	Obs	May-Oct 1917	
Johns R A P	Lt.	Pilot	May 1917	
Johns F J 120214	Private	AG	Sept-Oct 1917	
Johnson F 6391	Sgt	Pilot	Sept-Mar 1917/18	
Johnston A R	Captain	F. Cdr	Feb-Apr 1917	Killed 24.04.1917
Johnston E H	Major	CO	Oct-Apr 1918/19	
Johnston J E	Captain	Obs	Sept-Dec 1917	
Johnston H E	Lt.	Pilot	Sept 1918	
Johnstone	1/AM	AG	Jan 1917	
Jones E Trafford	Lt.	Pilot	Mar-May 1916	Killed 16.05.1916
Jones P G	2/Lt.	Obs	Apr-June 1918	Killed 02.07.1918
Jones P S	2/Lt.	Obs	Mar 1918	
Jooste G D	Captain	Pilot	Sept-May 1917/18	
Joslyn H W	Lt.	Pilot	May-Aug 1917	Killed 17.08.1917
Jourdan W T	2/Lt.	Obs	Sept-Feb 1916/17	
Keevil	1/AM	AG	Feb 1917	
Keith A D	Lt.	Obs	Nov-Feb 1917/18	
Kemp G H	2/Lt.	Obs	Mar-June 1918	Killed 01.06.1918
Kennard N D	2/Lt.	Obs	June 1917	
Kidd J F	2/Lt.	Obs	Oct-Nov 1918	Killed 01.11.1918
Kiermander A D	Lt.	Pilot	Sept 1917	
Kinder	2/AM	AG	Feb 1916	
Kirby H	2/Lt.	Pilot	May 1917	
Kirkman R K	Captain	F. Cdr	Aug-Mar 1917/18	

Names	Rank	Grade	Dates	Casualties
Kirkpatrick J C	Lt.	Pilot	Sept–Dec 1917	Killed 10.12.1917
Kirkpatrick T W	Lt.	Obs	19.09.18	
Kirton J P	2/Lt.	Pilot	Sept 1915	
Knight A A A	Captain	F. Cdr	Oct–Dec 1917	
Knowles R M	Captain	Obs	Dec–Apr 1916/17	
Kragstad R B	2/Lt.	Pilot	Dates unknown	
Kydd F.J.	2/Lt.	Obs	Apr–Aug 1917	
Lale H P	Captain	Pilot	June–Nov 1918	
Lankin C G	Lt.	Pilot	Mar–Apr 1918	
Lapraik D M	2/Lt.	Obs	Oct 1918	
Lascelles E H	Lt.	Obs	July–Aug 1916	
Latimer D	Captain	F. Cdr	Jan–Aug 1918	
Latta J	2/Lt.	Pilot	Sept. 1915	
Lawson J	2/Lt.	Pilot	Feb–Apr 1917	
Le Blanc– Smith M	2/Lt.	Pilot	Sept 1916	
Learmond G V	Lt.	Obs	July–Nov 1918	
Lee	1/AM	AG	Jan 1917	
Lee A C	Lt.	Pilot	May 1917	
Lee G S	Lt.	Pilot	June–Sept 1917	
Lee L C	Lt.	Pilot	Late 1918	
Leigh– Pemberton RD	Lt.	Pilot	Dec–Mar 917/18	
Leonard W T	2/Lt.	Pilot	Aug–Sept 1918	
Lewis	Cpl	AG	Jan 1917	
Lewis T A M S	2/Lt.	Obs	Apr–July 1917	
Lindup E	Lt.	Pilot	Feb–May 1918	
Lindup L	2/Lt.	Pilot	Dec–Jan 1917/18	
Lingard W	2/Lt.	Obs	May–July 1917	
Little R H	2/Lt.	Pilot	Jan 1918	
Livingstone A F	2/Lt.	Pilot	July–Sept 1916	
Lloyd C 11192	Private	AG	May–June 1917	
Lucas T C H	Lt.	Pilot	Aug–Feb 1916/17	Killed 06.02.1917
Luchford H G E	Captain	F. Cdr	May–Dec 1917	Killed 02.12.1917
Lyall K	2/Lt.	Pilot	1915	
Lyon S F	Lt.	Obs	Nov 1917	
MacAskill W R	Lt.	Obs	May–June 1917	Killed 19.06.1917
Maclean	2/AM	AG	Feb 1916	
Macleod J E 200280	Private	AG	June 1917	Killed 23.06.1917
MacMaster	1/AM	AG	Jan 1917	
Madill R M	Lt.	Obs	June–July 1917	Killed 21.07.1917
Magee E A	Lt.	Pilot	Apr–June 1918	
Mahony-Jones G J	Captain	F. Cdr	Dec–Apr 1916/17	Killed 07.04.1917
Makepeace R M	Captain	Pilot	Jun–Jan 1917/18	

Names	Rank	Grade	Dates	Casualties
Malcolm G J	Major	CO	Mar–July 1916	Killed. 09.07.1916
Maller F S	2/Lt.	Obs	Jan–Apr 1916	
Malpas D P/100024	Sgt	Obs	May–July 1918	Killed 25.07.1918
Mann A 406495	Cpl	AG	Dec–Jan 1917/18	Killed 22.01.1918
Mansfield W H C	Major	CO	July–Oct 1916/17	
Markham W H	Lt.	Pilot	Aug 1918	
Marsh W C	2/Lt.	Pilot	01.01.17 –	
Marshall B S	2/Lt.	Pilot	May–June 1918	Killed 07.06.1917
Martin A W	2/Lt.	Pilot	Feb–May 1917	
Masding S H P	Lt.	Obs	Nov–May 1917/18	
Masson R G	Lt.	Pilot	May 1916	Killed 23.05.1917
Mather M B 20624	Sgt	Obs	Oct–June 1917/18	
Matthews B 407022	2/AM	AG	Oct–Feb 1917/18	
Matthews H F 1712	2/AM	AG	Oct–Sept 1917	Killed 06.09.1917
Matthewson K	2/Lt.	Pilot	Dates unknown	
Maule E B	Lt.	Obs	Dec–Feb 1916/17	Killed 06.02.1917
Maxwell R S	Captain	Pilot	May–Dec 1916	
May E	Cpl	AG	June 1916	
May T '3791'	Sgt	AG	Feb–Mar 1916	
May	2/A.M.	AG	May 1917	
Mayne	Sgt	AG	Oct 1917	
McAllister A J	2/Lt.	Pilot	May–July 1918	Killed 04.07.1918
McBride A M	Lt.	Pilot	Sept–Oct. 1918	
McBride J G	2/Lt.	Obs	May–Oct 1918	Killed 08.10.1918
McCreary H C	Lt.	Pilot	June–July 1918	Killed 02.07.1918
McCudden J T	Sgt	Pilot	July–Aug 1916	
McCall M	Lt.	Pilot	June '17–late '18	
McEwen B C	2/Lt.	Pilot	Sept. 1915	
McGoun D M	Captain	Pilot	Sept–Mar 1917/18	
McHardy A W	2/Lt.	Pilot	Oct–Nov 1918	Killed 10.11.1918
McHattie J W	Lt.	Obs	Mar–Apr 1918	Killed 25.04.1918
McKay	1/AM	AG	Jan1917	
McKenzie M A	Lt.	Obs	Aug 1918	
McLean J M	2/Lt.	Pilot	Aug 1917	
McLean T W	2/Lt.	Obs	July–Sept 1917	Killed 21.09.1917
McMaster	Cpl	AG	Jan 1917	
McMechan J 36564	2/AM	AG	Aug–Oct 1917	
McNaughton N G	2/Lt.	Pilot	Jan–Apr 1916	
Melbourne S W 54494	1/A.M.	Obs	Mar–June 1918	
Middleton T P	Captain	Pilot	Apr–Sept. 1918	
Miller	F. Sgt	AG	Feb 1916	
Miller F D	2/Lt.	Obs	Dec–Feb 1917/18	Killed. 04.02.1918

Names	Rank	Grade	Dates	Casualties
Mills A	Lt.	Obs	Mar 1918	
Mitchell E J 34093	Sgt	Obs	Sept 1918	
Moore W G 3836	Cpl	AG	June–Sept 1916	Died of injuries 01.09.1916
Moors R 78179	Cpl	AG	Dec 1918	Killed 03.12.1918
Morden	Sgt	AG	Jan 1917	
Morgan	1/AM	AG	Jan 1917	
Morris R S V	2/Lt.	Obs	Sept 1917	
Morton R F S	2/Lt.	Pilot	Jan 1916	
Mottershead T1396' V.C. (Posth.), DCM	Sgt	Pilot	Nov–Jan 1916/17	Died of wounds 12.01.1917
Mowatt S A	2/Lt.	Pilot	Nov–Dec 1917	
Moyes W B	2/Lt.	Obs	Jan–Apr 1917	Killed 07.04.1917
Myers F M	2/Lt.	Obs	Dec 16 – 14.02.17	Killed 14.02.1917
Mynott	1/AM	AG	Jan 1917	
Nash W H	2/Lt.	Obs	Dec–Mar 1917/18	
Neville R H G	2/Lt.	Pilot	Sept. 1915	Killed 09.05.1917
Neville H G	2/Lt.	Obs	Apr–May 1917	
Newbold L A	2/Lt.	Pilot	Dec–Feb 1915/16	
Newland A 67168	Sgt	Obs	Mar–Oct 1918	
Nicholls	2/A.M.	AG	Feb 1916	
Nicholson H R	Lt.	Obs	Mar–Apr 1917	Killed 24.04.1917
Nicolson J	Lt.	Pilot	Aug–Sept 1918	Killed 23.09.1918
Noble H T	2/Lt.	Obs	Sept 1917	Killed 28.09.1917
Noble W	Lt.	Obs	Dec–July 1917/18	
Noel T C	Lt.	Obs	Mar–Aug 1918	Killed 22.08.1918
Noon G	2/Lt.	Obs	Oct–Nov 1917	Killed 29.11.1917
Oades S A	Lt.		Apr 1918	
Oberst C R	Lt.	Pilot	Sept 1918	
O'Neill W 236154	Sgt	Obs	May–June 1918	
Owen A 35716	Gunner	AG	July–Aug 1917	Killed 15.08.1917
Page L F	2/Lt.	Pilot	Sept. 1915	
Patterson J R	2/Lt.	Pilot	June 1917	
Pattinson L A	2/Lt.	Pilot	Jan 1917	
Paul A R	2/Lt.	Pilot	Dec–Jan 1917/18	Killed 22.01.1918
Pearce A D	Lt.	Pilot	May 1916	
Pearce G W	Lt.	Obs	Sept 1918	
Pearson K N	2/Lt.	Pilot	Sept–Jan 1915/16	
Pemberton A L	Lt.	Pilot	Dec–Apr 1917/18	
Pennal H L	Lt.	Pilot	Sept–Oct 1918	Killed 23.10.1918
Penrose K	2/Lt.	Obs	July–Sept 1918	Killed 03.09.1918
Perkins A C T	Lt.	Pilot	Oct 1918	

Names	Rank	Grade	Dates	Casualties
Perry E O	2/Lt.	Pilot	Feb–Apr 1917	
Peters N	Lt.	Obs	March–Apr 1918	
Phelps L H	Lt.	Obs	Oct–Apr 1917/18	
Pike S N	2/Lt.	Pilot	Feb–Apr 1917	
Pilbrow S E	Private	AG	July–Aug 1917	Killed 15.08.1917
Pile C J	2/Lt.	Obs	Jan 1916	
Pilkington J O	Lt.	Pilot	Sept 1917	Killed 06.09.1917
Pilling	2/A.M.	AG	Jan 1917	
Pinder W L	2/Lt.	Obs	Mar–Apr 1918	
Poellnitz H von–	Lt.	Pilot	Pre Dec 1915	
Pope K W	2/Lt.	Pilot	Jan 1918	
Pope	2/A.M.	AG	Sept 1916	
Potter F A P/2425	Sgt	AG	June–Sept 1917	Killed 11.09.1917
Price L M	Lt.	Pilot	Apr–Aug 1918	
Price	Cpl	AG	Jan 1917	
Prosser D H	2/Lt.	Obs	Dec–Mar. 1917/18	
Purcell J M	2/Lt.	Pilot	Feb–Aug 1918	
Purvis R C	2/Lt.	Obs	Sept–Feb 1917/18	
Quinn J R	Lt.	Pilot	Feb 1918	
Rabagliati CEC	Captain	Pilot	Oct. 1915	
Ralph F J	2/Lt.	Obs	Apr–Sept 1918	Killed 03.09.1918
Randall G E	Lt.	Pilot	Sept–Dec 1918	
Ray W C 7389	F/Sgt	AG	Nov–Dec 1917	
Reeves W A	2/Lt.	Pilot	Jan–Feb 1917	
Reid G P S	2/Lt.	Pilot	Jan–Sept 1918	
Reid G R M	Lt.	Pilot	June–Dec 1916	
Reid R W	2/Lt.	Pilot	Oct–July 1916/17	
Rendle S.	2/Lt.	Pilot	Aug – Sept 1918	
Riach C M2/051774	Cpl	AG	Feb/Mar 1917	
Richards C R	2/Lt.	Pilot	May–Aug 1917	
Roberts L P	2/Lt.	Pilot	Jan–Feb 1918	Killed 23.02.1917
Roberts W H 332	Sgt	Pilot	Sept 1917	Killed 11.09.1917
Robertson K L	Lt.	Pilot	Feb–Apr 1917	
Robins E	2/Lt.	Pilot	June 1917	
Robinson T V	2/Lt.	Obs	June–July 1918	Killed 04.07.1918
Rodger W A	2/Lt.	Obs	Oct–Nov 1918	Killed 10.11.1918
Rodwell J T	2/Lt.	Pilot	Nov 1915	
Ross J	2/Lt.	Obs	May–June 1918	
Rowan O A	Lt.	Obs	Sep–Mar 1917/18	
Russell C G	Lt.	Obs	Sept 1918	
Salmons	Pte	AG	Feb–Mar 1917	
Salter G C T	Lt.	Obs	Mar–May 1918	Killed. 28.05.1918

Names	Rank	Grade	Dates	Casualties
Sampson R D	2/Lt.	Pilot	Apr-June 1916	
Samson M S '2910'	Sgt	Obs	May-July 1918	
Sanders N M	Lt.	Obs	Sept-Dec 1917	
Satchell H L	Captain	Pilot	Jan-Dec 1917	
Saunders E	Sgt	AG	May 1916	
Sawden W N	2/Lt.	Pilot	Jan-June 1917	Killed 05.06.1917
Sawle	1/A.M.	AG	Jan 1917	
Sayers E H	Sgt	AG	Mar-July 1917	
Scaramanga J J	2/Lt.	Obs	Dec-Apr 1917/18	
Schorah O 4407	Sgt	Pilot	December 1917	
Scott D 50821	2/A.M.	AG	Feb 1918	
Scott L H	2/Lt.	Obs	July to Oct 1916	
Scott P G	2/Lt.	Pilot	Jan-Apr 1916	
Scott W P	2/Lt.	Pilot	May 1917	
Scott W	2/AM	AG	Feb 1918	
Segrave P	2/Lt.	Pilot	Sept-Nov 1918	Killed 01.11.1918
Segui H W	Lt.	Pilot	Apr-May 1918	
Seward W J	2/Lt.	Pilot	Sept 1917	
Shaw G L	2/Lt.	Obs	July-Aug 1918	
Shearer F J	2/Lt.	Pilot	July 1918	Killed 25.07.1918
Shell W H	Lt.	Pilot	July 1918	
Simpson C B	2/Lt.	Pilot	July-Nov 1917	Killed 06.11.1917
Sinclair A D	2/Lt.	Obs	Nov 1918	
Skelton J E L	2/Lt.	Obs	Aug-Sept 1917	
Slade R B	2/Lt.	Pilot	Sept-Oct 1917	
Smart E J	Lt.	Pilot	Mar 1917	
Smith D E	Lt.	Pilot	Mar-Aug 1918	Killed 14.08.1918
Smith H O 328	Sgt	Pilot	Dec-Jan 1917/18	Died of wounds 15.07.1918
Smith L G	2/Lt.	Pilot	Sept 1918	Killed 26.09.1918
Smith R	2/Lt.	Pilot	Jan-Apr 1917	Killed 06.04.1917
Smith	1/A.M.	AG	Jan 1917	
Smith	Sgt	AG	Feb 1917	
Snoulton C M 9035	Private	AG	Sept-Oct 1917	
Solly A N	Lt.	Pilot	Apr-Aug 1917	Killed 11.08.1917
Solomon F H	2/Lt.	Pilot	Nov 1918	
Soulby H W	2/Lt.	Obs	Oct-Apr 1916/17	
Spain G Dixon-	Captain	Obs	Feb to Sept. 1916	
Spatz	Major	Pilot?	Feb 1918	
Speakman L R	Captain	Obs	Nov-Feb 1917/18	
Spicer E D	2/Lt.	Obs	July-Feb 1916/17	Killed 01.02.1917
Spratt WA	Lt.	Pilot	Feb. 1916	

Names	Rank	Grade	Dates	Casualties
Stacey D W	2/Lt.	Pilot	June 1917	Killed 18.06.1917
Stac T A	Sgt	Obs	Sept 1918	
Stanley A 6717	2/AM	AG	July-Sept 1916	
Starfield B.	2/Lt.	Pilot	Oct-Jan 1917/18	Killed 19.01.1918
Starsfield A 49324	Sgt	Pilot	Apr-May 1918	
Stead J K	Lt.	Pilot	July-Feb 1916/17	Killed 04.02.1917
Steele C R	Captain	Pilot	Dec-Jan 1918	
Stelling	1/A.M.	AG	Jan 1917	
Stevens D E	Lt.	Obs	Mar 1918	Killed 13.03.1918
Stevens F D	Captain	Pilot	Feb-Sept 1917	
Stewart A G	Lt.	Obs	Jan/Feb 1917	
Stewart D A	2/A.M.	AG	Feb 1916	
Stott C C	2/Lt.	Obs	Sept-Dec 1916	
Strachan A R	Lt.	Pilot	June-Sept 1918	Killed 20.09.1918
Strange B	Lt.	Pilot	June 1917	
Stratton D C	2/Lt.	Pilot	Sept-Nov 1917	
Stream J H	Lt.	Obs	Dec-Feb 1917/18	Killed 19.02.1918
Stringer J W 10068	Cpl	AG	Mar-July 1916	Killed 20.07.1916
Sugden J E W	Lt.	Pilot	Mar-June 1918	
Summers J D P555236	Sgt	Obs	June-July 1918	
Sweeney E W	Lt.	Pilot	June-Sept. 1918	
Swinnerton	Private	AG	April 1916	
Talbot	2/A.M.	AG	Feb 1916	
Tapp R B	Lt.	Pilot	Oct-Nov 1918	
Tasker H	2/Lt.	Obs	Mar-Apr 1918	
Tattersall F V	2/Lt.	Pilot	Nov-Dec 1917	
Taylor A G V	Captain	Pilot	Feb-Oct 1917	Killed 17.10.1917
Taylor F J	2/Lt.	Pilot	Feb 1917	
Taylor N N	Captain	Obs	Dec-May 1917/18	
Taylor S	2/AM	AG	Sept 1916	
Teale G N	Captain	Pilot	July 1916	Killed 20.07.1916
Tennant J	2/Lt.	Obs	June-Oct 1917	
Tester G T/2 10816	Driver	AG	Sept 1917	Killed 28.09.1917
Thayre F H	Captain	F. Cdr	Apr-June 1917	Killed 09.06.1917
Thompson F H	2/Lt.	Pilot	Aug-Nov 1917	
Thompson S F	Lt.	Obs	June-Aug 1917	
Thomson W M.	Lt.	Pilot	Mar-Sept 1918	
Thomas H 36233	1/AM	AG	Oct-Jan 1917/18	
Tod M	2/Lt.	Obs	Mar-Aug 1917	
Tomlin H F	2/Lt.	Pilot	Sept. 1917	Killed 28.09.1917
Townsend 78606	2/AM	AG	Oct-Nov 1917	
Traill T C	Captain	Pilot	May-Nov 1918	

Names	Rank	Grade	Dates	Casualties
Trevethan R M	Lt.	Pilot	June–Sept 1917	
Trotter S F	Lt.	Obs	June–July 1917	Killed 06.07.1917
Tulloch J	2/Lt.	Obs	Apr–May 1918	
Tupman	Cpl	AG	Feb 1917	
Turner F E	2/Lt.	Pilot	Sept 1918	Killed 27.09.1918
Turner R W	2/Lt.	Obs	Mar 1918	
Tyrell A R 47292	1/AM	AG	May 1917	
Tyrell F J	2/Lt.	Pilot	July 1916	
Urquhart A	2/Lt.	Obs	July–Aug 1917	Killed 17.08.1917
Vage C 35678	2/AM	AG	Jan 1917	
Veacock S J	Lt.	Obs	Sept–Oct 1917	Killed 17.10.1917
Veale E P71991	Cpl	Obs	Sept–Feb 1917/18	
Vickers O H D	2/Lt.	Pilot	June–Aug 1917	
Waddington M N	Lt.	Obs	June–Dec 1917	
Wainwright R B W	2/Lt.	Pilot	June–Feb 1916/17	
Wait T E 265376	Sgt	AG	May 1917	
Wakefield H C	2/Lt.	Pilot	Dates unknown	
Walrand-Skinner D D	Captain	Pilot	Sept–Oct 1917	
Wallis F B	2/Lt.	Obs	Oct–Nov 1917	
Walter D P	2/Lt.	Pilot	Jan–Feb 1917	
Walters S	Lt.	Pilot	Sept–Nov 1918	
Ward C R J	Lt.	Obs	July – Sept 1917	
Ward		AG	Apr 1916	
Warden R H	Captain	Obs	Oct–Jan 1917/18	
Washington W F	2/Lt.	Pilot	Sept 1918	Killed 03.09.1918
Watney H C G	2/Lt.	Pilot	July 1917	
Watt W H	2/Lt.	Obs	June–July 1917	
Wear A E	2/Lt.	Obs	June–Sept 1917	Killed 11.09.1917
Welsh W H	2/Lt.	Obs	Oct–Nov 1918	
Weston D J	Lt.	Pilot	Dec–July 1917/18	
White H G	Lt.	Pilot	July–June 1916/17	
White R W	Lt.	Obs	Sept–Jan 1916/17	
White V R S	Lt.	Obs	Sept–Oct 1917	
White	1/A.M.	AG	Jan 1917	
Whiteside H L	2/Lt.	Obs	March 1917	
Wilkinson H R	2/Lt.	Obs	Sept–May 1916/17	
Williams F S	2/Lt.	Pilot	Jul – Aug 1918	
Williamson T W	Lt.	Pilot	Apr–May 1918	
Wilson B W	2/Lt.	Obs	Apr–Sept 1918	Killed 23.09.1918
Wilson C.W.	Major	CO	Oct–Mar 1915/16	
Winch P2633	Sgt	Obs	Sept 1918	
Wise F H V	Sub/Lt.	Pilot	Jan 1917	

Names	Rank	Grade	Dates	Casualties
Woodbridge A E	2/Lt.	Obs	May-July 1917	
Woods C H C	Lt.	Pilot	Sept 1917	Killed 21.09.1917
Woods M E	2/Lt.	Pilot	Dec-Feb 1916/17	
Woolley D B	Lt.	Obs	Mar 1917	
Wootton	Cpl	AG	Jan 1917	
Wornum A P	Lt.	Obs	Oct-Jan 1917/18	
Worthing G	2/AM	AG	May 1917	Killed 05.05.1917
Wyatt	Cpl	AG	Jan 1917	
C S Wynne-Eyton C S	2/Lt.	Pilot	Sept –Dec 1915	
Zellers G H (U.S.A.S.)	Lt.	Pilot	June-July 1918	Killed 30.07.1918

Appendix 2

Officers & Men Serving in a Ground Duties Role

This list provides the names of just a small fraction of those who served on the ground. It has not been possible to provide a fuller list as no muster roll survives. It should also be borne in mind that the majority of the Air Mechanics and NCOs shown in Appendix 1 as having flown with 20 Squadron would probably have had regular ground duties to fulfil when not flying.

Officers				
Achurch G P	2/Lt.	EO	1916/1917	
Ackey C	2/Lt.	Tech	1918	
Bankes C D R O	Captain	Padre	Mar–Apr 1918	Rev. C of E.
Barrett S H	2/Lt.	EO	June–Apr 1918/19	R.A.F.
Bryant W E G	2/Lt.	RO	Jan–Oct 1917	Royal Fusiliers
Castle E E	2/Lt.	EO W/T	To April 1916	Gen. List (N.Z.)
Churcher L G	2/Lt.	Int.	1918	
Finney J L	2/Lt.	EO	Dec. 1915	
Fraser K	2/Lt.	MO	Dates Not Known	
Hall H G	Lt.	AO	From Nov 1917	Gen. List
Heald C B	Lt.	MO	Apr 1916	R.A.M.C.
Jacques G	2/Lt.	EO W/T	April – July 1916	R.F.C. (SR)
Logan R A	2/Lt.	EO	Dec. 1915	R.F.C. (SR)
Martyne V C	Captain	MO	Dates Not Known	R.A.M.C.
Mechan H R	Lt.	Tech	Mar 1918	R.F.C.
Oliver R V	2/Lt.	Int.	Nov 1917 onwards	Border regiment (T)
Packham A T	Lt.	RO	Jan 1918	N Staffs Reg't
Porteous H B	Captain	MO	Nov–Apr 1917/18	R.A.M.C. (T)
Prynne G M F	Lt.	AO	Up to Nov 1917	Border Reg't
Purvis R L	2/Lt.	RO	Dates Not Known	Gen. List
Towler M N	Captain	Int.	Feb–Apr 1918	Army Cyclist Corps
Wallace-Smyth J W	Captain	Padre	Early 1918	Rev. C of E
Wight J E	2/Lt.	Tech.	May – June 1917	R.F.C. (SR)
Wood R B M	Lt.	RO	Dates Not Known	Indian Army
Woodhill C	Captain	Int.	03.12.17 –	N Hants Yeo. (TF)
Wright E W	2/Lt.	EO	Jan–Feb 1916	
Wright F W	2/Lt.	EO W/T	Feb 1917 (Air 76)	R.F.C. (SR)

Ground Duties - Other Named Ranks

Barnes J 240119	Private	Int.	Nov 1917 –	Border Reg't
Billing B 232	Sgt.Maj.	Tech	Nov–Feb 1915/19	Died Belgium 16.02.1919
Bradey 245529	Sapper	Int.	Nov 17 –	R.E.
Bullet E 52244	2/AM	Photog	Early 1918	
Burnes J. 240119	Private	Int.	Nov 1917	
Crabbe W J SS/1530	Sgt	Int.	Nov 17 –	AS.C.
Drew A 65150	2/AM	Photog	02.01.18 –	
Farmer	Cpl	Tech?	July 1916	
Fenton A 77635	2/AM	Photog	02.01.18	
Griffiths I 30009	2/AM	Photog	24.01.18	
Harvey W 542245	2/AM	Photog	19.02.18	
Herriott F 5245	1/AM	Mech.	Up to Feb 1919	Died Belgium 23.02.1919
Hughes	Cpl	Tech?	July 1916	
Kennard D 245951	Sapper	Int.	22.11.17 –	R.E.
Kerr	Ft. Sgt	Tech?	July 1916	
McGrath W 77890	2/AM	Photog	Early 1918	
Perring F J 95910	2/AM	Photog	24.012.18 –	
Reid	Sgt	Tech?	July 1916	
Simpson F 57907	2/AM	Photog	19.02.18	
Sudds T E 1811	Private	Int.	Nov1917 –	Surrey Reg't
Watts J E 244271	Sapper	Int.	Nov 1917 –	R.E. (FSC)
Webb H J 106391	Private	M. Ord	20.11.17 –	

Appendix 3

Decorations and Awards

The Following Officers and Men of 20 Squadron Were Decorated for Their Service
Victoria Cross (Posthumous)
Sergeant T. Mottershead, 1396, D.C.M.   London Gazette 29937: 09.02.1917

Distinguished Conduct Medal

Sergeant J.J. Cowell, 78171, M.M. & Bar.	London Gazette 30188: 18.07.1917
Sergeant E. Deighton.	London Gazette 30932: 03.10.1918
Sergeant F. Hopper, 2015.	London Gazette 30601: 28.03.1918
Sergeant M.B. Mather, 20624.	London Gazette 30664: 01.05.1918

Military Cross

2/Lt. W. Beaver	London Gazette 30761: 21.06.1918
2/Lt. G.G.W. Burkett	London Gazette 30466: 08.01.1918
2/Lt. W.C. Cambray	London Gazette 30787: 14.09.1917
Lt. D.G. Cooke	London Gazette 30813: 23.07.1918
Lt. H.G. Crowe	London Gazette 30813: 23.07.1918
Captain F.C. Cubbon	London Gazette 30188: 09.07.1917
Captain F.C. Cubbon	London Gazette 30188: 17.07.1917 (Bar to M.C.)
Captain G. Dixon-Spain	London Gazette 29765: 26.09.1916
Lt. W. Durrand	London Gazette 30431: 14.12.1917
Captain E.W. Forbes	London Gazette Air 1/689/21/20/20 (23.05.1916)
2/Lt. G. Gordon-Davies	London Gazette 29981: 09.03.1917
Lt. W.E. Gower	London Gazette 29968: 02.03.1917
2/Lt. R.F. Hill	London Gazette 30583: 15.03.1918
Lt C.A. Hoy	London Gazette 30787: 14.09.1917
Captain R.K. Kirkman	London Gazette 30597: 22.03.1918
Captain R.M. Knowles	London Gazette 29981: 09.03.1917
Captain D. Latimer	London Gazette 30910: 13.09.1918
Lt. R.D. Leigh-Pemberton	London Gazette 30761: 21.06.1918
2/Lt. T.A.M.S. Lewis	London Gazette 30466: 08.01.1918
2/Lt. E. Lindup	London Gazette 30761: 21.06.1918
Lt. H.G.E. Luchford	London Gazette 30583: 15.03.1918

Captain H.G.E. Luchford	London Gazette 30614: 05.04.1918 (Bar to M.C.)
2/Lt. R.M. Makepeace	London Gazette 30466: 08.01.1918
Lt. Lt. T.C. Noel	London Gazette 30901: 13.09.1918 (Bar to M.C.)
2/Lt. G.P.S. Reid	London Gazette 29765: 26.09.1916
Lt. G.R.M. Reid	London Gazette 29837: 29.11.1917
Captain G.R.M. Reid	London Gazette 29837: 25.11.1916 (Bar to M.C.)
2/Lt. C.R. Richards	London Gazette 30787: 14.09.1917
2/Lt. L.H. Scott	London Gazette 29837: 25.11.1916
Captain F.H.J. Thayre	London Gazette 30188: 09.07.1917
Captain F.H.J. Thayre	London Gazette 30188: 17.07.1917 (Bar to M.C.)
Lt. W.M. Thomson	London Gazette 30901: 13.09.1918
2/Lt. R.M. Trevethan	London Gazette 30787: 14.09.1917
2/Lt. V.R.S. White	London Gazette 30614: 06.04.1918 (Bar to M.C.)

Military Medal

Sergeant B. Aldred, '11449'	London Gazette 30172: 09.07.1917
Sergeant. W.J. Benger '88288'	London Gazette 30431: 14.12.1917 & 20.10.1917
Sergeant. J.J. Cowell '78171'	17.09.1917 (Bar to M.M.) Air 1/689/21/20/20
2/A.M. S. Pilbrow '44340'	London Gazette 30312: 25.09.1917
2/A.M. F. Potter '2425'	London Gazette 30287: 14.09.1917

Distinguished Flying Cross

2/Lt. C.G. Boothroyd	London Gazette 31170: 07.02.1919
2/Lt. H.E. Edwards	London Gazette 31046: 03.12.1918
Captain F. Godfrey	London Gazette 30827: 03.08.1918
Captain V.E. Groom	London Gazette 30989: 01.11.1918
Lt. E. Hardcastle	London Gazette 30989: 01.11.1918
Lt. A.T. Iaccaci	London Gazette 30827: 03.08.1918
Lt. P.T. Iaccaci	London Gazette 30913: 20.09.1918
Captain H.P. Lale	London Gazette 31046: 03.12.1918
Captain D. Latimer	London Gazette 30913: 20.09.1918
Captain F.P. Middleton	London Gazette 30827: 03.08.1918
Lt. A. Mills	London Gazette 30827: 03.08.1918
Lt. W. Noble	London Gazette 30827: 03.08.1918
Lt. F.J. Ralph	London Gazette 30989: 01.11.1918
Lt. G.E. Randall	London Gazette 31170: 07.02.1919
Lt. W.M. Thomson	London Gazette 30989: 01.11.1918
Captain T.C. Traill	London Gazette 31170: 07.02.1919
Lieut. L. W. Burbidge.	London Gazette 31170: 07.02.1919
2/Lt. R.W. Turner	London Gazette 30989: 01.11.1918

Lt. D.J. Weston   London Gazette 30827: 03.08.1918

Distinguished Flying Medal

Sergeant. A. Newland '67162'   London Gazette 30913: 21.09.1918

Sergeant. A. Newland, D.F.M.,'67162'   London Gazette 03.12.1918 (Bar to D.F.M.)

Foreign Awards

Captain J.H. Hedley   Croix de Guerre (Fr.) 28.04.1918 – Air
                                          1/689/21/20/20

2/Lt. R.C. Purvis   Croix de Guerre (B) 04.02.1918 – Air
                                          1/689/21/20/20

2/Lt. H.M. Soulby   Croix de Guerre (Fr.) 11.02.1917 – Air
                                          1/689/21/20/20

2/A.M. J. McMechan   Croix de Guerre (B) 04.02.1918 – Air
                                          1/689/21/20/20

Sergeant. E. Sayers   Medaille Militaire 31.05.1917 – Air
                                          1/689/21/20/20

Meritorious Service Medal & Mentioned in Despatches

232 Sergeant. Major B. Billing '232'   Air 1/689/21/20/20

Order of the British Empire

Major E.H. Johnston   Air 1/689/21/20/20

******

V.C.	1
D.C.M.	4
M.C.	34 (including six Bars)
D.F.C.	19
M.M.	5 (including one Bar)
D.F.M.	2 (including one Bar)
M.S.M.	1
O.B.E.	1
Foreign Awards	5
Total Awards:	**72**

******

Appendix 4

Official Documents

History of 20 Squadron R.F.C./R.A.F.:	Air 1/689/21/20/20
20 Squadron Record Book Volume 1:	Air 1/167/15/156/2
20 Squadron Record Book Volume 2:	Air 1/167/15/156/3
20 Squadron Record Book Volume 3:	Air 1/168/15/156/4
20 Squadron Record Book Volume 4:	Air 1/168/15/156/5
20 Squadron Record Book March/April 1918	Air 1/1540/204/77/16
20 Squadron Records of Combats Aug 1917 to Nov 1918	Air1/168/15/156/6
20 Squadron Decisive Combats, May 1917 to Nov 1918	Air1/168/15/156/7
20 Squadron: Combat Records: Feb 1916 to Nov. 1918	Air/1/1220/204/5/2634
20 Squadron summary of Work	Air 1/1358/204/20/2
Account of an Air Fight involving F.E.2D's of 20 Sqn.	Air 1/733/185/4
2nd Brigade War Diary	Air 1/1579/204/81/2
2nd Brigade War Diary	Air 1/2229/209/41/12-34
2nd Brigade Operations Orders 10th Feb – 31st Aug 1916	Air 1/1275/204/10/25
2nd Brigade Operations Orders: Jan – March 1918	Air 1/882/204/5/602
5 Brigade Moves of Units 1918 Nov. - Dec.	Air 1/1025/204/5/1413
5 Brigade Movement of Unit instructions 1918 Nov.	Air 1/1/1152/204/5/2400
11th Wing R.F.C. Combat Reports to October 1917	Air 1/1827/204/202/13-18
11th Wing R.F.C. Combat Reports to Jan 1918	Air 1/1828/204/202/19
11th Wing R.F.C. Combat Reports to Sept 1918	Air 1/1829/204/202/20– 23
11th Wing Combat Reports	Air 1/1825-1830 (part)
11th Wing Battle Operations Order, May 1918	Air 1/1826/204/202/9
11th Wing Routine Orders	Air 1/1982/204/5/1159 & 1160
22nd Wing Operations Orders 1918 Aug - Oct.	Air 1/1591/204/83/10
22nd Wing Daily Routine Orders 1918 Oct. - 1919 Mar.	Air 1/1930/204/242/7
Individual Service Records:	WO 339, WO 374, Air 76, Air 79
The Battle of Arras – Preparatory Period:	Air/1/676/21/13/1872
The Battle of Messines: 7th – 14th June 1917	Air/1/676/21/13/1872
Notes on Fokker Fighting by 'An F.E.2B Observer'	Air1/129/15/40/191
Gun Mountings:	Air 1/867/204/5/528 &
	Air 1/1124/204/5/2103
Pilot and Observer Casualties	Air 1/967/204/5/1097 + 1098

Pilot and Observer Casualties   Air 1/968/204/5/1099 + 1100
Pilot and Observer Casualties   Air 1/969/204/5/1101 + 1102
'Rough History of 20 Squadron R.F.C. and R.A.F.'   R.A.F. Museum, Hendon: AC
                                                       73/73/62

Second Lieutenant B. Wilson Observer's Logbook   R.A.F. Museum Hendon

Appendix 5

Select Bibliography

The History of No 20 Squadron, R.F.C./R.A.F.	N J Roberson
Flying Fury – Five Years in the Royal Flying Corps	James McCudden
Wings Over France ('Up and At 'Em' in the USA)	Harold Hartney
With a Bristol Fighter Squadron	Walter Noble
Flying an Ugly Duckling	Michael Cambray
Into The Blue	Norman Macmillan
The War in the Air	Raleigh & Jones
Bristol F2B Fighter	Chaz Bowyer
The Roll of Honour R.F.C. and R.A.F. 1914 – 1918	H J Williamson
The Red Air Fighter	Manfred von Richtofen
Hunting with Richtofen	Bodenschatz
Germany's War in the Air	Peter Kilduff
The Red Baron Combat Wing	Peter Kilduff
Airfields and Airmen of the Channel Coast	Mike O'Connor
The Royal Flying Corps in France	Ralph Barker
Tumult in the Clouds	Nigel Steel & Peter Hart
The First Great Air War	Richard Townshend Bickers
The R.F.C./RNAS Handbook 1914-18	Peter G Cooksley
The Guns of August	Barbara W Tuchman
Undertones of War	Edmund Blunden
The First World War	John Terraine
To Win a War	John Terraine
To The Last Man – Spring 1918	Lyn Macdonald
1918 The Unexpected Victory	J H Johnson
The Sky Their Battlefield	Trevor Henshaw
Above The Trenches	C Shores, N Franks & R Guest
Above The War Fronts	N Franks, R Guest & G Alegi
Casualties of the German Air Service	N Franks, F Bailey & R Duiven
The Jasta War Chronology	N Franks, F Bailey & R Duiven
The Jasta Pilots	N Franks, F Bailey & R Duiven
Above The Lines	N Franks, F Bailey & R Guest
Under The Guns of the German Aces	Norman Franks & Hal Giblin
Who Downed the Aces in WW1?	Norman Franks

Appendix 6

Abbreviations

British Army Grades & Ranks used in the Royal Flying Corps

AG	Air Gunner
Int.	Intelligence Branch
Obs	Observer
M. Ord.	Medical Orderly
Photog.	Photography Branch
Tech.	Technical Branch
Pte	Private
L. Corporal	Lance Corporal
Corporal	Corporal
Sergeant	Sergeant
Sergeant. Maj.	Sergeant Major
W.O.	Warrant Officer
1st/Lt.	First Lieutenant – a U.S.A.S. rank
2/Lt.	Second Lieutenant
Lt.	Lieutenant
Capt.	Captain
Maj.	Major
Lt. Col.	Lieutenant Colonel
Col.	Colonel

British Military Decorations & Awards

D.C.M.	Distinguished Conduct Medal
D.F.C.	Distinguished Flying Cross
D.F.M.	Distinguished Flying Medal
M.C.	Military Cross
M.M.	Military Medal
M.S.M.	Meritorious Service Medal
O.B.E.	Order of the British Empire
V.C.	Victoria Cross

British Army Regiments & Corps

A.F.C.	Australian Flying Corps
A & S. H.	Argyll & Sutherland Highlanders
A.S.C.	Army Service Corps
Bn.	Battalion
C.E.F.	Canadian Expeditionary Force
D.C.L.I.	Duke of Cornwall's Light Infantry
D.L.I.	Durham Light Infantry
D.O.W.L.I.	Duke of Wellington's Light Infantry
Fus.	Fusiliers
Gen. List	General List (of officers)
H.A.C.	Honourable Artillery Company
I.A.R.O.	Indian Army Reserve of Officers
K.O.S.B.	Kings Own Scottish Borderers
K.R.R.C.	Kings Royal Rifle Corps
M.G.C.	Machine Gun Corps
N.Z.	New Zealand
R.A.M.C.	Royal Army Medical Corps
R.E.	Royal Engineers
R.F.A.	Royal Field Artillery
R.G.A.	Royal Garrison Artillery
R.H.A.	Royal Horse Artillery
R.M.L.I.	Royal Marines Light Infantry
S.A.	South Africa
T.F.	Territorial Force
Yeo.	Yeomanry

Re Combats & Casualties

A.L.G.	Advanced Landing Ground
Archie	R.F.C. slang for ANTI-AIRCRAFT
C.O.P.	Close Offensive Patrol
D.O.P.	Distant Offensive Patrol
S.O.P.	South Offensive Patrol
N.O.P.	North Offensive Patrol
O.I.C.	Officer in Charge
a/c	Aircraft
ANTI-AIRCRAFT	Anti Aircraft
Acc.	Accident

Alb.	German Albatros aircraft
'C' or C-type	German 2-seater aircraft
Cap.	Captured
Cr.	Crashed
'D'	German scout aircraft, as in Alb. 'D'
DDD	Driven Down Damaged
DD	Driven Down
Des.	Destroyed or Broke up in the air
D. Inj.	Died of Injuries
DOW	Died of Wounds
'E' or E-type	German monoplane fighting scout
E.A. or H.A.	Enemy or Hostile aircraft
EoL	East of the Lines
F	Destroyed In Flames
FTL/ftl	Forced to land
FL	Forced landing
Halb.	German Halberstadt aircraft
Inj. Acc.	Injured in air accident
Inj.	Injured
KIA	Killed in Action
KIFA	Killed in Flying Accident
OOC	Out of Control
POW	Prisoner of War
WIA	Wounded in Action
WoL	West of the Lines

German Air Service Units

F.A.	Flieger Abteilung	Reconnaissance Squadron
Jasta	Jagdstaffel	Fighter/scout Squadron

German Ranks

Gefr	Gefreiter	Lance Corporal
Uffz	Unteroffizier	Corporal
Vfw	VizeFeldwebel	Sergeant
Fw	Feldwebel	Sergeant
Fw Ltn	Feldwebel-Leutnant	Sergeant-Major
OfStv	Offizierstellvertreter	Warrant Officer
VzflugMstr	Vizeflugmeister	Aviation Chief Petty Officer

Ltn	Leutnant	Lieutenant
ObLtn	Oberleutnant	First Lieutenant
Rittm	Rittmeister	Cavalry Captain
Hptn	Hauptmann	Captain